G000096103

Reproductive Change in India and Brazil

Reproductive Change in India and Brazil

Reproductive Change in India and Brazil

edited by

George Martine, Monica Das Gupta,
and Lincoln C. Chen

DELHI
OXFORD UNIVERSITY PRESS
CALCUTTA   CHENNAI   MUMBAI
1998

Oxford University Press, Great Clarendon Street, Oxford OX2 6DP

Oxford New York
Athens Auckland Bangkok Calcutta
Cape Town Chennai Dar es Salaam Delhi
Florence Hong Kong Istanbul Karachi
Kuala Lumpur Madrid Melbourne Mexico City
Mumbai Nairobi Paris Singapore
Taipei Tokyo Toronto

and associates in
Berlin Ibadan

ISBN 0 19 564291 0

Typeset by Rastrixi, New Delhi 110 070
Printed at Pauls Press, Okhla, New Delhi 110 020
and published by Manzar Khan, Oxford University Press
YMCA Library Building, Jai Singh Road, New Delhi 110001

To
Carolina and Luis-Felipe
Timir and Mihir
Alexis and Greg

Preface

Comparison of recent demographic changes in developing countries present intriguing findings, in that some countries which are very different in their population policies and socio-economic characteristics experience reproductive change at much the same time. The contrasts between India and Brazil, two of the more important countries undergoing change, are particularly challenging. To advance understanding of reproductive change in these two countries, a series of seminars was conducted at the Harvard Center for Population and Development Studies in 1995 and 1996. A cross-country comparison of reproductive change in these two diverse countries was considered to be important for theoretical and practical purposes.

This volume represents the product of that interactive seminar process. The eleven chapters in this book provide fresh perspectives on the causes and consequences of reproductive change. The contributors of the chapters, all scholars from the two countries, were encouraged to probe recent data and explore afresh their interpretation of recent changes. The aim was to gather together a critical mass of scholarship that would stimulate, question, and advance the intellectual foundation of the determinants of reproductive change and its consequences for women in India and Brazil, as well as having implications for understanding other countries' experience. The results challenge established theories of reproductive change.

We would like to thank the John D. and Catherine T. MacArthur Foundation and the India office of the United Nations Development Programme for their generous support for this work. We also thank the editors of *Population and Development Review* for permission to reprint two articles: 'Brazil's Fertility Decline 1965–95: a fresh look at key factors', which appeared in the March 1996 issue of the journal, and 'Mortality, Fertility and Gender Bias in India: a district-level analysis', which appeared in the December 1995 issue of the journal; and the editors of *Population Studies* for permission to reprint the article 'Fertility Decline in Punjab, India:

parallels with historical Europe', which appeared in the November 1995 issue of their journal. We are indebted to Christopher Cahill, Kerry Malloy, Irene Ngaiza, and Laura Reichenbach for their help in preparing this volume for publication.

Contents

Contributors

ELZA BERQUÓ is Senior Researcher at the Brazilian Center for Analysis and Planning (CEBRAP) and the Population Studies Nucleus (NEPO/UNICAMP), and President of the Brazilian National Commission on Population and Development.

P.N. MARI BHAT is Director of the Population Research Centre, Vidyagiri, Dharwad, India.

LINCOLN C. CHEN is Taro Takemi Professor of International Health at the Harvard School of Public Health and Director of the Harvard Center for Population and Development Studies, Harvard University, USA.

MONICA DAS GUPTA is Senior Fellow at the Center for Population and Development Studies, Harvard University, USA, and Associate Director of the National Council of Applied Economic Research, New Delhi, India.

JOSÉ ALBERTO MAGNO DE CARVALHO is Director at the Centro de Desenvolvimento e Planejamento Regional (CEDEPLAR), Belo Horizonte, Brazil.

JEAN DRÈZE is Visiting Professor at the Centre for Development Economics, Delhi School of Economics, India.

ANNE-CATHERINE GUIO is Associate at the Center de Recherche en Economie du Developppment, Namur, Belgium.

ANRUDH JAIN is Deputy Director of the Program Division, Population Council, New York, USA.

T.N. KRISHNAN is Honorary Fellow at the Centre for Development Studies, Trivandrum, India.

GEORGIA KAUFMANN is David E. Bell Fellow at the Center for Population and Development Studies, Harvard University, USA.

GEORGE MARTINE is Senior Fellow at the Center for Population and Development Studies, Harvard University, USA.

MAMTA MURTHI is Research Associate at the STICERD, London School of Economics and Lecturer in Economics, University of Sussex, UK.

D. NARAYANA is David E. Bell Fellow at the Center for Population and Development Studies, Harvard University, USA.

LAURA WONG is Professor of Demography at the Centro de Desenvolvimento e Planejamento Regional (CEDEPLAR), Belo Horizonte, Brazil.

Introduction

Reproductive Change in India and Brazil: Implications for Understanding Fertility Decline

Monica Das Gupta, George Martine, and Lincoln C. Chen

INTRODUCTION

India and Brazil are among the demographic giants of the world. At the time of the latest census (1991), India with a population of 846 million, is second only to China in terms of population size, aside from being geographically the largest country in South Asia. Brazil with 146 million people is the largest country in Latin America in population and geographical size. Combined, these two countries have a population more than twice the size of all of sub-Saharan Africa or Western Europe.

Rapid and profound reproductive changes are taking place in these two countries. Yet the factors underlying these changes and their consequences for women are poorly understood. India, the first country in the world to adopt a population policy in 1952, has been generally considered a 'demographic laggard', trapped in the stagnation of persistently high fertility and rapid population growth. Except for the often-cited exceptional experience of Kerala, where reproductive change has been marked despite low income, the spectacular fertility declines of Asia have occurred outside South Asia: in East Asia and also in Southeast Asian countries like Thailand and Indonesia. Brazil's population situation has received relatively little international attention, perhaps because it eschewed government policies to reduce fertility, and also because it appears to have such enormous land resources. Greater attention has been devoted to environmental and ecological issues in Brazil, largely because of the significance of its tropical forest and land resources.

India and Brazil present enormous contrasts in features closely related to reproductive behaviour. Important among these are current land-man ratios and extent of urbanization, themselves the product of very diverse historical formations and settlement patterns. India has had high population density and few possibilities of opening up new land for cultivation for over a century, while Brazil has low density and vast expanses of underutilized land. In India, some three-quarters of the population still lives in rural areas. In contrast, Brazil has experienced rapid urbanization since the 1950s, and three-quarters of its population is urban, subject to the various forces in urban areas which make for altering reproductive behaviour. Finally, it is particularly interesting that India was the first country to undertake large-scale, publicly-financed and -administered family planning programmes; in India, the State has actively supported family planning service delivery for more than three decades. Conversely, Brazil is probably the largest developing country in the world not to have adopted a widespread family planning or population control programme, because the pronatalist and/or laissez-faire stances of various actors did not lend support to this.

Despite these contrasts, both countries have experienced substantial fertility decline at much the same time, and they show both important differences and commonalties in their fertility transitions. This makes it of considerable interest to compare the experiences of the two countries, to understand more about the applicability of existing theories of fertility decline to these countries' experience, and their policy implications. We begin this introduction by outlining the dimensions of reproductive change in India and Brazil and putting them in an international perspective. This is followed by a brief review of the similarities and contrasts between the two countries, and an analysis of the factors underlying their reproductive change, along with their implications for theories of fertility decline and policy formulation. Finally, we examine the implications of gender equity for reproductive change, and of reproductive change for gender equity.

REPRODUCTIVE CHANGE

India and Brazil are in the midst of a rapid fertility decline. Over the past two decades, total fertility in Brazil declined by over half, from 5.8 births per woman in 1970 to 2.6 in 1991. Albeit more modest in magnitude, India has similarly experienced fertility decline, from a total fertility of 5.2 in 1971 to 3.6 in 1991.

In both countries, all groups in all regions have participated in these reproductive changes, although marked differentials are found between groups and regions. In Brazil, earlier change characterizes the better-off, urbanized Southern regions, while the poorer and more rural Northeast and Amazon regions have lagged behind. Thus, for instance, the onset of fertility decline in the Northeast began later, but after decline began, it has also been more rapid: from a total fertility of 7.0 in 1970 to 3.7 in 1991. This less developed region produces one more child than the national average. In similar fashion, more rapid fertility decline has been registered in India's Southern states than the large Central states. Kerala's fertility is at replacement level and Tamil Nadu's is near replacement level. Because the Central Indian states are extremely populous, the relative weight of the demographic laggards has tended to slow the national pace of change. Nevertheless, these Central states also show noticeable fertility decline.

To gain a sense of the pace of these remarkable reproductive changes, Figure 1 shows the time trend of fertility decline in India and Brazil, in comparison to South Korea, Sweden and the United Kingdom. As noted by Watkins (1989:41) reproductive change is much more rapid in the developing world today than it was in historical Europe. We believe that contemporary contextual forces, distinctive to our times, are responsible for this accelerated pace of fertility decline. A number of new factors are at work. For instance, technological development has generated an explosion of media outreach, accelerating the spread of information in general, bringing new consumption aspirations to people's homes, as well as disseminating information on contraception and on the social and economic benefits of having fewer children. Contraceptive technology has also improved dramatically in recent decades, substantially reducing the difficulties associated with avoiding births. Improved transport and communications in general have also contributed to this process, and form part of the social and economic transformations which are taking place more rapidly in present day developing countries than in nineteenth century Europe. As a result of these changes, the pace of reproductive change has been sharply accelerated.

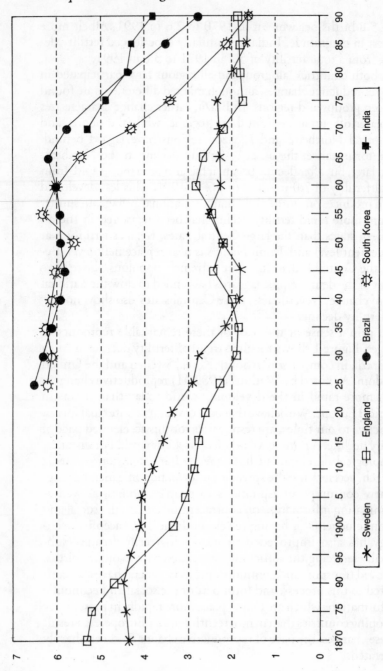

FIG. 1: *Sweden, England, Brazil, South Korea and India; Total Fertility Rates*

Similarities and Contrasts between India and Brazil

In many ways, these two countries are very different, and yet they also possess many similarities. An understanding of their respective backgrounds provides insight into the nature of their reproductive change. In comparing reproductive behaviour in India and Brazil, four areas stand out. These are history, land-man ratios and socio-economic structures; urbanization; marriage and gender relations; and population policies and programmes.

History, Land-man Ratios and Socioeconomic Structures

The first and most obvious difference between India and Brazil is that the former belongs to the Old World and the latter to the New World. It is well known that India has been settled since pre-historic times, and that a complex civilization evolved there millennia ago. Complex political structures have evolved, with dynasties and kingdoms replacing each other over the centuries, and these have built up complex administrative structures regulating economic and social life. Parallel to this evolved the complex structures of the caste and kinship systems, which regulate economic and social life at the local level. India also has a long history of interaction with other cultures, both through land routes (with West Asia, Central Asia, Europe, and China), and through sea routes (especially with the Arab world and Europe). Since large parts of India's land is highly fertile, it not only attracted invasions over the centuries but also permitted a high population density to grow. Even before the modern surge of population growth accompanying mortality decline in this century, large parts of India were already densely settled and offered little if any scope for people to open up new land to cultivate.

In contrast, Brazil belongs to a continent which was almost untouched by outside influences before it was colonized in the sixteenth century. It was a vast continent with a very small population and enormous unexploited natural resources. The Portuguese colonizers did not encounter densely populated areas nor complex social, political, or administrative structures among the indigenous population of Brazil. The occupation of this huge area over the next few centuries occurred as the result of a succession of spatially-differentiated extractive and agricultural cycles. Colonizers had a get-rich-quick mentality, centred on external markets, which did not favour the permanent and massive settlement of the interior. As late as the 1930s, the Brazilian population was still largely congregated in isolated regions, mostly along its vast coastline. Cities were entrepôts for men and riches, serving as coastal springboards for forays into the interior. The vastness of the land area, the labour-intensive production practices, together with the peculiarities of the settlement process, shaped a positive attitude towards immigration, population size and the rate of growth. Until a few decades ago, Brazilians were primarily concerned with increasing their population in order to occupy the vast interior and access the apparently unlimited resources.

Currently, India and Brazil both have a large internal market and a strong industrial base. Both have recently gone through periods of economic crisis and are now undergoing structural transformation. At the same time, both have sizeable and vigorous informal sectors which have generated a good proportion of the new jobs in the economy and mitigated the brunt of their respective economic crises. During the 1970s, Brazil's annual growth rate of GDP per capita was 8.1 per cent, far higher than India's 3.4 per cent. However, a prolonged crisis in the 1980s in Brazil reduced the rate to 2.5 per cent, while that of India rose to 5.4 per cent (World Bank 1993:240–1).

Both Brazil and India are marked by great social and economic diversity and regional disparities. Brazil has some of the greatest inequalities in income and land distribution in the world. India has less economic inequality, but the caste system makes for great social inequalities. Regional disparities in levels of living are glaring in both countries: in Brazil the Amazon and the Northeast, and in India the Central states are far less developed, economically and socially, than other regions. Both countries present extremely differentiated cultures, social class structures, climates, topographies, and other geographic characteristics, but India's social differences are considerably more conspicuous and deeply rooted. Notable in this is the caste structure, but there is also enormous diversity in religion, culture, language, and ethnicity. Brazil, given its size and heterogeneity, is often referred to as a mosaic. Nevertheless, it is united by a common language and by intense interchange and communications. Unquestionably, India is even more of a mosaic and this diversity could be a factor in the slower diffusion of fertility observed in that country (Watkins 1989:45).

These inequalities affect the demographic transition profoundly, as discussed below.

Urbanization

One of the most important differences between the two countries from the point of view of reproductive change is that in levels of urbanization. Already by 1940, at a time when nearly 90 per cent of India's population was rural, nearly a third of Brazil's population lived in urban areas. This differential has widened since then, because of massive waves of rural-urban migration in Brazil, particularly in the 1960s and 1970s. By 1991, three-quarters of Brazil's population was urban-dwelling, while in India the same proportion was living in rural areas. It should be noted, though, that in much of India people live in fairly large villages connected by good transport services to urban areas.

Nevertheless, the faster rate and higher level of urbanization of Brazil favour more rapid fertility decline, with people being exposed to more information, new modes of livelihood, cramped living areas, and new values and aspirations. All these make for lower desired family size, in order to be able to invest more in children and also to be able to meet new consumer expectations. Moreover, the nature of rural-urban migration in Brazil entails a significant break with the past: the majority of migrants settle permanently in the cities, and therefore adopt urban lifestyles and values more rapidly. By contrast, in India, there is a large volume of circular migration, with rural families sending one member off to the urban area for work and maintaining the village home base. Contact is maintained for years through visits and remittances, slowing down the pace of integration with urban, values and lifestyles. At the same time, it is common for families to have some contact with urban areas for employment and services of various kinds. This interaction together with the penetration of the media, expose rural people to many of the influences to which urban people are exposed, though obviously to a much lesser extent.

Marriage and Gender Relations

The context of family and marriage systems within which reproductive decisions are made also present sharp contrasts, as India is characterized by highly stable marriages, while Brazil is marked by considerable fluidity and instability of union. In India, marriage is mostly monogamous and rates of divorce are very low. Strong sanctions ensure negligible levels of premarital birth. In Brazil, marriages are far less stable, although divorce was only legalized two decades ago. Many unions are processual, with children being born outside the realm of stable unions or before the parents formalize their union. Double standards of morality prevail and secondary relationships outside marriage are not unknown. Moreover, the role of the church is diminishing: there is a drop in the proportion of unions which are formalized with religious or other ceremonies; the divorce rate is rising, and the proportion of single-parent households (mostly female-headed) is rising (Berquó, Oliveira, and Cavenaghi 1994).

Gender relations also pose some contrast. Gender inequalities are far more deeply rooted in India, where they are dramatically manifested in excess female mortality. In Brazil, women are subordinated to male machismo, but do not suffer from excess mortality as a consequence. In both countries, there are double sexual standards, unequal access to jobs, income and social amenities, thus making women dependent on men. At the same time, both countries have notably active feminist movements, and levels of female labour force participation as well as female education are rising.

Population Policies

India and Brazil have completely different histories of State involvement in family planning. India officially recognized the importance of reducing population growth as early as 1952, as part of its overall development strategy. At this time it initiated a State-backed family planning programme, but the approach at the beginning was largely clinical. In the mid-1960s, when the country was faced with a succession of harvest failures, the government embarked on an urgent programme to increase agricultural output on the one hand, and to reduce population growth on the other. It was then that a strategy of extending the outreach of the family planning programme, especially to the rural areas of the country, was designed and rapidly implemented. Since then, the State has tried to propagate family planning as aggressively as it dares, using targets for the staff and incentives for clients. One government was actually overthrown for being too forceful in pushing the population control agenda. The programme is financed by the Central Government, financial outlays have been steadily rising, and the family planning message reaches people in a myriad of ways in their daily life.

Brazil was still in the process of trying to occupy its vast interior when the first global concerns with the 'population explosion' were being expressed. At the time that the massive sterilization campaigns were going on in India, Brazilians of different political leanings were defending population growth for political, geopolitical, religious, or economic reasons. From the outset, discussions of family planning have caused considerable controversy there, and family planning initiatives have been denounced as part of an international conspiracy or as undue interference by the government in private lives. Until recently, the lawbooks severely reprimanded the dissemination of contraceptive information. Brazil first recognized that individual couples had the right to decide the size and spacing of their families only in 1974, at the World Population Conference in Bucharest. To this day, State family planning initiatives are hesitant and capable of meeting only a small part of the existing demand.

FACTORS INFLUENCING REPRODUCTIVE CHANGE

Why did fertility decline in India and Brazil? How well do current theories of fertility behaviour help explain these transformations? Few topics have received as much attention in the social sciences during the last few decades as fertility decline. Yet, there is a sense of frustration among students of fertility behaviour with the slow progress made in understanding the dramatic changes which have taken place in the last two hundred years (Szreter 1993:660). Two contrasting interpretations of fertility decline have been put forward. One attributes the decline to improved contraceptive availability, and the other to reductions in the desire for children as the result of socio-economic change. Little progress is being made in reconciling the two.

The debate originated in an early formulation by Notestein (1953), based on the experience of historical Europe. His view was that a gamut of changes associated with a shift to industrial occupations, urbanization, education, and mortality decline, had brought about Europe's fertility decline. The specter of rapid population growth in the developing world was already beginning to haunt the world by the time Notestein developed his theory:

indeed, his work was motivated by a sense of the urgency of initiating fertility decline in the developing world.

Existing theories of fertility decline have evolved with a logic of their own, and from this logic has emerged a long-standing debate between those who believe that fertility decline is 'demand-led', namely, that it comes about as a result of structural changes which reduce desired family size, and those who believe that the decline can be 'supply-led', that is, it can be induced by active efforts to propagate contraceptive use, even in the absence of other structural changes.

Lant Pritchett (1994) vigorously argues the case that fertility decline is driven by changes in the demand for children, stating that 'Analyses purporting to demonstrate the dominant importance of the provision of family planning practices are typically based on analytical errors . . . we show that to a striking extent the answer to why actual fertility differs across countries is that desired fertility differs, Pritchett laconically admits that contraception may have a role, albeit a very secondary one: 'Of course, it is always true that changing fertility desires *and* increased contraceptive access cause fertility reductions in the same trivial sense that gin *and* tonic makes you drunk.' (1994:52). As discussed below, Cleland et al (1994) vigorously argue that the demand for children can be driven down by increasing the availability of contraceptives.

Many policy-makers were concerned at the prospect of having to wait for structural shifts similar to those of Europe to take place in the developing world before the rate of population growth would slow down. Instead, they saw hope in the fact that modern contraceptive technology had made rapid advances. This opened up the possibility that technology could substitute for structural changes in bringing about fertility decline, just as modern medical technology had gone far in enabling mortality decline without the need for radical alterations in health behaviour or level of socio-economic development. Accordingly, energetic family planning programmes were devised in many developing countries in the 1960s and 1970s.

These programmes did not meet with overwhelming success in their early years. Since increasing the supply of contraceptive technology and information did not seem to be enough in itself, interest then shifted to the question of how to reduce the demand for children: namely, what factors could reduce people's desired family size. This field was dominated by the powerful economic theories of fertility behaviour which had recently been formulated, applying theories of consumer behaviour relating to the demand for goods, to the question of the demand for children.

Several variants of the basic theory of the costs and benefits of childbearing have emerged. Some hinge around the view that, in many agrarian settings, high fertility brings net economic advantages to parents, and, conversely, when this situation changes people will want fewer children (Caldwell 1976; Cain 1977). More recently it has been suggested that fertility decline can be 'poverty-led', that is, when people become impoverished over time, they can no longer afford to have as many children as before (Mencher 1980; Basu 1986). A variety of theories regarding childbearing as a form of insurance also exist, stressing the importance of children for ensuring old age support, for insuring against a variety of environmental risks (Cain 1981), and for insuring against high probabilities of child mortality.

Meanwhile, a very different set of ideas was generated by the Princeton study of European fertility decline (Coale and Watkins 1986). This study could not find generally applicable 'thresholds' of child mortality, education levels, urbanization, etc., associated with fertility decline. On the contrary, they found enormous variation in the levels of the indicators at the time of the fertility transition. They also found considerable homogeneity in fertility behaviour within linguistic zones. This shifted interest to the power of communication in influencing fertility and, in particular, suggested a focus on the power of diffusion of ideas within particular culturally-defined regions.

The 'diffusion' theory of fertility decline has two radically different forms. One assumes that people are rational actors: not in the narrow sense that they are in a position to make decisions with full knowledge of the outcomes, but in the sense that they have a broad understanding of the implications of alternative courses of action. It is so difficult to have full knowledge of the likely outcomes of childbearing (will they survive? what sex? what personality? what opportunities will be available to them when they grow up?) that one cannot take any narrow view of rational decision-making in the sense of parents weighing up the costs and benefits of each child. As Pollack and Watkins (1993:476) point out, 'critics of all versions of the rational actor model object that the assumption of maximizing behaviour grossly exaggerates the ability of individuals to store, retrieve and process information, and to make decisions.' In the real world, not all behaviour is planned or rational all the time. Yet this does not mean that childbearing decisions are not informed by rational choice.

Diffusion of smaller family size norms can take place through rational decision-making. For example, demographic innovators who are early to respond to altered circumstances make it easier for others to follow suit because they demonstrate that the innovation carries low risks and high gains, and they also make the new behaviours more socially acceptable. Thus individual strategies can shape and alter group norms. Coale (1973), for example, emphasizes that for fertility decline to take place, fertility control must be advantageous for the household and the act of controlling fertility must be ethically and morally acceptable. In this formulation of diffusion theory, the fact of diffusion is simply a description of *how* rational actors alter their behaviour, and we still have to turn to other theories to explain *why* they do so.

Another variant of diffusion theories of fertility decline drops the assumption that people are rational actors. This variant focuses on the possibility of 'pure' diffusion, on the power of ideas to communicate themselves. In this model, people alter fertility behaviour simply because the new suggestion gains currency in a setting, whether or not circumstances have altered people's demand for children. This brings us back full circle to the 'supply-led' view of fertility change, whereby it is deemed possible to reduce fertility by intensive family planning programme activity, without necessarily wasting time on the structural changes which reduce the demand for children.

In recent times, this view has perhaps been expressed most influentially by Cleland et al (1994) in their study of fertility decline in Bangladesh. They conclude that 'The evidence for Bangladesh suggests that the relative importance and primacy of the demand and supply side factors should be reversed. The crucial change that has taken place concerns acceptability of and access to birth control and *not* structural change that has driven down the demand for children.' (1994:134). This is despite the fact that they document much evidence of changes consistent with reduced demand for children: improved levels of living, rapid integration of rural people into non-agrarian sources of income, growing need to invest in children's education, and exposure to urban values and altered consumption aspirations. Similar arguments have been put forward by Robey et al (1993) and Larson and Mitra (1992).

Other studies of Bangladesh argue that, on the contrary, desired family size has fallen in Bangladesh following major structural shifts. To begin with, rapid population growth put intense pressure on land resources and drove people to seek income sources outside the agrarian sector (Adnan 1990; Kabeer 1994; Das Gupta and Narayana 1996). Fortunately for them, the manufacturing and trade sectors grew rapidly in the past few decades, enabling a massive shift of labour out of agriculture and into these sectors. These changes have gone far to reduce the demand for children in Bangladesh, and the family planning programme has only helped people meet their demand for reducing fertility.

Comparing India's and Brazil's experience in the area of reproductive change makes it immediately apparent that the active implementation of organized family planning programmes is neither a necessary nor a sufficient condition for fertility to decline. India has had such a programme since 1966, while Brazil has not had one at all. Despite this, Brazil's fertility decline has been considerably more rapid than India's. One could argue that large parts of India have low levels of socio-economic development and urbanization, so one cannot expect fertility decline there to be very rapid. In this regard, South Korea's experience is of relevance, as it has had both a very well-run family planning programme as well as very rapid economic growth and urbanization, so that both the 'supply' and 'demand' factors associated with fertility decline are abundantly at play and reproductive change should be expected to be amongst the most rapid observed. It is significant that South Korea's fertility decline has proceeded at much the same pace as that of Brazil (Figure 1), suggesting that 'supply' factors are of little consequence compared with 'demand' ones.

Reproductive Change in India

Perhaps the most striking feature of reproductive change in India are the enormous regional differences in the timing and pace of fertility decline. By 1991, parts of South India approached replacement fertility levels and the majority of states had moderate fertility levels of around 3 children per woman, while the Central states continued to have high levels of fertility of around 4.5 – 5 children per woman. Not only is fertility higher in the Central states, but also the pace of decline in them continues to be far lower than in the rest of the country (Table 1). Four of the papers in this volume address the factors underlying reproductive change in India.

TABLE 1: TOTAL FERTILITY RATES,
1981 AND 1991, FOR MAJOR STATES OF INDIA

State	1981	1991	% decline 1981–91
South			
Andhra Pradesh	4.0	3.0	25.00
Karnataka	3.6	3.1	13.89
Kerala	2.8	1.8	35.71
Tamil Nadu	3.4	2.2	35.29
North-Centre			
Bihar	5.7	4.4	22.81
Madhya Pradesh	5.2	4.6	11.54
Rajasthan	5.2	4.6	11.54
Uttar Pradesh	5.8	5.1	12.07
Northwest			
Haryana	5.0	4.0	20.00
Punjab	4.0	3.1	22.50
West			
Gujarat	4.3	3.1	27.91
Maharashtra	3.6	3.0	16.67
East			
Orissa	4.3	3.3	23.26
West Bengal	4.2	3.2	23.81
India	4.5	3.6	20.00

Source: Sample Registration System 1981, 1991.

India being such a large and heterogeneous country, in-depth studies of reproductive change have been carried out for specific parts of the country and not for the whole. However, although the explanations for reproductive change put forward for the different regions seem at first sight to be supported by completely different theories, on closer examination there is in fact an underlying pattern of similarity to be found.

Kerala is widely known to have almost completed its demographic transition, with levels of infant mortality, life expectancy, and fertility approaching that of developed countries. This achievement is especially remarkable in view of the fact that it is far from being the most prosperous state in India, and very far behind the economic levels of the developed world. Kerala is therefore often held up as a model of what can be achieved in low-income settings if the State is committed to the human development of its people. Kerala's economy also benefits from the high level of investment in its people, as substantial volumes of remittances are sent home by people working all over India and the world.

Fertility decline in Kerala is attributed to energetic efforts to provide universal education and health care, starting from the nineteenth century when an enlightened ruler espoused these causes (see Krishnan in this volume). Subsequently, there have been several popular socialist movements, such as those to keep wage levels high and protect workers' welfare. The population is almost universally literate and uses its literacy actively, with high proportions reading newspapers and using the public libraries available to both urban and rural dwellers. More importantly, the population is highly politicized and aware of its rights, and ensures that public facilities for health care and other services are properly run. Kerala, then, presents an impressive example of the 'human development model' of fertility and mortality decline.

At the other end of the spectrum is the state of Punjab, which represents the path of economic development (see Das Gupta in this volume). Punjab has by far the highest per capita income amongst the Indian states, and has been relatively prosperous through most of this century. Much of Punjab's prosperity derives from agriculture, which received an enormous boost with the development of canal and well irrigation around the turn of the century, and again during the time of the Green Revolution in the mid-1960s. Subsequent growth of industry and agro-business opened up new non-agrarian sectors of employment. Income levels have risen steadily for all groups of people.

The emphasis in development initiatives in Punjab has always stressed economic growth, and placed far less emphasis on social development. This is reflected in the health indicators, which show that Punjab enjoys better health than most other Indian states, but far less than Kerala. Education has also spread quite recently, especially among women, such that older people are largely uneducated, while high proportions of the young have been educated. Faced with rapid population growth stemming from steady mortality decline since around 1920, people began to reduce fertility by restricting marriage and controlling childbearing through the use of folk methods such as withdrawal and abstinence. People were enabled to respond quickly to the growing population pressure by reducing fertility, because of the same development efforts which reduced mortality. These efforts brought security against the epidemics and famines caused by the sharp fluctuations in harvests which had earlier generated tremendous insecurity in many aspects of life. Greater stability of expectations and security of livelihood were critical factors enabling people to reduce fertility (see Das Gupta in this volume).

It is notable that fertility began to decline in Punjab around 1940, a quarter of a century before the spread of modern contraceptives. The age distribution of Kerala suggests that fertility decline also began around the same period. It is also notable that this happened in Punjab under conditions of high infant mortality (over 150 per thousand births), low life expectancy, negligible levels of literacy, and no access to modern contraception. Moreover, although agricultural yields were rising steadily, levels of living in Punjab in the 1940s were low and remained low until the recent Green Revolution.

Tamil Nadu is also approaching replacement level fertility, and, has the lowest fertility in India, after Kerala. There is, however, less consensus about the reasons for fertility decline in Tamil Nadu than in Kerala. Tamil Nadu has gone the path of social development mixed with economic development (Kishor 1994; Ramasundaram 1995). Levels of social development in Tamil Nadu are not as high as in Kerala, with education and mortality levels which compare favourably with the rest of India, although noticeably less favourable than those of Kerala. During the 1950s and 1960s, the state underwent steady industrialization and emerged as one of the most industrialized and urbanized states in India (Kishor 1994, quoting Gough 1989). This period was also one in which public irrigation facilities were rapidly expanded, enabling rapid agricultural growth. When the 'Green Revolution' technology was introduced in the mid-1960s, further rapid rise in agricultural output was generated. Despite these efforts, however, Tamil Nadu (along with Kerala) ranks below average among the Indian states in terms of per capita income.

Turning to social development initiatives, levels of literacy, including female literacy, have risen rapidly in Tamil Nadu during recent decades, and as Kishor (1994) points out, the emphasis in education has been on increasing the spread of elementary education. Equity-oriented efforts also abound in the state. Land reform and tenancy legislation, aimed at protecting the poor, were passed, fixing limits on the amount of land that a family can hold, on the rent that can be charged from tenants, upholding the legal rights of tenants, and setting minimum wages for agricultural labourers (Kishor 1994; Ramasundaram 1995). While these reforms were not fully implemented, they, nevertheless, represented a serious thrust towards equity. Health service provision has been greatly expanded, and innovative nutritional supplement programmes carried out. In particular, since 1982 there has been a free lunch programme for children aged 2–10 years, registered in child welfare centres and elementary schools, which is found to have improved diets and reduced poverty (Kishor 1994). Perhaps the most notable feature of the state in this regard is the fact that it has a unique record of aggressive, affirmative action efforts to raise the status of the lower social classes (Ramasundaram 1995; see also Mari Bhat in this volume).

Since Tamil Nadu is not the leading state in terms of either social or economic development, which Kerala and Punjab, respectively, are, alternative hypotheses have been put forward for its rapid fertility decline. One is that it has had a particularly effective family planning programme, but Mari Bhat points out in this volume that this is not substantiated by the data. Another argument, put forward by Kishor, is that the development of the state has been 'exclusionary' of the poor, and this has left them with no choice but to shift over to investing in their children's education and training to enter the urban job market. The consequent need to reduce the quantity of children in order to improve their quality is sharpened by rising aspirations. However, Mari Bhat again finds no evidence that the fertility decline is in any sense 'poverty-led', as the decline amongst the poor lags behind that among the richer. He points out that the electronic media are especially widespread in Tamil Nadu, and that they seem to have an especially strong negative effect on fertility in this state.

Much of the apparent contradiction between the explanations of fertility decline in various parts of India are resolved when they are contrasted with the Central states of the country. These states are the most disadvantaged, both in terms of economic as well as social development. They have the lowest per capita income levels in the country and show poor performance on agricultural as well as industrial development indicators. They also show far lower levels of literacy and health than any other part of the country.

This suggests that whether states have placed greater emphasis on economic or on social development, is of far less consequence than whether they have placed emphasis on development at all. Both forms of development have in common the feature that they make for greater security of life and aspire to improved living conditions, thus motivating and enabling people to plan under conditions of far less uncertainty about the future. Both social and economic development increase people's control over their lives and, in Ansley Coale's words, brings fertility control 'within the calculus of choice'. It is to be noted that even in Punjab, people did not initiate fertility decline because of a direct income effect, since income levels there were still quite low in the 1940s, but because of greater security of life and livelihood.

Greater emphasis on social development seems to make for more rapid improvement in people's control over their lives than a greater emphasis on economic development. This is consistent with the fact that more rapid fertility and mortality decline have taken place in regions which have stressed social development over economic development. The parts of the country which have lagged in social as well as economic development are also those which have lagged in their demographic transition, and continue to have high mortality and fertility rates. These are the parts of the country where the environment of risk in daily life remains far higher than elsewhere, whether it be in terms of earning a living wage or in terms of the likelihood that one's child will survive. The slow penetration of some economic and social development has also been accompanied by a gradual decline in mortality and fertility.

The Indian experience suggests that the growing pressure of population on resources, which was experienced all over the country, generated a latent demand for reducing family size, but that improved security of life and changing aspirations were a critical condition enabling people to respond to their perceived pressure on resources. This interpretation is consistent with Mari Bhat's findings in this volume, that the regions of India characterized by the highest population density, the highest female literacy, and the lowest child mortality rates were those with the lowest fertility rates. The highest fertility regions were the most sparsely populated, economically the most backward, and with the lowest levels of female literacy.

Reproductive Change in Brazil

Causes[1]

In contrast to the variety of patterns witnessed in India, Brazilian fertility decline can be attributed to the same set of interrelated factors in all regions, although it occurred at varying rates in different parts of the country. That is, throughout the country, the same broad array of factors coalesced, in a sociologically intricate manner, to change reproductive behaviour. Brazil's fertility reduction has been rapid and unexpected — from a total fertility of about 6.0 in the early sixties to below 2.5 in the mid-nineties. No simple explanation can be proffered for this decline: Brazil has never had any widespread official or private family planning programmes, and much less has it supported any effort to control population growth. No abrupt changes or sudden cataclysms have occurred. Nor can the change be attributed to rapid and sustained economic growth; indeed, the decline began during a period of accentuated growth and was later intensified during the worst economic crisis ever experienced by the country. Some international circles have adopted the glib explanation that Brazil's fertility reduction is due to massive sterilization abuse; this hypothesis is vastly oversimplified. No other uni-faceted explanation stands up to examination. The rapidity and extent of Brazil's fertility decline, thus, presents a special analytical challenge.

[1] The following discussion of the causes of fertility decline in Brazil basically summarizes information in the chapter by George Martine in this volume.

At the level of proximate determinants, there is considerable agreement that the vastly increased control of marital fertility is at the root of Brazil's fertility decline. Yet, technological advances which would permit women or couples to control fertility cheaply and safely were not forthcoming, nor were effective family planning services made available to significant segments of the population. The postures and policies adopted by some of the most influential social actors in the population domain resulted in a standoff, and had the practical effect of limiting the range of contraceptive alternatives.

Unquestionably, the motivation to reduce births expanded enormously after the mid-1960s, due to the combined influence of a great variety of compelling factors — many of which were linked to some form of modernization. During the postwar period, and particularly after 1965, Brazil underwent rapid social change which progressively altered the nature of economic activity as well as the composition of the labour force. Migration of all types was intensified, but especially to urban areas. The country was transformed from a predominantly rural agrarian nation, to one in which the majority of the population lived in cities, many of these in large cities. Formal education improved significantly but, just as importantly, informal education and access to all sorts of information expanded enormously, as a result of improved transport and communication and the intensification of social interaction between social groups and regions. Women began to participate in large numbers in the job market. Simultaneously, structural change had significant impacts on proletarianization and on consumption patterns and thereby on the motivation to regulate fertility.

The specificities of the urban transition in Brazil are particularly helpful in understanding the velocity of its fertility decline. The impact of urbanization on Brazilian fertility decline is consistent with the general lines of the modernization theory. However, the particularities of its urbanization process warrant greater attention. Basically, Brazil's rapid urbanization began earlier than most developing countries. Rapid urbanization and transitions in urban life have had an enormous impact on the dissemination of fertility control motivation and information; they also had an impact on the practical ability to regulate fertility. In turn, rapid fertility decline has itself accelerated the urban transformation.

On another level, seminal research by Faria (1989) has drawn attention to the unintended impacts of government policies in other apparently unrelated domains on reproductive behaviour. Significant institutional changes — particularly during the military regime, (1964–85) — affected the spread of new ideas, having a direct and immediate bearing on the way people thought about sex and reproduction, and facilitating the massive adoption of modern contraception. Transformations in the politico-administrative structure, which were instituted during this period, radically altered consumer credit, health care, social security and telecommunications. These different policies ended up influencing the demand for children, the legitimacy of birth control, and the manner of access to modern forms of contraception, particularly sterilization.

The role of the mass media was particularly critical in this combination. When access to the media is widespread and where it occupies an important part of people's leisure time, as in Brazil, the media can significantly influence people's conceptions as to a wide range of social values and roles. Investments in the communications area made by the military government in the late 1960s, had the effect of linking the country through radio and television. An immensely popular genre — the *novelas* — had a significant impact on levels of information and on mindsets. Among other things, it had an influence on behaviour in the reproductive sphere, helping to bring traditional roles and authority into question, to erode traditional male authority, and to redefine sexually-approved roles. A particular family image — small, egalitarian, unstable, and consumeristic — was promoted. New themes, such as extramarital sex, family instability, female empowerment, and non-traditional family arrangements were portrayed on the screen and, as a result, became part of daily discourse. Various indirect messages, such as the advantages of separating sexuality from reproduction, the cult of corporeal beauty, the 'advantages' of remaining single, of working outside the home, etc., could be viewed. This combination has evidently had an impact on mindsets, choice of lifestyles, and values.

Overall, it is clear that key economic and social policies had a significant impact on changes in the thinkability of fertility control, on the value of children, on the practical availability of birth control methods, and thereby on the motivation and capacity for fertility control. Changes in the desire and ability to use effective birth control methods ultimately produced the country's observed rapid fertility reduction. In short, the motivation for reproductive change in Brazil stemmed from widespread and rapid social change.

From the foregoing, four main characteristics of the Brazilian process of fertility decline warrant highlighting. First are the high rates of abortion and the unusually rapid diffusion of the practice of sterilization. This is linked, in part, to the attitudes and policies of different social forces which resulted in the practical unavailability of other effective methods; sterilization is also attributable to the institutional changes which were implemented, during the military regime, in the areas of health and social security. Second, the widespread institutional changes, which were introduced by the military regime as part of its efforts to induce rapid modernization, and which had multiple and interlinked implications for fertility reduction. Third, within the institutional changes, the enormous influence of the mass media on social behaviour, including that in the area of reproduction; this influence is derived in part from the nature and dimension of the investments made in the area of communications by the military regime, and in part from the particular character of the message which permeates the Brazilian media, particularly through the novelas. Lastly, all of the other factors were catalyzed by an extremely rapid process of urbanization which, together with the fertility decline, helped bring about an early urban transition.

Consequences

Brazil's rapid fertility decline provides a window of opportunity for future social improvements. This can best be seen by examining the impact which changing patterns of growth have had on the country's age structure, as Carvalho and Wong show. Fertility decline produced not only a reduction in the rate of population growth in the short term, but also a profound change in age distribution in the medium and long terms. This demographic change has economic and social implications, and the structure of social demands has been completely altered.

Currently, the labour force is increasing in both absolute and relative terms and hence, despite population aging, the dependency ratio during coming years is quite favourable. The possibility of expanding investments in pre-school care and in education (both coverage and quality) is favoured by the relatively slow growth of the younger population. Investments in both these groups at the present time might be doubly profitable, since this cohort will go into the labour force in 10 to 15 years time, when the elder dependency ratio will start to increase at a faster rate. If society invests in the quality of the current stock of children, the economy will certainly experience a much better performance and the state will have more resources to invest in social security and the care of the elderly. Viewed in a long range perspective, one may say that Brazil has recently entered a 'golden' demographic stage, in which conditions are favourable for working out some of the social problems which plague the country. Exceptional opportunities for reallocating resources for child welfare: health, nutrition, education, training, and so on now exist. Since the demand for quantity is falling, investment and resources should increasingly go to quality.

Lessons from Comparing India and Brazil

Looking at India alone, it is difficult to avoid the conclusion that the pressure of population on resources, combined with development efforts, have been responsible for generating a powerful demand for reducing fertility. This has happened regardless of whether the focus was essentially on social or on economic development. The desire to reduce fertility has been so strong that it began to be implemented as early as 1940 in Punjab, at a time when modern contraceptives were unavailable, levels of literacy and income were low, and infant mortality rates were high. Despite these obstacles, people brought fertility down by delaying marriage and reducing the age at last birth through abstinence, withdrawal, and abortion.

In those parts of India where little development effort was made, namely the Central states, fertility levels remain high and have been slowest to decline, although rates of population growth have been high. This suggests that pressure on resources is not enough by itself to make for reduced fertility, although it can generate a latent demand for it. To translate the latent demand into actual demand, it is evidently necessary to create the conditions in which people feel that they can gain control over their lives and improve their lives through their own efforts. Increased expectations and a stable, predictable environment then, appear to be the critical factor enabling people to plan their family size as part of their overall effort to plan their lives.

Turning to Brazil, it would seem at first sight that a very different set of factors have been at work to reduce fertility. The main force making for fertility decline there seems to have been the rapid urbanization and modernization of the country. This included increased access to education and to other forms of information, increased participation of women in the labour force, enhanced consumption ambitions, changing values and aspirations, all affecting traditional stances towards childbearing.

State policies — in the economic and social rather than in the family planning domain — had an enormous impact on Brazilian fertility. First, they improved access to social security as well as to medical and hospital services: this not only helped to reduce dependence on the family for old age insurance and for help in medical crises, but also increased medical influence on the entire childbearing process while also paving the way for eventual access to sterilization. Second, credit policies directed to lower-income populations intensified consumption aspirations — which, in turn, are consistent with having smaller families. Third, they promoted capital-intensive modernization of agriculture which reduced employment opportunities in rural areas while stimulating rapid urbanization. As people moved en masse to urban areas, they were confronted with the problems of raising large urban families in reduced physical space, the need to invest in children's education, and the desire to increase consumption expenditure. Awareness of the implications of these changes for planning family life-styles and childbearing was greatly accelerated by the expansion of a mass communication system (Faria 1989: *passim*).

Several common features emerge from India's and Brazil's apparently divergent experiences. Firstly, in neither country was the decline driven primarily by the family planning programme. In the case of Brazil, such a programme did not exist until recently, and even today it covers only a small part of the demand. In the case of India, a strong family planning programme has been in place since the mid-1960s. However, it has met with differing success in different parts of the country. Those regions which have seriously tried to implement social or economic development, are also those in which the family planning programme has been most successful. This is despite the fact that family planning is financed and directed by the Central government, and thus there is far more homogeneity in the family planning input in the different states of India than in almost any other part of their development efforts. Apparently the fertility decline has not been essentially 'supply-driven', even in a country with a strong programme, but has instead been 'demand-led'.

The demand for reduced fertility thus seems to have been generated largely as a spin-off of State policies related to economic and social development. Many of these policies increased people's control over their lives. For example, the State in Brazil set about providing basic education to the population, and introduced social welfare programmes, including medical insurance for a majority of people. The Indian State has also provided health and education, though far less comprehensively than Brazil, except in the case of Kerala. In some other parts of India, increased control over life has come as a by-product of rapid economic development. In both countries, the regions which were relatively left behind in the developmental process (the Northeast and the Amazon regions in Brazil, the Central states in India) were the 'demographic laggers', being the last to experience the onset of fertility decline.

In both countries, people have found it difficult to remain as peasants living off the land. This lifestyle, in which the potential burdens of large family size are somewhat diffused, became unsustainable in both settings, and people increasingly turned to the growing modern economy to seek their living. In India this happened simply as a consequence of the growing pressure of population on land, although the State sought consciously to encourage labour-intensive cultivation techniques. In Brazil, it happened despite the low man-land ratio, because of the highly skewed distribution of land, combined with the State's encouragement of labour-substituting technologies and emphasis on land-extensive cultivation. The shift to the non-agrarian employment sector brings with it the need to invest in children's education, and introduces aspirations to lifestyles with higher levels of consumption, all of which are consistent with a demand for smaller families. The mass media contributed to altering people's aspirations more rapidly, propagating messages of how people with small families could achieve higher levels of living.

The demand for children in India and Brazil influenced by structural changes, often resulting from the unintended consequences of State policies. These triggered changes in group norms about family size through a process of ideational change. Having smaller families not only became advantageous for people, but also became socially acceptable. The more rapid pace of urbanization and also the more permanent nature of the rural-urban move in Brazil almost certainly helps explain the more rapid fertility decline in that country.

WOMEN'S POSITION AND REPRODUCTIVE CHANGE

Since women are centrally involved in the matter of reproduction, it is unsurprising that a substantial literature has developed around the subject of women's position and reproductive change. Three of the papers in this volume bring a fresh focus to the question of how gender equity contributes to reproductive change, while two deal with the more neglected question of how reproductive change affects gender equity.

Kaufmann discusses how the social construction of sexuality, gender, and family relations influence both reproductive behaviour (including demographic outcomes) and the wider political context of reproductive rights. Patterns of marital stability and the underlying system of gender relations strongly influence sexual and reproductive behaviour and, in this way, have a significant influence on family planning outcomes. Women's reproductive behaviour cannot be viewed in isolation from that of men. In Brazil, concepts of masculinity (*machismo*) are forceful and often deeply entwined with notions of fecundity and paternity. In such a cultural milieu, it is barely in their interest to embark on family planning. Because of men's disinterest, the women are left to act alone. Hence, reproductive control is up to women.

The degree to which the women interviewed by Kaufmann were in control of their lives, or were relatively more empowered, affected the level and type of contraceptive practice. Marital instability tended to reduce women's control over their own fertility: the women who were most secure in their marital relationship and who lived in the most controlled environment were the most effective contraceptors. Precarious sexual relationships not only generated a sensation of powerlessness in a woman's life, but also made it more difficult for her to have access to the means of fertility control.

Narayana argues that a rise in the proportion of female teachers has contributed to fertility decline. Women's participation in the labour force in general means that other women have role models to follow in terms of their own education, employment, and reproductive behaviour. However, higher levels of female participation in the education and health sectors has a more direct impact on these, because such women are in a position to train women directly. They become effective channels for the diffusion of information and technologies, and opinion leaders to other women in their community.

The same theme of gender equity contributing to fertility decline is explored by Jain. He notes the huge regional disparities in India in gender equity, fertility levels, and education, and suggests that Central financing of female education should redistribute the potential savings from fertility decline in low-fertility states to those which have low female literacy and high fertility. As in the Brazilian case, Jain points out that the freeing up of per capita resources resulting from fertility decline does not necessarily mean that the State will invest more per capita in human development. He also shows that the relationship between female education and fertility changes as fertility declines: fertility falls sharply with education where levels of female education are low, but this gap is small where fertility levels are low.

A relatively neglected question is that of how fertility decline can help promote gender equity and the condition of women as a whole. There are many reasons to predict that this will happen, but nevertheless there is a need for monitoring the process and attempting to maximize it. For example, it has often been suggested that lower fertility will enable women to participate more actively in the labour force. Yet studies in Britain suggest that the constraints placed by having any children at all may hinder women's economic participation substantially (Joshi 1992). More effort needs to go into evaluating policies which constrain women's full participation in the labour force and lead to high rates of poverty among unmarried women with children.

There is also considerable evidence that, in families with smaller numbers of children, girls stand a higher chance of receiving education (Lloyd 1992; Sathar and Lloyd 1993; Garg and Morduch 1996). As household resources are freed up by a reduction in the dependency burden of young children, the pattern of allocation of household resources can be expected to change, in favour of females. Yet in some settings with strong son preference, fertility decline may actually result in an increase of excess mortality of girls relative to boys (Das Gupta and Bhat 1997; Nizamuddin and Alam

1996). This is because the number of sons desired falls less steeply than the number of children desired, leaving less room for tolerating daughters and increasing parent's motivation to manipulate the sex composition of their children in order to meet their desired number of sons. Research and policy need to be directed towards trying to ensure that girls and women benefit as far as possible from the gains of fertility decline.

The analysis by Murthi, Guio and Drèze suggests that not only does increased female literacy reduce fertility and improve child survival, but that it also improves gender equity in child survival. Female labour force participation also improves the survival of girls relative to boys. Excess female child mortality appears to be amplified by variables related to development and modernization. The driving force behind gender bias in child mortality does not seem to be poverty, which might have been expected to force hard decisions on intrafamilial resource allocation. Instead, this bias seems to be mitigated by poverty.

Few factors can improve women's reproductive health as effectively as having fewer children, and, therefore, being subject to the stresses which culminate in poor reproductive health. This is evident in the closing gap between male and female mortality in the peak reproductive ages in India and Sri Lanka (Das Gupta and Visaria 1996; Nadarajah 1983). Yet, as Berquó points out, inadequate attention to women's health can result in a situation in which maternal mortality rates change little in response to fertility decline.

The rapid decline in the average number of children per woman and the high rate of contraceptive use in Brazil would suggest that Brazilian women are in good control of their reproductive lives, but Berquó shows that, in fact, there has not been a marked improvement in reproductive health. Absolute levels of maternal morbidity and mortality declined significantly with reduced exposure to childbearing, but the average risk associated with a pregnancy or childbirth did not improve noticeably. This is because much of the fertility decline occurred in a period of severe economic and social difficulties, accompanied by an increase in poverty and a gradual reduction in public funds allocated for health care. Since a high proportion of women depend on the public sector for health care, this has had negative implications for women's health in general, and for reproductive health in particular.

Berquó shows that access to medical attention during the pre-natal period as well as at childbirth and in the post-partum stage is often deficient, particularly among the lower-income strata. Several of the main causes of maternal mortality, such as pregnancy-related toxaemia, which accounts for 30 per cent of all deaths, could be easily prevented. Moreover, deaths resulting from self-induced or otherwise unsafe abortions accounts for 12 per cent of maternal deaths. Although health care resources saved from reduced child-bearing loads could have been used to improve maternal health services, even simple gynaecological examinations are accessible to only a small part of the female population, particularly in poorer regions such as the Northeast.

The fact that the State failed to back family planning did not prevent people from using it, but it made the conditions of use more difficult and dangerous than it might otherwise have been. The Brazilian case provides a good illustration of how women's health can suffer when official health services mostly ignore the domain of reproductive health, and poor people have to depend totally for their family planning services on the 'markets', which are monopolistically controlled by one or two producers. Women have had to make frequent recourse to self-induced abortion, ex-acting a severe toll on their health and lives.

CONCLUSIONS

A cross-country approach is very useful for shedding light on the factors underlying fertility decline. This forces one to move away from the specificities of a particular experience, and to test the validity of broader analysis. For example, conclusions coming out of one region of India need to be generalized in the light of those coming out of, apparently, very different conditions elsewhere in India. Another level of generalizability has to be reached when the experience of Brazil is also incorporated.

The comparison of India's and Brazil's experience offers several lessons for theories of fertility decline and for policy formulation. Firstly, they clearly suggest that the decline was driven by a demand for smaller families, and not by the propagation of a family plan-ning programme. Moreover, they suggest that most of the theories on the economic factors underlying the demand for children may be too unidimensional in their approach. The demand for smaller families was driven by a gamut of socio-economic changes relating to a shift from agrarian to non-agrarian occupations, improved mortality conditions, the spread of education, and and increased pressure on resources including on living space. This gamut of changes is far closer to Notestein's original formulation of the factors making for fertility decline in historical Europe than the more specific economic theories of fertility decline. Of course, the availability of modern contraceptive technology and the mass media have helped greatly to accelerate the speed of fertility decline in countries undergoing the transition today.

The specificities of which social and economic changes help initiate fertility decline can be expected to differ in different settings. In this sense, it is inappropriate to conclude, as many have done, that Notestein's view of demographic transition was disproved by the lack of common thresholds of variables, such as literacy and urbanization, associated with fertility decline in various regions of Europe. We should not logically expect to find specific thresholds common to all settings. Different combinations of structural changes can make for shifts in desired fertility, and these need to be studied in the context of the setting in question. Despite the different specificities of the causes of fertility decline in different settings, it is clear that certain changes which have swept the globe during the past century have triggered fertility decline across it (Das Gupta 1997). Amongst these changes are the development of the nation-state, with interventionist administrations bringing policing, credit, education, health, and other services to its citizens, replacing many of the roles of the family. Also critical is the growth of a rationalist scientific tradition and scientific advances which gave people a sense of mastery over their environment and helped bring fertility control 'within the calculus of conscious choice'.

Since fertility decline is now well under way in most of the developing world, it is also important to think about the consequences of fertility decline. One set of research and policy questions hinge around how to spend the resources which are freed up by this process: for example, Carvalho and Wong point to the possibility of improving the quality of educational facilities with the funds freed up from having to build new schools. The same logic clearly applies to health and other social services. On the other hand, fertility decline also generates new demand for resources. A common example of this is that the gradual ageing of populations create a need to make careful assessments of the ability to provide adequate State and familial care for the aged. These issues have already been the subject of considerable thought in present-day developed countries, and much can be learnt from them by the developing world.

More neglected is the question of how women benefit from fertility decline. For women, there is an unambiguous benefit from having fewer children in that the burden of reproductive morbidity and mortality is reduced. They are also freer to participate in the labour market. Yet, as the Brazilian case shows, if inadequate attention is paid to women's reproductive health, the gains from lowered childbearing will be reduced. For girls, too, the consequences of fertility decline can be ambiguous. In most settings, they are likely to benefit from having fewer siblings and gain greater access to schooling and health care. However, in settings such as India which have strong son preference, fertility decline puts greater pressure on families to get rid of unwanted female children, thereby raising levels of excess female child mortality. Thus some girls will not survive to benefit from the greater access to education and health associated with smaller family size. The studies in this volume have thrown up many insights into the causes of reproductive change, as well as some of its consequences: insights which are pertinent to both academic and policy debates. Above all, it demonstrates the power of cross-country comparison to further understanding of the reproductive transition.

REFERENCES

Adnan, Shapan (1990), *Annotation of Village Studies in Bangladesh and West Bengal: A Review of Socio-economic Trends over 1942–88* (Kotabari Comilla: Bangladesh Academy for Rural Development).

Basu, Alaka M. (1986), 'Birth Control by Assetless Workers in Kerala: The Possibility of a Poverty Induced Fertility Transition', *Development and Change*, 17(2):265–82.

Berquó, Elza, Maria Coleta Oliveira, and Suzana M. Cavenaghi (1994), 'Family and Household Structure in Brazil, 1970–1989' (Campinas: NEPO/UNICAMP), mimeograph.

Cain, Mead (1977), 'The Economic Activities of Children in a Village in Bangladesh', *Population and Development Review*, 3(3):201–27.

—— (1981), 'Risk and Insurance: Perspectives on Fertility and Agrarian

Change in India and Bangladesh', *Population and Development Review*, 7(3):435–74.

Caldwell, John C. (1976), 'Toward a Restatement of Demographic Transition Theory', *Population and Development Review*, 2(3–4):321–66.

—— (1978), 'A Theory of Fertility: From High Plateau to Destabilization', *Population and Development Review*, 4(4):553–77.

Cleland, John and Christopher Wilson (1987), 'Demand Theories of the Fertility Transition: An Iconoclastic View', *Population Studies*, 41:5–30.

Cleland, John G., James F. Phillips, Sajeda Amin, and G.M. Kamal (1994), *The Determinants of Reproductive Change in Bangladesh* (Washington D.C.: The World Bank).

Coale, Ansley J. (1973), 'The Demographic Transition Reconsidered', in *International Union for the Scientific Study of Population*, International Population Conference, Liege, 1973, vol. 1:53–72.

—— (1986), 'The Decline of Fertility in Europe Since the Eighteenth Century as a Chapter in Human Demographic History', in Ansley J. Coale and Susan C. Watkins (eds.) *The Decline of Fertility in Europe* (Princeton: Princeton University Press).

Crook, Nigel and Tim Dyson (1982), 'Urbanization in India: Results of the 1981 Census', *Population and Development Review*, 8(1): 145–55.

Das Gupta, Monica (1994), 'What Motivates Fertility Decline?: A Case Study from Punjab, India', in B. Egero and M. Hammarskjold (eds.) *Understanding Reproductive Change* (Lund: Lund University Press).

—— (1997), 'Liberté, Égalité, Fraternité: Exploring the Role of Governance in Fertility Decline', Harvard University Center for Population and Development Studies Working Paper 97.06

Das Gupta, Monica and D. Narayana (1997), 'Bangladesh's Fertility Decline from a Regional Perspective', *Genus*.

Das Gupta, Monica and Leela Visaria (1996), 'Son Preference and Excess Female Mortality in India's Demographic Transition', in Korea Institute for Health and Social Affairs and United Nations Population Fund, *Sex Preference for Children and Gender Discrimination in Asia*, KIHASA Research Monograph 96–02.

Das Gupta, Monica and P.N. Mari Bhat (forthcoming), 'Fertility Decline and Increased Manifestation of Sex Bias in India', *Population Studies*.

Dyson, Tim and Mick Moore (1983), 'On Kinship Structure, Female Autonomy and Demographic Behaviour in India', *Population and Development Review*, 9(1):35–60.

Faria, Vilmar (1989), 'Politicas de Governo e Regulacao da Fecundidade: Consequencias Nao Antecipadas e Efeitos Perversos' (Government

Policies and Fertility Regulation: Unanticipated Consequences and Perverse Effects), *Ciencias Sociais Hoje* (Sao Paulo: ANPOCS, Editora Revista dos Tribunais).

Friedman, Debra, Michael Hechter, and Satoshi Kanazawa (1994), 'A Theory of the Value of Children', *Demography*, 31(3):375–96.

Garg, Ashish and Jonathon Morduch (1996), 'Sibling Rivalry, Resource Constraints and the Health of Children: Evidence from Ghana', paper presented at the Harvard-HIID-MIT Economic Development and Growth Workshop, April 1996.

Gough, Kathleen (1989), *Rural Change in Southeast India: 1950s to 1980s* (Delhi: Oxford University Press).

Joshi, Heather (1992), 'The Cost of Caring', in C. Glendinning and J. Millar (eds.) *Women and Poverty in Britain, the 1990s* (New York: Harvester Wheatsheaf).

Kabeer, Naila (1994), 'Re-examining the "Demand for Children" Hypothesis in the Context of Fertility Decline in Bangladesh' (Copenhagen: Centre for Development Research) Working Paper 94.6.

Kishor, Sunita (1994), 'Fertility Decline in Tamil Nadu, India', in B. Egero and M. Hammarskjold (eds.) *Understanding Reproductive Change* (Lund: Lund University Press).

Larson, Ann and S.N. Mitra (1992), 'Family Planning in Bangladesh: An Unlikely Success Story', *International Family Planning Perspectives*, 18(4):123–44.

Lloyd, Cynthia B. and Anastasia Gage-Brandon (1992), 'Does Sibsize Matter?: The Implications of Family Size for Children's Education in Ghana' (New York: The Population Council), Research Division, Working Papers No. 45.

Malhotra, Anju, Reeve Vanneman, and Sunita Kishor (1995), 'Fertility, Dimensions of Patriarchy and Development in India', *Population and Development Review*, 21(2):281–305.

Mencher, Joan (1980), 'The Lessons and Non-lessons of Kerala: Agricultural Labourers and Poverty', *Economic and Political Weekly*, 18(19–21):877–900.

Nadarajah, T. (1983), 'The Transition from Higher Female to Higher Male Mortality in Sri Lanka', *Population and Development Review*, 9(2):317–25.

Nizamuddin, Mohamad and Iqbal Alam (1996), 'Nature of Sex Preference for Children and Gender Discrimination in Asia', in Korea Institute for Health and Social Affairs and United Nations Population Fund, *Sex Preference for Children and Gender Discrimination in Asia*, KIHASA Research Monograph 96–02.

Notestein, Frank W. (1953), 'Economic Problems of Population Change', in *Proceedings of the Eighth International Conference of Agricultural Economists* (London: Oxford University Press).

Phillips, James F., Ruth Simmons, Michael Koenig, and J. Chakraborty (1988), 'Determinants of Reproductive Change in a Traditional Society: Evidence from Matlab, Bangladesh', *Studies in Family Planning*, 19(6):313–34.

Pollak, Robert A. and Susan C. Watkins (1993), 'Cultural and Economic Approaches to Fertility: Proper Marriage or Misalliance?', *Population and Development Review*, 19(3):467–96.

Preston, Samuel H. and P.N. Mari Bhat (1984), 'New Evidence on Fertility and Mortality Trends in India', *Population and Development Review*, 10(3): 481–503

Pritchett, Lant H. (1994), 'Desired Fertility and the Impact of Population Policies'. *Population and Development Review*, 20(1):1–55.

Ramasundaram, S. (1995), 'Causes for the Rapid Fertility Decline in Tamil Nadu: A Policy Planner's Perspective', *Demography India*, 24(1):13–21.

Robey, Bryant, Shea O. Rutstein, and Leo Morris (1993), 'The Fertility Decline in Developing Countries', *Scientific American*, December, pp. 60–7.

Sathar, Zeba and Cynthia B. Lloyd (1993), 'Who Gets Primary Schooling in Pakistan: Inequalities among and within Families' (New York: The Population Council), Research Division, Working Papers, No. 52.

Srinivasan, K., Shireen J. Jejeebhoy, Richard A. Easterlin, and Eileen M. Crimmins (1984), 'Factors Affecting Fertility Control in India: A Cross-Sectional Study', *Population and Development Review*, June, 10(2): 273–96.

Szreter, Simon (1993), 'The Idea of Demographic Transition and the Study of Fertility Change: A Critical Intellectual History', *Population and Development Review*, 19(4):659–701.

Watkins, Susan C. (1986), 'Conclusions', in Ansley J. Coale and Susan C. Watkins (eds.) *The Decline of Fertility in Europe* (Princeton: Princeton University Press).

—— (1989), 'The Fertility Transition: Europe and the Third World Compared', in J. Mayone Stycos (ed.) *Demography as an Interdiscipline* (New Brunswick and Oxford: Transaction Publishers), 22.

World Bank (1993), *World Development Report 1993* (New York: Oxford University Press).

Factors Influencing Reproductive Change

1

Social Development and Fertility Reduction in Kerala

T.N. Krishnan

INTRODUCTION

Fertility decline can be perceived as a response to a shift in family size preferences. In the presently-developed countries, such a shift occurred as a gradual process during the course of economic development. It was accompanied by a massive transfer of the population from agricultural activities to industry and services and by a significant infusion of new technology. It is true that these countries also passed through major social transformations at the same time. However, because these changes occurred simultaneously, it is difficult to isolate the impact of social development on fertility decline. This paper shows how social transformation has been an important factor in changing the family size norm, and thus in promoting a rapid demographic transition, in Kerala. Low rates of economic development in Kerala make it easier to identify the social factors underlying its demographic transition.

BACKGROUND

Kerala state — a narrow strip of land about 600 km long and 115 km wide — is situated on the southwest coast of India. Its total area constitutes 1.3 per cent that of India. The present Kerala State was constituted by integrating the Malabar district with the former states of Travancore and Cochin in 1956; as will be seen, each of these components has had its own particular history of social evolution.

The author was extremely grateful to the editors of this volume for their editorial assistance in the preparation of this paper.

The 1991 census estimated Kerala's population to be 29 million, forming 3.4 per cent of India's total population. The significance of the Kerala story becomes fully obvious only in the context of a comparative setting. Kerala reports the lowest birth rates in India: 17.7 as compared to 29.2 for the entire country in 1992. It also has the lowest death rates in the country, resulting in a life expectancy of close to 70 years compared to about 59 years for India. Kerala surpasses all other states in levels of human development. Its HDI (Human Development Index) is estimated to be 0.775, compared to 0.744 for Punjab, which has a per capita state domestic product twice that of Kerala's.

Another unique feature of Kerala among the Indian states is its favourable sex-ratio. While there are only 927 females for every 1,000 males for India as a whole, the ratio in Kerala reaches 1,036 females per 1,000 males (Samuel 1991). The 1991 census also recorded a literacy rate of 90 per cent for Kerala, compared to 52 per cent for India as a whole. The female literacy rate increased from 38.9 per cent in 1961 to 86.9 per cent in 1991. The corresponding change in Punjab was only from 14.1 to 49.7 per cent. Life expectancy at birth was estimated at 67.6 years for males and 73.8 years for females for the period 1988–91. The infant mortality rate is 17 in Kerala, compared to 61 in Punjab. Data shown in Table 1 summarize the comparative position of Kerala among the major states in India with respect to some of the key economic and social parameters of development.

TABLE 1: STATE-WISE DEMOGRAPHIC INDICATORS 1992–93

State	TFR (15–49)	Birth rate	Infant mortality rate	% of prenatal check-ups by physician	% of institutional child-births	Female literacy rate
India	3.39	28.9	78.5	39.8	25.6	43.1
North						
Delhi	3.02	26.7	65.4	73.0	44.4	70.6
Haryana	3.99	33.1	73.3	29.5	16.7	45.9
Him. Pradesh	2.97	28.2	55.8	32.1	16.1	56.7
Jammu Regn. of J&K	3.13	28.0	45.4	48.8	21.7	51.0

Social Development and Fertility Reduction 39

State	TFR (15–49)	Birth rate	Infant mortality rate	% of prenatal check-ups by physician	% of institutional child-births	Female literacy rate
Punjab	2.91	25.0	53.7	34.4	24.8	52.1
Rajasthan	3.63	27.2	72.6	15.6	11.6	25.3
Central						
Madhya Pradesh	3.90	31.9	85.2	27.1	16.0	34.0
Uttar Pradesh	4.82	36.0	99.9	21.1	11.3	31.6
East						
Bihar	4.00	32.3	89.2	21.4	12.1	28.4
Orissa	2.92	26.6	112.1	33.6	14.2	41.4
West Bengal	2.92	25.9	75.3	60.5	31.5	55.2
Northeast						
Arunachal Pradesh	4.25	34.6	40.0	46.3	19.8	42.3
Assam	3.53	31.0	88.7	35.4	11.1	50.8
Manipur	2.73	24.0	42.4	59.7	22.6	63.1
Meghalaya	3.62	32.0	64.2	45.0	29.7	60.1
Mizoram	2.26	20.3	14.6	43.0	48.7	88.9
Nagaland	3.19	30.9	17.2	31.8	6.1	72.0
Tripura	2.68	23.3	75.8	58.3	30.2	63.6
West						
Goa	1.90	17.2	31.9	92.1	87.1	72.9
Gujarat	2.99	27.2	68.7	39.6	35.7	50.4
Maharashtra	2.86	26.7	50.5	61.0	44.1	55.4
South						
Andhra Pradesh	2.59	24.5	70.4	61.6	33.0	38.0
Karnataka	2.85	26.4	65.4	59.5	37.6	46.3
Kerala	2.00	19.6	23.8	95.9	88.4	82.4
Tamil Nadu	2.48	23.6	67.7	70.6	63.6	54.9

Note: TFRs and birth rates are for the three-year period prior to the survey. Infant mortality, percentage of prenatal check-ups, and institutional births are for the four years prior to the survey.

Source: International Institute of Population Sciences, *National Family Health Survey 1992–93*, Introductory Report, Bombay, October 1994.

Given these favourable social indicators, it is surprising to find that Kerala's per capita income is low compared, to not only many low-income countries, but also to many states in India. Indeed, it is noteworthy that Kerala ranked only ninth from the top among the Indian states in terms of per capita state income in 1993. Kerala ranked twelfth in terms of per capita consumer expenditure in 1973–4, but this has improved dramatically and Kerala now occupies the fourth rank from the top. In 1973–4, 60 per cent of Kerala's population was estimated to be below the poverty line but this declined to 32 per cent in 1987–8 (Planning Commission 1993). Kerala ranked the fifth highest in 1973–4 in terms of the size of the poverty ratio but moved down to twelfth position in 1987–8. Since poverty in India is measured on the basis of the distribution of per capita consumer expenditure, the decline in poverty in Kerala is a direct reflection of the improvement in per capita consumer expenditure. During this period, a large number of Kerala workers migrated to the Gulf countries and their remittances were primarily responsible for this rise in per capita consumption (Krishnan 1995).

Thus, a relatively high level of poverty and a relatively low level of per capita income have hindered neither improvements in literacy rates and mortality levels nor fertility decline in Kerala. It will be argued in this paper that access to education and health care is primarily responsible for this state's favourable situation. Access to education and health care is a prerequisite for social transformation, economic advancement, self-improvement, and the well-being of the family. The following section examines the history of changes in social conditions in India, and their particular evolution in Kerala.

SOCIAL CONDITIONS IN INDIA AND KERALA: CASTE AND SOCIAL SEGMENTATION

Patterns of social organization prevailing in India during the colonial period and the period immediately following independence were impediments to social change. They slowed the pace of social improvements and improvements in levels of living for a large segment of the population. The caste structure formed a major facet of social organization.

The caste structure follows a hierarchical order with the highest caste (brahmins) at the top and the scheduled castes and scheduled tribes (the so-called untouchable castes) at the bottom with numerous castes in between. These differentials have in turn led to social and cultural segmentation of Indian society along caste lines. During the periods when such segmentation was practiced rigidly, different caste groups never intermingled; social interactions like eating together and intercaste marriages were taboo; even regulations on the types of food and the dressing patterns for different castes were respected.

Each caste represented a separate social entity living in total cultural isolation. Some of the lower castes were not only denied any occupational mobility, but the traditional occupations they practiced were rigidly specified. Social segmentation was a universal phenomenon in Indian society, the intensity and severity of the practice varying somewhat from region to region. Income and wealth distributions were closely correlated with the distribution of the castes. As one moved down the caste hierarchy, both income and wealth declined, meaning that the lowest castes possessed practically no assets of their own. Political power and positions in the bureaucracy were also monopolized by the upper castes.

A central tenet of the caste hierarchy was 'social pollution'. The basis of caste segmentation lay in social distance. Social pollution was translated into 'social distance' and the social distance between any two castes increased as one moved down the caste hierarchy. The concept of social distance had embedded itself in the practice of physical distance. For an upper caste person, the distance to be kept away from a person depended on the position the lower caste person held in the caste hierarchy. Caste pollution prevented a person belonging to the top echelons of the hierarchy from entering the inner portions of his own household or partaking of food before purifying himself by bathing. Thus, segmentation prevented socialization between higher and lower castes and the evolution of common social values. Upper castes who had easy access to education and health care constituted less than 20 per cent of the total population of the state.

Though the hierarchical caste structure was a descending continuum with increasing social distances, broadly the population could be aggregated into three groups. The top group enjoyed unrestricted access to all private and public facilities; the middle group, consisting of backward communities, had partial access; and the bottom group, consisting of depressed classes, was denied access to most public facilities. Since the Christian and the Muslim communities were outside the caste structure, they did not fall under the purview of 'social distance'. Thus, as far as access to educational and health facilities is concerned, they were on a par with the top group.

As elsewhere, the rigidity of the caste system in Kerala kept the social environment frozen. Kerala was highly segmented along caste lines until about the closing decade of the nineteenth century (Rao 1981). In fact, Kerala was reputed to have had the worst forms of caste segmentation in the country during the nineteenth century. As a result, access to education and health care was denied to large segments of the population because of caste status. For instance, lower caste children were not allowed to sit inside classrooms for fear of polluting the upper caste children and the upper caste teachers, despite admissions being granted to them. For the same reasons, they were not allowed to seek medical help or to enter hospitals for medical consultations. How did Kerala transform such a moribund society to one of universal access to education and health care?

SOCIAL DEVELOPMENT IN KERALA STATE

Ultimately, Kerala overcame the caste impediments to social progress through a complex process of social intermediation. Social intermediation is understood here as interventions at different levels of the society, by various agents, to change the social and behavioural attitudes within the then prevailing social environment, to achieve desired social outcomes (Kabir and Krishnan 1992). Social intermediation was instrumental in democratizing access to education and health, and thereby eventually influencing fertility patterns.

The history of the development of education and health in Travancore and Cochin is mainly one of mutual interactions between the state and the society and the responses of the state and caste-based communities to social intermediation. Social processes in Malabar evolved along different lines as Malabar was under the direct rule of the British for a long time. Its progress in education and health was as slow as in the rest of India, until it officially became part of Kerala state.

The backward communities and depressed castes constituted nearly half the population of Kerala and, unless this group improved as well, the level of human development achieved in the state would have remained distorted and incomplete. Education of the lower castes, along with other economic changes, altered the social environment itself whereby the attitudes of the lower castes began to change towards access to health, education, and public employment (Kabir and Krishnan 1992). A generalized concept of social intermediation provides a framework of analysis which endogenizes the process of human development in Kerala.

This process had its origins in the early decades of the nineteenth century. At that time, the State of Travancore was a native state ruled by a royal family under the tutelage of the British Resident — *Dewan*. Steps were taken in Travancore to establish a government bureaucracy to streamline the administration. The Queen of Travancore, at the behest of the British Agent, declared universal education a noble goal of the State. However, this goal remained elusive for a long time since caste barriers were too strong to allow children of backward and untouchable communities to attend schools.

The first external shock to this stagnant situation was the entry of Christian missionaries into the field of education in the beginning of the nineteenth century. Denial of admission by the government schools to children belonging to the backward and depressed communities presented an opportunity for the missionaries — who saw educating these children as an easy route for large-scale conversion of a section of the Hindu community to Christianity. They opened English language schools, which incidentally helped to inculcate the values of equality and social justice and, thus, planted the seeds of the social revolution in Travancore which began in the late nineteenth century.

The depressed classes quickly realized that conversion to Christianity helped them break the shackles of the caste barrier. The missionary educational efforts, however, did not help significantly in spreading education in Travancore for three important reasons: first, the state itself withdrew its support, fearing large-scale conversion to Christianity; for similar reasons, the upper castes did not allow their children to attend missionary schools; and finally, the indigenous Christian community resented the missionary efforts as intrusions which undermined their traditional cultural values. Whatever the end result, the missionary schools, by educating a number of children from the backward and depressed communities, had unwittingly created a group of people who would later play critical roles in initiating the process of social intermediation. They also paved the way for large-scale entry of indigenous communities into the fields of education and health at a later date.

English education under state auspices was begun in 1834 (Gopinathan Nair 1989). Later, from the 1850s, the Travancore government also established allopathic hospitals to improve the health of its people (Kabir and Krishnan 1992). The policies in the neighbouring Cochin State closely followed those of Travancore, and in both these states the governments took the lead in establishing schools and hospitals.

The Travancore government articulated a more coherent and consistent policy for the development of education in the second half of the nineteenth century. This policy consisted of the expansion of government schools, encouragement of vernacular schools (whose medium of instruction was Malayalam), and provision for financial incentives to the private sector to establish schools through a system of grants-in-aid. The policies adopted for the development of education in Cochin state were similar. Although the number of schools and the enrollment rose substantially by the last decade of the nineteenth century, the children of backward and depressed castes were still denied entry to government schools (Gopinathan Nair 1989).

The forces of social intermediation were gathering strength during this period, and by the end of the last century they were able to articulate their demands more forcefully. The Ezhava community, the largest of the backward castes, took a pioneering role in mobilizing the forces of social intermediation to gain entry to schools. This community had greatly benefited from the land reforms of the 1860s and prospered by the favourable economic conditions of this period, caused mainly by a price revolution in coconut and coconut products.

Children from some of the more prosperous Ezhava families managed to receive education in the missionary schools and thus became intensely conscious of the social suppression which victimized them. They felt a deep need to improve their social standing in society, and there emerged from among them a spiritual and social leader, Sri Narayana Guru. Narayana Guru's ideas on social reforms were extraordinarily revolutionary for his times, since he advocated '*one caste, one religion, one God*' as the cardinal principle of human interaction. He advocated a combination of spirituality and material progress as the basis for uplifting the poor and the downtrodden. He saw the lack of education and poor hygiene as the root causes for the observance of 'social distance' and caste pollution. Therefore, access to education and health care became the cornerstones for social development and for the convergence of social values.

Inspired by the actions of Narayana Guru, Ayyankali, a spokesperson for the depressed castes, took courage to articulate the demands of these communities for entry into educational institutions and hospitals. During 1911 and 1912, the efforts of these communities finally resulted in the opening up of all government schools to the children of all communities. As a result, school enrolments doubled within a decade and there has since been a steady and increasing growth in enrolments and literacy rates (Gopinathan Nair 1989).

The forces of social change were similar and parallel in many respects in Travancore and Cochin. In Malabar, the direct British rule, the continuation of the feudal structure of the society, and the prevalence of high degree of inequalities in land and wealth distribution weakened the forces of social intermediation and stifled the progress of social development. While various social movements did create popular demand for education and health, the effective demand for these was confined to the upper castes in Malabar. These inter-regional differentials within the area persisted until the formation of the state of Kerala in 1956. By that time, however, the social environment of Travancore and Cochin had undergone a complete transformation.

The social intermediation process begun by Sri Narayana Guru culminated in the famous Temple Entry Proclamation of 1936, through which all the temples were opened up for worship to all Hindu communities. This Proclamation heralded a new social environment in Kerala, in which caste hierarchy no longer determined, nor even dominated, one's social position. Since then, the social status of a person has been determined largely by his/her economic position. Caste has yielded place to class, even though caste has assumed a new role among the erstwhile 'oppressed' communities as a claim for preferential treatment in education and employment.

EDUCATION AND HUMAN DEVELOPMENT

The basic strategy adopted for human development in Kerala was to ensure access to education and health to every individual. Access to education, in this context, involved locational, economic, and social access. Locational access implied having schools within walking distance from homes. Economic access was ensured by making education progressively free up to and including high school. Later, needy children were also provided noon meals at the schools. Social access was vital to ensure that children of backward and depressed communities were not denied enrollment in schools. It is basically social access which was provided through the process of social intermediation. These policies had been followed in Travancore and Cochin since the early decades of this century, with the result that these two regions were well ahead of Malabar when Kerala was constituted in 1956.

Another important policy was the integration of the private sector into the mainstream of education. During the 1860s, when a large number of public schools were opened in Travancore and Cochin states, the governments realized that they would not have enough resources to build schools for all the school-age children in their territories. The mechanism of grants-in-aid to private schools was devised to alleviate this resource constraint, and it became a powerful incentive to various communities for starting schools. Although these policies have been modified over time, they are an important factor in explaining the high proportion of current revenue expenditure on education in Kerala.

When Kerala was constituted in 1956, Malabar lagged behind the southern region in access to schools for children in different parts of the district. The number of government schools were few and the grants-in-aid scheme was not as comprehensive as in Travancore and Cochin. The first priority upon formation of the new state was, therefore, to redress the imbalance in the regional distribution of educational facilities by opening a large number of government schools in Malabar. The government also extended all the other facilitating measures, such as payment of salaries to private school teachers, the noon meal programme, etc., to the Malabar region. As a result, the number of schools in Malabar increased from 126 in 1956 to 5,477 in 1991.

By 1990, Kerala had one school for every 2400 population and the regional disparity in access to schools had been completely eliminated. Almost all children in the age-group of 5 to 15 years attended schools in all the districts of Kerala. In April 1991, Kerala achieved the distinction of becoming the first state in the country to be declared totally literate. The total literacy campaign in Kerala was a cooperative venture by government, political parties, a large number of NGOs, and individuals. It involved the free services of about 400,000 volunteers to teach the illiterates (State Planning Board 1992). Thus the programme for the eradication of illiteracy in Kerala represented the *summum bonum* of the process of social intermediation begun during the closing decades of the last century.

The current literacy rate of the population aged six years and over is around 91 per cent. The gap in literacy levels between males and females has declined and is now insignificant. The data on enrolment rates indicate that, in Kerala, the rates have been similar for boys and girls in the age-group 6 to 11 since 1960–1. Around 95 per cent of children in the age-group 5 to 14 are now in school.

The achievement of total literacy, the continuous rise in mean years of schooling, and the elimination of gender differentials in education in Kerala have their origins in the closing decades of the last century. The policies initiated at that time have proved to be unerring in their objectives and have continued to guide the development of education to this day. With the formation of the state of Kerala, these policies were extended to Malabar. By this time, the social conditions in Malabar had undergone a drastic change and the dominance of the caste hierarchy was also declining.

WOMEN AND EDUCATION

Numerous studies have commented upon Kerala's notable efforts at women's education and the role of women in Kerala's social development (Jeffery 1992). High female literacy and women's education are considered important factors in explaining the demographic transition and the high levels of health status in Kerala. Social barriers to women's education continue to retard female literacy levels in many parts of India. These barriers began to crumble in Travancore and Cochin in the second half of the nineteenth century itself. Again, the forces of social intermediation played an important role in this change. While the first girls'

schools in Travancore were opened on the initiative of missionaries, Cochin used local efforts to lobby for women's education.
Initially, separate schools for girls were established to overcome
the social resistance but, ultimately, coeducational schools began
to outnumber these. As a result of all of these measures, the
female literacy rate in Travancore and Cochin, while lower than
that for males, was the highest in India at the turn of the century.
The female literacy rate in Malabar, although initially lower,
gradually approached that of Cochin and Travancore.

Literacy rates among women in 1891 indicate that it was
highest among Brahmins, Nairs, and Christians. The Brahmins
constituted a minuscule proportion of the total population, and
numerically, Nairs, Christians, Ezhavas, Muslims, and depressed
classes made up the majority of the remainder. Therefore, the
history of female literacy and women's education is really the
story of how these groups responded to the schooling of girls.

Upper caste women, especially among the economically better
off Nair community, had a long tradition in functional literacy
since they had to read religious works like the *Ramayana* and
Mahabharata in Malayalam. Thus, girls from these families were
allowed to learn to read and write under the tutelage of the village
teacher. Therefore, when the indigenous schools were converted
to vernacular schools, girls from the upper castes continued to
attend. Their attendance was also encouraged by the opening of
separate girls' schools.

The Nair girls were especially helped in attending schools because
of the prevalence of the matrilineal system, which enabled them to
move outside their homes freely and independently. Since Nair women enjoyed a higher status within the family and a girl child was
necessary for the continuation of the family line, girl children enjoyed considerable social freedom within the family, and there were
no cultural or social barriers to their attending schools.

Though the matrilineal system was a factor in the rapid spread
of literacy among Nair women, Christians followed their example
closely. The establishment of a large number of schools under
the grant-in-aid scheme by the indigenous Christian community
opened the doors of education to Christian girls who had also
enjoyed a freedom of mobility similar to that of the Nairs.
Christian women also prized functional literacy as it enabled them
to read the Bible. In addition, the Church enjoined on the

Christian families to send their girls to schools and they also set up separate girls' schools run by nuns under the management of the church. Literacy rates among Christian women were equal to, or exceeded, those of the Nairs, by 1941. In fact, the highest female literacy rates in 1991 were in those districts where the Christian population is concentrated.

With the abolition of caste barriers, the Ezhava girls also began attending schools in large numbers. A section of the Ezhavas also practiced matriliny, but it would be wrong to attribute the progress of female literacy among them largely to this factor. Except for Namboodiri Brahmins and Muslims, women in Kerala do not practice the custom of purdah. They thus enjoyed some measure of movement outside their homes. The tradition of purdah is considered a powerful barrier for raising the literacy levels as well as the status of women in the backward Hindi-speaking states (Minturn 1993). Comparatively higher female literacy rates among the Southern states might be partly due to less practice of purdah in this part of the country.

HEALTH AND SOCIAL INTERMEDIATION

There is some indirect evidence for advancing the hypothesis that health conditions had begun to improve in Travancore and Cochin by the end of the nineteenth century. Thus, Kerala had a higher growth rate than India until 1971, due to the fact that its mortality rates were lower. With the formation of the state of Kerala, mortality in Malabar also began to fall and, now it is almost identical in both regions.

While a multiplicity of factors account for the health transition in Kerala, the acceleration of this process in recent years has taken place largely due to the emphasis placed on, and the extension of, maternal and child health. The emphasis on maternal and child health by itself also illustrates an important link between health and demographic transitions whereby feedback mechanisms between mortality levels and fertility decisions are set in motion.

Infant mortality is a key factor in the health transition of a population, as the life expectancy at birth and the general mortality rate are dependent on its level. It appears from the population census estimates that infant mortality in Kerala declined from 220 in 1921–30 to 120 in 1951–60. Panikar (1984) has attributed the decline in mortality rates during this period to preventive measures such as the spread of smallpox and cholera vaccinations, improvement in sanitation, and the extension of drinking water schemes. Kerala has the lowest infant mortality rate among all the states in India. In 1992, as shown in Table 2, its infant mortality in the rural sector was down to 17, which was about a fourth of the rate in India as a whole.

TABLE 2: CHANGES IN INFANT MORTALITY IN RURAL KERALA

Year	Infant Mortality Rate	Percentage Decline
1951–60	120	–
1966	68	43.33
1976	55	19.12
1986	27	50.90
1992	17	37.04

Source: Sample Registration in Kerala, Rural Annual Reports 1980 and 1988. Sample Registration Bulletin 1994.

The life expectancy at birth in Kerala is fifteen years longer than that in India as a whole. The death rate in rural Kerala is half that of rural India. How did Kerala achieve this transition from a moderate mortality region to a low mortality region within a span of thirty-five years? What were the instruments and policies which brought about this transformation? What lessons can Kerala offer to societies with similar levels of income?

The health status of a population at any particular moment in time, as pointed out by Mosley and Chen (1984) and by Caldwell (1986), is a result of multiple interactions and feedbacks among a number of factors — socio-economic as well as biological. While socio-economic factors determine the intensity of desire and the ability to seek health care, the biological factors interacting with the quality of health care determine the outcome of the actions taken in response to illnesses. This section focuses primarily on the socio-economic factors that have aided and accelerated the process of health transition in Kerala.

The reduction in the death rate and in infant mortality in Kerala must be partly attributed to policies aimed at improving locational and economic access to health care for lower income groups. If health care centers are located farther away from home, the opportunity costs must be added to the direct cost of medical care. Therefore, a measure of equity in making health care available is not only important for its use, but especially important for the poorer sections of the population.

Kerala stands apart from the other states in India in terms of access to health care. It not only has the lowest population-bed ratio among all the states, but the facilities are almost evenly divided between rural and urban areas. Although rural populations make up the large majority of the total population in most states, less than 20 per cent of the public-sector hospital beds are located there. If the private sector facilities are also considered, the disparities are much larger. In the case of Kerala, nearly 55 per cent of total hospital beds are in rural hospitals and clinics. Recent data indicate that the cost of treatment is also closely related to access to health care. Kerala reports the lowest cost of treatment among all the major states in India. Moreover, the burden of treatment is one of the lowest for the poorer income groups in Kerala (Krishnan 1994).

Data on causes of death for all ages indicate major shifts in the causes, even between 1959 and 1965. Smallpox accounted for 1.9 per cent of reported deaths in 1959, but declined to 0.1 per cent in 1965. The number of deaths due to diarrhoea, respiratory diseases, and fevers declined from 27.8 per cent of the total in 1959 to 16.0 per cent in 1965. The expansion of health care facilities, especially in the Malabar area, and the vaccination programmes against infectious diseases, have mainly been responsible for the rapid decline in mortality rates and the increase in the expectation of life during the first phase of the health transition.

The data presented in Table 3, on the percentage distribution of childbirths in rural Kerala by type of medical attention received, show that the percentage of births taking place in institutions rose from 26 in 1973 to 91.5 in 1991. Only about 3.5 per cent of childbirths were attended by untrained professionals in 1991, whereas it had been nearly 53 per cent as recently as 1973. This explains why, as late as 1980, no deaths were reported from complications arising from childbirth. Nor were there infant deaths due to malposition, cord infection, or malnutrition reported in 1980. This result could be attributed to the extension of prenatal care of pregnant women. Various inquiries have shown that the extent of coverage of tetanus toxoid immunization of pregnant women is almost universal in all parts of Kerala (NFHS Survey 1992–3, see IIPS 1992).

TABLE 3: PERCENTAGE DISTRIBUTION OF BIRTHS IN
RURAL KERALA BY TYPE OF MEDICAL ATTENTION RECEIVED —
1973, 1978, 1988, AND 1991

Year	Institutional	Trained professional	Untrained professional	Non professional
1973	26.0	20.0	36.6	17.4
1978	40.8	16.4	40.6	2.2
1988	86.0	5.6	6.8	1.5
1991	91.5	5.0	3.5	0.0

Source: (1) Sample Registration — Kerala, Annual Reports; (2) Sample Registration System 1991.

In short, various interventions, at different levels of society, by various agents, began to change the social and behavioural attitudes within the then prevailing social environment to achieve the desired social outcomes (Kabir and Krishnan 1992).

CONSOLIDATION AND CONVERGENCE

The present Kerala State was constituted by integrating Malabar district with Travancore-Cochin State in November 1956. Under the direct rule of the British, Malabar lagged significantly behind Travancore-Cochin in literacy levels and in access to health care. The history of social development since the formation of Kerala State shows how these differentials were eliminated or narrowed and what policies and programmes were adopted for this purpose.

The basic strategy in both the education and health sectors was the same: extension of the policies and programmes followed earlier in Travancore and Cochin to the Malabar region. This involved a combination of public and private investment in education and health, and provision of financial incentives for the private sector to establish and operate educational institutions. The private sector has also played a major role in health care delivery, especially since 1975, but there were no financial or other incentives in this case.

In the annual budgets of the Kerala state, a larger share of investments in education and health was earmarked for the Malabar region so that, over the years, the disparities in the number of public
institutions between the two regions have considerably narrowed.
The result of these developments in the increasing social infrastructure was that literacy rates and infant mortality rates in Travancore,
Cochin, and Malabar regions have now converged.

THE SOCIAL IMPLICATIONS OF INCREASED ACCESS TO HEALTH AND EDUCATION

Progress in education and health, as described above, had a catalytic
effect on other forms of social change in Kerala. Such progress not
only requires changes in social and behavioural attitudes but also
advances in education and health systems. In fact, Caldwell describes the health transition as a process that includes 'the social
and behavioural changes that parallel the epidemiological transition and may do much to propel it' (Caldwell et al. 1989). That is,
the health outcomes in a society are not a function of health technology alone but very much depend upon social change. This is
equally true for education. The process of social intermediation in
the health transition of Kerala made possible a more equitable distribution of health care among the severely deprived segments of
the society (Kabir and Krishnan 1992).

These processes of social change had, in the long run, important
implications for, *inter alia*, changes in the size of family norm. The
formation of social values can be seen as the result of interactions in
three distinct spaces: family, educational institutions, and workplace.
The educational level of parents and the economic circumstances of
the family play a significant role in changing the family's perceptions
about society and in molding social attitudes towards family. The
school is another social institution where children from different
castes and classes intermingle and social distinctions become blurred.
The educational environment also fosters common outlooks and
common values. The third environment for social interaction is the
workplace. If occupational mobility exists, persons from different
castes will find opportunities for social intercourse and will forge
common ties and develop similar outlooks on life and society.

The Indian caste system had long remained an impediment
for social interaction and prevented the emergence and eventual

convergence of a common set of values regarding family size norm. The earlier rigid segmentation of the society restricted the scope for the demonstration effect to operate through observation and acceptance of the small family size norm of the upper castes who had received modern education and moved on to non-traditional occupations. Families of lower castes engaged in low-productivity traditional occupations and the illiterate saw little value in education; naturally, therefore, they seldom encouraged children to go to school or, if enrolled, to pursue further studies. In the pre-independence period, children of the lowest castes were even denied admission to schools in many parts of the country. The scope for occupational mobility is extremely limited in India on account of the low rates of growth of the economy and the large size of the labour force in each occupational category. Most non-traditional occupations are confined to urban areas, which account for less than 30 per cent of the total population.

Social development in Travancore and Cochin took nearly a full century. However, the lessons of the development experience in Travancore and Cochin were successfully applied to policies and programmes in Malabar and produced similar outcomes within a span of thirty-five years. The wide differentials in literacy, birth, death, and infant mortality rates have almost disappeared since the integration of the two regions, as the result of socially conscious policies. This is a clear demonstration that deliberate and targeted social policy can indeed lead to significant improvements in levels of human development even in situations with low per capita incomes. If such policies are complemented with moderate increases in consumption levels, then the results are quite impressive. In the case of Kerala, such moderate increases in per capita consumption were made possible by migrant workers' remittances.

SOCIAL DEVELOPMENT AND REPRODUCTIVE CHANGE IN KERALA

The history of Kerala's fertility decline is an integral part of its social development. Within it, three major factors are worth highlighting: increased access to education, particularly for women; explicit social policy; and, increased access to the means of fertility regulation.

Women's Education, Changing Values and Fertility Decline

While the level and spread of education achieved by a society is an important instrument for social change, it is women's education that is most critical for changes in social attitudes towards desired family size. Numerous studies have attributed a critical role to women's education in Kerala's high level of social achievement. The question is: how did Kerala succeed, while many other states struggled in this matter?

One important factor is that Kerala had the matrilineal system, in which women enjoyed considerable freedom of movement outside their homes. Upper caste Kerala women visited temples every day, and thus were accustomed to socializing outside their homes. The same was true of Christian women who frequented their churches. It was the mother who took prime responsibility for bringing up children under the matrilineal system since the father did not cohabit continuously with his wife. There was also no sex discrimination under this system, there being no preference for male children.

From time immemorial Kerala had also observed a distinction between reading and writing. While a large number learned to read, only a few cared to learn writing. Many upper caste noble families employed writers to maintain their accounts and correspondence, a practice considered a mark of prestige for the head of the household (Bhaskaranunni 1988). This tradition in reading included women as well. They learned to read the Indian epics as part of religious observance during certain periods of the year. As a result, they could read other literature as well. Similarly, Christian women had a tradition of reading: primarily, the Bible.

These practices had a significant influence on society as a whole, since about a quarter of the population of Travancore and Cochin followed the matrilineal system of inheritance. The Christians and the matrilineal communities together constituted over 40 per cent of the total population in the two states of Travancore and Cochin, and they set an example to other communities by sending their girls to schools, when 'modern' institutional education was introduced.

The increase in the number of girls attending schools had various consequences for reproductive behaviour. First, it had a direct influence on fertility by raising the age at marriage. Generally speaking, child marriages were uncommon in Kerala, and the state's traditions in this matter were reinforced through educational expansion. As the average number of years of schooling continued to increase over a long period, so did the age at marriage. Though India had incorporated family planning since 1952, its programmes became seriously operational only in the mid-1960s. Therefore, it is justifiable to attribute the pre-1966 decline in fertility in Travancore and Cochin, at least in part, to the increase in age at marriage brought about by the spread of female education.

Second, education had an obvious impact on value formation. A notable feature of the history of fertility decline in Kerala is its convergence between the regions, as well as among the different communities. The total fertility rate in Malabar was estimated at 5.5 in 1970, as compared to 3.2 in Travancore-Cochin. By 1991, this had declined to 2.2 and 1.8, respectively. The major factor which facilitated these trends towards lower fertility convergence was the rapid spread of education, particularly women's education, in Malabar, at a rate higher than in Travancore and Cochin areas. In short, the importance of female education in universalizing the small family norm cannot be overstated.

The Acceleration of Social Change through Explicit Policies

While the beginnings of social change through education and access to health care may be traced to the latter half of the nineteenth century in Travancore and Cochin, Malabar remained unchanged until late in this century. Total literacy rates, as well as those for females, were lower and the mortality rates were higher in Malabar than in Travancore and Cochin. These differences could be attributed to the differentials in access to schooling and health care between the two regions.

However, upon formation of the state of Kerala, the political parties and the government leadership realized these disparities and resolved to rectify them. Additional resources were allocated to the Malabar region to promote more rapid development of schooling and health care facilities than in the rest of the state. As a result of this conscious policy, the number of schools and enrolment increased at a higher rate in Malabar and, by 1991, the differentials in literacy rates between Malabar and Travancore-Cochin regions had substantially narrowed.

Similarly, the inadequacy of health care facilities in the Malabar region were an important factor explaining the higher mortality rates which prevailed there. In 1970, the crude death rate was estimated at 10.5 in Malabar as compared to 8 in Travancore-Cochin. The death rates had become almost identical in the two regions by 1991. Similar changes have also occurred in the case of infant mortality rates for Malabar, which declined from 62 per 1000 live births in 1970 to 15 in 1993, similar to the figure for the Travancore-Cochin region.

A disaggregated analysis of the data on a community or religious basis provides further insights into the importance of convergence in Kerala's fertility decline. For instance, the birth rate among the Muslim community in 1980 was 34 per 1000 population in Malabar, compared to 27.6 in the Travancore-Cochin region; the corresponding rates for the Hindu community were 25.8 and 20.6, respectively. For the Muslim community, it declined to 29.4 and 23.0 per thousand, respectively, by 1990 (Sample Registration Report 1980, 1990). The reason for the relatively higher figures for this community is the late entry of Muslim girls to secular schooling and the still higher levels of illiteracy among Muslims than among the Hindus and Christians. In fact, levels of education and literacy rates are the highest among Christian women, a fact that seems to be reflected in their fertility behaviour as well; fertility rates among Christians are the lowest in Kerala.

Though differences still persist in fertility rates among the three major religious communities, the fact is that the decline has been rapid among all the communities and that Kerala has already achieved an over-all total fertility rate of less than two. The most significant point to note in this context is that this was achieved in a period of about thirty years. The important message of Kerala's experience is not that it took about 150 years in Travancore and Cochin to complete the social transformation, but that it took only thirty years for Malabar to catch up, with social change consciously guided through a preferential policy of accelerated development of education and health care in that region.

Access to the Means of Fertility Regulation: The Importance of Health Care

Social development, while creating a favourable environment, could not by itself have brought about a significant fertility decline. Access to the means of fertility regulation was essential for translating a desire for smaller family size into reality. In turn,

effective provision for the means of fertility regulation also involved a favourable health care setting.

Provision of contraceptive means is particularly critical in the
Indian context. From the beginning of the 1980s, the dominant
method of fertility regulation in India has been female sterilization.
The Indian programme did not deny access to other methods of
fertility regulation but, owing to various socio-economic and cultural factors, female sterilization seems to have remained the most
preferred method. The complementary factors which account for
the success of the sterilization programme in Kerala also explain
why it has so far failed in other states.

The critical factor in the success of Kerala's sterilization programme was the easy access to health care which contributed to
fertility regulation in diverse ways. Since 1975, as a consequence of
the inflow of remittance incomes from the Kerala migrant workers
in the Middle East, substantial expansion in the provision of private
health care occurred. This has supplemented the public health care
facilities in those areas to which remittance incomes were flowing
in significant volume.

The availability of affordable health care, combined with greater
health consciousness, has dramatically altered the quality of care
sought at childbirth in Kerala. As a result, the proportion of childbirths occurring in medical institutions has risen sharply from 26
per cent in 1973 to 91 per cent in 1991 (Krishnan 1991). This
increase has contributed to a reduction in infant mortality, through
a reduction in perinatal mortality. It has also led to a reduction in
maternal mortality by ensuring immediate medical attention to
complications of childbirth.

Along with the institutionalization of births, a great sense of
concern with the conditions of maternal and child health has also
developed. This concern is being translated into a number of programmes relating to the care of pregnant women, such as the distribution of vitamin and iron supplements, tetanus immunization,
etc. Similarly, the immunization of newly-born children has shown
far greater compliance in Kerala than elsewhere in the country.
These health interventions are reflected in the extremely low rates
of infant, child, and maternal mortality rates attained by Kerala.

The success of Kerala's fertility decline may thus be attributed
to the inculcation of the small family norm brought about by
social development and to the provision of health facilities to

attain that objective. A careful examination of the elements of the population policy as implemented in Kerala will show that the state had, though not consciously, followed what in modern parlance is known as a reproductive health approach. The maternal and child health programmes in Kerala together contained most of the components of the modern reproductive health package. This conclusion is also supported by data on the distribution of patients treated in hospitals. For instance, of the total number of persons treated in government hospitals and clinics in 1986–7, women and children constituted 42 per cent and 29 per cent, respectively (Krishnan 1991). Data on the numbers treated by private hospitals and physicians are unavailable, but if these were to be considered, the corresponding proportions would undoubtedly be much higher.

The transformation of the population programme to a reproductive health programme is partly due to the inclusion of the maternal and child health components; but a great deal of credit is due to the increased demand generated by the people themselves. And the importance attached to maternal and child health has been increasing over time as a consequence of the fertility reduction itself. Thus, these two aspects of fertility reduction have been mutually reinforcing.

LESSONS FOR OTHER STATES IN INDIA

How does a society overcome social segmentation and universalize the small family norm? The Kerala experience would indicate that there are three necessary conditions. The first is the universal acceptance of education of children as a means of social and economic mobility. The second is the assurance to parents of the feasibility and desirability of the small family norm by ensuring the survival of their children. The third is the creation of conditions which make it possible for those who opt for the small family norm to carry out their decision. Essentially, these conditions imply that access to education and health care is the important prerequisite for the universal acceptance of the small family norm.

In this paper, I have endeavoured to show, on the basis of the Kerala experience, how the generalization of access to education and health care can play an important part in the demographic transition and how lack of access is probably the major reason for the persistence of high fertility rates in most of the less developed states in India.

The early history of social development in Kerala suggests that vigorous public action can transform a region's level of social development and cause major improvements in social indicators, even at low levels of per capita income. Kerala is unique in that its per capita income is lower than the average of other Indian states and yet it has high levels of education and health care (Sen 1994). High income growth can also promote or accelerate social development, but there may exist a substantial time-lag before the social transformation manifests itself. While private initiative may raise growth rates of income, the trigger for social development is invariably public action. A comparative study of the levels of social development among the Indian states supports this proposition. On its own, an increase in per capita income is insufficient to accelerate the rate of social development. The complementarity between income growth and social development is probably weak at low levels of per capita income, but it can be compensated by strong public action. This might not be true at high levels of income since there would be sufficiently strong incentives for private initiative in developing the institutional infrastructure necessary for social development. This might account for the lag in social development in the absence of public action at low levels of income.

Second, the Kerala story has shown that a major fertility transition is possible within the span of a single generation, even without significant economic growth. Upon observing Kerala's success in reduction of the total fertility rate to below two children, one must ask — what happened in the other states of India? Kerala's fertility transition is the result of the simultaneous operation of a number of factors; in this paper, we have attached considerable importance to the attitudinal changes brought about by social development and generalized access to health care as well as to family planning facilities.

One side of the Kerala story tells us that social development is a prolonged and slow process while the plot within the main story, namely, the process of social change and fertility transition in Malabar, shows how the period can be shortened dramatically by conscious policy interventions. One of the reasons for the continuing low levels of human development in some other Indian states is the degree of inequality in the distribution of the benefits of human development. There, social intermediation processes did not develop in the past, nor did a targeted policy of social transformation evolve since Independence. Therefore, the social inequalities which had existed in these states for a long time continue to dominate social relations, and the small family norm has yet to take root in these states. In addition, even though the components of the population programme being implemented in the other states are the same as in Kerala, they are ineffective for the simple reason that access to health is very limited or even lacking to rural populations in most of these states (See Table 1).

In this view, the present approach to population programmes in the other states is less likely to succeed simply because there is no health infrastructure in these states to implement a reproductive health programme. In this sense, the lessons of Kerala's fertility decline may be of limited relevance to other states in India. On the other hand, Kerala is a demonstration of how powerful a reproductive health approach to fertility transition can be.

REFERENCES

Berman, P. (1995), 'Financing of Rural Health Care in India', Paper presented at the International Workshop on Health Insurance in India, September.

Bhaskaranunni (1988), *Kerala of the Nineteenth Century* (in Malayalam) (Trichur: Kerala Sahitya Academy).

Bhat P.N., Mari and I. Rajan (1990), 'Demographic Transition in Kerala Revisited', *Economic and Political Weekly*, September.

Caldwell, J.C. (1986), 'Routes to Low Mortality in Poor Countries', *Population Development Review*, 12 (2) June.

Caldwell, J.C., and S. Findley et al. (eds.) (1989), *What We Know About Health Transitions — The Cultural, Social and Behavioural Determinants of Health*, vols. 1 and 2 (Canberra, Australia: The Australian National University).

Department of Economics and Statistics (1987), *Report of the Survey on the Utilisation of Gulf Remittances in Kerala* (Trivandrum: Government of Kerala).

Directorate of Economics and Statistics (1980–90), Sample Registration System — Annual Report, Trivandrum.

Franke, R.W., and B.H. Chasin (1992), *Development Through Radical Reform* (New Delhi: Promilla & Co.).

George, K.K. (1993), *Limits to Kerala Model of Development — An*

Analysis of Fiscal Crisis and its Implications (Trivandrum: Centre for Development Studies).

Ghurye, G.S. (1992), 'Features of the Caste System', in D. Gupta (ed.), *Social Stratification* (Delhi, New York: Oxford University Press), pp. 28–49.

Gopinathan Nair, P.R. (1981), *Primary Education, Population Growth and Socio-economic Change: A Comparative Study with Particular Reference to Kerala* (Delhi: Allied Publishers Private Limited).

—— (1989),' Universalisation of Primary Education in Kerala', in P.R. Panchamukhi (ed.), *Educational Reforms at Different Levels*. Studies in Educational Reform in India, Volume II (Himalaya Publishing House).

Government of Kerala (various years), Budget in Brief

International Institute for Population Sciences (1994), *National Family Health Survey, 1992–1993*, Introductory Report, Bombay.

Jeffery, R. (1992), *Politics, Women and Well-Being — How Kerala Became 'A Model'* (Oxford: Oxford University Press).

Joseph, T.A. (1990), *Educational Development in Kerala* (Nattakam, Kottayam: Government College).

Kabir, M. and T.N. Krishnan (1992), 'Social Intermediation and Health Transition — Lessons from Kerala', Working Paper 251 (Trivandrum: Centre for Development Studies).

Kannan K.P., and K. Pushpangadan (1988), 'Agricultural Stagnation in Kerala', *Economic and Political Weekly, Review of Agriculture*, September.

Kannan, K.P. et al. (1991), *Health Status in Rural Kerala — A Study of the Linkages between Socio-economic Status and Health Status* (Integrated Rural Training Centre, Kerala Sastra Sahitya Parishad).

Krishnan, T.N. (1976), 'Demographic Transition in Kerala — Facts and Factors', *Economic and Political Weekly*, vol. XI, nos 31–3, Special Number, August.

—— (1992), 'Population, Poverty and Employment in India', *Economic and Political Weekly*, vol. XXVII, no. 46.

—— (1994), 'Access to Health and Burden of Treatment in India — An Inter-state Comparison', Discussion Paper Series, Number 2, Project of the United Nations Development Programme, Centre for Development Studies, July.

—— (1991), *Kerala's Health Transition: Facts and Factors* (Cambridge, MA: Harvard Center for Population and Development Studies and Centre for Development Studies).

—— (1995), *'The Route to Social Development in Kerala — Social Intermediation and Public Action', A Retrospective Study 1960–1993'* (Trivandrum: Centre for Development Studies).

Minturn, L. (1993), *Sita's Daughters Coming Out of Purdah* (New York: Oxford University Press).

Mosley, H.W. and L. Chen (1984), 'An Analytical Framework for the Study of Child Survival in Developing Countries', *Population and Development Review, Supplement,* 10:25–45.

Murray, C.J.L., and L. Chen (1990), 'A Conceptual Approach to Morbidity in the Health Transitions', Working Paper, Number 2 (Cambridge, MA: Harvard Center for Population and Development Studies).

Panikar, P.G.K. and C.R. Soman (1984), *Health Status of Kerala: The Paradox of Economic Backwardness and Health Development* (Trivandrum: Centre for Development Studies).

Pillai, G.P. (1994), *Malayala Manorama Daily,* 31st May.

Planning Commission (1993), 'Perspective Planning Division', Report of the expert group on estimation of proportion and number of poor, New Delhi: Government of India, July.

Rao, M.S.A. (1981), 'Changing Moral Values in the Context of Social-cultural Movements', in Adrian, C.M., *Culture and Mortality* (New Delhi: Oxford University Press).

Rajan, I., Misra, and Sarma (1993), 'Aging in India: A Demographic Assessment of Past and Future, Background chapter prepared for the India case-study of aging, Centre for Development Studies, Trivandrum & Social Development Section, UN, Bangkok.

Sample Registration Bulletin, Office of the Registrar General of India, 1994, vol. xxviii, no. 2, Ministry of Home Affairs, New Delhi, July.

Sample Registration System, *Annual Report, 1980, 1990, 1991,* Office the Registrar General of India, Ministry of Home Affairs, New Delhi.

Samuel, N.M. (1991), Census of India — Kerala, Series-12, Paper 2 of 1991, Population Totals — Kerala.

Sen, A. (1993), 'Life Expectancy and Inequality in Development and Change', in P. Bardhan, M. Dutta-Chaudhari and T.N. Krishnan, *Development and Change: Essays in Honour of K.N. Raj* (Bombay: Oxford University Press).

—— (1994), 'Population and Reasoning', Working Paper Series No. 94–6, June (Cambridge, MA: Harvard Center for Population and Development Studies).

Sivanandan, P. (1989), 'Caste and Economic Opportunity', A study of the effect of educational development and land reforms on the employment and income earning opportunities of the scheduled castes and scheduled tribes in Kerala. Ph D. Thesis, University of Kerala.

Srinivas, M.N. (1992), 'Varna and Caste'. in D. Gupta (ed.), *Social Stratification* (Delhi, New York: Oxford University Press), pp. 28–49.

State Planning Board, Social Service Division (1992), *Status Paper on Literacy in Kerala — A Regional, Gender and Social Analysis*, Government of Kerala, September.

Thankappan, K.R. Private discussion with author, September, 1995.

Tilak, J.B.G. (1995), 'Costs and Financing of Human Development in India: A Review of Issues, Problems and Prospects'. Studies on Human Development in India, Discussion Paper Series No. 5, Trivandrum, May.

United Nations (1975), 'Poverty, Unemployment and Development Policy', A case-study of selected issues with reference to Kerala, New York.

Zachariah, K.C. (1984), The Anomaly of the Fertility Decline in India's Kerala State', World Bank Staff Working Papers No. 700. Washington, D.C.: World Bank.

Zachariah, K.C., and S. Patial (1982), 'Trends and Determinants of Infant and Child Mortality in Kerala', World Bank, Population and Human Resources Division, Discussion Paper No. 82–2, January.

Zachariah, K.C., et al. (1994), *Demographic Transition in Kerala in the 1980s* (Trivandrum: Centre for Development Studies).

2

Fertility Decline in Punjab, India: Parallels with Historical Europe[1]

Monica Das Gupta

INTRODUCTION

An enormous amount of research has been done on the causes of fertility decline in developed and developing societies. Looking at this literature, it is interesting to note that there seem to be almost two separate universes of discourse: one relating to the decline in historical Europe, the other to the decline currently under way in the developing world.

This may be partly explained by the differences in the disciplinary backgrounds, data utilized, and analytical approaches between those working on these regions. The bulk of research on historical Europe has been done using the methods and materials of social historical research, and looking at events in the context of changes over a long sweep of time. In contrast, research on developing countries has with few exceptions focused on changes over a relatively short period of time, frequently relying primarily on cross-sectional survey data.

[1] This paper is reprinted here with permission from *Population Studies*, where it was originally published in November 1995, pp. 481–500.

Comments from Lincoln Chen, Nigel Crook, Gene Hammel, David Kertzer, Bob Levine, Morris D. Morris, Tony Wrigley, and an anonymous reviewer have been very helpful in revising this paper. Tim Dyson has contributed a great deal to this paper by estimating the total fertility rate and by commenting on the paper.

The survey data presented in this paper were collected with the help of a grant from the International Development Research Centre, Canada, to the National Council of Applied Economic Research, New Delhi. The support of both these institutions is gratefully acknowledged, as also the support from a grant by the Mellon Foundation to the Population Studies and Training Center, Brown University, USA, for preparing this paper. This is a revised version of Working Paper 1993–11 of the Population Studies and Training Center, Brown University.

Whatever the reasons may be, the conclusions from these two bodies of work appear to be at odds with each other, although both address themselves to the same realm of human behaviour. The research on developing countries emphasizes the importance of various aspects of development and modernization in bringing about fertility decline. These include, the need to improve levels of infant and child survival; improve levels of education (especially female education); expand employment opportunities; and increase the outreach of modern health and family planning facilities. Conversely, findings from historical Europe show that fertility decline became well-established under conditions of higher levels of infant mortality and illiteracy than prevail in developing countries today, and this without the benefit of modern contraceptive technology.

Another major difference between these two bodies of work lies in the existence (or implied lack) of the Malthusian 'preventive checks'. It is widely known that, long before the onset of marital fertility decline in Europe, a substantial degree of population control was achieved by postponing marriage or permanent celibacy when resources were scarce.[2] This homeostatic mechanism helped to regulate the balance of population and resources. Apart from Japan,[3] this form of 'preventive check' is not discussed in the context of other developing country societies. In fact, the existing literature points out that in South Asia, in particular, the dominant system is of joint families with partible inheritance and early universal marriage, a system viewed as being incompatible with such homeostatic mechanisms (Davis 1955, Hajnal 1982). With a few notable exceptions,[4] there has been little attempt to bridge the perspectives arising from research in these different parts of the world.

The potential pitfalls of cross-sectional studies of fertility in developing countries are well demonstrated in the study area discussed in this paper. Having looked at one of the villages studied in this paper, Mamdani (1972) argued that one should not expect fertility decline in this region because children are crucial economic assets

[2] See for example L.K. Berkner (1972); Mc Netting (1981); Viazzo (1989); and Wrigley and Schofield (1981). See also the collection of papers in P. Laslett and R. Wall (1972), and Wall, et al (1983).

[3] See Hanley and Yamamura (1977), and Smith (1977).

[4] See, for example, Crook (1989); Hajnal (1982); Knodel and van de Walle (1986); and Lesthaeghe (1980).

for the household. This argument appealed simultaneously to the more conservative proponents of the Chicago School, and to a more radical audience. Mamdani's theories have been very influential and have received wide attention. Yet as soon as one examines economic and demographic trends in this region, it becomes apparent that he was quite mistaken.

This paper combines the approaches of historical and anthropological research with that of demographic surveys, to understand the process of fertility regulation and decline in rural Punjab. It shows that peasant families in this society traditionally used marriage regulation to keep family size in line with available land, as did their counterparts in Europe. It also shows that, as in historical Europe (Knodel and van de Walle 1986), fertility decline became well-established while levels of infant mortality were very high, illiteracy was almost universal, there was substantial dependence on the agrarian economy, and modern family planning technology had not arrived. The fertility decline was, nevertheless, clearly related to developmental inputs. Thus, the study of Punjab throws light on the aspects of development which are crucial for fertility decline to take place.

DATA SOURCES

The data used in this paper are derived from a field study, archival records, and secondary sources. The fieldwork consisted of a restudy of the eleven villages in Ludhiana District, Punjab, which were originally studied in the 1950s by John Wyon and John Gordon (1971) in the well-known Khanna Study, and restudied by Das Gupta (1977) in 1984–8. The primary data used in this article draw on: (a) the survey data from the baseline household census of 1984 and the pregnancy histories of all ever-married women aged 15–59 in the study population; (b) qualitative anthropological data; and (c) vital registration data. Administrative records and secondary source materials were also used.

As a point of clarification, it should be mentioned that the Khanna Study villages are located in Ludhiana District, one of the districts of the present-day Indian state of Punjab. The Punjab Province of the colonial era was partitioned in 1947 between India and Pakistan. The Indian Punjab was further divided in 1966 into the states of Haryana and Punjab. Thus, the Indian

Census and other official data on 'Punjab' refer, depending on the dates, to pre-partition or post-partition Punjab.

THE STUDY AREA: DEVELOPMENTAL INPUTS

Fertility has been declining rapidly since around 1940 in Ludhiana District, in which the study villages are located. This is indicated by the trend in the total fertility rate (Graph 1).[5] Mortality has also been falling sharply. The infant mortality rate in Ludhiana District fell from above 160 to 57 per thousand between 1940 and 1981. The pattern of decline in the crude death rate can be seen in Graph 2.

Punjab has benefited from a great deal of developmental inputs, and is today by far the richest state in India. The pace of economic and social development in Punjab has been such that most of the factors which are usually believed to help bring about fertility decline are in evidence in this region. They include rapidly rising standards of living, literacy, health, family planning facilities and off-farm employment opportunities. These changes have largely come about since around 1966. Yet, as is evident from Graph 1, fertility decline was well under way for decades before this, so the onset of the fertility decline cannot be attributed to this recent period of rapid improvements in economic and social development.

Much of the literature on Punjab discusses this region as it has evolved since 1966, that is, after the advent of the 'Green Revolution', a package of agricultural inputs and technology which raised yields dramatically. Per capita income has been rising sharply, and alongside this there has been a dramatic expansion in the social infrastructure. This impressive record of development in recent decades has tended to dominate the literature on Punjab so much that relatively little attention is paid to earlier developments there. However, the record of developmental efforts in Punjab during the century preceding 1966 is also extremely impressive. It laid the foundations for Punjab's economic and demographic progress.

The nature and pace of development have been quite different in these two periods, and both have influenced the fertility decline

[5] These were obtained through indirect standardization, using the decennial census age-distributions and the registered crude birth rates for Ludhiana District. For details of the methodology, see Dyson (1989).

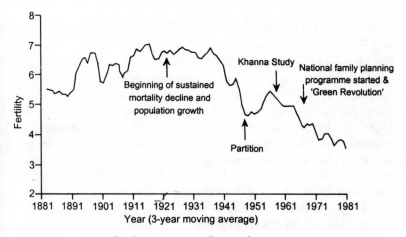

GRAPH 1: *Total fertility rate — Ludhiana district 1881–1981*
(3-year moving average)

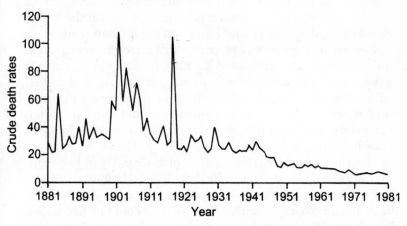

GRAPH 2: *Crude death rate — Ludhiana district 1881–1981*

in this area. The pre-1966 period was characterized by major
reductions in mortality crises from famines and epidemics, and
by a stabilization and gentle but steady growth of agricultural
yields. The post-1966 period was characterized by more rapid
increases in standards of living, along with the spread of education

and widespread availability of health and family planning services. These two periods are discussed separately below.

Developmental Efforts Before 1966[6]

A great deal of developmental activity had been taking place in Punjab even before the turn of the century, under the British colonial administration. The most important part of this was the expansion of irrigation through constructing canals and digging wells. These efforts began in the 1860s and accelerated in the 1880s and 1890s. By 1950, half of the cultivable land in Punjab was perennially irrigated. In this arid region, which was previously so dependent on the rainfall for successful cropping, the expansion of irrigation was critical in reducing the major fluctuations in crop yields which had made the villagers' lives highly vulnerable to famine and food shortages. Irrigation also helped raise overall yields, so both the 'level' and the 'variance' of yields were improved.

By the mid-1930s, large-scale agricultural extension programmes were under way, bringing improved seeds, agricultural technologies and livestock breeds to the farmers. While these efforts were not as spectacular in raising yields and incomes as the 'Green Revolution', they had a major impact on the agrarian economy.

Farmers in Punjab were especially well placed to benefit from these efforts at agricultural development, because of the relatively egalitarian distribution of land and the predominance of owner-cultivation, making for more careful land management than tenurial systems. The egalitarian nature of the land distribution was not an introduction of the colonial administration; it was found in place by them and maintained subsequently. The western parts of the Province (the 'Canal Colonies', which are today in Pakistan), were opened up for settlement by the colonial administration, and evolved in quite a different way, with large tracts owned by landlords and cultivated by tenant farmers. This could be one reason why the agricultural and demographic experience of present-day Indian Punjab and Pakistan Punjab have been dissimilar.

The mortality peaks associated with famines disappeared with the spread of irrigation, as well as with the construction of railroads which made it possible to transport grain to places suffering from

[6] The discussion in this section is based on my own fieldwork and archival data, as well as secondary sources. The latter include Calvert (1936); Darling (1947); Kessinger (1974); Lewis (1958); and Wyon and Gordon (1971)

crop failure. Efforts were also made to control mortality from infectious diseases through a variety of public health measures, including efforts to monitor and prevent the spread of epidemics. The first decade of this century was especially beset by major epidemics of plague and cholera, and the last mortality peak was that of the influenza pandemic of 1918. The effectiveness of agricultural development, transportation and public health efforts[7] at controlling mortality peaks is evident in the crude death rates (Graph 2).

While the economy of the rural areas of this region was overwhelmingly dependent on the land, there were some income sources available outside the village. The most important of these was the British Indian Army, which recruited heavily from Punjab. For many households, the Army provided an important supplement to their income from the agrarian economy.

The focus during this period was more on economic rather than social development. It was only in the 1930s that plans were considered for providing medical care to people in the rural areas. The level of educational infrastructure available to these people was such that only a few boys (and almost no girls) managed to receive an education. The villagers were further isolated from the amenities of the outside world by the lack of all-weather roads. However, this lack of social and physical infrastructure cannot eclipse the transformation wrought in these villagers' lives by the developmental inputs during this period: the atmosphere created was one of gradual improvement in levels of living, within an environment of a stable administrative and legal order.

Post-1966: The 'Green Revolution' and After

The mid-1960s was marked by major foodgrain shortage in the country, and difficulty in obtaining food aid from outside. This made the Indian government set aside other developmental goals temporarily and focus on raising the country's agricultural production by spreading the new agricultural technology of the 'Green Revolution', while simultaneously beginning to make serious efforts to control population growth.

The agricultural innovations were enormously successful, especially in Punjab. As a consequence, per capita income has been

---

[7] For a description and analysis of efforts to reduce cholera mortality, see Arnold (1989)

rising sharply, along with nutritional intakes. The growth of agriculture contributed to the rise of a wide range of agro-related and other industries, which provided off-farm employment for many. Moreover, people made considerable use of employment opportunities elsewhere in India and abroad. The combined volume of these employment opportunities was such that the erstwhile agricultural labourers found it unprofitable to take on agricultural work, even though the wages were the highest in India.

The mid-1960s was also the period in which social development infrastructure such as education, health, and family planning were built up rapidly. Levels of female literacy rose such that while only 11 per cent of women aged 45–9 in 1984 in the study villages had gone to school, 84 per cent of those aged 10–14 had some school education, that is, this area is approaching universal female education. Health and family planning facilities were extended to the rural areas. From the late 1960s, the number of Government rural health centres grew rapidly, such that by the 1980s people had access to such a centre in their own village or a neighbouring village.

Pre-Transitional Homeostatic Mechanisms

Before the demographic transition, a variety of adjustment mechanisms were used in this society to try to maintain the balance between population and resources. These were very important for families and communities to continue to thrive despite the substantial fluctuations in population size caused by large swings in mortality levels. This discussion of the homeostatic mechanisms in the study region is based largely on an analysis of genealogies and accompanying histories. These show how different branches of lineages grew or failed to grow, and some of the mechanisms used to cope with the problems such fluctuations caused.

Fertility Control

One way of responding to such fluctuations was through controlling fertility, but this could not resolve immediate problems because of the inherently long time-lag involved for the effects to be felt. For example, it takes a generation to replace working age adults in a decimated household. Conversely, if a household had good fortune in fecundity and survival and was growing too rapidly, there would be an equivalent time-lag before efforts to curtail future growth would show results.

Realignment of Population to Resources

A more immediately effective way of responding to the vagaries of mortality experience was to realign population groups and their access to resources. Mechanisms for such realignment existed at all levels of organization in this society, that is, the community (the village), the lineage, and the household.

A brief thumbnail sketch of the study villages' socio-economic organization will help in understanding the context in which these adjustment mechanisms worked. The village was divided broadly into two groups: those who owned the land, and those who were landless. In the traditional village economy, the landless derived a living through patron-client relationships with the landowners, (Wiser 1936, Lewis 1958) whereby they would perform a variety of services for them in exchange for (a) direct payment; (b) rights to free collection of many essentials; and (c) an assurance of help in crises to ensure survival, though at very low levels of living. These service relationships constituted property in ways analogous to land: both the landowners and the landless would pass on their property to their sons through a system of partible inheritance.

At the level of the community, the primary adjustment mechanism was that of controlled migration. For example, if it was felt that there was a shortage of landless labourers, the landowners would invite a person or a lineage from another village to settle in their village and take on specified hereditary service relationships. Conversely, if a landless lineage was growing too rapidly, some of its members would seek to migrate to another village.

An analogous process worked at the sublineage level. If a branch of a lineage was dying out, they had two options: either to adopt a son, or to bring in a larger group of working age men by asking a daughter's husband and his male kin to come and settle in the village. There were also more temporary and reversible ways of adjusting access to resources to shifts in demographic fortunes. One was to reallocate land temporarily through sharecropping or simple usufruct arrangements, or to reassign service rights in the case of the landless.

At the level of the household and the family, there were two basic strategies apart from adoption. One was for families ravaged by mortality to regroup with other kin so as to form a new unit large enough to be viable. The third strategy was to control growth through regulating marriage.

Marriage Regulation

Marriage was regulated on an *ad hoc* basis, to avoid rapid subdivision of property. When a household's demographic fortunes were such that many sons survived to reproduce, they frequently resorted to restricting their sons' marriages, especially if the household already had a small landholding because of earlier subdivision. Marriage was also postponed when times were hard for a household. Marriage regulation can, thus, be seen partly as a result of a perception of current impoverishment, as well as a desire to avoid future impoverishment. Take, for example, a family with five acres of land and four surviving sons. Five acres of land in this fertile region is adequate for a family's sustenance, but not for sustaining four families in the next generation. When such a family decided to let only one son marry, they were motivated not only by the immediate consideration of curtailing household expenses, but also by the long-term need to ensure that the next generation would have sufficient resources for their livelihood.

Those with larger landholdings did not restrict marriage to the same extent as those with smaller holdings. As long as each son would have enough land to sustain a family, land subdivision was not seen as a major concern. This is understandable, because before the sustained mortality decline, it was not uncommon to find a shrinking of numbers in a subsequent generation such that landholdings which had previously subdivided would be re-consolidated by reverting to the closest male kin.

Genealogy 1 shows how marriage was restricted in one sublineage of landowners, and illustrates some of the above points about how such decisions were made. It is evident that the strategy was resorted to by those branches of the sublineage which were growing most rapidly in terms of surviving sons and consequently experiencing rapid subdivision of land. Vigourously followed, this strategy could counter the effect of rapid growth. For example, the descendants of person A restricted marriage sharply in two consecutive generations, a fact which, combined with the normal probability of some marriages being sonless, would result in the

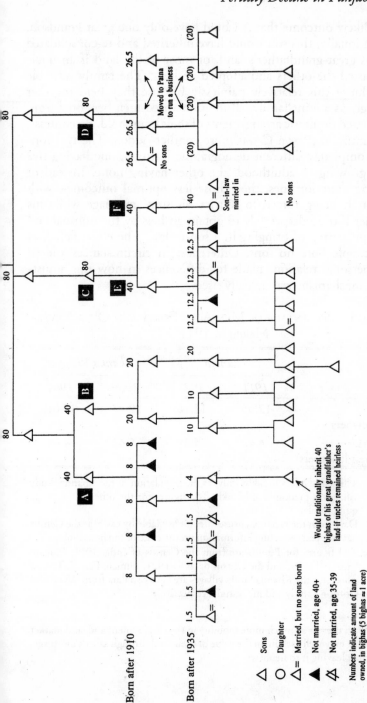

GENEALOGY 1: *Genealogy of a Jat lineage, Khanna villages*

Note: This genealogy was constructed from archival records, supplemented by additional information supplied by members of the family.

very likely outcome that A would have only one great-grandson. Traditionally, this son would have inherited and re-consolidated all his great-grandfather's land, or most of the land if an uncle distrusted the others and adopted an heir.[8] The family was able to achieve this relatively painlessly because they held together strongly as a joint family: all the unmarried men benefited from the shared domestic arrangements of their household. By contrast, the family of person C was more conflict-ridden. The two sons had completely different demographic fortunes, one having five sons growing to adulthood, the other having none. Instead of sharing their fortunes, they chose less optimal outcomes, with person E being forced to restrict his sons' marriage while his brother F tried desperately to obtain an heir by the unusual and unpopular step of bringing in a son-in-law. The effort failed, as this couple bore no sons. Differences in circumstances and in interpersonal relations made for differences in how this adjustment mechanism was actually used.

TABLE 1: PERCENTAGE OF MEN AGED FORTY AND OVER NEVER-MARRIED, 1911–84

Caste	Punjab		Khanna Villages	
	1911	1921	1969	1984
Jat (landowners)	12.05	13.10	22.77	17.61
Chamar (landless labourers)	4.41	4.88	5.43	4.08

Notes: This table refers to Sikhs only, as the population of the Khanna Study villages is predominantly Sikh. The figures for the other religions are quite similar.
Data from the recent Censuses are not available by caste, as the Census has stopped collecting information on the caste of the household.

Sources: The figures for Punjab are from the Census of India 1911, Punjab, Part II: Tables, and the Census of India 1921, Punjab, Part II: Tables. Those for the Khanna Study villages are based on data from Wyon and Gordon's study and my restudy, respectively.

[8] Today, there is so much more mobility in the employment and land market that people may well cash in on the value of their land through sale or mortgage, rather than leaving it to nephews.

That marriage regulation was motivated by a desire to prevent property division is also clearly enunciated by older men in the study villages today. (People would in any event prefer not to marry their daughters into households which were resource-poor.) It is interesting to note that marriage restriction was practiced relatively little amongst the landless labourers (Table 1), although they were far more resource-poor than the landowners. One reason for this could be that the landowners found it easier to relate their available resources to their numbers, as is discussed below (see the section on the reasons for the onset of fertility decline).

The regulation of marriage was combined with the practice of informal fraternal polyandry. Thus, for example, only one brother might marry, and the other brothers would share conjugal rights in the wife and derive a considerable degree of emotional satisfaction in raising the children together. The children were seen as *de jure* the offspring of the 'married' brother, but de facto those of all the brothers, and all the brothers' land would be divided amongst the resulting sons.

A potential contradiction existed between male celibacy and the culturally required universal marriage of women. Female celibacy was not culturally acceptable, as in Europe, or even in Nepal (McFarlane 1976:226). Yet the females who were born could not all be married if a substantial proportion of potential grooms were kept celibate by their households. This was resolved largely by maintaining an imbalance in the sex ratio through the infanticide and neglect of female babies. It could be argued that removing female children was in fact the only relevant instrument of population control, and that male celibacy was irrelevant. This is not quite the case, for two reasons. Firstly, it was the relevant mechanism at the level of the household for adjusting numbers to resources. Secondly, the stock of wives was fine-tuned to the number of men in a position to marry by importing women from other regions.[9]

Although male celibacy and excess female child mortality seem to mesh well in this cultural and demographic regime, they are the result of different decision-making processes. As is illustrated

[9] See, for example, Census of Punjab 1868. Personal communication with some older women in Bengal indicates that Punjabi wife-seekers would look as far as Bengal for brides. Hershman (1981) also mentions that Jats would, if necessary, marry women from lower castes, which had far lower levels of female infanticide.

in Genealogy 1, marriage regulation was the result of conscious decisions made by households in order to maintain collective prosperity. Excess female child mortality was the result of more complex forces.[10] Given the fact of exogamy and the time-lag between infancy and marriage, excess female child mortality cannot be seen as being deployed as part of the same immediate household strategy as nonmarriage. The ways in which numbers of marriageable girls were adjusted to fluctuations in male celibacy need to be studied.

Marriage regulation and fraternal polyandry were widely documented in the colonial administrative literature from the times of their first settlement in this region, and vestiges of it remain today. For example, the 1901 Census of Punjab[11] explicitly discusses male celibacy and fraternal polyandry as ways used to prevent the subdivision of property. This is followed up in the 1911 Census of Punjab,[12] which adds that another of the 'artificial methods of keeping down the population' is the practice of female infanticide. It is interesting to note that the colonial administrators perceived that fraternal polyandry and female infanticide amongst the Jats constituted part of their efforts to regulate their population. This differs from their analysis of female infanticide based on their earlier encounter with the phenomenon amongst the Rajputs in present-day Uttar Pradesh. This they perceived as being related to hypergamy, with families from higher Rajput echelons killing their daughters to make room for their sons to accept brides from families lower to them in the hierarchy. This is consistent with present-day anthropological perceptions of relative egalitarianism among members of the Jat caste and considerable stratification amongst the Rajputs.[13]

Limitations of these Adjustment Mechanisms

These adjustment mechanisms were geared towards coping with fluctuations in population size, in a situation where the overall rate of population growth was very slow and sometimes negative. They were quite inadequate in the situation which began around 1920,

---

[10] For a discussion of the reasons for excess female child mortality in this society, see Das Gupta (1987).

[11] Census of India 1901:223.

[12] Census of India 1911:65, 260.

[13] See Pradhan (1966); Lewis (1958); and Parry (1979).

that of sustained mortality decline and consequently steady and rapid population growth.

In fact, most of these adjustment mechanisms could operate only in a situation of alternating spurts of growth and shrinking of numbers, because they were based on reallocating access to resources between groups with differential growth, i.e., between groups who were experiencing different phases of such spurts. When a village, a lineage or a household was going through a phase of declining numbers, these mechanisms would help reallocate resources to those whose cycle was going in the other direction.

In the face of sustained population growth after 1921, a situation was quickly reached in which all groups were growing, and no resources were being opened up for reallocation. Marriage regulation was the only mechanism which was not dependent on resources being available to reallocate. With this exception, the other adjustment mechanisms were quickly abandoned. By the early decades of this century, people were no longer invited to settle in the village. This is evident from the genealogies, which indicate when a family migrated in, from where, and under what circumstances. In-migration after this period was rare (as also adoption), and done only for personal reasons without accompanying hereditary rights to land or service relationships.

The redistribution within the lineage of land and service relationships also petered out. In the case of service relationships, not only were they no longer redistributed, but over time they became too meagre a source of income to support all the families in these groups. The amount of land available for leasing reduced sharply, and the norm of keeping leasing arrangements within the lineage was largely abandoned.

METHODS USED TO CONTROL WOMEN'S FERTILITY

Male and Female Fertility

The combination of temporary or permanent male celibacy and female infanticide (or death through neglect) was, as discussed above, the traditional method of regulating population growth. As has been described above, families in which several boys survived would often keep some sons unmarried to reduce the number of potential heirs in the next generation. Faced with steady mortality decline after 1919, and increasing numbers of surviving sons, the response was to increase the proportions of men remaining permanently unmarried (Table 1, Genealogy 1).

As discussed, females were withdrawn from marriage by the simple expedient of killing some of them at birth or encouraging their death in early childhood. In response to the greater pressure to control fertility when mortality began to decline steadily, a major social innovation took place: the control of individual women's fertility.

For some decades, increasing male celibacy and curbing women's fertility were pursued as simultaneous strategies of reducing population growth. Gradually, the successful control of female fertility has made it possible to begin to reduce levels of permanent male celibacy in this society (Table 1). However, the levels of male celibacy remained high in 1984, reflecting the experience of men in the older cohorts in which large numbers of boys survived.

Female Fertility

The total fertility rate started declining quite steeply sometime around 1940 (Graph 1). These figures relate to the district to which the study villages belong. However, the total fertility rates implied by the vital registration data for the district correspond quite closely to those found from the surveys in the study villages.[14]

The disruption caused by the Partition of the country in 1947 seems to have caused an additional dip in fertility rates. This is followed by some limited recovery in fertility for a period of about fifteen years, suggesting that people were trying to recover from the effects of the previous Partition-induced disruption. After this, the decline continued on its earlier path. Within the four decades of 1940 to 1980, the TFR fell from around 6.5 to less than 3.5. By 1984, it was 3.26 in the study villages.

[14] For example, the study villages had a total fertility rate of 5.55 in 1957–9, 4.45 in 1966–8 and 3.26 in 1983–4 (Table 4), which are only a little higher than the district figures of 5.14 for 1957–9, 4.24 for 1966–8 and 3.38 for 1981. Part of this small differential may be due to the fact that the district contains the town of Ludhiana and some small towns, where fertility may be lower than in the rural population of the study villages. It may also be partly due to the fact that the data for the study villages derive from intensive surveys, and as such are likely to yield more complete coverage of births than the district vital registration system.

The success of people's efforts to curb their reproduction is also reflected in the age-distribution of the population. The age-distribution for 1959 (Wyon and Gordon 1971:95) still shows quite a steep increase in numbers at younger ages, which is common to societies with high fertility and rapid population growth. The 1984 distribution (Table 2) is in sharp contrast to this, and shows that new birth cohorts had not increased in size over the previous twenty years. This is despite the fact that the number of women in the reproductive age-groups has been growing due to the momentum generated by increasing size of birth cohorts in the past. In fact, this area's fertility decline appears to be not far behind that of Kerala (Table 2), the state which has for long been viewed as outstandingly ahead of the rest of the country in fertility and mortality decline. Kerala's fertility decline appears to have begun at about the same time as that of the Khanna villages.

TABLE 2: AGE DISTRIBUTION OF POPULATION,
KHANNA VILLAGES, 1984 (%)

Age	Total population	Landowners	Landless labourers	Kerala, 1981*
00–04	11.79	9.78	13.62	10.77
05–09	11.33	9.99	12.63	11.49
10–14	11.30	10.47	12.46	12.76
15–19	11.23	10.94	12.03	11.83
20–24	9.52	10.26	8.38	10.29
25–29	7.75	7.72	7.80	8.18
30–34	6.55	6.99	6.04	6.20
35–39	6.00	6.22	5.90	5.50
40–44	4.65	5.28	3.93	4.45
45–49	4.04	4.34	3.64	4.60
50–54	4.09	4.52	3.71	3.48
55–59	3.13	3.49	2.88	2.91
60–64	3.02	3.31	2.73	2.68
65–69	2.10	2.37	1.91	2.04
70+		3.51	4.31	2.33

* *Source:* Census of India, 1981.

It is notable that much of this decline had already taken place before 1966–70, which is when serious efforts began to be made to spread health and family planning services in the rural areas. By this time, the total fertility rate had already dropped to below 4.3, and the age distributions indicate that the overall growth of population had slowed down substantially.

How, then, was female reproduction restricted? Before the advent of modern contraceptive technology, impressive levels of reproductive control were achieved through the time-honoured means of restricting opportunities to procreate. This was done largely by reducing the reproductive span of women. The female age at marriage (cohabitation) rose rapidly (Table 3). They also brought forward the age of terminating childbearing, largely through withdrawal and abstinence. In 1955 (Wyon and Gordon 1971:137–8), about a quarter of the couples in the study villages stated that they had practiced birth control, using rhythm, withdrawal, or abstinence, or combinations of these. Induced abortion was and is also practiced in this society.

TABLE 3: AGE AT MARRIAGE OF WOMEN,[#]
KHANNA VILLAGES 1940s–84

Year	Age at marriage 1940s[*]
1940s	16.10
1959[**]	18.89
1984	21.36

[#]   This refers to the age at effective marriage, i.e., cohabitation. In the past, there was a gap of several years between the ritual marriage and the girl going to live with her husband.

       Note that the age at marriage very probably began rising before the 1940s. Data from that period are not available in this study, and the Census data provide figures only on *marriage*, not on, *cohabitation*.

       The figures for 1959 and 1984 are the singulate mean age at marriage, estimated by the Hajnal method. The figure for the 1940s is the mean age at marriage.

Source: [*]   Wyon and Gordon, *loc. cit.* in fn. 8, p. 154.

       [**] John Wyon, data on proportions single.

The rise in women's age at marriage was the main factor behind the fertility decline uptil the mid-1960s. This is reflected in Table 4, which shows that the total fertility rate fell much more rapidly than the total marital fertility rate until the mid-1960s. Control of fertility within marriage was accelerated after this period.

TABLE 4: DECLINE IN TOTAL FERTILITY RATES AND TOTAL MARITAL FERTILITY RATES, KHANNA VILLAGES, 1957–84

Year	TFR	% decline	TMFR	% decline
1957–59	5.55		6.68	
1966–68	4.45	20	6.15	8
1983–84	3.26	27	4.73	23

This accelerated control of fertility within marriage must have been helped enormously by the extension, after 1966, of modern methods of contraception. The effect of these efforts can clearly be seen in Table 5. Levels of contraceptive use rose little between 1959 and 1969. They rose very rapidly between 1969 and 1984. By 1984, levels of contraceptive use were as high as 66–70 per cent (ever-use) to and 60 to 64 per cent (current use) among women aged 30–9. The fact that the levels of current use are only a little lower than the levels of ever-use indicates a high degree of motivation to contracept in these women.

TABLE 5: PER CENT OF EVER-MARRIED WOMEN USING CONTRACEPTION, KHANNA VILLAGES, 1959–84

Age of woman	1959	1969		1984	
		Ever-use	Current use	Ever-use	Current use
15–19				6	6
20–24	16.7	15.7	14.6	26	23
25–29				54	46
30–34				66	60
35–39	28.4	39.7	36.4	70	64
40–44				56	47

Source for 1959 and 1969 data: John Wyon.

The Reasons for the Onset of Fertility Decline

The onset of fertility decline began in this society while levels of per capita income were still very low; there was almost no literacy among males or females; no modern methods of contraception; and an infant mortality rate above 150 per thousand. The onset of fertility decline was clearly not brought about by the factors usually associated in the demographic literature with fertility decline in developing countries.

What factors were responsible for the onset of the fertility decline? The answer seems to be that there were two sets of factors at work: mortality decline, population pressure, and the inadequacy of traditional homeostatic mechanisms to deal with this; and growing security of life and livelihood.

Mortality Decline, Population Pressure and the Inadequacy of Traditional Homeostatic Mechanisms

The sustained mortality decline after 1920 is reflected in the genealogies, which show the burgeoning of numbers in the generations born after 1920. As discussed in the section on pretransitional homeostatic mechanisms, most of the traditional mechanisms were helpful only as ways of adjusting to fluctuations in numbers. They were clearly inadequate for coping with a situation of steady growth of numbers, and most of them were abandoned during the early decades of this century.

Marriage regulation was the only traditional homeostatic mechanism which remained as an effective response in this new situation. This, too, had its limitations. It was useful as an ad hoc mechanism for adjusting to variations in household size before the beginning of the demographic transition, but there were problems in using it as the sole method of countering the steadily growing pressure of population.

Firstly, enormous human burdens are involved in having high and ever increasing proportions of men remaining permanently unmarried, and women correspondingly removed from growing to marriageable ages. Besides, this society perceives universal marriage to be the ideal if resources permit. While marriage might be postponed or denied when times are hard, it was one of the foremost consumption priorities when times were good. And, indeed with the control of famines and epidemics, and the growth of agricultural productivity, times were good in a way never experienced before. Clearly, a wider range of strategies for fertility control were required, and this was found in the innovation of restricting the fertility of individual women.

The effort to control population growth was not only multi-pronged, but intense and carried out at considerable human and social cost. Levels of male celibacy soared despite the drawbacks entailed. Restricting female fertility also involved considerable cost, and entailed a social revolution. As in much of South Asia, this society places enormous value on premarital chastity, and a rise in women's age at marriage involves considerable risk of loss of honour. Terminal abstinence and withdrawal also involves a major cost to the couple. Practiced at increasingly early ages (Table 4), the advent of modern contraceptives was a boon to these women.[15]

Mortality decline did not merely provide an initial impetus to control fertility. The continued reduction in both infant and adult mortality rates kept up a sustained pressure to maintain the tempo of fertility reduction, by partially offsetting its effectiveness in slowing population growth. Mortality decline was also very important in enabling people to shape their families and households as they thought best. As mortality levels fell, people were freed from a situation in which the vagaries of mortality could remove productive adults from the household, and prevent couples from reaching the number of surviving children they would like to have. Levels of child mortality are now low enough for the majority of women to achieve the family size they want and to terminate childbearing while still within their peak reproductive years.

Security of Life and Livelihood

It is very interesting to see the speed with which people in this society responded to the need to reduce fertility; within a generation after the beginning of the sustained mortality decline, fertility began to decline. The main reason people were able to respond so quickly lies in the developmental interventions carried out in this region. These were very important in creating the conditions for this fertility decline. They gave rise to a new security of life and livelihood, which was a crucial factor enabling the people to have

[15] Wyon and Gordon (1971:149) concluded that the early acceptors of modern contraceptive methods probably merely substituted these for the folk methods they were already practicing.

the confidence to shift over to a regime of tighter and more universal fertility control.

People were well placed to reduce fertility largely because of the very factors that had brought on the need to do so: security against mortality peaks and major food shortages. They no longer lived under the perpetual threat of disaster, of being wiped out financially, or by death. Moreover, although the economy of the study villages was overwhelmingly agrarian, some households had members participating in the outside economy and benefited from the income stabilization provided by these members' remittances.

Before the efforts to stabilize and increase agricultural yields in this region, large fluctuations in yields had caused severe famines in the worst years, and, more frequently, food shortages of varying severity. Frequent epidemics added to the tremendous insecurity to which this region had been subject, especially during the 1890s and 1900s. Wave after wave of serious famine and epidemic caused much mortality and disruption of life. The mortality peaks during this period were frequent and very high: in 1902 and 1918, the registered crude death rate soared above 100 per thousand, that is, villages were literally decimated.

Under these conditions of high mortality peaks, households could find that not only were their crops devastated, but also that key members had died, so that the household might not be in a position to cultivate its fields in the next season. The overwhelming concern, then, was with ensuring the continued viability of the household. This could be achieved by means of reproduction, and by maintaining a kinship structure in which people could link up with even distant agnatic kin and form a new viable household.

The developmental efforts had an incalculable impact on the security of people's lives. After 1920, these major mortality crises were a thing of the past, and both child and adult mortality levels fell. The reduction of adult mortality, in particular, made households much more secure against the threat of losing key productive members. With agricultural yields rising and becoming more predictable, security of livelihood was immeasurably enhanced. These people saw themselves as having emerged from their hard times. As the 1950s Khanna Study noted, when drawing up a calendar of major events in the villages:

> Significantly, up to 1920 nearly all the events referred to catastrophes, including three epidemics of bubonic plague. . . . After 1920, most of

the important time markers were positive events — the building of a flour mill and the establishment of schools, wells and temples (Wyon and Gordon 1971:63).

Perennial irrigation raised agricultural yields, but even more importantly, it reduced fluctuations in agricultural yields. This brought a new stability of expectation to people's lives and gave them a sense of being able to control and improve their lives through their own efforts. This psychological sea-change was commented upon by administrators at the time. Their observations are very pertinent to an understanding of the relationship between reducing the environment of risk and enabling people to move towards a low-fertility regime:

> The whole framework and order of society are changed, and men are no longer entirely at the mercy of nature and of fate. . . . The man-made canal is beginning to take the place of fate in men's minds, and it is only a step from this to realize that if man can make the canal, he can make much else besides; and that it is not 'as God wills' but as man works that he will be rich or poor. . . . The change is one of the subtlest influences now coming into play, and as it spreads, will do more than anything else to make agricultural progress possible (Darling 1974:146–7).

The tremendous uncertainties and insecurity of life buffeting people in this region in the early decades of this century are reflected in the life-histories of old people. By contrast, the histories of their children and grandchildren show the transformation wrought in the predictability of life in the subsequent decades. These younger generations were placed in a position of being able to plan their lives and make choices beyond the level of immediate survival.[16]

The rapid increase in the pace of economic and social development of this region since 1966 has also contributed to the fertility decline. In particular, the new efforts to develop the rural outreach of the family planning programme made more convenient methods of contraception available to people and improved the distribution of contraceptives. This enabled women to reduce their fertility more conveniently and effectively than through the traditional means of withdrawal, induced abortion and terminal abstinence. Improvements in health care outreach helped people to feel that they could do more to avoid child deaths, and thereby is likely to have helped

---

[16] See the life history of Siri Chand and his son in Das Gupta (1994:118–19).

reduce the 'hoarding' component of family size goals. The data indicate that the recent increase in female education has also contributed to the fertility decline (Das Gupta 1994).

Social Class Differentials in the Fertility Decline

The difference between social classes in the timing and pace of fertility decline confirms and further elaborates this hypothesis as to how the need to reduce fertility came to be felt and put into practice. The social classes discussed here are the landowners (Jat caste) and the landless labourers (Chamar caste).[17] Between them, they comprised over three-quarters of the total population of the study villages in 1984. The villages contain several other castes with small numbers of people, and an analysis of all these castes would involve much circumstantial detail which is outside the scope of this paper.

In this society, there is a clear differential between the landowners and the landless labourers, in that the landowners had earlier and more rapid fertility decline than the landless. This differential already existed in this area in the 1950s. Graph 3 compares the age-specific marital fertility rates of these two groups in the 1950s and the 1980s, and shows that while both groups had a sharp fertility decline, the landowners retained their position of being ahead in the decline. A comparison of the age-distribution of the landowners and the landless labourers (Table 2) indicates that the landowners initiated fertility decline at least five years before the landless labourers. The pace of the landowners' fertility decline has also been faster, such that the cohorts born after 1974 have actually been shrinking in size.

It is not surprising to find this differential between the landowners and the landless labourers. Firstly, the landowners benefited earlier than the landless from each effort to improve the security of life and livelihood. Secondly, the landowners had traditionally been the most sensitive to the need to regulate family size to the available land. Their custom of equal inheritance by each son made them vulnerable to rapid subdivision of holdings. The effects of rapid population growth in one generation were, therefore, very visible to them, in the very concrete terms of the amount of land inherited by each son. It was they who traditionally made more use of male

[17] The overlap of caste and class in preindustrial village India is discussed in Béteille (1965).

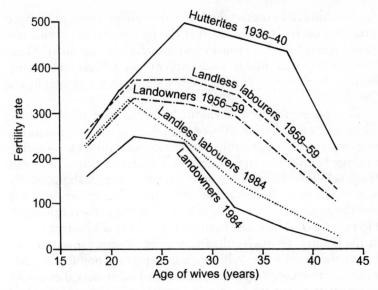

GRAPH 3: *Age-specific marital fertility rates by socio-economic status, Khanna, 1959 and 1984*

Source for the 1956–59 data: Wyon and Gordon, op. cit. in fn. 8
(1971) p. 141

celibacy to control the number of heirs born in the next generation (Table 1). Thus, a provision for population regulation existed in their 'cultural reservoir', which made it easier for them to respond quickly to the need for increased control of population growth. Studies in other parts of south Asia suggest the existence of similar 'cultural reservoirs' elsewhere in the region, especially amongst the landowning groups.[18]

The landless also had partible inheritance of property and income sources, the primary income source in their case being their patron-client service relationships. The subdivision of such resources was concretely less visible than that of land. This perception was

[18] Schuler (1987), and others have written on polyandry and marriage regulation in the Himalayan region as a means of conserving household resources. Even where marriage regulation is not practised, as amongst the Patels of Gujarat, the intercensal growth rates of landowners are far lower than that of landless. See (Breman 1974). The pattern of tighter marriage regulation amongst cultivators than amongst agricultural labourers has also been found in the European context (Kertzer 1991).

further diffused by the fact that the patron-client relationships were premised on the assumption that the patron would provide not only a living but also a generalized insurance to the client. Thus, the landless would find it much harder to see a direct relationship between having a large number of heirs and a threat to their future livelihood.

The landowners were, then, the leaders in the fertility decline. The logic of this decline diffused from them to the landless, just as in many other settings fertility decline diffused from the local élite to those below them in the social and economic hierarchy.[19] The landless followed after only a short lag. This was probably partly by way of imitating the behaviour of the dominant group, which is also the group perceived as the model of success in the community. However, it could not have been simply a matter of blind imitation, as the landless themselves had very good reasons for wanting to reduce their family size. While their perception of population pressure would be more diffuse than that of the landowners, they would nonetheless have felt considerable pressure. This perception was heightened by the fact that one of the ways in which the landowners coped with their own pressure on resources was to gradually abandon their patron-client relationships, leaving the landless with a shrinking income base.

The differential pattern of fertility decline between these socio-economic groups highlights the workings of the factors underlying the onset of the fertility decline in this society discussed above. That is, they emphasize the role of the perceived need for fertility decline, combined with the newly-found security and stability of expectations which made it possible for people to have the confidence to reduce their family size.

The fact that both the landowners and the landless labourers had rapid fertility decline contradicts Mamdani's (1972) theory about the economic imperative for high fertility in this society. He argued that all groups shared this imperative; that in the absence of high fertility, the landowners faced crippling costs of hiring labour, and the landless labourers would forgo the income from additional pairs of hands. In fact, fertility had declined substantially amongst all these groups, by the time Mamdani conducted his study. This

---

[19] This process of diffusion of changes in fertility behaviour down the social hierarchy is discussed in several studies from historical Europe. See, for example, Banks (1954); Kertzer and Hogan (1989).

indicates that their own perceptions of their childbearing impera-
tives were quite different from those of Mamdani.

CONCLUSIONS

Fertility began to decline steadily in Punjab as early as 1940, at a
time when the society was overwhelmingly agrarian, illiterate, had
infant mortality well above 150 per thousand livebirths, and was
without modern contraceptive technology. Two interesting features emerge from this study of fertility behaviour in Punjab. Firstly, it brings out the commonalities of peasant life and demographic
behaviour between this developing country setting and that of historical Europe. Secondly, it throws light on the aspects of developmental interventions most crucial for enabling people to reduce
their fertility.

The concept of regulating the balance between population and
resources was not new to this society. A variety of mechanisms were
used to try to achieve this balance, including reallocation of access
to resources and controlled migration. Marriage was also regulated,
to adjust to the availability of land and other resources. Permanent
celibacy was practised, most by the landowners, as they were in a
position to perceive pressure on resources much more sharply than
the landless labourers.

This runs counter to Davis' (1955) and Hajnal's (1982) view
that societies characterized by the joint family system necessarily
exhibit universal early marriage and lack a 'nuptiality valve' to
help balance household numbers with available resources. Their
argument rests on the assumption, that since the costs of child-
bearing in a joint family are borne by the household and not by
the couple, there are few constraints on high fertility. While it
is certainly true that the couple may be able to spread the costs
of childbearing, they overlook the possibility that the household
may want to regulate the number of new members born into it.
One way for the household to make effective joint decisions about
fertility is to regulate marriage. Another is for other household
members, such as the husband's parents, to make inputs into the
young couples' childbearing decisions — a feature of joint families
which is widely noted in south Asia.

With the exception of marriage regulation, the traditional
mechanisms for balancing population and resources could cope

only with fluctuations in numbers, and had to be abandoned in a situation of steady growth in numbers. Thus, the sustained mortality decline made it necessary to increase celibacy rates at first, while shifting over to alternative ways of controlling the growth of family size. The fertility decline began among the landowners, who were the quickest to perceive the negative effects of population growth, because partible inheritance brought these consequences home to them vividly and concretely. With a short lag, the landless labourers also began to reduce their fertility. By the time Mamdani visited this area and concluded that for these people reducing fertility would mean 'courting economic disaster', the total fertility rate had already fallen by nearly 40 per cent, and all the socio-economic groups in these villages were engaged in rapid fertility decline.

Yet mortality declines far more impressive than that of Punjab in the 1930s have now been experienced all over south Asia, and have not necessarily triggered off such an early and rapid response in fertility behaviour. In much of the rest of northern India, particularly, fertility decline has been slow. The crucial factor which seems to have made it possible for people to move towards rapid fertility decline in Punjab is the security generated by the nature of the developmental interventions in this region. The emphasis placed on rural development in Punjab preceded that in the rest of northern India. Thus, although levels of living were still quite low in Punjab when fertility decline was established, the havoc wrought in people's lives by uncertainties surrounding food availability and the survival of the household's productive adults had been relegated to the past, and a sense of fatalism replaced by a feeling that people could shape and improve their lives by dint of their own efforts. This feeling is glaringly lacking in parts of rural north India even today, because of the slow pace of improvement in most dimensions of physical security.

After 1966, that is, several decades after the onset of the fertility decline, Punjab began to experience rapid social as well as economic development. Levels of income and education rose very sharply, and health and family planning services were made widely available to the people. Had fertility decline not already begun, these and related developmental efforts would almost certainly have initiated a fertility decline. In this case, they facilitated the continued decline.

The Punjab case suggests that it is important to redefine what we understand to be the features of socio-economic development which are crucial for fertility decline. The more dramatic forms of development widely viewed in the literature since Notestein's (1953) formulation as being associated with fertility decline may be less important than some more basic forms of development. Of the greatest importance in Punjab were those interventions which generated a feeling of stability of expectations, of an ability to control and improve one's life, instead of simply responding to shifts in fortune. They built up a demand for fertility control such that very substantial fertility decline took place long before the advent of the family planning programme, and also made for quick acceptance of the new contraceptive technologies offered by the family planning programme when it was introduced. This is consistent with Cain's thesis (1981) that the reduction of risk and uncertainty is a critical factor in inducing fertility decline.

Viewed from this perspective, there are strong parallels between the situations prevailing in late-nineteenth-century Europe, when rapid fertility decline began in most countries (Knodel and van de Walle 1986:394–5), and Punjab of the 1940s. In both, the majority of people were illiterate and poor, with high (though falling) infant mortality rates. The fact that fertility fell under these conditions does not suggest that development is irrelevant to fertility decline. On the contrary, in both these cases major developmental transformations were under way, which made people's lives more secure and enabled them to reduce family size. The changes which took place in Punjab have been described. In the European context these efforts are familiar. Apart from agricultural and industrial development, there were many other efforts by the newly conscious nation-states to improve their citizens' lives, including improvement of housing and various public health and sanitary reform efforts. Development and fertility decline are closely linked, and the essential feature of this link is the generation of a sense of stability and control over life.

REFERENCES

Arnold, Devid (1989), 'Cholera Mortality in British India', in T. Dyson (ed.), *India's Historical Demography* (London: Curzon Press).
Banks, Joseph A. (1954), *Prosperity and Parenthood* (London: Routledge and Kegan Paul)

94 *Reproductive Change in India and Brazil*

Berkner, Lutz K. (1972) 'The Stem Family and the Developmental Cycle
of the Peasant Household', *American Historical Review*, 77:398–441.
Béteille, Andre (1965), *Caste, Class and Power* (Berkeley: University of
California Press).
Breman, Jan (1974), *Patronage and Exploitation: Changing Agrarian Relations in South Gujarat, India* (Berkeley, California: University of
California Press).
Cain, Mead (1981), 'Risk and Insurance: Perspective on Fertility and
Agrarian Change in India and Bangladesh', *Population and Development Review*, 7(3):435–74.
Calvert, Hugh (1936), *The Wealth and Welfare of the Punjab* (Lahore:
Civil and Military Gazette Press)
Census of Punjab, 1868, *Report on the Census of the Punjab*.
Census of Punjab, 1901, Punjab, Part I: *Report.*
Census of Punjab, 1911, Punjab, Part I: *Report* and Part II: *Tables.*
Crook, Nigel (1989), 'On the Comparative Historical Perspective: India,
Europe and the Far East', in T. Dyson (ed.) *India's Historical Demography* (London: Curzon Press)
Darling, Malcolm (1947) *The Punjab Peasant in Prosperity and Debt,*
Fourth Edition (London: Oxford University Press) (first published
in 1925).
Das Gupta, Monica (1987), 'Selective Discrimination Against Female
Children in Rural Punjab, India', *Population and Development
Review*, 13(1):77–100.
—— (1994) 'What Motivates Fertility Decline? A Case Study from Punjab, India', in B. Egero and M. Hammarskjold (eds.), *Understanding
Reproductive Change* (Lund, Sweden: Lund University Press).
—— (1997) 'Methodology and Main Findings on Child Survival of the
Khanna Restudy, 1984–1988', in M. Das Gupta et al. (eds.), *Prospective Community Studies in Developing Countries* (Oxford: Clarendon
Press).
Davis, Kingsley (1955), 'Institutional Patterns Favouring High Fertility
in Underdeveloped Areas', *Eugenics Quarterly*, 2:33–9
Dyson, Tim (1989), 'The Historical Demography of Berar', in T. Dyson
(ed.), *India's Historical Demography* (London: Curzon Press).
Hajnal, John (1982), 'Two Kinds of Preindustrial Household Formation
System', *Population and Development Review*, 8(2):449–94.
Hanley, Susan B. and K. Yamamura (1977), *Economic and Demographic
Change in Preindustrial Japan, 1600–1968* (Princeton: Princeton
University Press).
Hershman, Paul (1981), *Punjabi Kinship and Marriage* (Delhi: Hindustan Publishing Corporation).

Kertzer, David I. (1991), 'Reflections on the European Marriage Pattern: Sharecropping and Proletarianization in Casalecchio, Italy, 1861–1921', *Journal of Family History*, 16(1):31–45.

Kertzer, David I. and Denis P. Hogan (1989), *Family, Political Economy and Demographic Change: The Transformation of Life in Casalecchio, Italy, 1861–1921* (Madison: University of Wisconsin Press).

Kessinger, Tom (1974), *Vilyatpur* (Berkeley: University of California Press)

Knodel, John and Etienne van de Walle (1986), 'Lessons from the Past: Policy Implications of Historical Fertility Studies', in A.J. Coale and S. Watkins (eds.) *The Decline of Fertility in Europe* (Princeton: Princeton University Press)

Laslett Peter and Richard Wall (eds.) (1972), *Household and Family in Past Time* (Cambridge: Cambridge University Press)

Lesthaeghe, Ron (1980), 'On the Social Control of Human Reproduction', *Population and Development Review*, 6(4):527–48.

Lewis, Oscar (1958), *Village Life in Northern India* (New York: Vintage Books)

Mamdani, Mahmood (1972), *The Myth of Population Control* (New York and London: Monthly Review Press).

McFarlane, Alan G. (1976), *Resources and Population* (Cambridge: Cambridge University Press).

Netting, Robert McC. (1981), *Balancing on an Alp* (Cambridge: Cambridge University Press)

Notestein, Frank (1953), 'Economic Problems of Population Change', in *Proceedings of the Eighth International Conference of Agricultural Economists* (Oxford: Oxford University Press).

Parry, Jonathon (1979), *Caste and Kinship in Kangra* (London: Routledge and Kegan Paul).

Pradhan, M.C. (1966), *The Political System of the Jats of Northern India* (Bombay: Oxford University Press)

Schuler, Sidney R. (1987), *The Other Side of Polyandry* (Boulder: Westview Press)

Smith, Thomas C. (1977), *Nakahara* (Stanford: Stanford University Press).

Viazzo, Pier Paolo (1989), *Upland Communities* (Cambridge: Cambridge University Press).

Wall, Richard, Jean Robin, and Peter Laslett (eds.) (1983), *Family Forms in Historic Europe* (Cambridge: Cambridge University Press).

Wiser, William H. (1936), *The Hindu Jajmani System* (Lucknow: Lucknow Publishing House).

Wrigley, Ernest A. and Roger Schofield (1981), *The Population History of England, 1541–1871* (London: Edward Arnold).

Wyon, John B. and John E. Gordon (1971), *The Khanna Study* (Cambridge MA.: Harvard University Press).

3

Contours of Fertility Decline in India: An Analysis of District-Level Trends from Two Recent Censuses

P.N. Mari Bhat

> This is the first and most essential thing to learn about India,
> that there is not, and never was an India, or even a country
> of India, possessing according to European ideas any sort of
> unity, physical, political, social and religious; no Indian na-
> tion, no people of India, of which we hear so much.
>
> Sir John Strachey

INTRODUCTION

India, the second most populous country in the world, and the first to launch an official family planning programme aimed at reducing population growth, is undergoing fertility declines of notable proportions. However, neither the speed of the decline, nor the reasons contributing to it are a matter of complete unanimity. Although there are multiple sources of demographic data for India, each source has limitations. Further, they tend to disagree on what is actually occurring in India. The matter is further complicated by the long delay in publishing the bulk of the 1991 census results. This paper attempts to make sense of various, and apparently diverging sources, and tries to determine the actual course of fertility trends in different parts of the country. Since this book is directed to a broader audience, the analysis presents a minimum of technical detail concerning demographic calculations or statistical data base. (For a more detailed analysis, cf. Bhat 1996).

An assessment made following the 1981 census by the Panel on India, constituted by the Committee on Population and

Demography of the National Research Council, concluded that
fertility levels in India were falling faster than generally believed
(Bhat, Preston, and Dyson 1984; Preston and Bhat 1984). But
in the years that followed, India's main source of information
for yearly trends in vital rates, namely the Sample Registration
System (SRS), indicated the stalling of the fertility decline. Subsequently, in the late 1980s, the SRS began to show a decline in
the birth rate. In spite of this most recent decline, information
from the latest (1991) census indicated that, so far, the growth
rate of the population seemed unaffected by the reduction in
fertility. The census evidence on the growth rate, however, must
be interpreted in the light of other demographic data it provides.
In this paper, information released from the 1991 census on the
size of the population in ages 0–6 years (India, Registrar General
1993) is used to unravel some of the mysteries surrounding Indian
demographic trends, to assess future prospects, and to analyse the
spatial patterns of fertility change. Data from the SRS and the
National Family Health Survey (NFHS) of 1993 are also used
to arrive at a more precise estimate of fertility change in India.

Data and Methods

The principal objective of this paper is to assess recent trends in
Indian fertility from census data. The most direct means to achieve
this would be to make use of the data on live births in the year
preceding the one during which the census was conducted. This can
be accomplished by using Indian censuses since 1971. We do not
use this approach, however, because the data gathered on live births
for the preceding year in the last two censuses were found to be
defective, and estimates of fertility made directly from the data had
grossly understated actual levels (India, Registrar General 1989).
Although some of the deficiencies in the data could be corrected by
using the well-known 'P/F procedure', this method is unsuitable to
populations experiencing rapid fertility declines (United Nations
1983). There is also little reason to expect a drastic improvement in
the quality of census data in 1991; thus, it could not be utilized
without adjustment. Consequently, other avenues have to be explored.

The recent release of data on children in the age interval 0–6 years
provides an opportunity to examine the accuracy of the trends in

Indian fertility indicated by the Sample Registration System — a dual recording system which has operated on a continuous sample basis since the mid-1960s. Such a crosscheck is deemed essential because of the erratic nature of the fertility trends indicated by the annual SRS data. Moreover, the census analysis is of additional value because the data on the size of population under 7 years of age are generated at the village level in rural areas and at the ward level in urban areas. This provides us with a means to study levels and trends in fertility at administrative divisions smaller than the state, for which the SRS data are unreliable owing to inadequacies of sample size.

To estimate the levels of fertility, the 'reverse-survival' method was applied to the population in ages 0–6 years from the 1981 and 1991 censuses for over 300 districts in 14 major states of India. These district-level estimates of fertility fill an important data gap. Altogether, estimates derived from the 1991 census should be considered as provisional (because of the approximate nature of the estimates of child mortality used in their calculations); the figures are fully expected to reflect reality.

ALL-INDIA TRENDS IN FERTILITY

A convenient starting point for our discussion is a review of country-level trends in fertility. In Table 1, we have compiled the estimates of the total fertility rate for the country as a whole from all major sources in the last 20 years. In Figure 1, we have plotted the trends in fertility suggested by the three sources: the SRS, the NFHS, and the indirect estimates derived from censuses and other surveys.

The SRS, the major source of information on annual trends, had indicated that total fertility had fallen quite rapidly from around 5.2 in 1971 to 4.5 in 1978. But during the next five years, fertility levels showed no signs of decline. Two explanations for this can be proffered. In substantive terms, this period of stagnation coincided with the postemergency imbroglio when the family planning programme assumed a low political profile. In methodological terms, this was also the period when the sampling units of the SRS were modified to make them conform to the 1981 census count. Be that as it may, the SRS again began to register a fertility decline from 1984 onwards, and by 1991, the TFR had reportedly fallen to 3.7 births per woman.

TABLE 1: ESTIMATES OF TOTAL FERTILITY RATE FOR ALL-INDIA FROM DIFFERENT SOURCES, 1970–91

Data source	Method of estimation	Approximate reference year								
		'71	'73	'77	'78	'80	'85	'87	'90	'91
1972 SRS Survey	P/F adjustment	5.6	–	–	–	–	–	–	–	–
1979 SRS Survey	Modified P/F method	–	–	–	4.7	–	–	–	–	–
1981 Census	P/F adjustment	–	–	–	–	4.9	–	–	–	–
1981 Census	Child-woman ratios	–	5.4	–	4.7	–	–	–	–	–
1981 Census	Reverse-survival	–	–	4.9	–	–	–	–	–	–
1991 Census	Reverse-survival	–	–	–	–	–	–	4.1	–	–
NFHS, 1992–93	Birth history analysis	–	–	–	–	4.8	4.5	–	3.4	–
SRS	Three-year average	5.2	5.0	4.6	4.5	4.5	4.3	4.1	3.8	3.7

Source: Bhat, Preston and Dyson (1984); Rele (1987); India, Registrar General (1989); and International Institute for Population Sciences (1995).

In its assessment of fertility trends during the 1970s, the Panel on India (Bhat, Preston, and Dyson 1984) had come to the conclusion that the SRS was underestimating both the level of fertility and the pace of its decline. Our application of the reverse-survival procedure to census data on children under 7 years of age now shows that, while the SRS was underestimating the birth rate in the 1970s, it is now almost fully complete. The improved coverage can be attributed to the switching over of the sampling units drawn on the basis of the 1961 census results to conform to the 1981 census results. Such a procedure not only made the system more representative, but also enabled the system managers to take corrective action, especially in regions where a special survey in 1980–1 had indicated below-par performance. Recently, more timely publication of the SRS results is one indication of the changes brought about in the system during the early 1980s. This improvement in data quality is also supported by various other types of evidence.

The analysis of birth history data from the recent National Family Health Survey (NFHS), modeled along the lines of the Demographic Health Surveys, provides a somewhat different picture of fertility change in India (International Institute for Population Sciences 1995). For all-India, this survey suggests a decline of 28 per cent in TFR between 1980 and 1990, while the SRS indicates a decline of only 16 per cent during the same period. However, like the SRS, the NFHS data also suggest a stagnation of fertility levels in the early 1980s and an acceleration of the decline in the late 1980s (see Figure 1). The NFHS evidence on levels and trends in fertility may be flawed by what is called the 'Potter effect' (Potter 1977); that is, older women have a tendency to misreport the date of birth of their children retrospectively. This 'backward displacement' of births causes an inflation of fertility levels in the earlier part of the reporting period, and an exaggerated reduction in more recent years (see Bhat 1995).

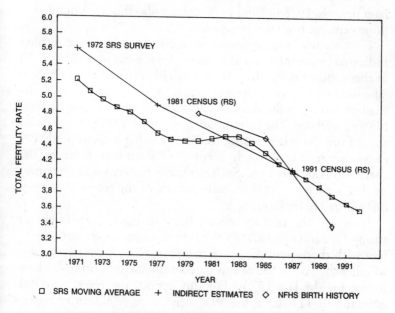

FIG. 1: *Trends in total fertility rate, India, 1971–91*

On the whole, the evidence reviewed thus far suggests that total fertility declined from a level of 5.6 births per woman around 1971, to 4.7 around 1978. After stagnating at this level for some time, it fell to 3.7 around 1991. The census analysis suggests that although SRS birth reporting is now nearly complete, its birth rate estimate had a significant downward bias in the 1970s. Consequently, it understated the pace of fertility decline in India. In contrast, the NFHS suggests a more rapid decline in fertility in the 1980s than either the census or the SRS, but this may well be exaggerated. These conclusions also derive strength from the state-specific comparisons made below.

LEVELS AND TRENDS IN MAJOR STATES

Table 2 presents the estimates of TFR derived from reverse-surviving the population enumerated in ages under 7 years in the 1981 and 1991 censuses for major states of India, as well as for rural and urban areas of all-India. For purposes of comparison, the average estimates from the SRS for the corresponding periods, namely, 1974–80 and 1984–90, and estimates from the NFHS for slightly later periods, 1978–82 and 1988–92, are also shown. A number of points emerge from this comparison.

First, there is a great deal of similarity in the regional fertility indicated by the three sets of estimates for the end of the 1980s. All of them show the familiar north-south divide in levels of fertility. The similarity between the census and SRS based estimates is particularly strong, as the state-level estimates from the two sources are highly correlated. The correspondence of the NFHS estimates with those from the other two sources is somewhat weaker, partly because they refer to a slightly later period. Even here, however, the correlations are very high. Such symmetry between sources assures us that we have a fairly accurate picture of the recent state-level differentials in fertility.

However, the correspondence between the sources is not as strong for earlier periods. As the NFHS estimates are less consistent with those from the other two sources, we have to consider whether the SRS or the census-based estimates constitute our best source for the late 1970s. For this period, the reverse-survival estimates of TFR from the 1981 census are significantly higher than the SRS estimates for Rajasthan, Karnataka, Maharashtra,

TABLE 2: RECENT TRENDS IN TOTAL FERTILITY RATE IN MAJOR STATES OF INDIA AS INDICATED BY CENSUSES OF 1981 AND 1991, SAMPLE REGISTRATION SYSTEM, AND NATIONAL FAMILY HEALTH SURVEY, 1992–93

Major states	Census reverse survival estimates			Sample registration system			National family health survey			% Fall from 1978–82 to 1988–92 in SRS	SRS birth under-registration 1980–81*
	1974–80	1984–90	Percent-age decline	1974–80	1984–90	Percent-age decline	1978–82	1988–92	Percent-age decline		
	(1)	(2)	(3)	(4)	(5)	(6)	(7)	(8)	(9)	(10)	(11)
India											
Total	4.9	4.1	16	4.6	4.1	11	4.8	3.4	28	16	3.2
Rural	5.2	4.5	12	4.9	4.4	10	5.1	3.7	27	14	NA
Urban	4.0	3.1	21	3.5	3.1	11	3.9	2.7	30	20	NA
Kerala	2.9	2.0	30	3.1	2.2	31	3.3	2.0	38	35	2.0
Tamil Nadu	3.5	2.3	35	3.7	2.7	27	3.6	2.5	30	32	2.0
Andhra Pradesh	4.3	3.2	26	4.3	3.5	18	3.7	2.6	29	24	5.9
Karnataka	4.3	3.4	21	3.7	3.5	5	4.4	2.9	33	12	11.1
Maharashtra	4.1	3.7	9	3.7	3.5	6	4.1	2.9	28	12	2.5
Gujarat	4.3	3.2	25	4.9	3.7	26	4.3	3.0	31	26	1.1
Rajasthan	6.0	5.2	14	5.2	5.0	5	5.6	3.5	37	13	4.9

Table 2 (contd.)

Major states	Census reverse survival estimates			Sample registration system			National family health survey			% Fall from 1978–82 to 1988–92 in SRS	SRS birth under-registration 1980–81*
	1974–80	1984–90	Percentage decline	1974–80	1984–90	Percentage decline	1978–82	1988–92	Percentage decline		
	(1)	(2)	(3)	(4)	(5)	(6)	(7)	(8)	(9)	(10)	(11)
Punjab	4.2	3.5	17	4.4	3.4	21	4.4	2.9	34	18	2.0
Haryana	5.1	4.5	13	5.3	4.4	18	5.4	4.1	24	20	1.2
Uttar Pradesh	6.3	5.4	15	5.9	5.4	8	6.1	4.9	20	10	2.3
Madhya Pradesh	5.5	5.0	9	5.5	4.9	11	5.2	3.8	27	13	0.2
Bihar	5.3	5.1	5	NA	5.3	NA	5.7	4.1	27	14	NA
Orissa	4.5	3.9	15	4.4	3.9	12	4.6	3.0	34	18	NA
West Bengal	4.0	3.6	12	NA	3.6	NA	4.4	3.0	32	22	NA
Assam	NA	4.1	NA	4.2	3.9	8	5.6	3.7	34	15	9.0
Correlation coefficient (r)	0.916	0.979	0.738	0.817	0.917	0.158	0.949	0.907	0.316	0.349	
Columns	1 & 4	2 & 5	3 & 6	4 & 7	5 & 8	6 & 9	7 & 1	8 & 2	9 & 3	10 & 9	

NA Not available.

* From India, Registrar General (1984).

and generally in urban India. Several pieces of evidence indicate that these discrepancies can basically be attributed to underestimation by the SRS. One such evidence comes from the SRS coverage evaluation study conducted in 1980–1 which disclosed a large undercount of births in Rajasthan and Karnataka (India, Registrar General 1984). However, no supporting evidence could be found from the SRS evaluation study for the discrepancies in the TFR estimates for Maharashtra and Gujarat — which are also evident for the 1984–90 period (see Table 2).

Besides the SRS evaluation study, estimates of TFR available from other sources for the 1970s provide more support for the reverse-survival estimates of fertility than the SRS estimates. For example, state-specific estimates of TFR derived by Rele (1987) for 1976–81, using the census child-woman ratios, show a correlation of 0.97 with the reverse-survival estimates and 0.90 with the SRS estimates. The estimates of TFR derived by applying the P/F procedure to the 1981 census fertility data are more strongly correlated with our reverse-survival estimates than the SRS-based TFR (correlation of 0.96 vs. 0.89). Even the NFHS estimates of TFR for 1978–82 are more strongly correlated with the reverse-survival estimates than the SRS estimates (0.95 vs. 0.82).

Moreover, the SRS birth rate changes are unable to account for the large declines in the growth rate of the population registered by the 1991 census in Karnataka, Rajasthan, and generally in urban areas of India (see Table 3). These are precisely the areas where the SRS is suspected of understating fertility levels during the 1970s.

In short, the reverse-survival estimates of TFR appear to provide a more accurate picture of fertility trends than the SRS estimates. How much do the more reliable estimates of TFR from the reverse-survival method change our perception of fertility trends in the Indian states? First, they confirm the large reductions in fertility shown earlier by the SRS in Kerala and Tamil Nadu during the 1980s. In particular, what needed substantiation was the dramatic, yet uneven, fall in fertility in Tamil Nadu recorded by the SRS during the 1980s. The SRS birth rate for the state was almost static, then fell dramatically and then fluctuated. The report that over half of the decline in birth rate had occurred in one year naturally raised questions about the reliability of the SRS data. In addition to confirming the overall trend, the reverse-survival estimates derived from the 1991 census suggest that

TABLE 3: SOME ADDITIONAL INDICATORS OF TRENDS IN
FERTILITY LEVELS IN MAJOR STATES OF INDIA, 1971–91

Major states	Children ever-born to women aged 40–49	Total fertility rate for ages 15–49		Implied percentage fall in total fertility		Percentage fall in growth rate from 1971–81 to 1981–91
	NFHS, 1992–93	P/F adjusted estimate from 1972 SRS survey*	Direct estimate from SRS 1990–92	With NFHS cohort fertility, ages 40–49**	With TFR estimated from 1972 survey	
	(1)	(2)	(3)	(4)	(5)	(6)
India						
Total	4.8	5.6	3.7	25	34	3.1
Rural	5.1	NA	4.0	24	NA	-3.4
Urban	4.2	NA	2.7	36	NA	18.4
Kerala	3.7	4.5	1.8	51	60	23.9
Tamil Nadu	4.2	4.6	2.3	47	51	11.2
Andhra Pradesh	4.1	4.8	3.0	28	39	-4.3
Karnataka	4.7	5.5	3.1	34	44	19.2
Maharashtra	4.3	4.9	3.1	28	38	-4.3
Gujarat	4.4	6.0	3.2	27	46	21.3
Rajasthan	5.0	6.4	4.6	11	29	12.2
Punjab	4.2	5.6	3.1	25	44	11.8
Haryana	5.2	6.6	3.9	27	42	8.3
Uttar Pradesh	6.0	6.5	5.2	16	20	0
Madhya Pradesh	5.2	6.2	4.6	14	26	-5.5
Bihar	5.2	NA	4.6	14	NA	2
Orissa	4.9	5.5	3.3	33	40	0.5
West Bengal	4.7	NA	3.2	34	NA	-6
Assam	5.7	6.4	3.4	41	46	NA
Correlation coefficient (r)		0.855			0.901	
Columns		(1 & 2)			(4 & 5)	

*   From Bhat, Preston and Dyson (1984).

**   In this case, TFR for ages 15–44 from the SRS has been used to
compute the percentage decline.

NA   Not available.

fertility levels in Tamil Nadu may now be even lower than what is indicated by the SRS.

The reverse-survival estimates show that fertility declines in the two other South Indian states, Andhra Pradesh and Karnataka, were also sizeable, but not as high as that recorded by the two southern most states. In western India, fertility decline during the 1980s was much more rapid in Gujarat than in Maharashtra. In fact, the pace of fertility decline in Maharashtra during the 1980s was one of the lowest observed among the major states. Fertility has also fallen in all the northern states, though the pace of the decline during the 1980s was much lower than that experienced in south India (12 per cent vs. 27 per cent). The estimates from the reverse-survival procedure also suggests that fertility had declined much more rapidly in urban areas than in rural areas, a fact which may partly explain why the growth rate of the·urban population was lower in 1981–91 than in 1971–81.

Earlier, we had rejected the NFHS recent trend data on Indian fertility because it was suspected of being influenced by the erroneous declaration (backward displacement) of birth timings by older women. There is, however, one piece of information from the survey that might be useful in the assessment of fertility trends. It is the average number of children ever-born to women at the end of the reproductive span. This information is completely free from reference period biases and, because the NFHS had probed birth histories of women, it is also less likely to be affected by recall errors. Table 3 shows the mean completed family size of women aged 40–49 at the time of the survey for major states and for rural and urban areas of all-India. As this is a cohort measure, it reflects the level of total fertility at approximately 17–18 years before the survey, or around 1975–6. This can be usefully compared with the TFR for 1990–1 from the SRS to gauge the extent of fertility decline.

For India as a whole, the completed family size of women aged 40–49 was 4.8 live births, which is comparable to our reverse-survival estimate of a TFR of 4.9 around 1977. The NFHS data on cohort fertility suggests that fertility has declined more rapidly in urban areas (36 per cent) than in rural areas (24 per cent), which confirms the pattern observed in our estimates of TFR. These data also show that the fertility decline was not confined to a few states in South India, although they certainly had more rapid declines in recent years. The survey data on cohort fertility suggest that fertility may have fallen by at least one-third in eastern India, comprised of the states of Orissa, West Bengal, and Assam. This is a comparable decline to that of neighbouring Bangladesh, now being described as a family planning success story (Cleland et al. 1994). Even in the demographically backward regions of northern India, the NFHS data on cohort fertility indicate a noticeable decline.

Another useful benchmark for assessing the state-specific trends in fertility are the estimates made by the Panel on India, through the application of the P/F method, to the 1972 SRS survey data. In Table 3, we have compared these with estimates of total fertility from the SRS for 1990–2 (as the SRS appears to be more complete now), to gauge the trends in fertility during the last twenty years. For India as a whole, this comparison shows that the TFR has fallen from 5.6 to 3.7, or by about one-third, between 1971 and 1991. The size of the decline (34 per cent) is higher than that implied by the comparison with NFHS cohort fertility data (25 per cent) since the NFHS data refers to a more recent and shorter time period. At the state level, this comparison shows that in Kerala and Tamil Nadu, TFR levels have been reduced by 50–60 per cent during the last 20-year period. In other parts of South India, as well as in western, eastern, and northwestern frontier regions, fertility decline was also sizeable, of the order of 40 per cent. In the heartland of northern India, the decline was slower, but here as well, a fall of 20–30 per cent in TFR appears to have occurred during the last two decades. We can be more confident of these spatial patterns in fertility decline because they show a strong correlation with the pattern of change implied by the NFHS data on completed family size.

In short, cumulative evidence, thus, strongly favours the conclusion that fertility is on a rapid downward course in India and that the decline is much more widespread than is commonly believed. The earlier indication of this decline from the SRS was flawed because it was underestimating fertility levels in a number of places in the 1970s. While the NFHS period-specific estimates of fertility appear to overstate the extent of recent fertility decline in India, the survey information on completed family size is consistent with evidence from other sources. Our preferred estimates of TFR for the major states of India are those derived by the Indian Panel for 1971–2 (Table 3) and reverse-survival estimates from the 1981 and the 1991 censuses for circa 1977 and 1987, respectively

(Table 2). For even more recent years, estimates taken directly from the SRS could be used without any adjustment.

DISTRICT-LEVEL ESTIMATES

Estimates of crude birth rate and total fertility rate have been derived from the reverse-survival procedure for 326 districts in 14 major states of India in 1981 and 362 districts in the same states in 1991 (not shown). For 17 smaller states and union territories, the estimates have been made for their respective total geographical area only.

A variety of consistency checks were applied to these data (see Bhat 1996). These demonstrate that our district-level estimates of fertility are generally accurate. While there are some discrepancies, they could be due to the fact that none of the tests performed are completely error-free. A state-by-state examination of district level estimates reveals more inconsistencies, partly because intrastate variations in fertility and related measures are relatively small and thus sensitive to data errors. Nonetheless, throughout all the checks, the only state to perform poorly is Haryana. However, for various reasons, we are confident that the levels of fertility we have estimated are reasonably close to their true values, even in Haryana.

Spatial Distribution of Fertility

The crude birth rate estimates derived from the 1991 census for the 362 districts show a range of variation from a high of 45.4 per 1000 in a tribal district of Madhya Pradesh (Jhabua) to a low of 16 per 1000 in the metropolitan district of Calcutta. The estimates of TFR also show a similar variation, from a level of 7 births per woman in Jhabua to a level of around 1.6 births in a cluster of districts in southern Kerala and northwestern Tamil Nadu. Although Calcutta had the lowest TFR (2.0) in the country in the late 1970s, and continues to have the lowest CBR, in terms of TFR it now ranks only twelfth from the bottom. Its relatively low birth rate is due partly to its peculiar age-sex structure, shaped largely by migration.

The frequency distributions of districts, by their level of TFR in 1974–80 and 1984–90, are shown in Table 4. In order to facilitate the comparison of the distributions at the two points in time, wherever new districts were formed, the estimates derived

TABLE 4: FREQUENCY DISTRIBUTION AND SELECTED DESCRIPTIVE STATISTICS OF DISTRICT-LEVEL ESTIMATES OF TOTAL FERTILITY RATE FOR 1974–80 AND 1984–90

Major states	Period	Total Fertility Rate							Total districts	Descriptive statistics*		
		Less than 2	2–3	3–4	4–5	5–6	6–7	7 or more		Mean	Standard deviation	Skewness
India*	1974–80	0	12	41	108	88	62	15	326	5.05	1.140	−0.034
	1984–90	12	40	76	73	102	22	1	326	4.28	1.208	−0.241
South	1974–80	0	11	29	51	5	0	0	96	3.99	0.743	−0.479
	1984–90	11	35	31	13	6	0	0	96	3.13	0.958	0.513
Kerala	1974–80	0	7	4	1	0	0	0	12	2.96	0.659	0.850
	1984–90	7	4	1	0	0	0	0	12	2.04	0.502	2.000
Tamil Nadu	1974–80	0	4	8	4	0	0	0	16	3.46	0.583	−0.128
	1984–90	4	11	1	0	0	0	0	16	2.23	0.417	0.076
Andhra Pradesh	1974–80	0	0	5	14	4	0	0	23	4.44	0.544	0.065
	1984–90	0	8	11	4	0	0	0	23	3.30	0.490	0.405
Karnataka	1974–80	0	0	4	15	0	0	0	19	4.24	0.466	−0.291
	1984–90	0	10	4	3	2	0	0	19	3.38	0.911	0.843
Maharashtra	1974–80	0	0	8	17	1	0	0	26	4.21	0.563	−0.306
	1984–90	0	2	14	6	4	0	0	26	3.87	0.857	0.522
North	1974–80	0	0	6	37	54	58	15	170	5.69	0.954	−0.129
	1984–90	0	4	30	43	72	20	1	170	4.85	0.961	−0.304
Gujarat	1974–80	0	0	4	10	4	1	0	19	4.57	0.596	0.735
	1984–90	0	4	12	2	1	0	0	19	3.45	0.687	1.126

Major states	Period	Total Fertility Rate								Descriptive statistics*		
		Less than 2	2–3	3–4	4–5	5–6	6–7	7 or more	Total districts	Mean	Standard deviation	Skewness
Rajasthan	1974–80	0	0	0	0	13	12	1	26	6.00	0.478	0.552
	1984–90	0	0	0	12	10	4	0	26	5.10	0.608	0.704
Punjab	1974–80	0	0	2	10	0	0	0	12	4.24	0.294	0.153
	1984–90	0	0	11	1	0	0	0	12	3.50	0.270	0.701
Haryana	1974–80	0	0	0	3	9	0	0	12	5.14	0.450	−0.422
	1984–90	0	0	1	9	2	0	0	12	4.53	0.621	1.067
Uttar Pradesh	1974–80	0	0	0	6	10	29	11	56	6.27	0.798	−0.464
	1984–90	0	0	4	9	33	10	0	56	5.27	0.731	−0.584
Madhya Pradesh	1974–80	0	0	0	8	18	16	3	45	5.79	0.807	−0.106
	1984–90	0	0	2	10	26	6	1	45	5.23	0.764	0.038
East	1974–80	0	1	6	20	29	4	0	60	4.91	0.798	−0.928
	1984–90	1	1	15	17	24	2	0	60	4.50	0.886	−0.468
Bihar	1974–80	0	0	0	4	23	4	0	31	5.45	0.440	−0.593
	1984–90	0	0	1	6	22	2	0	31	5.15	0.493	−0.475
Orissa	1974–80	0	0	1	10	2	0	0	13	4.57	0.359	−0.763
	1984–90	0	0	6	7	0	0	0	13	3.97	0.357	0.129
West Bengal	1974–80	0	1	5	6	4	0	0	16	4.14	0.829	−0.850
	1984–90	1	1	8	4	2	0	0	16	3.69	0.837	−0.100

Note: The distribution for 1984–90 is for the districts as of 1981.
The all-India distribution is for the districts in the 14 major states only.

* Not weighted by population size of districts.

from the 1991 census were combined so as to reflect the level of fertility for the district territories in the 1981 census.

The table clearly emphasizes the large interdistrict variation in fertility and the significant changes taking place in the spatial distribution of fertility. Out of the 326 districts in 1974–80, there was not a single district with a TFR under 2, which signifies a level of fertility below replacement. At the other end of the distribution, there were a total of 77 districts in 1974–80 having over 6 births per woman.

After ten years, the shift to a lower fertility category was observed in every state, confirming that the fertility decline is an all-pervasive phenomenon. Some 12 districts are below the replacement level; all of these, except Calcutta, are a part of either Kerala or Tamil Nadu. Meanwhile, only 23 now had TFR levels above 6.

Subcultures of Fertility

It is now common knowledge that there are large north-south differences in fertility levels in India (e.g., Dyson and Moore 1983, Basu 1992). The SRS data have also emphasized differences between states within the same region. A one-way analysis of variance of our district-level estimates of TFR for 14 major states showed that if the districts were grouped into four conventional geographical zones — north, south, east, and west — between-zone variation in fertility levels accounted for about half of the total variation in our district-level estimates of TFR. On the other hand, if the districts were grouped according to the state they belonged to, variation in fertility between the 14 states 'explained' as much as 70 per cent of the total interdistrict variation. Using estimates for 1974–80 or 1984–90 did not change the percentage of variance explained.

In order to further identify 'subcultures' of fertility existing in the vast Indian landscape, we have mapped the district-level estimates of TFR, from 1974–80 and 1984–90, in Figures 2 and 3, respectively. It is clear from these maps that contiguous districts, though not necessarily in the same state, have similar levels of fertility. Thus, we see the fertility decline in South India sweeping across the coast and moving inland. This has left a central core in the Deccan plateau, comprising mainly districts of the Hyderabad state; but also in Andhra Pradesh, Karnataka and Maharashtra. In north India, fertility is relatively low in the northwestern frontier region as well as in the eastern plateau and Gangetic delta. Highest

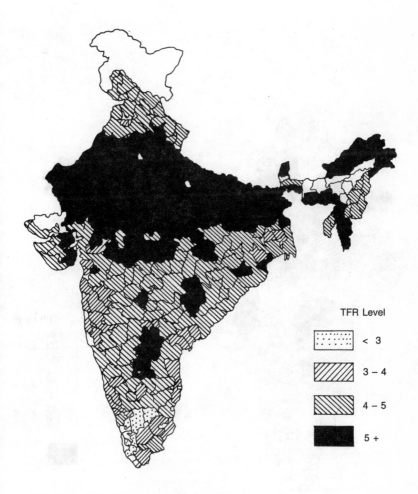

FIG. 2: *Total fertility rate, 1974–80*

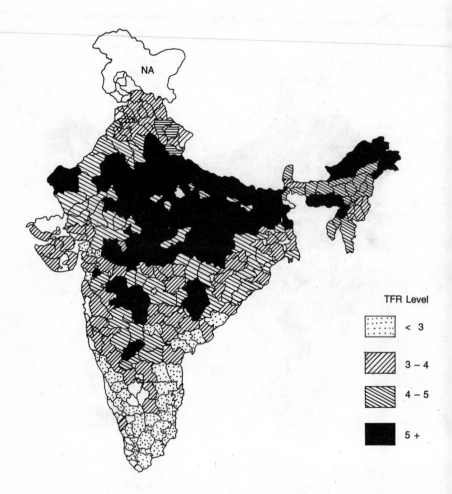

FIG. 3:   *Total fertility rate, 1984–90*

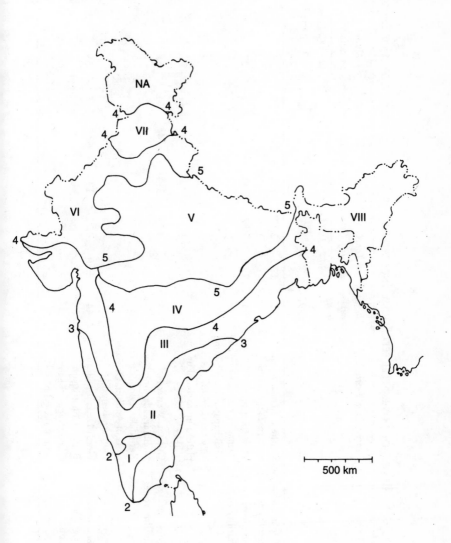

Fig. 4: *Fertility zones in India, 1984–90*

116 Reproductive Change in India and Brazil

TABLE 5: LEVELS OF SOME SELECTED SOCIAL INDICATORS FOR EIGHT FERTILITY ZONES OF INDIA, 1981–91

Fertility zones	Geographical location	No. of districts in 1991	Total Fertility Rate		Pop. density (per sq. kms)	CMIE development index	Male workers in agriculture	Work participation		Female literacy (7+)	Media exposure*
			1984–90	1974–90				Women (7+)	Children (5–14)		
1. Replacement fertility zone	Southern Kerala, north-western Tamil Nadu	12	1.75	2.57	588	130	50	22	5	73	80
2. Southern low-fertility zone	West coast up to Ratnagiri; east coast up to Visakhapatanam; adjoining hilly tracts; south Deccan plateau up to Tumkur district	53	2.66	3.82	333	121	58	27	8	51	70
3. Moderate fertility zone	Gujarat, Western Maharatwada; Bombay-Karnataka region, eastern parts of Andhra, Orissa, southern Bengal	64	3.38	4.14	314	174	54	18	7	46	55
4. Southeastern high fertility zone	North Deccan plateau, Bastar, Chhattisgarh Chota Nagpur region, central Bengal plains	44	4.40	4.72	197	68	68	35	12	37	56

Fertility zones	Geographical location	Joint family	Female age at first marriage	Males per 1,000 females	Percent Muslims	Percent Scheduled Tribes	Under-5 mortality rate, c. 1988	Health personnel for 100,000 rural pop.		CPR, 1989	
								Doctors*	ANMs*	Sterilization	All methods
1. Replacement fertility zone	Southern Kerala, northwestern Tamil Nadu	12	19.2	1,001	8	1	53	6	24	47	59
2. Southern low-fertility zone	West coast up to Ratnagiri; east coast up to Visakhapatanam; adjoining hilly tracts; south Deccan plateau up to Tumkur district	13	17.6	1,017	10	3	98	5	22	39	49
3. Moderate fertility zone	Gujarat, Western Maharatwada; Bombay-Karnataka region, eastern parts of Andhra, Orissa, southern Bengal	18	17.1	1,073	10	10	120	3	19	36	45
4. Southeastern high fertility zone	North Deccan plateau, Bastar, Chhattisgarh Chota Nagpur region, central Bengal plains	23	16.1	1,049	13	15	132	4	21	36	45

Table 5 (contd.)

Fertility zones	Geographical location	No. of districts in 1991	Total Fertility Rate		Pop. density (per sq. kms)	CMIE development index	Male workers in agriculture	Work participation		Female literacy (7+)	Media exposure*
			1984–90	1974–90				Women (7+)	Children (5–14)		
5. Northern high fertility zone	Uttar Pradesh excl. Uttarakhand, northern Bihar, central Madhya Pradesh, northeastern Rajasthan	141	5.41	6.08	336	67	74	13	6	24	38
6. Northwestern high fertility zone	Western and tribal Rajasthan, Ujjain, Haryana, Delhi, Uttarakhand of U.P.	43	4.32	5.20	163	215	55	17	8	35	48
7. Northwestern moderate fertility zone	Punjab, Himachal Pradesh, Chandigarh, Ambala district	26	3.43	4.21	254	230	56	7	6	51	50
8. Northeastern zone	Northeastern states, Assam, northern Bengal	67	4.11	4.62	139	42	68	20	6	43	48

Fertility zones	Geographical location	Joint family	Female age at first marriage	Males per 1,000 females	Per cent Muslims	Percent Scheduled Tribes	Under-5 mortality rate, c. 1988	Health personnel for 100,000 rural pop.		CPR, 1989	
								Doctors*	ANMs*	Sterilization*	All methods
5. Northern high fertility zone	Uttar Pradesh excl. Uttarakhand, northern Bihar, central Madhya Pradesh, northeastern Rajasthan	24	15.9	1,122	14	6	198	2	19	21	31
6. Northwestern high fertility zone	Western and tribal Rajasthan, Ujjain, Haryana, Delhi, Uttarakhand of U.P.	20	16.6	1,111	6	10	145	3	19	26	41
7. Northwestern moderate fertility zone	Punjab, Himachal Pradesh, Chandigarh, Ambala district	20	18.4	1,117	1	1	105	10	27	36	58
8. Northeastern zone	Northeastern states, Assam, northern Bengal	12	18.0	1,081	18	24	137	3	20	23	25

* Since data were available at the state-level only, zonal estimates were derived by assuming that there was no district-level variation within the state.

levels of fertility are found in the upper Gangetic plain and in the adjoining uplands in Central India. These spatial patterns probably arise out of a complex interaction of diffusion of fertility norms with pre-existing sociocultural and linguistic differences.

We can identify at least eight spatially integrated fertility sub-cultures or zones in the Indian subcontinent. The isoquant map in Figure 4 shows their boundaries (i.e., isoquant lines) according to the levels of TFR in 1984–90. Table 5 gives an account of the geographical areas included in these zones and also the zone-wise levels of some selected socio-economic indicators. At the southern-most tip of India, a cluster of 12 districts of southern Kerala and north-western Tamil Nadu form the replacement fertility zone where TFR was under 2 births per woman even by 1984–90. The region, with an average population density of 88 per sq. km in 1991, is the most densely populated of the eight fertility zones and is marked by high population pressure on the land. Although in terms of economic development the region is only marginally better than the rest of India, it has a number of features that favour low fertility. It has the highest literacy rate among females (73 per cent), the lowest incidence of joint family (12 per cent), the highest female age at marriage (19 years), the most balanced sex ratio of population (1,001 males per 1,000 females), and the lowest level of under-five mortality (3 per 1,000).

Surrounding this is the southern low-fertility grid which stretches up to Ratnagiri district of Maharashtra in the west coast, and Visakapatanam district of Andhra Pradesh in the east coast. The region includes the Ghats (hilly tracts) adjoining the coastal lines, and the south Deccan plateau up to Tumkur district in Karnataka. About 80 per cent of the districts in this zone had a level of TFR between 2 and 3 births per woman in 1984–90. Others were very close to this range. The region is generally less densely populated than the replacement fertility zone and ranks second only to this zone in all the indicators listed above, which could explain its relatively low fertility levels.

A narrow strip of land that separates the low fertility zone in the south from the high fertility zone in the north forms the moderate fertility zone. This region extends from Gujarat in the west to Bengal in the east, and is socioculturally the least homo-genous of the fertility zones we have identified. Besides Gujarat and southern Bengal, this zone includes the Konkan coast above

Ratnagiri, western Maharashtra, Bombay-Karnataka region, parts of Talengana and Rayalaseema of Andhra Pradesh, and almost the entire Orissa. In this zone, two-thirds of the districts had a level of TFR between 3 and 4, and others were around this range in 1984–90. The average population density in this region is not much different from that of the low-fertility zone.

Because of the inclusion of several metropolitan districts (Calcutta, Bombay, Hyderabad, and Ahmedabad), the region is, on average, more economically prosperous than the first two zones, despite the inclusion of the less prosperous Orissa state. Also, female literacy is not significantly different from that of the low-fertility zone. Fertility levels are apparently higher here because of a greater incidence of joint family, a higher percentage of scheduled tribes in the population, and the lower status of women as indicated by greater imbalance in the sex ratio and lower female age at marriage.

The southeastern high fertility zone is comprised of the northern Deccan plateau which includes parts of Maharashtra, Karnataka, and Andhra Pradesh, the eastern plateau which includes the Bastar and Chattisgarh regions of Madhya Pradesh and the Chota Nagpur area of Bihar, and the central Bengal plains. In about half of the districts in this zone, TFR was between 4 and 5 in 1984–90. Others had TFR levels either just under 4 (23 per cent) or slightly above (28 per cent). The region is sparsely populated and one of the least developed. It has a large tribal population (14 per cent), and has the highest work participation rate among women (34 per cent) as well as children (12 per cent). Other significant features of the region include a significant Muslim population (in nontribal areas), a relatively high incidence of joint households, low levels of female literacy, and low age at marriage.

Uttar Pradesh, excluding Kumaon Himalaya in the northwestern corner (Uttarakhand), the plains of Bihar, the central highlands of Madhya Pradesh, and eastern Rajasthan form the northern high fertility zone where the highest levels of fertility are found. Here, TFR was generally higher than 5 (in 90 per cent of the cases) and often above 6 (19 per cent). The region is more densely populated than the southeastern zone, but only one-third of the agricultural work force is comprised of casual labourers. With three-fourths of the male work force engaged in agriculture, it is economically the most backward among the eight zones. It also has the lowest level of female literacy (24 per cent), the highest incidence of joint family

(24 per cent), the lowest female age at marriage (16 years), the largest imbalance in the sex ratio (1,122) and the maximum rate of under-five mortality (198 per 1,000). Undeniably, these are all characteristics that favour high fertility.

In the sub-Himalayan range of Uttar Pradesh, Haryana, western and southern Rajasthan, and in parts of eastern Madhya Pradesh (eastern Malwa) fertility levels were high, but in 90 per cent of the census TFR was under 5 births per women. The region is very sparsely populated (163 per sq. km), and has the lowest percentage of casual workers in agriculture (20 per cent). It is also economically more prosperous, and, on all other indicators, fares better than the northern high-fertility zone. Falling within the same geographical area, the districts of Punjab, Himachal Pradesh, Chandigarh, and the Ambala district of Haryana had levels of TFR under 4 births per woman. This moderate fertility zone is economically the most prosperous in India but women's participation in economic activity is extremely rare (7 per cent). However, the region has comparatively high levels of female literacy, later age at marriage, and a high child survival rate.

Lastly, Assam, the northeastern states, and the northernmost parts of Bengal form another geographical region where fertility levels are probably moderate with an average TFR of around 4 births per woman. Owing to the paucity of data, the demographic estimates for the region are suspect; nonetheless, there are indications that the region may not be homogenous with respect to fertility levels. The river valleys probably have low fertility (e.g., Manipur, Mizoram, Tripura, Assam) while hilly terrains have high fertility (e.g., Arunachal Pradesh, Meghalaya, Nagaland). The region on the whole is sparsely populated (139 per sq. km) and the least economically developed. However, on social indicators such as literacy, female age at marriage, sex ratio of population, and the percentage of joint families, it compares favourably with the rest of India.

While fertility declined in all of the eight zones in the 1980s, it was lowest in the southeastern high fertility zone (0.3 births per woman) and highest in the southern-low fertility zone (1.2 births per woman). Estimates of the couple protection rate, derived from official statistics, indicate a weak correspondence with our estimates of zonal fertility levels. As expected, the percentage of eligible couples protected through sterilization is estimated to be highest in the replacement fertility zone (47 per cent) and lowest in the northern high fertility zone (21 per cent). The differences in couple protection rates between the north and northwestern fertility zones are also in the expected direction. However, while the official estimates show that the prevalence of contraception is about the same in zones 2, 3, 4, and 7, there is, in fact, significant variation in their TFR levels. Further, according to the official figures, there is no significant difference in the levels of contraceptive use between the northern high fertility zone and the northeastern zone; yet, levels of fertility in the latter are significantly lower. While some of these discrepancies could perhaps be explained by the differences in female age at marriage, this criterion is inadequate for the rest.

Finally, it is of interest to know what portion of the interdistrict variation in fertility originates from interzonal differences. The one-way analysis of variance applied to data for 320 districts in 14 major states showed that between-zone variation in fertility accounted for as much as 83 per cent of the total variation in TFR in 1984–90, and 75 per cent of the variation in 1974–80. Thus, with seven fertility zones (excluding the northeastern zone) we were able to account for greater proportion of the interdistrict variation in fertility than the variability accounted for by the 14 states (70 per cent).

Pace of Fertility Decline

As elsewhere, much of the reduction in fertility in India is due to the use of contraception by married couples. As per the NFHS, 41 per cent of currently married women in the age interval 15–49 were using a method of family planning in 1992–3, and over three-fourths of the couples practicing contraception were sterilized (see International Institute for Population Sciences 1995). The diffusion of contraceptive use, like many other technological innovations, could be characterized by an S-shaped acceptance curve over time (see, for example, Mahajan and Peterson 1985). The maximum rate of diffusion normally occurs around the halfway mark when the interaction between the potential acceptors and the current adaptors is the greatest. However, in the case of fertility control, there is also the possibility that the process may slow a bit in the middle because the transition from a three-child norm to a two-child norm may prove difficult, especially in societies with a strong son preference, as it would involve a substantial proportion of couples deciding to cease child-bearing

. after having only one son, or no son. It is, therefore, of interest to know whether our data show any evidence of middle-level stagnation or acceleration, in fertility decline.

In Table 5 we have presented two types of data to examine this issue. First, from our district-level estimates, we have computed the average decline in TFR between 1974–80 and 1984–90 by the level of TFR at the initial period. Also shown for each TFR interval in 1974–80 in the table are the percentage of districts that moved to a lower class during the ten-year period. Both types of data indicate that, if the stagnation occurs at all, it takes place quite early in the transition. Those districts with a TFR in the range of 5–6 births per woman in 1974–80 have shown the least reductions in fertility (average of 12 per cent) during the subsequent ten-year period. After this threshold, fertility decline seems to accelerate until re-placement level is reached. Similarly, we find that out of the 88 districts that had a TFR in the range of 5–6 in 1974–80, less than half (4 per cent) had moved to a lower fertility interval during the subsequent ten-year period. Districts belonging to all other TFR class intervals experienced higher rates of decline. Out of the total of 326 districts, two-thirds had moved to a lower interval during the ten-year period.

The slowing of fertility decline at the neighbourhood of 5 births per woman could be due to gender preference. It may be recalled that, years ago, Sheps (1963) showed that if couples did not cease childbearing until their family included at least two boys and one girl — a typical Indian norm — the average family size would be 4.4 children. If these same couples are also assumed to allow for child mortality, the required number of children to reach this norm would be greater than 5 births per couple. It is equally important to note, however, that a large number of districts had crossed the threshold and experienced rapid fertility declines during the 1980s. Have these districts experienced these declines because of a low preference for sons? Or, did they have access to new technologies which make the practice of female foeticide easier?

In spite of the clearly defined regional variation in son preference in India, the actual difference revealed in desired family size cannot account for more than a difference of one birth per woman, whereas the difference in total fertility is typically more than three times this value. Similarly, because of an interest in sensationalizing the issue, reports appearing in the media on female foeticide cannot be relied upon to estimate the actual prevalence of the practice. In particular, it is hard to believe that the technology to determine the sex of the child *in utero* has become so accessible to the rural poor that it is now an important determinant in the fertility transition. While media attention has focused on a slight decline in the sex ratio of the population reported by the 1991 census, few noticed that wherever fertility has reached low levels, the census data also show that the number of living male children per woman has declined by about as much as the number of female living children. It is, thus, clear that couples, in general, have opted for a small family which does not consist of sons alone.

Rapid declines in fertility in the continued presence of strong son preference would not be viewed as a paradox if the attention were shifted from the utility of sons to the cost of daughters. In particular, the cost of female children may have increased in recent years because of the rising costs of marriage and dowry. Although the dowry inflation has undoubtedly made parents worse off collectively, it should not be forgotten that each parent is willing to provide a dowry because it is viewed as an investment in the daughter's future. In fact, according to one leading comparative sociologist, dowry transaction is a form of 'diverging devolution' that arises out of the concern of parents to maintain or improve the status of their daughters in stratified societies (Goody 1976). In contemporary India, parents may also feel that the chances of securing a better- or equal-status marriage alliance for their daughter are greater if she is also educated and has acquired the skills to be an 'ideal' daughter-in-law. These quality considerations must have raised the cost of daughters, and in deciding to control fertility, it is probably the risk of having another daughter that is more important to parents than what another son may bring in by way of dowry or security in old age. There is, thus, nothing contradictory in the parental decision to regulate fertility and increase allocation to female children but, at the same time, their fertility outcomes have continued to suggest strong preference for sons.

FUTURE PROSPECTS

How do the trends in fertility estimated in this paper affect our expectations regarding the country's future population prospects?

The Expert Committee constituted by the Planning Commission, which had earlier assumed that India would reach the net reproduction rate of unity by 2001, has postponed the date to 2011–16 (India Planning Commission 1992). The projections made by the United Nations (1995) and the World Bank (Bos et al. 1992) assume a replacement-level fertility in India five years later (i.e., 2016–21).

If the TFR falls at an average rate of 0.8 births in 10 years, as estimated in this paper for the last decade, Indian fertility could well reach the replacement-level around 2015. But we should be cognizant of the fact that fertility would not fall far below replacement levels in south India and much of the future reductions would have to come from north India, where declines have been slower. Because the pace of fertility decline could be a function of the initial fertility level, a technically more rigorous way to address this question is to project the distribution of districts by the level of TFR, employing the 'transition' rates observed in the base period (i.e., 1974–80 to 1984–90), and then to estimate the implied average rate of decline for the country as a whole.

In doing so, we find that if the rate of transition to lower fertility class remains at the level observed during the last decade, the percentage of districts that have completed the transition would progressively increase from 4 per cent around 1987 to 15 per cent in 1997, 33 per cent in 2007, 49 per cent in 2017, and 64 per cent in 2027. As more and more districts attain replacement fertility, the average fall in fertility will progressively diminish, and the TFR should slowly fall from 4.1 in 1987 to 3.4 in 1997, 2.8 in 2007, and 2.3 in 2017. Thus, the country as a whole could hope to attain the coveted goal of replacement fertility only after 2020. Interestingly, the levels of TFR projected in this manner are almost identical to those assumed in the UN medium projections until the end of the first decade of the next century. Thereafter, however, our calculations suggest slower convergence to replacement level fertility. On the other hand, the World Bank projections assume rapid reductions in the initial years but considerable deceleration in the later years, as our computations had suggested.

For several reasons, we expect the transition to replacement fertility in India to be faster than what these projections suggest. First, our computations were made on the assumption that trends observed for the period 1977–87 would apply to the future as well.

Yet, this was the period that saw the adverse impact of the emergency excesses. Available evidence now indicates that fertility decline did accelerate in the late 1980s.

Second, television as a medium of social change began to exert influence in India only after 1982, and only in 1992 did access to television broadcasts reach a coverage of 80 per cent (India Ministry of Information and Broadcasting 1993). While prodevelopment soap operas such as *Hum Log* have demonstrated the potential of television in propagating socially desirable behaviour (see Singhal and Rogers 1989), when they were first experimented with, in the mid-1980s, their viewership was quite limited, and largely confined to the urban areas of Hindi-speaking regions. Now, with programmes in regional languages, the television audience is expanding quickly and is relatively gender-neutral. We, therefore, expect television to play a major role in influencing lifestyle preferences, social values, and reproductive goals in the future.

Thirdly, as more areas attain replacement fertility, there will be pressures placed on high fertility regions to concur. Already we see this effect in terms of a greater flow of national and international assistance to population control programmes in northern states. Consequently, we do not expect the transition rates of the last decade to apply to the future. Reaching replacement fertility at around 2015 does not seem impossible for India; however, for this to happen, fertility decline must accelerate in high fertility regions of northern India.

CONCLUSIONS

The analysis of birth rates based on census data confirms that a secular fall in fertility is currently under way in much of India. Moreover, the estimated speed and spread of the decline is larger than what the Sample Registration rates had indicated. The total fertility, which had fallen from 5.6 births per woman in 1971 to 4.9 in 1977, is estimated to have declined further to 4.1 in 1987. The SRS, whose levels appear to be more complete now, showed that the downward trend reached a TFR level of 3.7 by 1991. Thus, total fertility in India has declined by about two births per woman, or by one-third, in the twenty-year-period between 1971 and 1991. The recently concluded National Family Health Survey suggests even larger reductions in fertility in recent years, but its estimates appear to be affected by the 'backward displacement' of births of older women in the survey.

The reverse-survival estimates of fertility, derived from the population in ages 0–6 years from the 1981 and 1991 censuses, suggest large regional variations in the levels and in the pace of fertility decline. In 1984–90, the estimated levels of the total fertility rate varied from a high of 7 live births per woman in a tribal district of Madhya Pradesh to a low of about 1.6 children in a cluster of districts in southern Kerala and northwestern Tamil Nadu. A total of 15 districts in the country (including the two in Goa) had reached below-replacement level fertility by 1987, but 23 districts still had TFR levels of 6 or more. In the ten-year period between 1977 and 1987, two-thirds of the districts had moved to a lower TFR class interval, or experienced roughly a decline of one birth or more in total fertility. The pace of fertility decline was slowest in districts with TFR levels between 5 and 6 in 1977, among whom less than half moved to a class interval of under 5 births per woman.

The deceleration of fertility decline at around a TFR level of five births per woman could be attributed to gender preference. If the desire is to have at least two surviving sons and a daughter, then a woman would have to give birth, on an average, to about five children, after some allowance is made for child mortality. Although we find a slowing down of the transition at this threshold, the majority of districts have crossed this barrier and experienced sustained declines in fertility during the last decade. In areas where TFR has fallen considerably below five, parents are probably not willing to have many daughters because of their rising cost and they often accept sterilization early, even if it means having less sons than they initially desired. It is quite logical for couples not to have another child even if the addition of a son to the household is expected to result in net gain (thus showing son-preference), but it is less than the net loss expected from the addition of a daughter.

In South India, fertility decline is sweeping across the coast to the inland but has yet to penetrate the central plateau region. In north India, a pocket of low fertility is expanding in the frontier region of the north-west, which includes Punjab, Himachal Pradesh, parts of Haryana, and the hilly tracts of Uttar Pradesh. In East India, fertility has fallen considerably in districts in the southern part and in river valleys. We were able to distinguish at least 8 distinct 'sub-cultures' of fertility within the Indian landscape. These fertility zones account for over 80 per cent of the district-level variation in fertility.

Although we have shown that under the current rates of change, declines in fertility in India were larger than commonly believed, it is projected that the country could hope to reach the replacement-level fertility only after 2020. This is because, as more and more areas enter the posttransitional phase, the average rate of decline is bound to fall. It is, however, suggested here that India would reach the coveted goal earlier because (i) the rate of change observed during the period of backlash against the emergency excesses is unlikely to persist; (ii) the impact of the electronic media, especially that of television, on lifestyle preferences is bound to increase in the future; and (iii) as more and more areas attain replacement-level fertility, the pressure on other states to lower their fertility will increase.

ACKNOWLEDGMENT

The research work reported in this paper and the one following was funded under the UNDP financed Research Project on Strategies and Financing Human Development in India. The author is thankful to the late Dr. T.N. Krishnan, former National Coordinator of the project, for financial and moral support.

REFERENCES

Basu, A.M. (1992), *Culture, the Status of Women and Demographic Behaviour* (Oxford: Clarendon Press).

Bhat, P.N. Mari (1996), 'Contours of Fertility Decline in India: A District-level Study Based on the 1991 Census', in K. Srinivasan (ed.), *Population Policy and Reproductive Health* (New Delhi: Hindustan).

—— (1995), 'On the Quality of Birth History Data of the National Family Health Survey, 1992–93', *Demography India*, 24(2):245–57.

Bhat, P.N. Mari, S.H.T. Preston, and T. Dyson (1984), 'Vital Rates in India, 1961–81'. Committee on Population and Demography, Report No. 24 (Washington, D.C.: National Academy Press).

Bos, E., M.T. Vu, A. Levin, and R.A. Bulato (1992), *World Population Projections: 1992–93 Edition* (Baltimore and London: The John Hopkins University Press).

Cleland, J., J.F. Phillips, S. Amin, and G.M. Kamal (1994), *The Determinants of Reproductive Change in Bangladesh: Success in a Challenging Environment* (Washington, D.C.: The World Bank).

Dyson, T. and M. Moore (1983), 'On Kinship Structure, Female Autonomy and Demographic Behaviour in India', *Population and Development Review*, 9(1):3–60.

Goody, J. (1976), *Production and Reproduction: A Comparative Study of the Domestic Domain* (Cambridge: Cambridge University Press).

India, Registrar General (1984), 'Report on the Intensive Enquiry Conducted in a Subsample of SRS Units', Occasional Paper No. 2 of 1983 (New Delhi: Office of the Registrar General).

—— (1989), 'Fertility in India: An Analysis of 1981 Census Data', Occasional Paper No. 13 of 1988 (New Delhi: Office of the Registrar General).

—— (1993) 'Final Population Totals: Brief Analysis of Primary Census Abstract', Paper No.2 of 1992 (Delhi: Controller of Publications).

India, Ministry of Information and Broadcasting (1993), *Mass Media in India, 1992* (New Delhi: Publications Division).

India, Planning Commission (1992), *Eighth Five Year Plan, 1992–97*, vol. 1 (Delhi: Controller of Publications).

International Institute for Population Sciences (IIPS) (1995), *National Family Health Survey (MCH and Family Planning), India 1992–93* (Bombay: IIPS).

Mahajan, V. and R.A. Peterson (1985), 'Models for Innovation Diffusion'. Sage University Paper Series on Quantitative Applications in Social Sciences, Series No. 07–048 (Beverly Hills and London: Sage Publications).

Potter, J.E. (1977), 'Problems in Using Birth History Analysis to Estimate Trends in Fertility', *Population Studies*, 31(2):33–364.

Preston, S.H. and P.N.M. Bhat (1984), 'New Evidence on Fertility and Mortality Trends in India', *Population and Development Review*, 10(3):481–3.

Rele, J.R. (1987), 'Fertility Levels and Trends in India, 1971–81', *Population and Development Review*, 13(3):13–30.

Sheps, M.C. (1963), 'Effect on Family Size and Sex Ratio of Preferences Regarding the Sex of the Child', *Population Studies*, 17(1):66–72.

Singhal, A. and E.M. Rogers (1989), *India's Information Revolution* (New Delhi: Sage Publications).

United Nations (1983), 'Manual X: Indirect Techniques for Demographic Estimation', *Population Studies*, 81 (New York).

—— (1995), *World Population Prospects: The 1994 Revision* (New York).

4

Emerging Regional Differences in Fertility in India: Causes and Correlations

P.N. Mari Bhat

> Starting out from the proposition that 'India is many', the ethnography could as easily be made to show the opposite. Neither proposition is wrong, nor does the truth lie somewhere in the middle. . . . both models, the divergent and the convergent, need one another for their own completion, and both are needed for a complete apprehension of the data.
>
> Thomas Trautmann

INTRODUCTION

In my previous paper in this volume, the nature of geographical variation in fertility in India was explored using the census data. From that discussion, it ought to be clear that any interpretation of Indian fertility decline must take a regional perspective. There is already a growing body of literature attempting to do just this (e.g., Ratcliffe 1978; Caldwell, Reddy, and P. Caldwell 1982; Krishnan 1976; Nag 1983; Kishor 1994; Das Gupta 1994; Srinivasan 1995). Although immensely important, a reinterpretation of the causes of the decline is beyond the scope of this paper. However, the quantitative information that has become available at the district-level could be useful for identifying the important correlates of fertility variation and preparing the ground for a more informed debate on the causes of fertility change. Although there were a number of such attempts in the past using state-level information (e.g., Jain 1985; Jejeebhoy 1981), the analyses were constrained by the small number of cases. However, very recently, attempts have been made to analyse, somewhat belatedly, the 1981 census information of district-level fertility (Malhotra, Vanneman, and Kishor 1995; Murthi, Guio, and Drèze 1995).[1] In contrast, we propose to analyse the 1991 census fertility data which show greater regional differentiation than was present in 1981. Moreover, while the previous attempts had focused on gender issues, we analyse the data from a more general perspective that takes into account other competing explanations for the demographic transition. Technically, it may seem that we have the advantage of having district-level information on fertility at two points in time. However, we have not taken benefit of this due to a lack of information on the relevant explanatory variables at two points in time. Also, estimates of fertility change during this decade are not as well measured as the level of fertility.

We propose to begin the discussion by providing an account of the variables used in the analysis, with the objective of placing our analysis in the context of previous writings on fertility change in India, and developing hypotheses for statistical testing. This would be followed by a presentation of the results of the multivariate analysis. Subsequently, three specific issues would be taken up for special treatment, namely, reasons for north-south differences in fertility, significance of exposure to mass-media to fertility change and, the unusually low levels of fertility found in the state of Tamil Nadu.

CHOICE OF VARIABLES

Table 1 shows the means and standard deviations of the explanatory variables used in the analysis and their expected relationship with fertility in a multivariate context. The selection of the variables was based on a reading of the current theoretical debate on fertility determinants, as well as on the availability of quantified data. Broadly, five categories of variables were considered: (i) structural elements of the economy that have a bearing on fertility behaviour; (ii) social, religious, and gender differentials affecting fertility; (iii) factors governing ideational change and individual modernity; (iv) indicators of child health and family planning programme effort; and (v) factors

---

[1] As a matter of fact, much of the analysis presented in this study was completed before we had the opportunity to read these papers.

of unknown origin represented by state or regional dummies. Conceptually, we view the first two categories of variables as representing the superstructure which, although slow to change, can facilitate or regulate the impact of the third and fourth variable groups.

TABLE 1: DESCRIPTION, MEAN, AND STANDARD DEVIATION OF EXPLANATORY VARIABLES USED IN THE MULTIVARIATE ANALYSIS, AND THEIR EXPECTED RELATIONSHIP WITH TOTAL FERTILITY RATE

Variable name	Description	Mean	Standard deviation	Expected relationship
Economic Structure				
Male workers in agriculture	Proportion of agricultural workers among total male workers (main), 1991 census	0.663	0.158	+
Agricultural labourers	Proportion of agricultural labourers among total agricultural workers (main), 1991 census	0.387	0.170	?
Female work participation	Proportion of main workers among females aged 7 years and over, 1991 census	0.200	0.130	−
Child labourers	Proportion of main and marginal workers among children in the age interval 15–14 years, 1981 census	0.081	0.047	+
Bank offices	Banks offices per 100,000 population, March 1986	6.8	2.5	−
CMIE development index	Index of economic development around 1985, constructed by Centre for Monitoring the Indian Economy, Bombay	94	99	−
Social Structure				
Joint family	Proportion of lineally or collaterally joint households, 1981 census	0.204	0.054	+
Female age at marriage	Mean age at first marriage of ever-married females as reported in the 1981 census	16.63	1.35	−

Table 1 (contd.)

Variable name	Description	Mean	Standard deviation	Expected relationship
Population sex ratio	Males per 1,000 females, 1991 census	1,080	68	+
Muslims	Proportion of Muslims in the population, 1981 census	0.098	0.091	+
Scheduled tribes	Proportion of scheduled tribes in the population, 1991 census	0.090	0.152	?
Ideational Factors				
Female literacy	Female literacy rate in ages 7 and over, 1991 Census	0.359	0.176	−
Media exposure[#]	Proportion of couples regularly exposed to mass media (either newspaper, radio, television, or cinema), ORG survey, 1988	0.493	0.142	−
Cinema exposure[#]	Proportion of married women who see a movie at least once in three months, ORG survey, 1988	0.127	0.121	−
Transport & communication	Transport and communication workers per 1,000 population, 1991 census	8.4	5.7	−
Population density	Population density per sq. kilometre, 1991 census	622	2123	−
Health & Family Planning				
Under-five mortality	Under-five mortality rate derived from 1981 census	0.205	0.068	+
Target achievement[#]	Proportion of sterilization targets achieved, 1984–91	0.809	0.126	−
Unmet need[#]	Unmet need for contraception for limiting and spacing, NFHS, 1992–3	0.196	0.063	+
Residual Factors				
Kerala	Dummy variable for districts of Kerala	0.037	0.189	−
Tamil Nadu	Dummy variable for districts of Tamil Nadu	0.049	0.216	−

Variable name	Description	Mean	Standard deviation	Expected relationship
Coastal districts	Dummy variable for coastal districts	0.156	0.364	–
BIMARU states	Dummy variable for districts of Bihar, Madhya Pradesh, Rajasthan, and Uttar Pradesh	0.485	0.501	+

Only state-level data are available. In the regression analysis the districts were assigned a value equal to their respective state-average.

Source: Census of India, 1981 and 1991; Yearbooks of Dept. of Family Welfare; Centre for Monitoring Indian Economy (1987); Operations Research Group (1990), and International Institute for Population Sciences (1995).

Economic Structure

The structural aspects of the economy are represented in the analysis by proportion of male workers in agriculture, proportion of agricultural labourers among total farm workers, female work-participation rate, child work-participation rate, number of banks per 100,000 population, and an index of overall economic development. The proportion of male workers in agriculture, including those in fishing and animal husbandry, is expected to capture the effect of industrialization and urbanization which the original proponents of demographic transition theory described as a prerequisite for fertility decline. The share of agricultural labourers among farm workers could be taken as a rough proxy for poverty. The traditional view has been that poverty leads to high fertility because of the need for family labour in poor households. But during a period of rising material aspirations, and the spread of an egalitarian outlook, the poor may actually attempt to limit their family size in order to provide a better life for themselves and their children. Interestingly, it is possible to argue that when the cost of fertility regulation is sufficiently small, deteriorating economic conditions may also induce the poor to limit their family size because of their inability to provide for their offspring. Such possibilities have led some to hypothesize that much of the fertility decline in south Asia is poverty-led (Mencher 1980; Basu 1986). There is also a common view that high incentives offered for sterilization might have acted as a further inducement for the acceptance of family planning among the more disadvantaged. Thus, the association

between fertility and wage employment in agriculture remains unclear, although, under the present context, reasons for expecting an
inverse relationship are strong.

In accordance with the economic perspective, female work participation is expected to raise the opportunity cost of childbearing
and thus reduce the demand for children. We are aware of the possibility of reverse or joint causation here, which, however, can be
dismissed as relatively unimportant. The regional variation in the
sexual division of labour is a longstanding one, likely to have been
shaped by agricultural systems and population density (Boserup
1970), whereas the fertility variation for which we seek explanation
is of recent origin. Even in the modern, urban environment, wage
employment of women is held in check by various cultural constraints. Negligible change in female work participation rates in areas
experiencing rapid fertility declines appears to confirm this view.

In contrast, work participation of children is expected to raise
the demand for births as it implies low investment in children and
greater returns from them, at least in the short run. It is to be noted
that the census data employed here probably underestimate the
economic contribution of both women and children. But, as there
is no strong reason to suspect that the degree of this underestimation varies from region to region, the use of census data is unlikely
to introduce large biases in our statistical results.

Since 1969 there has been a rapid expansion of banking institutions in rural areas. We expect this to have a negative influence on fertility for two reasons. First, banks symbolize the
monetization of costs and a movement from a subsistence to a
market economy. Caldwell, in particular, stresses monetization
as an instrument of social change in south India (Caldwell, Reddy,
and P. Caldwell 1982). According to him, when commodities
were exchanged through barter or services were rewarded through
the *jajmani* system (see Wiser 1958), people were not very conscious of relative costs, especially for large families. For Caldwell,
the villagers' repeated assertion that inflation is the reason they
were having smaller families indicated that monetization of costs
as well as a change in the concept of child care was occuring.[2]

---

[2] Interestingly, inflation was also the most commonly cited reason in Tamil
Nadu for adopting the small family norm, according to several focus-group
studies reported at a recent workshop held at Madras on the theme of Demographic Transition in Tamil Nadu.

Second, there is an impressive body of literature suggesting that in much of south Asia, children are a source of insurance against risk (e.g., Cain 1981). Modern banking and other financial institutions provide a superior platform for meeting credit and investment needs and thus can reduce the need for investing in children for deriving such support.

In some model specifications, we have used a summary index of economic development constructed by the Centre for Monitoring the Indian Economy (1987). According to its developers, the index was intended as a rough proxy for per capita income and was computed as a weighted average of nine indicators on agriculture, mining and manufacturing, and service sector performance. The index was derived so that the level of all-India was 100 in 1985.

Social Structure

An attempt to measure the impact of patriarchy and social structure on fertility has been undertaken by analysing the proportion of joint families, female age at first marriage, sex ratio of the population, and the proportion of Muslims and scheduled tribes in the population. The extended family system is often assumed to promote high fertility. As in joint families costs and care of children are shared, young couples, especially women, enjoy less autonomy, and resistance to new ideas and innovations is likely to be strongest. The census information on coresidence used here most probably understates the actual magnitude of extended kinship ties and obligations (see Caldwell 1976), but it suffices for our purposes as long as the two can be assumed to be strongly interrelated.[3]

The two measures of female autonomy used here are the female age at marriage and the sex ratio of the population. Female mean

[3] There are two types of data on residential joint families in the census volumes of 1981. The household tables give the distribution of households by number of couples (Table H-3) and social and cultural tables give the distribution of family types based on the information on relation to the head of the household and marital status of members (Table C-10). At the all-India level, the percentage of households with two or more couples was about the same as the proportion of households which were either lineally or collaterally joint (20 per cent). As the data on number of couples in the household were reported as missing for a large number of cases in some states, we have made use of the data given in the social and cultural tables, except for Tamil Nadu. Original census schedules were reportedly lost when tabulation work was taken up on family types in this state, hence for Tamil Nadu we have used the information given in the household tables.

age at first marriage is a proximate determinant of fertility and thus could directly influence the supply of children. However, we expect it to have a greater influence than just its direct effect on childbearing. Female age at marriage is regarded to be a powerful indicator of the status of women, with early marrying populations characterized by low female autonomy (Mason 1984). Recently, Coale (1992) has drawn attention to the fact that in historical European populations, *marital* fertility began to decline earlier where female age at marriage was later. He also notes a similar trend in contemporary Indian states. Another index that does well in capturing the regional variation in female autonomy in India is the sex ratio of population (see Dyson and Moore 1983). The excess of males over females in the population, which is unique to the south Asian region, is widely regarded as an outcome of long-standing gender discrimination. Besides being affected by sex differentials in mortality, the sex ratio of the population is also influenced by differences in migration rates by sex. In regions where endogamous marriages are more common, females would have lower rates of out-migration (Malhotra, Vanneman, and Kishor 1995), and the population sex ratio would be more favourable to females. In this sense too, it would be appropriate to use the sex ratio of population as a measure of female autonomy.[4]

Attitude towards contraception and family size may also be shaped by religious and moral upbringing; therefore, we have considered the percentage of Muslims and scheduled tribes in the population as possible determinants of fertility. The higher fertility of Muslims in India is a politically-charged issue, especially after the 1991 census revealed that the population growth rate during 1981–91 was significantly higher among Muslims (2.8 per cent per annum) than Hindus (2.1 per cent). Although few dispute the existence of the religious differential, its magnitude

[4] The district-level data on female mean age at marriage is derived from a question asked to all married women in the 1981 census (India, Registrar General 1988). As just one variable doesn't appear to capture the regional variation in female autonomy well, we decided to use at least two proxies for it. For example, female age at marriage is relatively late in Punjab but population sex ratios indicate the presence of strong gender discrimination. In predominantly urban districts, population is extremely masculine but female age at marriage is high. Therefore, the two indicators together appear to complement each other well in capturing the elusive concept of female autonomy than one of the two independently.

and causes are vigourously contested. This is sometimes attributed to the relative poverty and illiteracy of Muslims (in spite of their greater concentration in urban areas and larger villages), and sometimes to the religious dogma and the minority status of Muslims. Based on his microresearch in south India, Caldwell reports that there were no significant fertility differentials in his study area by socio-economic status, except by religion (Caldwell, Reddy, and P. Caldwell 1982). He goes on to comment that the difference could be explained largely by sterilization acceptance which is proscribed in the Koranic Law, and almost wholly by the addition of a difference in the practice of postnatal sexual abstinence.

The scheduled tribes, found mainly in the highlands of central and northeastern India, are generally least impacted by modernization. Consequently, we would expect them to exhibit higher fertility. Yet, it is also believed that when these tribes come into contact with modern civilization, they are more likely to accept family planning methods, either because of greater autonomy of women among tribals, or because of incentives. Therefore, the impact of the size of the scheduled tribe population on fertility is somewhat ambiguous.

Ideational Factors

In explaining fertility change, the impact of education in modern schools and exposure to mass media in emphasizing maternalism and egalitarianism cannot be overlooked. As Caldwell has reported from his fieldwork in Nigeria, 'mass infusion of European manners, however, has been relatively recent and it has had two interrelated vehicles: mass education and the mass media' (Caldwell 1982:150). For fertility change, two aspects of this cultural diffusion seem particularly relevant — a widening spectrum of materialistic wants and a changing conception of childcare, consistent with the inculcation of Western norms and values. The almost simultaneous increase in the desire for consumer durables and preference for higher 'quality' children could have had strong effects on fertility decline. In order to capture the effect of this ideational change, we have included female literacy and exposure to mass media as possible determinants of fertility levels in the analysis.

Our interpretation of female literacy as primarily an ideational variable may need some further clarification. While arguing that mass education is the determinant of the timing of fertility decline, Caldwell (1982) had listed five possible mechanisms by which education could influence fertility. Among them, two pathways involving direct and indirect costs of educating children could be regarded as purely demand-side variables (Raftery, Lewis, and Aghajanian 1995). However, further reflection indicates that they are actually products of a parental decision to send children to school and thus more properly attributed to factors that prompt this decision. In fact, it is possible to argue that a decline in educational cost per child, especially through increased access to schools, made it possible for parents to educate their children in large numbers. Even if educational costs were rising, the most important question is why parents (or the patriarch, in P. Caldwell's exposition) decided to bear these costs. In part, it might have been due to population pressure on arable land and the simultaneous availability of urban, public-sector employment, as Caldwell himself has noted in the case of south India (Caldwell, Reddy, and Caldwell 1985), and in part from an ideational change brought about by the diffusion of Western values. It is, however, doubtful that the decision of first-generation parents to send children to school had a simultaneous impact on their fertility as Caldwell has claimed. As Caldwell notes from his research in south India (Caldwell 1983), illiterate parents selectively send the later born children to school, as the elder ones are required for work on the farm, or at home. Since such adjustments are possible only when one has a large family (thanks to the reduction in child mortality), we see the effect of education on fertility principally in the educated second generation who are likely to send *all* of their children to school.

Female literacy is also thought of as a variable that represents the status of women. This view, however, is now being challenged because education alone does not appear to be sufficient to ensure female autonomy in developing countries (Kaufmann and Cleland 1994). Even if education is found to enhance female autonomy, it does not necessarily weaken our hypothesis that female literacy should be viewed as a vehicle of an ideational change. If, however, as some have argued (e.g., Jeffery 1976), the extent to which females are educated in a society is conditioned by the degree of autonomy granted to women by its culture, then the former should be viewed as a variable representative of the larger social structure. Since variables such as female age at marriage, sex ratio of the population, and female employment, are included in our analysis, it is unlikely that female literacy will explain the cultural dimension of the social structure.

Literacy and education are also said to reduce the cost of providing information on contraception. Due to vigourous programmatic efforts during the last quarter century, knowledge of at least one method of contraception is now fairly well-diffused in India. To the extent the awareness of a range of contraceptive methods is important to the regulation of fertility, the cost of direct information may be influenced by the prevalence of female literacy. But the overriding effect of female literacy must be examined in terms of preferences regarding quality and quantity of children desired, and the readiness to accept a contraceptive device whenever the situation demands.

Exposure to mass media is another variable that could have potentially important effects on one's lifestyle preferences as well as on parental aspirations for their children. The recent survey of the Operations Research Group (1990) has revealed significant regional variation in the exposure to mass media. The results released from the National Family Health Survey (NFHS) of 1992–3 appear to confirm this. As the variable could be potentially important in explaining fertility variation, we decided to use the data on mass media exposure from the ORG survey even though data are available at the state-level only.[5] In the ORG survey, the regular exposure to mass media was defined as reading a newspaper, listening to the radio, or watching television at least once a week, and going to the cinema at least once every three months. From the published data of the survey, we have selected two indicators, the percentage of couples who are classified as exposed to at least one of the four media, and the percentage of married women in ages 15–44 who are regularly exposed to cinema. The emphasis on cinema in the analysis is based on the consideration that it is a medium that even poor and illiterate women are exposed to, and is often cited by village elders in south India as the source of 'corruption' of young minds (e.g., see Caldwell, Reddy, and P. Caldwell, 1982:697). As the data are available only at the state-level, all the districts belonging to a state are assigned the same value (the state-average) on these two indicators.

[5] We have preferred the ORG data on exposure to mass media over that of NFHS because the former included the exposure through the print media.

Ideational changes are facilitated by improvements in transport and communication. However, it is difficult to get data on these aspects at the district-level; the best we could do is to use the data on the number of transport and communication workers per 1,000 population from the 1991 census as a proxy for the development of transport and communication networks at the district-level.[6] A variable that we think also facilitates ideational change is the density of population. It could, of course, influence fertility in multiple ways. An increase in density would raise the pressure on arable land and thus create a need for population control; reduce the cost of providing transport and communication services owing to the economy of scale; may partly stand for the level of urbanization and the effect of urban residence on tastes and preferences; and, more generally, could reduce the cost of fertility regulation by accelerating the diffusion of contraceptive use by word of mouth or through demonstration. In part, these effects are probably captured by other variables used in the analysis (e.g., proportion of labourers among farmworkers, workers in transport and communication sectors), but not all may be so (especially, ideational ones).

Health and Family Planning Effort

As postulated in the demographic transition theory, a decline in child mortality is expected to reduce the demand for live births and thus negatively influence fertility level. However, the problem of reverse or joint causation arises because fertility levels may also influence child mortality levels. We are of the view that, while such a possibility does exist, it is more of a problem in the micro than the macrolevel data.[7] Even at the microlevel, when the associated factors are controlled, the observed impact of fertility on child mortality is generally a small one (Bongaarts 1987). In our data, a more serious problem of simultaneity may arise from the fact that child mortality estimates were used in computing the fertility rates; hence, the errors in the two variables may be correlated. As a partial remedy to these

[6] In addition to transport and communication workers, the census category on which the data are based includes workers in storage facilities. As their numbers are small, the contamination is not expected to be consequential.

[7] At microlevel, the effect of fertility on child mortality mainly operates through birth interval differences. At the macrolevel, especially during a secular fall in fertility, variations in fertility are caused largely from the decision to limiting childbearing than from spacing children.

problems, we have lagged the child mortality variable by about 10 years by employing the estimates of the under-five mortality rate derived from the 1981 census data on children ever-born and children surviving. A technically better strategy would have been to use the instrumental variable approach, but it was difficult to find data for a variable(s) that was strongly correlated with child mortality but theoretically unrelated to fertility.[8]

It is now generally accepted that family planning programme efforts can reduce the cost of fertility regulation and thus quicken the decline in fertility where the demand for children has decreased. Unfortunately, data are not available on family planning inputs or on programme effort scores to measure the cost of fertility regulation at the district-level. Nonetheless, owing to the importance of the variable, we have reported results that used two indicators which were available only at the state-level. These are, the number of sterilization targets achieved during 1984–91, and the unmet need for contraception as measured by the NFHS in 1992–3. In an attempt to translate the national goals through layers of bureaucracy and to evaluate worker performance, a system of assigning method-specific targets was routinely followed since the inception of the family planning programme, and pursued more vigorously in the 1980s. A practice of rewarding the states on the basis of their target achievement was also instituted during this period. This generated immense competition among the states and pressure on the workers, resulting in some cases of falsified records. It appears, however, that acceptor data on reversible methods are more questionable than on sterilization. Therefore, target achievement on sterilization could still serve as a rough indicator of the programme effort in different states.[9] The unmet need for contraception is a

[8] Source of drinking water and toilet facility were the possible instruments on which we had data, but they were not found to be strongly correlated with child mortality.

[9] Family planning targets as an indicator of family planning effort has two components; one is how ambitious the target is, and the other is the percentage of the target actually achieved. In order to capture both the dimensions, we have divided the annual sterilization acceptors (A_i) by the target for sterilization for the previous year (T_{i-1}). That this index contains both the dimensions is evident by the relation:

$$\frac{A_i}{T_{i-1}} = \frac{T_i}{T_{i-1}} \times \frac{A_i}{T_i}$$

direct measure of programme efficiency, since the primary task of any family planning programme is to ensure that all those women who do not wish to have children are not exposed to the risk of pregnancy. Information on this measure was taken from the NFHS of 1992–3, and it included the unmet need for limiting as well as for spacing (International Institute for Population Sciences 1995).

There are probably large intrastate variations in these two indicators of programme effectiveness but, owing to the lack of data, we are forced to assume that there are none. Such an assumption is likely to underestimate the contribution of the programme effort. Nonetheless, because nearly three-quarters of the variation in our estimates of district-level fertility originate from interstate differences, a truly powerful variable is unlikely to be rendered insignificant, even when state-averages are employed in its case.

Residual Factors

In my previous paper in this volume, I have shown that fertility is near replacement levels in Kerala and Tamil Nadu, and is generally low in coastal districts of south India. On the other hand, fertility remains high in the four, large, north Indian states of Bihar, Madhya Pradesh, Uttar Pradesh, and Rajasthan. In order to explore whether there are any additional factors at work in these regions, we have included dummy variables representing each of these regions in some model specifications. It is to be noted that the failure to detect the independent significance of these variables would be an indicator of our success in explaining the geographical variation in fertility in India.

REGRESSION RESULTS

The data for 326 districts in 15 major states of India were subjected to ordinary least-squares regressions with the estimated TFRs for 1984–90 as the dependent variable.[10] Before performing

---

The average of this measure for the years 1984 to 1991 has been used as an indicator for family planning effort.

[10] We have not corrected the regressions for the possible presence of spatially correlated errors. Even in the presence of such errors, the OLS estimates of the coefficients are known to be unbiased though the results of significance tests could be questioned. Spatially correlated errors often arise from the omission of relevant explanatory variables. As we have assembled a large array of covariates and are

the regression analysis, the dependent variable and the independent variables other than those that were measured in proportions (female literacy, agricultural labourers, Muslims, scheduled tribes, etc.) were transformed to the logarithm scales, so that the regression coefficients would give estimates of the percentage change in TFR associated with a one-per cent change in the independent variable (i.e., elasticity). The under-five mortality rate was transformed to the logit scale so as to linearize its relationship with fertility at low levels.

The results obtained under five different model specifications are reported in Table 2. In the first model, all the relevant variables have been included except the regional dummies and the overall index of economic development. The model is found to explain as much as 90 per cent of the district-level variation in fertility. While most of the variables are significant and show their effects in the expected direction, a few variables do not. Among the variables standing for economic structure, child labour, and banks show a significant and expected relationship with fertility, whereas the effects of the proportion of the male labour force in agriculture and the work participation of females are found to be insignificant. The wage employment in agriculture shows a positive and significant relationship with fertility, although we expected a negative relationship.

The variables representing social structure, however, perform much better, as all of them show significant effects on fertility in the expected directions. Among these, the estimated positive effects of the joint family and Muslims on fertility are found to be particularly strong. The two variables for womens's status, age at marriage, and population sex ratio, are independently significant and, perhaps, appear to be less important than others only because they share the same overall impact. The proportion of scheduled tribes, the direction of whose impact we were not sure of, shows a significant positive effect on fertility, much the same way as agricultural labourers.

All variables representing the ideational change, except workers in the transport and communication sectors, are found to be significant. In particular, exposure to mass media and cinema show

---

able to explain most of the geographical variations in fertility (R^2 being over 0.9), any bias arising on this account is unlikely to be large enough to discredit our results.

TABLE 2: RESULTS OF OLS REGRESSION WITH TOTAL FERTILITY RATE FOR 1984–90 AS DEPENDENT VARIABLE

Explanatory variables	Model 1		Model 2		Model 3		Model 4		Model 5	
	Parameter	t-ratio	Parameter	t-ratio	Parameter	t-ratio	Parameter	t-ratio	Parameter	t-ratio
Economic Structure										
Male workers in agriculture	−0.0953	1.08	–	–	–	–	–	–	–	–
Agricultural labourers	0.1055	2.04	0.0843	1.74	0.0737	1.55	−0.0512	0.99	−0.0021	0.04
Female work participation	−0.1229	1.21	–	–	–	–	−0.3547	3.46	−0.3498	3.50
Child labourers	0.5947	2.07	0.5718	2.50	0.5359	2.33	0.8373	2.65	0.7111	2.38
Bank offices*	−0.0606	2.54	−0.0323	1.28	−0.0545	2.11	−0.0314	1.11	−0.0692	2.53
CMIE development index*	–	–	−0.0361	1.98	−0.0341	1.82	−0.0057	0.27	−0.0242	1.17
Social Structure										
Joint family	1.4063	8.25	1.3627	8.70	1.4244	8.10	1.9255	11.67	1.3800	7.84
Female age at marriage*	−0.3987	3.08	−0.2965	2.68	−0.1150	0.93	−0.4197	2.93	−0.2955	2.11
Population sex ratio (M/F)*	0.3003	1.95	0.5381	3.56	0.5248	3.46	0.5694	3.21	0.4911	2.88
Muslims	0.6014	7.78	0.6045	8.32	0.5398	7.29	0.4993	6.24	0.4413	5.64
Scheduled tribes	0.1419	2.63	0.1120	2.28	0.0939	1.94	0.2193	3.84	0.1811	3.31
Ideational Factors										
Female literacy	−0.4449	4.84	−0.3679	4.66	−0.3292	4.19	−0.2768	3.06	−0.2658	2.96
Media exposure#	−0.5842	3.47	−0.6442	5.09	−0.8166	4.09	–	–	–	–
Cinema exposure#	−0.3488	2.62	−0.3521	2.86	−0.0329	0.18	–	–	–	–

Explanatory variables	Model 1		Model 2		Model 3		Model 4		Model 5	
	Parameter	t-ratio	Parameter	t-ratio	Parameter	t-ratio	Parameter	t-ratio	Parameter	t-ratio
Transport & communication*	-0.0093	0.49	–	–	–	–	–	–	–	–
Population density*	-0.0312	2.84	-0.0178	1.78	-0.0191	1.92	-0.0502	4.51	-0.0353	3.29
Health & Family Planning										
Under-five mortality†	0.1006	4.63	0.0975	4.95	0.1093	5.30	0.1127	4.83	0.1000	4.20
Target achievement#	0.0529	0.63	–	–	–	–	-0.1675	2.08	0.0586	0.66
Unmet need#	0.1487	0.71	–	–	–	–	1.1012	6.64	0.5496	2.64
Residual Factors										
Kerala	–	–	–	–	0.0285	0.44	–	–	-0.1641	3.13
Tamil Nadu	–	–	–	–	-0.1465	3.97	–	–	-0.2397	6.63
Coastal districts	–	–	–	–	0.0028	0.14	–	–	-0.0209	0.96
BIMARU states	–	–	–	–	0.0081	0.32	–	–	0.0914	3.21
Constant	0.9429	1.17	-0.9928	1.06	-1.3185	1.07	-1.2788	1.30	-1.0245	1.25
Adjusted R²	0.895		0.897		0.901		0.871		0.887	
N	326		326		326		326		326	

– Not included in the model.
* Information was available only at the state-level.
\# Used in logarithmic form.
† Used in logit form.

strong negative impact on fertility, in spite of the fact that we only had state-level information. Female literacy shows the expected negative impact on fertility, as does population density. Among the health and family planning variables, child mortality is found to have a strong positive effect on fertility, but neither the unmet need for contraception nor the family planning target achievement show any additional explanatory power, perhaps because they are measured only at the state-level.

The insignificance of several economic variables in Model 1 suggests that their independent effects cannot be assessed accurately with the available data owing to multicollinearity. Similarly, the failure of the transport and communication variable to show the expected influence might be due to the fact that it is intrinsically connected to economic development. Therefore, in Model 2 we have dropped these insignificant variables and, instead, have introduced a composite index for economic development constructed by the CMIE, Bombay.

Another area of concern is the insignificance of the family planning variables. We experimented with several indicators such as the per capita expenditure on family planning, the size of the field workers stationed in rural areas, etc., but none were found to be significant (results not presented). While the measurement of these indicators is certainly problematic, this cannot be the sole reason for their lack of significance because, as was shown by the media variables in Model 1, the effect of a truly powerful variable can be revealed even when measured at the state-level. We shall return to a discussion of the probable cause(s) later in the paper. For now, we have dropped all the family planning variables from consideration in Model 2.

Almost all the variables included in Model 2 are statistically significant and show their effects in the expected direction. The composite index of economic development has a statistically significant negative impact on fertility. It's inclusion, however, renders the importance of banks to insignificance and reduces the influence of wage employment in agriculture and population density, although they remain significant at around the 10 per cent level. The effect of child labour remains as statistically significant as before, and so do all variables representing social structure, ideational change, and child survival. This parsimonious model explains about as much variation in fertility as Model 1.

In Model 3, we retained all the variables of Model 2 but added dummy variables for Kerala, Tamil Nadu, the coastal districts, and the four north Indian states. Among these, only the dummy variable for Tamil Nadu shows strong statistical significance. This is an indication that variables included in Model 2 are able to explain most of the geographical variation in fertility, barring the exceptionally low fertility in Tamil Nadu. It is to be noted that the introduction of the dummy variable for Tamil Nadu in Model 3 has almost completely drained the effects of the cinema exposure and female age at marriage variables, although at the same time the significance of the overall media exposure variable and of banking institutions has increased. This suggests that Tamil Nadu's low fertility was partly responsible for making the effects of cinema exposure and female age at marriage variables significant in Models 1 and 2.

In Models 4 and 5, we have explored the effect of dropping the powerful media variables on which we have only state-level data. Some dramatic changes result. In Model 4, which does not include the regional dummies, we find that dropping the media variables makes the two family planning variables, target achievement and unmet need for contraception, statistically significant as well as the female work participation rate variable. All three show the expected relationship with fertility. The exclusion of the media variable also has the effect of rendering the impacts of the CMIE development index, banks and wage employment in agriculture insignificant, and raising the importance of all variables representing social structure except the variable for Muslims. Overall, the model explains a significantly lower percentage of the variation in TFR than Model 2 (0.87).

When the regional dummies are included (Model 5), some of the unexplained variation in fertility is recaptured owing to the significance of all of the dummies except the one representing the coastal districts. Although the positive effect of unmet need for contraception remains statistically significant, the family planning variables lose some of their significance. The effect of female work participation rate continues to be important and the banking sector regains its explanatory power.

These results indicate that when both mass media and family planning variables are measured at the state-level, there is a considerable amount of collinearity between the two, and as a result, we are unable to precisely estimate their independent effects on fertility.

When both are included in the model, the mass media variables, being more powerful, capture the entire effect. Only when we exclude them do the family planning variables become statistically significant; however, they are still unable to account for all variations in fertility, as suggested by the significance of the regional dummies in Model 5.

DECOMPOSITION OF NORTH-SOUTH DIFFERENCE

The above regression results can be used to obtain a quantitative estimate of the contribution of each of the factors to the difference in fertility levels between north and south India. Such a decomposition of the north-south difference in fertility is essential for gaining a better understanding of the salient factors responsible for the regional variation in fertility in India. This is accomplished in Table 3 by employing group means of variables for the four 'BIMARU' states of north India and for the four south Indian states of relatively low fertility. Two alternate sets of estimates are given, each one corresponding to the estimated coefficients of Model 3 and Model 5. In 1984–90, the average TFR was 5.24 for the north Indian states and 2.84 for the south Indian states. Although the difference between the north and the south is quite sizeable in some indicators of economic structure, their net contribution to the difference in fertility between the two regions is estimated to be quite small. Their net impact is near zero in Model 3, which employed the mass media variables, and about 10 per cent in Model 5, which utilized the family planning variables. The difference in the two estimates is almost entirely due to the impact of the female work participation rate which was significant only in Model 5.

As in both the models, about one-third of the north-south variation in fertility could be attributed to the differences in social structure. Interestingly, joint family alone accounts for 20 per cent of the overall difference in fertility, leaving only about 10 per cent to be explained by the two status of women variables, female age at marriage and the sex ratio of the population. The percentage of Muslims and scheduled tribes do not contribute much to this difference, even though the former showed strong statistical significance in all the model specifications. The importance of the joint family system may seem surprising because, on the surface, its incidence doesn't vary a great deal between the north and the south

TABLE 3: REGRESSION DECOMPOSITION OF THE
DIFFERENCE IN TOTAL FERTILITY RATE BETWEEN
FOUR STATES OF NORTHERN AND SOUTHERN INDIA

Explanatory variables	Variable means #		Difference in log of TFR attributed to the variable (in per cent)	
	BIMARU states	Southern states	Model 3	Model 5
Economic Structure			−0.4	9.7
Agricultural labourers	0.310	0.568	−3.1	0.1
Female work participation	0.148	0.289	−	8.0
Child labourers	0.068	0.098	−2.6	−3.5
Bank offices*	5.9	7.6	2.3	2.9
CMIE development index*	68	116	3.0	2.1
Social Structure			30.9	32.6
Joint family	0.231	0.146	19.7	19.1
Female age at marriage*	15.9	17.3	1.5	4.0
Population sex ratio (M/F)*	1,112	1,022	7.2	6.7
Muslims	0.123	0.102	1.8	1.5
Scheduled tribes	0.083	0.036	0.7	1.4
Ideational Factors			58.8	11.3
Female literacy	0.245	0.485	12.8	10.4
Media exposure	0.381	0.711	43.9	−
Cinema exposure	0.053	0.342	1.5	−
Population density*	264	312	0.5	1.0
Health & Family Planning			10.7	19.2
Under-five mortality†	0.247	0.153	10.7	9.8
Target achievement	0.752	0.886	−	−1.3
Unmet need	0.256	0.136	−	10.7
Residual Factors			0.0	27.1
TFR, 1984–90	5.24	2.84	100.0	100.0
N	158	70		

Population-weighted averages.   − Not included in the model.
*   Used in logarithmic form.   † Used in logit form.

Note: BIMARU states comprise of districts belonging to Bihar, Madhya Pradesh, Rajasthan, and Uttar Pradesh.
Southern states are inclusive of districts belonging to Kerala, Tamil Nadu, Andhra Pradesh, and Karnataka.

(23 and 15 per cent, respectively). But the estimated effect of the variable is quite large, perhaps due to two reasons. First, what is relevant to fertility is not how many households are joint, but how many couples live in joint families. In this latter measure, the census data do suggest large differences between the north and the south (around 50 per cent and 30 per cent, respectively). Secondly, as stated earlier, beneath the difference in coresidence, there is probably a large difference in the extended family ties and obligations.

The two model estimates differ sharply in the amount of fertility variation attributed to what we have called the 'ideational factors'. According to Model 3, a surprising 59 per cent of the fertility difference is due to these factors, out of which as much as 46 per cent originates from the mass media exposure variables. Model 5, which does not include these variables, naturally assigns a minute 11 per cent to the ideational factors, almost all of which comes from the difference in the levels of female literacy. It should, however, be noted that Model 5 leaves a large percentage of fertility difference unexplained (27 per cent), which could be because the model does not include the mass media variables. If we assume this to be the case, then the ideational factors should be credited with about 40 per cent of the fertility difference, even under Model 5.

Health and family planning variables account for about 10 and 20 per cent of the variation in fertility as per Models 3 and 5, respectively. Both the models attribute about 10 per cent of the difference to child mortality, but Model 5, which includes the family planning variables, assigns an additional 10 per cent to the latter source.

In sum, the results of the decomposition suggest that no more than 10 per cent of the difference in fertility levels between north and south India could be attributed to the institutional factors of the economy. The differences in social structure explain at least 30 per cent of the difference, and ideational factors account for at least an additional 40 per cent. The difference in the level of child survival accounts for about 10 per cent of the fertility variation and family planning effort could explain no more than an additional 10 per cent of this difference.

It seems that previous literature on the subject appears to have overstated the case of patriarchy and female autonomy in causing the regional variation in fertility in India. The results of the above decomposition suggest that the two status of women variables included in the analysis account for only about 10 per cent of the north-south fertility difference. If we add the independent effect of the joint family, the share of patriarchy in causing the fertility variation rises to 30 per cent. If we also add the effect of female work participation, which, in our scheme of classification, is included under the economic structure, the impact of patriarchy rises to about 40 per cent (under Model 5). If we also include the effect of female literacy, which is treated as an ideational factor, the total impact of patriarchy and female autonomy rises to about 50 per cent. Thus, even under a very generous reallocation of variables, patriarchy and female autonomy can explain no more than half of the north-south difference in fertility. To their credit, Malhotra, Vanneman, and Kishor (1995) did note that regional peculiarities beyond the factors accounted by them could be responsible for the north-south difference in fertility. We identify these factors as mass media exposure and family planning programme effectiveness, in that order.

As pointed out by Koenig and Foo (1992), there are two different views on the role of patriarchy in explaining the persistence of high fertility in south Asia. Dyson and Moore, as well as Cain, have emphasized differentiation on the basis of sex in patriarchal systems, while Caldwell has stressed differentiation along the lines of age. Regarding this, our results appear to lean towards Caldwell's position, since among the measures used for patriarchy, incidence of joint family shows the strongest impact on fertility. In other words, what is suggested is that in patriarchal systems, not only is the autonomy of women at stake, but the freedom of younger generations as well. In an era of sweeping ideational change, younger couples are likely to hold more progressive views on reproductive matters which may not get translated into action in a joint family.

It must be remembered that the above assessment of the relative contribution of each of the factors was made in the context of cross-sectional variation in fertility. The results could be quite different if we analysed the change in fertility over time. The relative contribution of patriarchy and social structure to the decline in fertility could be minimal since they have not undergone rapid changes. On the other hand, contribution of ideational factors, child mortality, and family planning, to the fertility decline could even be higher than their estimated contribution to the regional variation in fertility. The contribution of economic factors is also likely to be higher, especially that of banking institutions. The branches of commercial banks in the country have gone up phenomenally from less than 3,000 in 1951 to over 60,000 in 1991. As rightly stressed by Caldwell, the monetization of the economy and the opening up of new avenues for meeting credit and investment needs could have contributed significantly to the decline of fertility. Unfortunately, the paucity of time series data on many of the variables make it difficult to analyse factors that have a bearing on fertility change.

ROLE OF MASS MEDIA

The most significant and probably the most controversial finding from the above regression analysis is the suggested importance of mass media exposure in shaping the regional variation of fertility in India. This calls for a detailed consideration of our results, especially in the context of the 'passing away' of the dominant paradigm in the field of development communication (Rogers 1976). The early enthusiasm about the role of mass media as the 'magic multiplier' of development has given way to a more cautious stance wherein mass communication is relegated to playing an indirect and contributory role. In this context, our findings assume additional significance.

It is easy to dismiss our regression results by pointing out that correlation does not prove causation. But the strength of the relationship we observe between mass media exposure and regional variation in fertility in India calls for a more careful examination of the evidence. The relationship holds its own even in the presence of such well-known causal factors as education and patriarchy, and in spite of the fact that the variable was measured at the state-level only. In Table 4, we present data on mass media exposure for the major states of India from the reports of the ORG survey of 1988 and NFHS, 1992–3. The regional patterns of exposure to mass media revealed by the two surveys are strikingly similar. Media exposure is substantially higher in the south and lowest in Hindi-speaking north India. This cannot be attributed to education levels alone because we observed the same pattern even among illiterate women. Also, it cannot be wholly ascribed to greater autonomy of women in the south either, because the north-south difference is

TABLE 4: DATA ON PERCENTAGE OF COUPLES OR MARRIED WOMEN EXPOSED TO MASS MEDIA FROM TWO NATIONAL SURVEYS AROUND 1990, FOR MAJOR STATES OF INDIA

| Major states | ORG Survey, 1988 | | | | | | NFHS, 1992–93 | | | | | |
| | Any media exposure* | | Exposure to cinema | | Exposure to TV | | Any media exposure† | | Cinema exposure of wife | TV exposure of wife | Exposure to F.P. message through media# | |
	All couples	Illiterate wife	Husband	Wife	Husband	Wife	All women	Illiterate women			All women	Illiterate
India												
Total	51.0	33.6	22.9	13.3	23.3	20.0	52.7	35.8	15.0	31.8	42.2	27.5
Rural	NA	NA	17.2	8.6	13.6	9.9	42.7	NA	10.6	18.9	33.0	NA
Urban	NA	NA	40.3	26.9	53.3	53.7	80.9	NA	27.6	68.2	68.5	NA
Kerala	85.2	75.1	26.4	19.3	17.8	23.8	79.2	55.3	18.3	42.2	55.9	33.5
Tamil Nadu	72.5	58.8	53.1	41.6	28.7	27.6	78.0	64.8	42.6	50.4	51.9	37.2
Andhra Pradesh	71.0	60.1	55.3	39.2	16.7	14.7	75.2	65.7	48.8	39.1	58.5	46.7
Karnataka	60.3	41.0	34.0	27.3	22.1	21.2	70.1	56.2	30.3	39.5	66.9	53.3
Maharashtra	59.5	36.7	26.7	11.5	30.8	29.6	62.8	42.5	14.9	46.4	51.5	31.8
Gujarat	61.7	41.6	37.1	15.0	44.0	38.7	55.4	35.0	9.5	39.4	47.4	26.8
Rajasthan	29.9	19.8	13.4	1.8	17.9	13.0	30.1	19.6	5.2	17.9	33.3	23.5
Punjab	47.4	25.0	6.6	2.5	38.8	35.4	65.5	46.3	2.3	57.3	59.9	39.9

Table 4 (contd.)

| Major states | ORG Survey, 1988 | | | | | | NFHS, 1992–93 | | | | | |
| | Any media exposure* | | Exposure to cinema | | Exposure to TV | | Any media exposure† | | Cinema exposure of wife | TV exposure of wife | Exposure to F.P. message through media# | |
	All couples	Illiterate wife	Husband	Wife	Husband	Wife	All women	Illiterate women			All women	Illiterate
Haryana	41.9	27.3	8.6	4.4	30.2	24.1	60.1	44.8	2.0	49.0	52.5	36.7
Uttar Pradesh	36.2	24.5	10.4	3.7	21.9	18.4	35.5	28.2	4.1	19.0	32.8	22.0
Madhya Pradesh	37.9	25.9	14.7	6.8	18.0	19.4	41.0	24.2	10.0	26.7	34.3	21.7
Bihar	42.1	31.0	17.8	8.6	16.8	11.9	29.5	18.2	5.2	12.7	26.6	15.8
Orissa	41.3	21.3	10.1	4.6	13.6	11.5	39.5	24.5	7.4	16.1	26.1	15.3
West Bengal	49.7	30.3	17.4	17.6	17.8	17.3	61.3	44.1	16.1	33.3	34.2	22.4
Assam	46.6	24.1	6.7	5.0	20.2	16.9	39.1	23.9	4.2	18.0	23.7	13.2

*   Who read newspaper or listen to radio or watch television at least once in a week, or see cinema at least once in three months.

†   Who listen to radio or watch television at least once in a week, or go to cinema/theatre once in a month.

Through radio or television in the month prior to the survey.

Source: Operations Research Group (1990), International Institute for Population Sciences (1995), and also state-level reports of NFHS.

observed even among men. Apart from being exposed to print media, people of the south go to the cinema and listen to the radio more often than their counterparts in the north. When the ORG survey was conducted in 1988, there was little difference between the north and the south with respect to exposure to television. But, by the time the NFHS survey was conducted about 5 years later, the south had forged ahead in this aspect too. Additionally, the NFHS data show that greater exposure to mass media has made women of the south more amenable to family planning messages through this channel than women of the north.

Without a detailed analysis of historical circumstances, it is difficult to pinpoint why the electronic media has been able to penetrate more sucessfully in the south than the north. However, we would postulate that, in general, it represents the overall lead the south has in the process of social development and adoption of Western norms and values in India. One crucial factor to note is that Western colonies were first established in the coastal lines of peninsular India and initially trading was done by sea. As a result, coastal regions in the south were the first to develop commercially and educationally and to come in contact with Christianity. Thus, one eminent Indian sociologist observed 'from a geographical point of view the inhabitants of coastal areas, especially those close to the fast-growing port towns, were favourably situated to undergo primary Westernization' (Srinivas 1966:62). He went on to add, 'it is possible to come across groups inhabiting rural areas which are more Westernized in their style of life than many urban groups. The former are to be found in areas where plantation or commercial crops are grown or which have a tradition of supplying recruits to the Indian army.' (Srinivas 1966:48). This impact is clear in the progress costal areas in the south and frontier regions in the north have made towards the demographic transition.

One of the main criticisms levelled at the dominant paradigm of mass media was that those who really needed new information had no access to mass media. While this was certainly the case in the 1960s and in the 1970s, the situation seems to be rapidly changing in many parts of India as exemplified in the south, where three-fourths of the population is now reported to be regularly exposed to at least one form of modern mass media. Consequently, mass media is poised to make a greater impact on social change than ever before. This is, however, not to deny the continued presence of both vertical and horizontal differentiation in the access to mass media. On the contrary, we attribute fertility variations primarily to differential access to media as illustrated by the north-south differences.

Disenchantment with the dominant paradigm in the communication field also grew out of its 'top-down' approach, ethnocentric bias, and lack of attention to traditional media. None of these arguments contradicts our position. These criticisms would have been valid had our contention been that fertility has fallen due to family planning messages through media or from the adoption of social marketing of contraceptives. In my view, the role of mass media is largely an indirect (or even unintended) one, since its main means of influence is probably through changing family size desires by altering lifestyle preferences, raising aspiration levels, and enlarging the range of felt needs. As Lerner (1958) has pointed out, media exposure provides 'clues to what the better things in life might be' and promotes an 'empathy' with the cultural stereotypes of the West. Such a cultural invasion is taking place precisely because of the ethnocentric bias in mass communication, and the emphasis on modern media, which are themselves goods produced and marketed by the modern economy.

On the other hand, some critics believe that mass media, such as the cinema, cannot have more than a superficial influence on social change because they do not fundamentally undermine traditional values (e.g., Hartmann, Patil, and Dighe 1989). Although this assessment is probably correct in some respects (on issues such as patriarchy, status of women, myths, and superstition), it underestimates the power of motion pictures in creating new role models and consumption standards for the youth by borrowing cultural stereotypes from the West. The popular cinema does portray, albeit in a crude way, exploitation, corruption, and injustice in society, and projects the protagonist as successfully fighting a tyrannical system, thus creating a role model to emulate. The commercial cinema does not glorify the simple, ascetic life idealized in the bygone era, but sells a technicolor dream that appeals to the basic instincts and romanticizes the worldly pursuits of love, wealth, and honour by mixing cultural stereotypes of the East and the West. Apparently, people find it easier to identify with the passion and saga of such fictional, 'masala' characters than the self-denying, otherworldly saints idealized in Hindu mythology. The fact that the semi-literate viewers do take these celluloid heroes and make-believe world somewhat seriously is borne out by the political clout film stars hold in Tamil Nadu and Andhra Pradesh (Kerala being a significant exception), where cinema going has become a favourite pastime among both young men and women. In these two states (as in southern Karnataka where Caldwell did his field work), more than 40 per cent of the women go to the cinema at least once a month, compared to less than 4 per cent in the north. When village elders blame the cinema for 'moral decadence' among the younger generation, they are clearly acknowledging the power of the medium in supplying role models and behavioural norms quite different from their own.

However, this is not to suggest that mass media does not lend itself to being used for the propagation of traditional values. As a matter of fact, when the British introduced printing in India, it made possible the transmission of epics, mythology, folklore, legends of saints, and other religious literature through books, pamphlets, and journals (Srinivas 1966). The same phenomenon was observed when radio, cinema, and television, were introduced in India. The use of cassette records in popularizing devotional songs and disseminating 'religious bigotry' provides yet another example. Perhaps this is what led Milton Singer to remark, 'the effect of mass media . . . has not so much secularized the sacred traditional culture as it has demo-cratized it' (quoted in Srinivas 1966:132). Clearly, it would be wrong to trivialize the contribution of mass media to social change. Com-munication researchers have known for sometime that *existing* basic attitudes and opinions are not subject to ready manipulation through mass media. However, the media do appear to be powerful in creat-ing *new* attitudes when clear opinions have not been formed on a given issue (e.g., Klapper 1960). Owing to selectivity in exposure, perception, and retention, mass communication probably reinforces traditional values among the older generation but among the young, who are less likely to have solidified their opinions on many issues, mass media can act as a powerful agent in shaping new attitudes and aspirations about quality of life, the quantity of children desired, and on the morality of using contraception. It is to be noted that this impact on fertility operates with a considerable time-lag, as it will only be manifest when children and adolescents exposed to mod-ern media become adults acquiring power to influence family size and other consumption decisions of the household.

Tamil Nadu Puzzle

Near replacement levels of fertility in the state of Tamil Nadu, with a population size as large as Thailand, have been a matter of considerable debate because its levels of female literacy and child survival are nowhere near that of neighbouring Kerala, nor is it as economically prosperous as Punjab or Haryana in the north. It is to be noted, however, that the state's position is extremely favourable on two counts — mass media exposure and joint family — which we found to be crucial in explaining spatial variation in fertility in India. If the exposure to mass media is high in Kerala because of the access to print media, in Tamil Nadu (also in Andhra Pradesh) it is because of access to electronic media. In addition, Tamil Nadu also has the lowest incidence of joint family in the country. Joint family residence, besides curtailing the freedom of younger couples in reproductive choices, appears to restrict the exposure of young women to mass media.[11]

However, the regression results reported above show that the variables employed in the analysis do not fully account for the low fertility in Tamil Nadu. The coefficient of the state dummy in the regression indicates that estimated level of TFR in Tamil Nadu is 14 per cent lower than the expected level. It is, therefore, necessary to explore what additional factors might be at work in Tamil Nadu. In this connection, we shall critically examine the three broad explanations offered in the literature, namely, poverty, programme effort, and backward-class movements in the state (Kulkarni et al. 1995).

Among the three, the first explanation is the easiest to dismiss because poverty or the 'exclusionary' process of development (Kishor 1994) is not unique to Tamil Nadu. There are states in India with higher levels of poverty and where the poor are more marginalized. The social movements in the earlier periods of this century have succeeded in transferring political power to the backward classes in the state which ought to make Tamils feel more in control of their destiny than elsewhere. Even if it is granted that

[11] The state-level data from the ORG survey of 1988 show that cinema exposure of the wife (CIN_w) is inversely related to the incidence of joint family (JF), even after controlling for husband's cinema exposure (CIN_h):

$$CIN_w = 16.6 + 0.64 \ CIN_h - 0.89 \ JF$$
$$(.07) \qquad (.27) \quad N = 14, \ R^2 = 0.94.$$

these movements succeeded in uplifting these groups' social status but not their economic conditions, there is no evidence to suggest that fertility decline in Tamil Nadu was more pronounced among the poor. On the contrary, the available data suggest that these groups lagged behind others in the transition process.[12] In our regressions using district-level data, the proportion of farm workers who have to eke out a living as agricultural labourers (a proxy for poverty) showed a positive effect on fertility. Even if this is assumed to be due to the use of population density as an additional regressor (which is found to have a negative effect on fertility), the independent significance of the dummy variable for Tamil Nadu is a strong negation of the poverty hypothesis.

Among programme administrators and supply-side academics, Tamil Nadu is a shining example of what a strong family planning programme can achieve. Interestingly, however, on such programme input indicators as expenditure on family planning and number of field personnel deployed in rural areas, Tamil Nadu does not have an exceptional record. But a high level of programme efficiency is claimed because of strong intersectoral linkages, administrative support, and political commitment coming from the highest ranks of the government (Anthony 1992; Srinivasan 1995). Because functional aspects of the programme are difficult to quantify, we have used programme output variables such as the percentage of targets achieved on sterilization and the unmet need for contraception as overall measures of programme efficiency. Surprisingly, even on these indicators, Tamil Nadu does not stand out as unique. On target achievement, Punjab, Kerala, and Maharashtra show better records than Tamil Nadu, and in reducing the unmet need for contraception Tamil Nadu ranks below Andhra Pradesh, Kerala, Punjab, Gujarat, and Maharashtra. Not surprisingly, when these measures are used as proxies for programme effort in our statistical analysis, Tamil Nadu's low

[12] Kishor (1994) presents some data from the SRS surveys that purportedly show that fertility has declined relatively more among the poor than the rich during 1972–84. But because of the likely presence of 'cultural lag', the observed pace of fertility decline by social class is likely to be highly sensitive to the time period chosen for the comparison. On the assumption that, before the transition, fertility differentials by social class were negligible (in fact, supply conditions were probably such that fertility was higher among the better-off sections), the data presented by Kishor clearly show that cumulated declines in fertility were higher among the rich than the poor at any time point chosen for the comparison.

fertility remains largely unexplained. Either our measures are flawed, or exaggerated claims have been made about programme achievements in Tamil Nadu.

What might explain the state standing apart from others is the Tamil-separatist movement of the early twentieth century. Although other states have also undergone similar backward-caste movements, none have been as militant and vehemently anti-Brahman and widespread as the one witnessed in Tamil Nadu. It is worthwhile to briefly review the history of this campaign because it vividly illustrates how ideational changes occur through a complex interaction of contact with alien culture and religion, rising levels of literacy, introduction of mass media (press, in this instance), and chance emergence of a charismatic leader. In describing the events that unfolded at the beginning of this century, we have relied mainly upon a fascinating study of the evolution of the Tamil-separatist movement made by Eugene Irschick (1969).

The foundation of this movement was laid in the eighteenth and nineteenth centuries by Christian clergymen who for purposes of their missionary work began to take interest in the Tamil language and literature. Their discoveries caused them to theorize that Tamil was a non-Aryan (Dravidian) language and of greater antiquity and sophistication than Sanskrit, which was brought by Aryan Brahman invaders from the north. It was also contended that the Brahmans brought with them a brand of Hinduism which embodied the worship of idols and differentiated groups along hereditary lines (i.e, castes). While there was probably substantial truth in this interpretation of Tamil history, it should not be forgotten that Christian missionaries had their own agenda, and Brahmans, being the custodians of religious faith in India, were seen as their main adversaries.

Stimulated by these early missionary writings, some educated non-Brahman Tamils began to take an interest in their own culture and literature. They also became acutely aware of the fact that Brahmans, by virtue of their long tradition of learning (non-Brahmans were predominantly farmers), had taken advantage of the educational opportunities offered by the British and occupied key positions in the administration, and were, thus, ready to seize power if the demand for home rule was granted by the British. A conflict began to develop between Brahmans and non-Brahmans for political, economic and educational privileges, with the British extending tactical support to the latter due to their alarm at the power wielded by the

Brahmans in the administration and by their active participation in the independence struggle. The discontentment that was brewing came into the open in 1916 with the formation of the Justice Party and the release of a *Non-Brahmin Manifesto*. In the wake of the boycott of the 1920 provincial election by the Indian National Congress, the Justice Party captured power in Madras and succeeded in passing a series of government orders designed to give power and reservations to non-Brahmans for government jobs. This was the beginning of the decline of Brahman dominance in Tamil Nadu, and their exodus to other parts of India in search of employment.

On the social sphere, the most virulent campaign against Brahmans was waged by E.V. Ramasamy Naicker (later to be known as 'Periyar'), the leader of the 'Self-Respect' movement. Although he was not well-educated, his two young lieutenants, first S. Ramanathan, and C.N. Annadurai in later years, were both college-educated Vellalas (a dominant, non-Brahman caste). The movement sought to give Tamils a sense of pride based on their Dravidian past, and contended that self-respect should come before self-rule. The propaganda organ of the movement was the Tamil language weekly newspaper *Kudi Arasu*, started by Periyar in 1924. While the Justice Party served the interest of a few educated elites among the non-Brahmans, the Self-Respecters targeted the semieducated in rural areas, including the untouchables, through inflammatory speeches, articles, and pamphlets decrying the Brahman hegemony and their caste-based society. Copies of Brahmanic texts were burnt and their idols disfigured. Much publicity was given to the Self-Respect weddings, which were often intercaste or widow remarriages arranged by the leaders of the movement and conducted without the services of Brahman priests. These weddings were used as a platform to mount scathing attacks on Brahmanic epics, especially for their portrayal of women as subservient to men.

With time, the reform campaign grew even sharper, and increasingly came under the rationalistic influence of the Ingersoll variety, especially after Naicker made a trip to Europe in 1931. The self-respect propaganda became influenced by materialistic jargons picked up from the West and turned anti-God and anti-religion. Women were urged to use contraception in order to unchain themselves from the age-old burden of childbearing, and even the abolition of the institution of marriage was advocated to free women from their enslavement. When attempts were made to make Hindi, an Indo-Aryan language, compulsory at schools, followers of the movement held violent demonstrations. Later, when the question of dividing India on religious lines came up, a separate nation-state for Tamil people was also demanded. These articulations for regional autonomy by the members of the movement ultimately led to the formation of a political party in the 1940s. In the post-independence era, the party lead by Annadurai, the able lieutenant of Periyar, seized power in the state election of 1967. Since then, one or the other splinter group of this party has been in power in Tamil Nadu.

What is the relevance of this social-reform movement of the late 1920s and 1930s to the fertility decline that occurred after the 1970s? It is to be noted that the radical positions the Dravidian movement had taken on a variety of issues were moderated once the leaders entered the terrain of electoral politics (Pandian et al. 1991). It is doubtful that the campaign for emancipation of women had a lasting influence on the public because Periyar had failed to lead by example, which allegedly led to division in the ranks during the 1940s (see Lakshmi 1990). With the institution of dowry and the incidence of female infanticide on the rise, the situation, rather than improving, seems to have escalated. However, the practice of political personalities attending wedding ceremonies, though rare, is still in vogue. Instead of making inflammatory speeches, the leaders — several of whom are from the world of cinema — now campaign for family planning and child immunization. That this may have had some impact on the younger generation cannot be denied.

Perhaps the lasting impact of the campaign was its projection of a separate identity for Tamils that is more progressive and secular than the Brahmanic culture of the north. While 'backward-class' movements witnessed elsewhere in the subcontinent could be characterized as an expression for caste mobility within the bounds of the Hinduism that is termed 'Sanskritization' (Srinivas 1966), the Dravidian movement had clearly rejected the superiority of the Brahmanic culture and tried to establish its own identity. The separatist feeling among the Tamils has probably reduced fatalism and increased Westernization. This, along with the preponderance of nuclear family and exposure to mass media, is the reason for the low levels of fertility in Tamil Nadu. Befittingly, the district from where Periyar hailed, and which now goes by his name, has the lowest level of TFR in Tamil Nadu (1.6).

CONCLUSIONS

In this paper I have attemped to test some of the competing explanations for the spatial variations in fertility in India using the district-level estimates of fertility derived from the 1991 census. A multivariate analysis of the data shows that no more than 10 per cent of the difference in fertility levels between northern and southern India could be attributed to the structural factors of the economy. Differences in social structure explain at least 30 per cent of the variation in fertility, and ideational factors account for at least another 40 per cent. The difference in the level of child survival accounts for about 10 per cent of the fertility variation. The family planning effort, measured primarily through the unmet need for contraception, appears to account for most of the remaining 10 per cent of the difference.

It is suggested that previous literature has overstated the case of patriarchy and female autonomy in causing the regional variation in fertility in India. Our analysis indicates that these variables do not explain more than half of the north-south difference in fertility. Conversely, the analysis does suggest that the exposure to mass media has played a key role in shaping the regional variation in fertility in India. However, it is cautioned that the importance of this variable in explaining fertility differences should not immediately be interpreted as representing the effectiveness of family planning messages through mass media or the success of the social marketing approach. The role of mass media is probably indirect, by changing lifestyle preferences, rising aspiration levels, and modifying childcare practices.

The near replacement level fertility in Tamil Nadu is puzzling because of its relatively high levels of illiteracy, poverty, and infant mortality. Our analysis identifies high exposure to mass media and weak patriarchal control as two plausible explanatory factors, but they do not fully explain the low levels of fertility in the state. We also find the arguments based on claims that it is a poverty-induced phenomenon or programme-promoted change to be unconvincing. Our belief is that the unusually low level of fertility in Tamil Nadu has its roots in the social-reform movements of the earlier part of this century which succeeded in transferring political power to backward classes. In particular, it helped to create an identity separate from mainstream Hinduism and brought the people of Tamil Nadu

closer to the secular and materialistic traditions of the West. It is to
be noted that the social-reform movement itself was a product of
contact with the European culture and religion, increasing literacy
levels, and the introduction of printing into the traditional society.

REFERENCES

Anthony, T.V. (1992), 'The Family Planning Programme: Lessons from
Tamil Nadu's Experience', Paper presented at the Symposium on
India's Development in the 1990s (New Delhi: Centre for Policy
Research).
Basu, A.M. (1986), 'Birth Control by Assetless Workers in Kerala: The
Possibility of a Poverty Induced Fertility Transition', *Development
and Change*, 17(2):265–82.
Bongaarts, J. (1987), 'Does Family Planning Reduce Infant Mortality
Rates?', *Population and Development Review*, 13(2):323–34.
Boserup, E. (1970), *Women's Role in Economic Development* (London:
Allen & Unwin).
Cain, M. (1981), 'Risk and Insurance: Perspectives on Fertility and
Agrarian Change in Rural India and Bangladesh', *Population and
Development Review*, 7(3):435–74.
Caldwell, J.C. (1976), 'Toward a Restatement of Demographic Transi-
tion Theory', *Population and Development Review*, 2 (3&4):321–66.
—— (1982), *Theory of Fertility Decline* (London, New York: Academic
Press).
—— (1983), 'In Search of a Theory of Fertility Decline for India and Sri
Lanka', in K. Srinivasan and S. Mukerji (eds.), *Dynamics of Popula-
tion and Family Welfare* (Bombay: Himalaya Publishing House).
Caldwell, J.C., P.H. Reddy, and P. Caldwell (1982), 'The Causes of
Demographic Change in Rural South India: A Micro Approach',
Population and Development Review, 8(4):689–727.
—— (1985), 'Educational Transition in Rural South India', *Population
and Development Review*, 11(1):29–51.
Centre for Monitoring Indian Economy (1987), *District-Level Data for
Key Economic Indicators with 70 Maps* (Bombay: Centre for Monitor-
ing Indian Economy).
Coale, A.J. (1992), 'Age of Entry into Marriage and Date of the Initiation
of Voluntary Birth Control', *Demography*, 29(3):333–41.
Das Gupta, M. (1994), 'What Motivates Fertility Decline?: A Case Study
of Punjab, India', in Egerio, B., and M. Hammarskjold (eds.), *Understanding Reproductive Change: Kenya, Tamil Nadu, Punjab, Costa
Rica* (Lund: Lund University Press).

Dyson, T., and M. Moore (1983), 'On Kinship Structure, Female Autonomy and Demographic Behaviour in India', *Population and Development Review*, 9(1):35–60.

Hartmann, P., B.R. Patil, and A. Dighe (1989), *The Mass Media and Village Life: An Indian Study* (New Delhi: Sage Publications).

India, Registrar General (1988), 'Female Age at Marriage: An Analysis of 1981 Census Data', Occassional Paper No. 7 of 1988 (New Delhi: Office of the Registrar General).

International Institute for Population Sciences (IIPS) (1995), *National Family Health Survey (MCH and Family Planning), India 1992–3* (Bombay: IIPS).

Irschick, E.F. (1969), *Politics and Social Conflict in South India* (Berkeley: University of California Press).

Jain, A.K. (1985), 'The Impact of Development and Population Policies on Fertility in India', *Studies in Family Planning*, 16(4):181–98.

Jeffery, R. (1976), 'Governments and Culture: How Women Made Kerala Literate', *Pacific Affairs*, 60(3):447–79.

Jejeebhoy, S.J. (1981), 'Status of Women and Fertility: A Socio-cultural Analysis of Regional Variations in Fertility in India', in K. Srnivasan and S. Mukerje (eds.), *Dynamics of Population and Family Welfare* (Bombay: Himalye Publishing House).

Kaufmann, G. and J. Cleland (1994), 'Maternal Education and Child Survival: Anthropological Response to Demographic Evidence', *Health Transition Review*, 4(2):196–9.

Kishor, S. (1994), 'Fertility Decline in Tamil Nadu, India', in Egerio, B. and M. Hammarskjold (eds.), *Understanding Reproductive Change: Kenya, Tamil Nadu, Punjab, Costa Rica* (Lund: Lund University Press).

Klapper, J.T. (1960), *The Effects of Mass Communication* (Glencoe, Illinois : Free Press).

Koenig, M.A. and G.H.C. Foo (1992), 'Patriarchy, Women's Status, and Reproductive Behaviour in Rural North India', *Demography India*, 21(2):145–66.

Krishnan, T.N. (1976), 'Demographic Transition in Kerala: Facts and Factors', *Economic and Political Weekly*, 11(31–3):1203–24.

Kulkarni, P.M., S. Krishnamoorthy and N. Audinarayan (1995), 'Review of Research on Fertility in Tamil Nadu', Paper presented in the workshop on Demographic Transition in Tamil Nadu, 21–2 August, Madras.

Lakshmi, C.S. (1990), 'Mother, Mother-Community and Mother-Politics in Tamil Nadu', *Economic and Political Weekly*, 25(42&43): WS72–83.

Lerner, D. (1958), *The Passing of Traditional Society* (New York: Free Press).

Mahajan, V. and R.A. Peterson (1985), *Models for Innovation Diffusion*, Sage University Paper Series on Quantitative Applications in Social Sciences, Series No. 07–048 (Beverly Hills and London: Sage Publications).

Malhotra, A., R. Vanneman, and S. Kishor (1995), 'Fertility, Patriarchy and Development in India', *Population and Development Review*, 21(2):281–305.

Mason, K.O. (1984), *Status of Women: A Review of its Relationship to Fertility and Mortality* (New York: The Rockefeller Foundation).

Mencher, J. (1980), 'The Lessons and Non-lessons of Kerala: Agricultural Labourers and Poverty', *Economic and Political Weekly*, 18(19–21): 877–900.

Murthi, M., A.C. Guio, and J. Drèze (1995) 'Mortality, Fertility and Gender Bias in India: A District Level Analysis', DEP No. 61 (London: London School of Economics).

Nag, M. (1983), 'Fertility Differentials in Kerala and West Bengal: Equity-fertility Hypothesis as Explanation', *Economic and Political Weekly*, 18(19–21):877–900.

Operations Research Group (1990), *Family Planning Practices in India: Third All-India Survey* (Baroda: Operations Research Group).

Pandian, M.S.S., S. Anandhi, and V. R. Venkatachalapathy (1991), 'Of Maltova Mothers and Other Stories', *Economic and Political Weekly*, 26(16):1059–64.

Raftery, A.E., S.M. Lewis, and A. Aghajanian (1995), 'Demand or Ideation? Evidence from the Iranian Fertility Decline', *Demography*, 32(2):159–82.

Ratcliffe, J. (1978), 'Social Justice and Demographic Transition: Lessons from India's Kerala State', *International Journal of Health Services*, 8(1):123–44.

Rogers, E.M. (1976), 'Communication and Development: The Passing of the Dominant Paradigm, in E.M. Rogers (ed.), *Communication and Development: Critical Perspectives* (Newbury Park, CA.: Sage Publications).

Srinivas, M.N. (1966), *Social Change in Modern India* (Berkeley: University of California Press).

Srinivasan, K. (1995), *Regulating Reproduction in India's Population: Efforts, Results and Recommendations* (New Delhi: Sage Publications).

Wiser, W.H. (1958), *The Hindu Jajmani System*, 2nd edn. (Lucknow: Lucknow Publishing House).

5

Brazil's Fertility Decline, 1965–95: A Fresh Look at Key Factors

George Martine

INTRODUCTION

Over the last thirty years, Brazil has experienced a remarkably rapid fertility decline. Its total fertility rate (TFR) fell by more than 50 per cent between 1970 and 1990. Rates of population growth thus decreased from 2.8 per cent per year during the 1960s to around 1.5 per cent in the 1990s. Although nothing short of spectacular, the abrupt reduction in Brazilian fertility has received comparatively little attention in the international literature. The tendency is to write off the Brazilian story as an anomaly. It is my contention that, on the contrary, the history of fertility decline in Brazil can be quite useful, not only for a reflection on population policy, but also for expanding the horizons of current fertility theory.

What has prompted this unexpected and rapid reduction? No simple and ready explanation can be proffered. Brazil has never had a widespread official or private family planning programme; much less has it supported any effort to control population growth. No abrupt changes or sudden cataclysms have occurred. Nor can the fertility decline be attributed to rapid and sustained economic growth; indeed, the decline began during a period of economic boom, then continued unabated during the grave economic crisis experienced in the 1980s. The glib explanation currently being offered by some observers is that Brazil's fertility reduction is due to massive 'sterilization abuse'. This hypothesis, which implies that fertility declined because massive numbers of women were coerced

Reprinted with the permission of the Population Council from *Population and Development Review*, 22(1) (March 1996):47–75. Additional information on the effects of urbanization has been added to this version.

into sterilization, is vastly oversimplified. Nor does any other single-cause explanation stand up to closer examination.

This article addresses the multiplicity of factors underlying Brazil's rapid fertility decline. Several studies have previously examined causation at different levels of generality, using a variety of approaches. However, many of these studies are difficult to access. Moreover, not enough has been done to compare their approaches and integrate their findings.[1] These findings are reviewed in the core section of this article, revealing considerable overlap but also important conceptual and methodological differences. The majority of existing studies are cross-sectional or have limited time-space reference points. I contend that understanding the Brazilian fertility transition requires an integrated and longitudinal view of sociodemographic processes, one that situates recent changes within the framework of their particular historical context.

THE TRAJECTORY OF FERTILITY DECLINE IN BRAZIL

At the turn of the century, Brazil's total population was about 18 million. During the next four decades, this number grew to 41 million. The subsequent rapid decline in mortality accelerated the rate of growth, and the population reached 145 million in 1990. It is now generally acknowledged that fertility began declining during the 1940s, but at a very slow pace. Until the 1960s, the reduction was restricted to better-off income groups and regions, particularly in urban areas, while the majority of the population showed high and even increasing fertility rates (Carvalho and Wong 1990; Chackiel and Schkolnik 1990).

Demographers began to perceive the first signs of an unanticipated and widespread fertility decline in Brazil during the late 1970s. Early analyses tread warily on these findings, yet each subsequent source of data has shown an even faster and more widespread decrease than that predicted by the experts in the preceding period (see Table 1). Several independent estimates of national fertility trends in Brazil, based on a variety of techniques and assumptions, all concur with respect to the overall timing and breadth

---

[1] For recent reviews see Rios Neto, McCracken, and Rodrigues (1991); Silva, Henriques, and de Souza (1990); and Lam, Sedlacek, and Duryea (1993).

of the decline (Bercovich, Oliveira, and Mendes 1993). The TFR has fallen from approximately 6.0 children per woman in the early 1960s to below 2.5 in the mid-1990s. This swift reduction has, since the 1980s, begun to produce an absolute reduction in the number of children born, resulting in a hollowed-out base in the current Brazilian population pyramid.

TABLE 1: TOTAL FERTILITY RATE, BRAZIL AND
NORTHEAST REGION OF BRAZIL, 1960–95

Years	Brazil	Northeast
1960–65	6.00	7.44
1965–70	5.75	7.11
1970–75	4.97	6.77
1975–80	4.17	5.97
1980–85	3.37	4.76
1985–90	2.82	3.97
1990–95	2.48	3.50

Sources: For Brazil, Camarano (1996); Bercovich, Oliveira, and Mendes (1993); Simões and Oliveira (1986). For the Northeast, Camarano (1996) and Wong (1994).

Practically all regions and social strata have been affected by the decline. Although important rural-urban and regional differences remain, it is particularly significant that Brazil's poorest socio-economic region, the Northeast, has undergone the fastest fertility reduction over the last twenty years: there, the TFR has fallen from around 7 in 1970 to 3.7 in 1990.

The speed of Brazil's fertility decline is comparable to that of other large developing countries that have implemented, over several decades, aggressive family planning programmes. As shown in Figure 1, the Brazilian fertility decline is somewhat slower than that in China and Thailand, and considerably faster than that in Mexico, India, and Bangladesh.[2]

[2] The TFRs for Brazil are estimates based on the available, and often deficient, statistical information; they should be taken as valid indicators of trends and orders of magnitudes, rather than exact numbers. The same caveat applies to the estimates of TFRs represented in Figure 1, based on the United Nations' latest

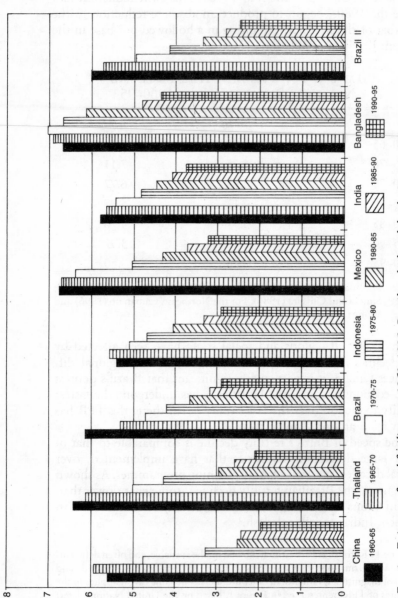

FIG. 1: *Estimates of total fertility rate, 1960–1995, Brazil and selected developing countries.*

Source: United Nations 1995. For Brazil II cf. Table 1 in this article.

DATA FOR FIGURE 1

Year	China	Thailand	Brazil	Indonesia	Mexico	India	Bangladesh	Brazil II
1960–65	5.61	6.42	6.15	5.42	6.75	5.81	6.68	6
1965–70	5.94	6.14	5.31	5.57	6.7	5.69	6.91	5.75
1970–75	4.76	5.01	4.7	5.1	6.37	5.43	7.02	4.97
1975–80	3.26	4.27	4.21	4.68	5.03	4.83	6.66	4.17
1980–85	2.5	2.96	3.65	4.06	4.3	4.47	6.15	3.37
1985–90	2.41	2.57	3.15	3.31	3.7	4.07	4.8	2.82
1990–95	1.95	2.1	2.88	2.9	3.21	3.75	4.35	2.48

I begin by reviewing evidence on the relative roles of the proximate determinants of fertility change in Brazil. I then turn to consideration of four factors that have been posited as affecting fertility decline in that country: the influence of key social institutions, the impact of modernization and socio-economic change, the effects of economic pressure, and the unintended outcomes of institutional changes and public policies. I critically examine each of these factors. In addition, I analyse separately the consequences of Brazil's unique urban transition for its fertility reduction.

THE PROXIMATE DETERMINANTS OF FERTILITY

The proximate determinants are defined as the biological and behavioural factors that directly influence fertility. Social, economic, and other factors operate through these intermediate variables. As Bongaarts has shown, four proximate determinants account for most observed variation in fertility worldwide: marital patterns,

---

revision of world population trends (United Nations 1995). For instance, the UN's numbers clearly overestimate current levels of Brazilian fertility (and possibly that of other countries, notably India and Bangladesh); nevertheless, I use this source for comparative purposes in Figure 1, in order to maintain consistency. In addition, estimates for Brazil from Table 1 are shown in Figure 1 as 'Brazil II'; these estimates suggest that Brazil's fertility decline was also faster than that of Indonesia, a country with energetic population control policies.

contraception, induced abortion, and postpartum nonsusceptibility, mainly due to breast-feeding (Bongaarts 1978).

When we consider these four factors in Brazil, we find first that variations in age at marriage cannot be held responsible for changing reproductive outcomes. Indeed, recent alterations in nuptiality patterns, expressed by a growing number of consensual unions and greater sexual freedom, operate in the direction of increasingly early exposure to sexual intercourse (Verdugo 1994:1). Recent studies in the northeast, which has traditionally had lower ages at marriage and higher fertility than the rest of the country, show that age at first union is actually decreasing (Camarano 1994). This alone should have led to higher fertility; in fact, fertility has been declining dramatically in that region. On the other hand, fertility rates of women under age 20 have remained stable while adolescent pregnancies are on the rise (Henriques, Silva, and Wulf 1989). However, the number of such early births is insufficient to offset the effect of the generalized fertility reduction in the age groups above 20.

A new and relevant factor in this context, whose impact on fertility requires further research, is the growing level of marital instability and, consequently, the increasing number of female-headed households (Berquó, Oliveira, and Cavenaghi 1994). It has been suggested that increasing marital instability results, in part, from the growing sex imbalance caused by the rapid changes in Brazilian vital rates, and that it is associated with sequential sharing of males by females (Greene and Rao 1992). Be that as it may, fertility is higher in consensual than formal unions, although there is a tendency toward convergence as fertility declines in both groups (Verdugo 1994:7). Existing differentials by type of union, however, may be countered by the fact that consensual unions do not last as long as formal unions (Henriques, Silva, and Wulf 1989).

A 1969 study in the city of Rio de Janeiro observed that poor young women often looked upon childbearing as a means of legitimizing and cementing a union; however, at least in the lower-income urban milieu, dissolution of the union was a more common outcome of pregnancy than formal marriage (Martine 1975). More recent research in the *favelas* (slum areas) of Belo Horizonte provided similar results (Kaufmann 1994). On the other hand, Goldani (1988), using indirect estimation techniques at the national level, concluded that premarital conceptions have contributed to increasing the number of marriages in Brazil.

A second proximate determinant of fertility — post-partum nonsusceptibility to pregnancy — also does not figure in the fertility decline. No significant changes in the frequency and duration of breastfeeding have been reported. Both the 1986 national Demographic and Health Survey (DHS) and the 1991 DHS carried out in the Northeast region investigated breastfeeding practices. These data show that breastfeeding has had little influence on Brazilian fertility. The average duration of breastfeeding did increase somewhat between the two surveys in the Northeast. Nevertheless, its effect is minor when compared with the impact of contraception (Camarano 1994:41).

Among the proximate determinants of fertility, the practice of birth control played the major role in generating Brazil's fertility decline. Prevalence of the practice has increased rapidly over time, although the range of methods used has remained limited. Two methods have had the most impact on fertility reduction: abortion and sterilization. Recourse to induced abortion as a birth control method appears to have been particularly important in the early years of the fertility decline. Since the latter half of the 1970s, when sterilization through tubal ligation was introduced on a large scale, that method has played an increasingly important role, in terms of both its prevalence and its impact on fertility reduction.

The hypothesis that abortion was the most important method of fertility control when accelerated fertility decline first began in the late 1960s and early 1970s is based on a simple process of elimination. At that time, the only contraceptive methods that were widely known and used were the oral contraceptive and the rhythm method. Given the general lack of knowledge concerning the reproductive process, the poor quality and inadequacy of contraceptive information, the frequent incorrect use of the pill, and the unavailability of other modern techniques, the practical effectiveness of those two methods is dubious (Martine 1975). Sterilization was not yet a factor: according to the 1986 national DHS, 85 per cent of all tubal ligations reported had been performed after 1975 (Costa 1991:3). These considerations strongly suggest that the birth control method that had the most impact in the early stages of rapid fertility decline was abortion.

Just how prevalent is abortion in Brazil? Its role has generally been understated, in part because of the lack of reliable data, either national or regional. Since induced abortion is not legal in Brazil, except in the case of rape or risk to the mother's life, it is rarely performed in public institutions. Hence, data on its incidence are not systematically collected. Detailed field research in São Paulo indicates that whatever data do exist tend to underreport the importance of abortion as a means of fertility regulation (De Souza e Silva 1992).

Local-area surveys reveal, however, that knowledge of methods of abortion is commonplace and that recourse to them is frequent (Berquó 1980). In-depth studies tend to reveal higher incidence of abortion than large-scale surveys. In Rio de Janeiro, a 1969 study among poor, young (aged 25–30) urban women showed that 22 per cent had already had an abortion; an additional 10 per cent of the sampled women had unsuccessfully attempted to provoke an abortion, using infusions, drugs, or injections, during their most recent pregnancy. Moreover, hospital workers in the two maternity wards where some of the women were interviewed indicated that approximately half of all hospital beds in those wards were regularly occupied by the victims of self-inflicted abortions (Martine 1975).

A recent study by Giffin and Costa (n.d.) documents a number of small-scale studies, all of which reveal high and increasing incidence of abortion. 'It seems that abortion is something that most women know how to do, or if self-help fails, they know where to go. Where contraception is hard to get, or difficult to use well, if the women do not want children they turn to abortion, regardless of its legality or risks' (Kaufmann 1994:24–5). Only middle- and upper-class women have access to safe clandestine abortions. Poor women resort to cheaper but dangerous methods. They sometimes deliberately provoke miscarriages to gain admittance to a public health facility, where an abortion can be concluded more safely than it could without medical help. Brazil is also the first country where a drug intended for treatment of ulcers (marketed under the brand name Cytotec) was widely pressed into service as a self-prescribed abortifacient (Barbosa and Arilha 1993).

Estimates of current abortion levels on a regional or national basis vary enormously (De Souza e Silva 1992; WHO/MHO/CEMICAMP 1994:6; Barbosa and Arilha 1993; Singh and Wulf 1994). Recent estimates reported by Singh and Wulf (1994) suggest that there are between 266 and 444 abortions for every 1,000 births, and between 210 and 308 abortions for every 1,000 pregnancies. Whatever the correct figures, there is no denying that abortion represents an important and understudied factor in the Brazilian fertility decline. In Latin America at large, an estimated one-third of deliberate fertility control has been attributed to abortion (Frejka and Atkin 1990). Similar levels of magnitude are probably valid for Brazil.

The prevalence of a few other methods of fertility control is relatively high in Brazil. The last national fertility survey, carried out in 1986, indicated that close to two-thirds of all women in marital unions between the ages of 15 and 44 were using a contraceptive method. Among all women in that age group, regardless of marital status, prevalence was 43 per cent (Berquó 1993). During the last few years, contraceptive prevalence has undoubtedly increased. In the Northeast region, for instance, the proportion of all women aged 15–44, in marital unions, who were using some form of contraception rose from 53 per cent in 1986 to 61 per cent in 1991 (Ferreira 1994).

Among nonabortive methods, female contraceptive sterilization has been particularly important. Its use rose by more than 100 per cent between 1978 and 1986 in São Paulo, and by almost 80 per cent in the Northeast between 1980 and 1986 (Rutenberg and Ferraz 1988:62). Sterilization and hormonal methods together accounted for some 80 per cent of use prevalence among women in marital unions in 1986 (see Table 2). In the 1990s, these two methods remain the most commonly known and used means of contraception. Periodic abstinence and withdrawal were the only other methods of any significance.

Oral contraceptives are readily available through commercial outlets. However, the pill is cited by the majority of respondents as the method to which they reacted most negatively. In view of inadequate knowledge and use, it is somewhat surprising that the pill's efficacy is reported to be high (Ferreira 1994). Nevertheless, the overall impact of the pill on fertility is probably reduced by high rejection and discontinuation rates. The oral contraceptive is universally known, and 70 per cent of married women of reproductive age had tried it at one time or another, according to the 1986 DHS. Contraceptive pills are the most easily obtainable method of contraception. They can be purchased without prescription and, until recently, at low cost. Price controls, subsidization of pharmaceutical products, and nonpayment of royalties to international laboratories helped spread the use of the pill (World Bank 1992).

TABLE 2: PER CENT OF WOMEN AGED 15–44
IN A MARITAL UNION WHO ARE USING CONTRACEPTION,
BY METHOD: BRAZIL 1986

Method	Per cent
Female sterilization	26.9
Pill	25.2
Withdrawal	5.0
Periodic abstinence	4.0
Condom	1.7
IUD	1.0
Vasectomy	0.8
Injections	0.6
Vaginal methods	0.5
Billings method	0.3
Any method	65.8

Source: BEMFAM/DHS (1986), as computed by World Bank (1991),
Table 2.1.

Of the two main contraceptive methods, female sterilization has had the greater impact on fertility. The incidence of sterilization has been rising in poorer regions, although it may be receding in more developed regions. Thus, the proportion of married women aged 15–44 in the Northeast who are sterilized rose from 25 per cent to 37 per cent between 1986 and 1991; meanwhile, use of the pill decreased from 17 to 15 per cent and the use of traditional and 'natural' methods dropped from 9 to 6 per cent (Ferreira 1994). In the municipality of São Paulo, hormonal contraception is now slightly more prevalent than sterilization (Berquó 1993).

At the same time, women are turning to sterilization at younger ages. In 1986, the median age at sterilization in the Northeast was 36.6 and in the municipality of São Paulo, 38.2. By the early 1990s, the median age had fallen abruptly to 29.7 and 31 years, respectively (Berquó 1993; Camarano 1994).

Of particular interest in Brazil is the close correlation of sterilization with the high rate of caesarean sections at childbirth. The country has one of the highest rates of caesarean sections in the world: 26 per cent of all births and 32 per cent of hospital births in the five years preceding the 1986 DHS were delivered by caesarean (Rutenberg and Ferraz 1988:63). According to the same survey, 75 per cent of women who underwent sterilization did so in the course of a caesarean; a 1992 study indicated that the coincidence was 80 per cent in the municipality of São Paulo (Berquó 1993:41).

The uncommonly high prevalence of both tubal ligation and childbirth through caesarean section can be attributed, in large part, to the peculiarities of the Brazilian health system (Faúndes and Cecatti 1991; Barros et al 1991). The great majority of women who have been surgically sterilized in that country during the last few decades had the procedure performed in state-subsidized hospitals and clinics. The cost of a caesarean is covered by the public health system, and the procedure is more profitable for the attending physician than natural childbirth. Tubal ligations, on the other hand, are not covered by the health system and thus require extra-institutional arrangements. A common ploy is for a doctor to have his patient classified as being at high risk for pregnancy complications. He then arranges for her to have a caesarean section, based on her high-risk status, and to have her privately defray the costs of the tubal ligation that will be carried out simultaneously. The financial advantages of this arrangement for the often underpaid medical attendants in the official health system can be seen as an important part of the explanation for Brazil's exceptionally high rates of caesarean sections and sterilizations.

The main point here is that sterilization is one of the two most widely used forms of fertility limitation in Brazil. Given the increasingly younger ages at which sterilization is being resorted to, and the fact that it terminates a woman's reproductive cycle, one must conclude that use of this particular birth control method has been the major proximate determinant of the recent decline in Brazilian fertility.

THE INFLUENCE OF KEY SOCIAL ACTORS AND INSTITUTIONS

Few studies have concerned themselves systematically with the roles of social actors and institutions in Brazil's recent history of reproductive change. On the other hand, a great deal of attention has been focused on the 'population establishment'. Accusations of undue

interference in the lives of individuals, leveled at internationally financed family planning institutions and non-governmental organizations, have been common. The facile explanation that sterilization
abuse (i.e., coercing women to undergo sterilization) has occurred,
that it is attributable to such interference, and that it lies at the root
of Brazilian fertility decline, is widespread.

This section investigates the roles played by several major actors
in the reproductive domain: the government, the Catholic Church,
women's groups, the international population lobby and its local
representatives, and professionals in the health sector.[3] I argue here
that the main impacts of these social actors on fertility decline were
largely unanticipated and unintended.

Direct Government Influence

Brazil has never adopted population targets, and the government
has become tentatively involved in family planning activities only
recently. Formerly, the government was officially pronatalist. Explicit laws prohibited the dissemination of birth control information or devices. At the Bucharest Conference in 1974, the government stated, for the first time, that couples were free to plan their
families and had a right to family planning information and contraceptive techniques.

Timid attempts at translating these principles into effective action
met with opposition from the Church as well as from both right
and left wing political factions and from feminist organizations. Although state and municipal authorities, particularly in the poor
Northeast region, had initiated local family planning programmes
with the support of private agencies in the 1970s, it was only in
1986, when the fertility transition was already well-advanced, that
the government launched PAISM (the Programme of Integrated
Assistance to Women's Health), the first significant reproductive
health programme. To this day, government-sponsored family planning programmes are of relatively little significance, either in terms

---

[3] For a more detailed analysis of the role of these actors (with the exception
of the medical profession) see Barroso (1987, 1988, 1989, and 1991). Pitanguy
(1994) provides an authoritative review of the evolution of feminist politics in
Brazil. McDonough and de Souza (1981) examine the politics of population
policy in Brazil, portraying the viewpoints of elites across the board, without
systematically differentiating them by origin or affiliation. The doctoral thesis by
Fonseca (1993) reviews the evolution of explicit population policies and views.

of the population covered or in terms of their influence in promoting access to effective family planning services (Giffin and Costa n.d.; Barroso 1989; Pitanguy 1994).

Government action in the reproductive health domain has been stymied by a variety of political, administrative, and financial problems. Yet, it is plausible to argue that the very ineffectiveness of the public sector in the field of family planning ended up prompting women to use those methods that were available in the private sector. This inadvertently heightened the practical importance of two highly effective birth control methods: abortion and sterilization. Similarly, government policies in the pharmaceutical sector ended up favouring the use of the pill. Furthermore, as I argue below, the government has played an unintended but important role in fostering fertility decline through policies pursued in several domains whose connections to fertility behaviour are indirect, and whose consequences were not anticipated or recognized.

The Role of the Catholic Church

The Catholic Church has traditionally opposed sexual activity without the intent to procreate, and it approved of periodic abstinence as a means of exercizing responsible parenthood only relatively recently.[4] In matters bearing on politics and public policy, the Church in Brazil has not always presented a united front. Its conservative segments have persisted in defending traditional positions. Its politically progressive elements have promoted grass roots political movements and have often allied themselves with liberal and leftist groups as well as with women's movements. Within this coalition of forces opposing the military government, arguments rejecting the legitimacy of foreign and government intervention in the private domain, such as family-building behaviour, prevailed, as did the argument that fertility regulation would not solve problems of poverty and underdevelopment. At the same time, the stance adopted by the lower clergy was generally permissive, with parish priests discreetly advising the faithful to adopt natural methods of fertility control.

In the 1980s, growing awareness that a large proportion of the population was making determined efforts to practice effective

[4] Protestantism is growing in terms of number of adherents, but its role and influence *vis-à-vis* the country's rapid fertility decline are still modest.

birth control helped force a change in the attitudes of most social actors in this debate, including the Church. The process of democratization in the mid-1980s dissolved the political alliances opposed to the military government, within which the Church had played a significant role. Since, under the civilian regime, government intervention in the area of family planning seemed inevitable, the Church began to support it on the condition that only natural methods would be promoted. In subsequent years, the Church maintained its support for natural methods and its staunch opposition to other methods. Paradoxically, by helping to retard access to a variety of modern methods of contraception, the Church has unwittingly contributed to steering women toward abortion and sterilization.

Women's Movements

The feminist movement in Brazil took root among educated middle-class women during the early 1970s. In the then-prevailing climate of political oppression, the central cause of the movement was the struggle for civil liberties. It was felt that an aggressive feminist approach, or even a concentration on specific women's issues, would be divisive, alienating such key partners in the battle for freedom of speech and democracy as leftist political movements and the Catholic Church. It was only later that specific women's issues were placed high on the feminist agenda.

During the 1970s, when fertility was already declining rapidly, women's movements opposed all organized family planning efforts and denounced foreign intervention in this area. This posture reflected their antigovernment and antiimperialist stance. Family planning issues were one of the fragments in what has been called the left's 'mirror reaction', which held that 'if it's good for the imperialists, then it must be bad for us'.

Given the low levels of information about means of contraception, such stances contributed to postponing the democratization of access to effective fertility regulation. 'Contraceptives were widely available — to those who could buy them' (Barroso 1991:60). This meant no access or considerable costs for poorer women.

By the end of the 1970s, the struggle of millions of women to control their reproduction had transformed family planning and reproductive health into critical national issues. New influences were changing social and economic expectations as well as behaviour patterns in the reproductive sphere. Poor women were determined to regulate their family size. However, that determination was resulting not only in declining fertility but also in wholesale damage to women's health.

In the early 1980s, feminists moved decisively from opposition to family planning to leadership in defense of a new agenda. Emphasis was eventually placed on the provision of family planning services as part of an integrated women's health approach. The uneasy alliance of feminists with the left and with the Church was largely dismantled as democratization began. Since then, representatives of women's movements have participated in the formulation of a succession of government initiatives aimed at providing comprehensive health care to women and to the population at large.

Paradoxically, the overall impact of women's movements on fertility decline in Brazil is ambiguous. Their support of family planning was begrudging and belated. It is still beset with political problems of various types in some subgroups. On the other hand, subsequent efforts of women's organizations in this domain did have a major influence in shifting the terms of the national debate to reproductive health issues. They were also influential in promoting women's reproductive rights and women's empowerment, as well as in fostering the reformulation of gender roles and values. Feminists played a critical role in undermining Brazil's long-standing pronatalist coalition made up of the Church, right wing nationalists, and leftist movements. They promoted sex education and gender awareness, both of which favour greater control over reproductive behaviour and thus, ultimately, promote fertility decline.

The Population Establishment

Concern over rapid population growth in developing countries spawned an affluent and influential assemblage of donors, activists, and associations, loosely referred to as 'the population establishment' and generically dedicated to spreading the practice of family planning. Large and fast-growing Brazil was one of the primary targets of these efforts back in the 1960s and 1970s (Fonseca 1993:91–6). Women's groups, leftist parties, and 'progressive' non-governmental organizations (NGOs) within the country, maintained that Brazil's fertility decline was initiated, instigated, financed, and otherwise abetted, by the international population establishment. The nature and degree of the population establishment's influence need to be examined more closely.

Two related influences have been repeatedly cited in this connection: the 'sterilization industry' and the family planning NGOs. Indeed, the facile explanation for Brazil's remarkable fertility decline making the rounds internationally in the post-Cairo era is that it is due to sterilization abuse, which, in turn, is frequently attributed to external interference.

Although the exact figures are hard to ascertain, substantial resources have undoubtedly entered the country since the mid-1960s, earmarked for 'population activities' (Rocha 1993). On the other hand, on a per capita basis, the totals invested in Brazil, if compared with allocations in other developing countries, appear to be insignificant. Moreover, the magnitude of their total impact on fertility decline is not self-evident. The largest and best known of the family planning agencies, and one of the largest in any developing country, is BEMFAM, an affiliate of the International Planned Parenthood Federation. Founded in 1965, it has had a turbulent and controversial history.

The impact that BEMFAM and other programmes have had on Brazilian fertility patterns has been, on the objective evidence, minor, at least in direct terms. According to the 1986 DHS conducted by BEMFAM, only one per cent of all users obtained their contraceptive methods from private family planning agencies and fewer than one per cent of the women sterilized received that service from such sources. In that same year, BEMFAM claimed to have provided some 528,000 couple-years of protection from pregnancy. This number appears impressive, but given the size of the demand in Brazil and the high prevalence of contraceptive use, it is not considered meaningful in terms of total family planning practice (Townsend et al. 1994:130). This evaluation is confirmed by the 1986 DHS, according to which BEMFAM was the source of supply among current contraceptive users in only 0.5 per cent of the cases.

BEMFAM's role was probably greatest in the Northeast. There, it had a more extensive operation at an early stage, as well as greater access to the population through agreements with state and municipal authorities. Since these agreements were established during the military regime, generally in precarious conditions, they were frequently criticized by the anti-fertility-control coalition. According to the 1991 DHS, 20 per cent of all sterilized women in the Northeast obtained their information from private clinics (including family planning clinics) or doctors, while government agencies were cited in 46 per cent of sterilization cases. Only 5 per cent of pill users cited private sources of supply (BEMFAM/DHS 1992).

According to Berquó (1993), it is likely that international assistance contributed to increased access to female sterilization more than to other methods. Moreover, the 1986 DHS showed that the more modern methods (IUDs, male sterilization, and the diaphragm) were more likely to be obtained from private sources than traditional methods; however, these methods, as shown earlier, have had little impact on the total fertility decline to date.

Despite the absence of a direct and significant impact, it can be argued that the population establishment has had an indirect influence on fertility decline (Martine and Faria 1988). It helped push the population question onto the public agenda and keep it there. Donor support for teaching and research on demographic questions helped place the population agenda onto more neutral, and therefore, more 'acceptable' grounds. The population establishment has maintained a permanent lobby in the legislature, which kept the topic in public view. It also financed numerous and varied publications that, in the long run, probably helped increase awareness of the possibility of separating sexuality from procreation — at a time when the opportunity costs of children were rising.

Finally and most importantly, the multiplicity of private clinics and institutions may have had a 'demonstration effect' beyond their direct and immediate clientele. Given changing expectations and the widespread unfulfilled demand for contraception, the presence of such agents in many parts of the country, however small their direct impact, may have had an important influence by increasing awareness of fertility-regulation possibilities among a wider population.

Health-Sector Professionals

Although no systematic study has been made of the role of public health workers and of the medical profession in Brazil's fertility decline, it can be hypothesized that it has been significant, albeit uneven. Investments made during the 1960s in public health and social security promoted sweeping changes in health policy and administration. A hybrid system of private medicine subsidized by the state was implemented nationally. The upshot of such efforts was the widespread 'medicalization' of health. The number of physicians greatly increased, though the quality of medical training deteriorated. This circumstance was accompanied by a greater concentration of medical services and health professionals in urban areas, particularly in larger cities. It was also marked by increased investments in curative/hospital treatment, rather than preventive medicine. Thus, between 1962 and 1982, preventive health expenditures decreased from 64 per cent to 15 per cent of the government's health-sector budget (World Bank 1991).

One result of these initiatives was that a new class of 'public--sector healthworkers' arose and quickly expanded. This sector soon proved to be highly politicized, its membership dominated by leftist party leaders. Predictably, these groups were vociferously opposed to family planning. Given the lack of clear elite support for family planning, the party line of the public healthworkers in this domain became, to a large extent, the official position of the health sector. It also had a considerable influence on other politicized progressive elements of society, including women's activists, journalists, and other intellectuals.

Nevertheless, a combination of influences began to alter this monolithic profile of health professionals in the late 1970s. First, the grassroots demand for assistance in the domain of fertility regulation challenged public clinics and hospitals. Maternity wards were filled with women suffering from abortion-related complications. In one hospital, 44 per cent of all maternal deaths between 1955 and 1977 were attributed to abortion complications (Paxman et al. 1993:210). At the same time, the population control/family planning controversy, which drew heated attention from many social groups (at a time when freedom of speech on many other issues was restricted), made its way into the rapidly growing medical schools. Similarly, the social problems encountered by professionals involved in the daily treatment of poor, multiple-parity women undoubtedly affected their perceptions of the need for contraception.

Such reactions were soon reinforced by pecuniary self-interest. Salaries of public-sector healthworkers were chronically inadequate. The multiplication of unnecessary caesarean sections, which were more profitable to healthworkers than natural childbirth, and the provision of birth control services, particularly through sterilization, became sources of extra income. Growing numbers of women and couples were seeking to limit childbearing, resorting to any measure, including illegal abortion or sterilization, to achieve this objective. Public health professionals responded to this demand, mainly through the performance of caesarean sections cum sterilizations (and, to a lesser extent, abortions, in clandestine clinics).

In sum, the impact of public-sector healthworkers and of the medical profession on fertility decline in Brazil has changed over time. Their influence during the early years of the decline was largely negative. Subsequently, the widespread demand of women for fertility regulation, and the pecuniary interests of health professionals themselves, ended up modifying, and then reversing, the direction of this influence.

MODERNIZATION AND THE SOCIO-ECONOMIC DETERMINANTS OF FERTILITY DECLINE

Several researchers working within the conceptual framework of 'modernization' have related Brazilian fertility patterns to such often cited variables as income, education, and female labour force participation. Their results generally confirm the time-honoured inverse relation between fertility on the one hand, and income and education on the other. The impact of labour force participation, by contrast, is less clear.

With respect to the explanation of Brazil's rapid fertility decline, however, studies using this approach have made limited progress. They suggest that Brazilian fertility changes are generally consistent with demographic transition theory and show correlations between particular socio-economic variables and fertility behaviour of given population groups at given points in time. But they are unable to explain specific features of Brazilian trends and they throw little light on how concomitant changes in fertility and socio-economic variables relate to broader historical trends. The following discussion focuses on some of the more pertinent studies that have used a modernization framework.

Merrick and Berquó (1983) were among the first to find strong empirical support for the argument that increased educational attainment of women contributed to the changing reproductive behaviour in Brazil. Thus, between 1970 and 1976, fertility decline was greatest among urban lower- and middle-income women, and educational attainment was judged to be a likely important contributor to that decline. Female labour force participation and household ownership of a television set were among factors cited as being related to the linkages between education and lower fertility.

Using 1986 DHS data, Silva, Henriques, and de Souza (1990) identified two main socio-cultural factors through which modernization affects fertility — wife's education and her religiosity — both of which indicate the importance of ideational change in the process of fertility transition. The impact of wife's education is complex since it increases family size through higher survival of children but also raises age at marriage. It also improves knowledge of contraception and thus increases the likelihood of effective fertility regulation. Overall, it tends to lower both desired and achieved family size. On the other hand, traditional values, as expressed by women's religiosity, increase both desired family size and the psychological costs of fertility regulation. Using the same data, Rios Neto, McCracken, and Rodrigues (1991) concluded that traditional variables such as education, income, and labour force participation, had little influence on the method of contraception chosen.

More recent data from the 1991 DHS-Northeast study reveal a high correlation between level of education, income, and socio-economic status of the household, on the one hand, and lower fertility on the other. Exploring these data, Wong finds that, among women aged 20 and over, the most important determinant of current fertility is education, followed by household socio-economic status and women's level of information (i.e., access to the mass media). Surprisingly, such traditional variables as race and rural-urban residence have little influence, once other socio-economic factors are controlled (Wong 1994:13–15).

The study by Lam, Sedlacek, and Duryea (1993) is the only one to systematically examine longitudinal data within the context of long-term societal processes. Specifically, it relates the reduction in Brazilian fertility levels to improvements in educational coverage, using retrospective fertility data from the 1984 PNAD (the annual national household survey of socio-economic and demographic trends). This source contains an extensive fertility and marital history supplement, allowing reconstruction of the fertility behaviour of women back to the 1930 birth cohorts. As expected, the empirical relationship between women's education and fertility in Brazil is strong. Women aged 45–54 with no schooling report an average of 7 live births, those with four years of schooling report 4.6 births, and those with ten years of schooling report 3 or fewer births.

The strength of the relationship suggests that education has played a fundamental role in Brazil's fertility decline. Comparing fertility profiles across cohorts, Lam, Sedlacek, and Duryea infer that fertility began to decline with the 1940 birth cohorts and appears to be strongly influenced by cohort effects. Coincidentally, they find that a substantial increase in the rate of growth of schooling also began with the 1940 cohort.

Locating the critical cohort that experienced both a marked improvement in educational attainment and a reduction in fertility levels is an important finding in itself. Nevertheless, three related points are worth mentioning in this connection. First, as the authors admit, the precise mechanism that would explain the relationship between schooling and fertility is not known. Expectations about the links between fertility, schooling, wages, and the opportunity cost of women's time are confirmed at high levels of education, but not at low levels (Lam, Sedlacek, and Duryea 1993:25).

Second, causality cannot be inferred from this study since its findings simply demonstrate the simultaneity of fertility decline and educational improvement. Significant changes in educational attainment cannot occur in a socio-economic and political vacuum. In order for critical improvements to occur, other changes usually have to take place first or simultaneously. These also affect fertility behaviour directly. In the case of the 1940 cohort in Brazil, the relevant fact is that its members began to attend school shortly after the end of World War II. They were the first generation of schoolchildren to benefit from the sweeping changes experienced in the post-war period. War-time interaction with the outside world had greatly accelerated technological advances and cultural interchange, while also improving systems of transport and communications in Brazil. Demand for urban labour was increased and industrial activity was intensified. The changing *mentalité* that was enhanced by such transformations placed greater emphasis on education, science, technology, and material development. The combination of these factors, combined with rapidly increasing population growth brought about by reduction of mortality, fostered intensive rural-urban migration, thus placing new demands on government and accelerating social change. Urbanization, in turn, made it easier to promote the generalization of school attendance and to improve the quality of instruction.

Third, although Lam, Sedlacek, and Duryea identified a high correlation between education and fertility, they were unable to explain the unique features of Brazil's fertility decline. As they point out, the negative correlation between educational attainment and fertility is one of the most widely observed empirical relationships in research on fertility. However, higher educational attainment, on the international scene, operates through labour force participation and later age at marriage; in Brazil, age at marriage has not been a factor in fertility decline since it actually decreased, and the effect of labour force participation has been ambiguous.

More importantly, higher educational levels should result in faster fertility declines. If Brazil's mean levels of education, for both men and women, are recognized to be 'disturbingly low by international standards' (Lam, Sedlacek, and Duryea 1993:1, 25), educational changes alone could not have accomplished what other countries, with better educational levels, failed to experience, namely a momentous change in fertility behaviour. Thus, without minimizing the obvious importance of education for fertility reduction, attributing most of Brazil's recent fertility transition to this factor is an oversimplification. It is highly unlikely that the improvements in education would have altered fertility patterns without other simultaneous transformations in socio-economic organization.

THE EFFECTS OF ECONOMIC PRESSURE, UNEQUAL GROWTH, AND POVERTY

Several researchers have suggested that the reduction of fertility in Brazil can be attributed to pervasive economic difficulties rather than to (or, in addition to) social changes linked to modernization. The reduction in fertility is seen to stem largely from a combination of such adverse factors as the prolonged economic depression, inappropriately conceived modernization, rapid proletarianization, growing socio-economic inequality, and widespread pauperization — most of these ills being attributed to the structural changes introduced by the military regime beginning in 1964.

The notion that deprivation is at the root of fertility decline has spawned various analyses. In the early 1980s, Carvalho, Paiva, and Sawyer (1981) pointed to the rapid social changes undergone by Brazil in the 1960s and 1970s, and to their impact on reproductive behaviour, particularly among the poorer classes. They observed that, prior to the 1960s, the majority of Brazil's population lived outside the money economy, with subsistence agriculture and non-wage labour being predominant. The subsequent rapid proletarianization drew the labour force into the money economy and resulted in the elimination of the advantages of larger families. Loss of purchasing power and higher costs of food, transportation, and housing forced the new working classes to limit the number of their offspring. The fact that real wages did not keep pace with rising costs of living in this period provided additional motivation for birth control.

Meanwhile, Carvalho, Paiva, and Sawyer argued, the country's pattern of uneven distribution of the returns to economic growth, in combination with the availability of new consumer durables, led to increasing expectations by the middle classes. Difficulties encountered in the pursuit of consumerism generated personal indebtedness. The gap between aspirations and personal consumption ended up stimulating fertility control. In this view, then, fertility decline was ultimately attributed to structural changes, which produced economic pressures and behavioural changes.

Later studies took up the same theme, focusing on household economics in rural areas (Paiva 1984) or in different social strata (Wood and Carvalho 1988). According to Carvalho and Wong (1990), Brazil's fertility decline was particularly accentuated during the early 1970s and the early 1980s, each of which periods was marked by a specific socio-economic crisis. In the same vein, the impact of the general Latin American crisis of the 1980s on reproductive behaviour has been the object of widespread discussion in the region (e.g., Potter 1990; Reher and Ortega 1990; Bravo 1990; Silva, Henriques, and de Souza 1990).

Although these studies have the advantage of situating fertility trends within their historical context, the specific argument that economic pressure is the primary force behind changing reproductive patterns is difficult to validate. Fertility decline has persisted in the face of dramatic changes in the Brazilian economy. It began in earnest during the second half of the 1960s, when the modernization policies of the military regime were being implemented. It accelerated during the boom years of the 'economic miracle' during 1968–76, and persisted unabated through the pervasive crisis of the 1980s, during which several short-term reversals of economic trends were observed.

Current data do not appear to support the assertion by Carvalho and Wong (1990) that the 1970–5 and 1980–5 periods were marked by either a more accentuated fertility decline or by a notable worsening of socio-economic conditions. In addition, the very notion of 'economic pressure' can be ambiguous within a context of rapid social change. Proletarianization, for instance, is an inevitable part of modernization and is conducive to lower fertility, whether or not it is associated with real pauperization. Rural-to-urban migration tends to alter people's value structure and aspirations, as well as the nature of their work and its form of remuneration; and women's participation in the labour force increases with urbanization, whether or not the economy is in crisis.

Moreover, both subjective and objective factors hold weight in the formation of 'economic pressure'. The challenge is to understand the particular factors that transform economic pressures into effective motivation for fertility regulation and to separate their effects from the effects of social change at large. That is, increasing aspirations can be as significant as objective deprivation in the formation of pressure to reduce family size — as correctly conveyed by the concept of 'relative deprivation'. Social and economic conditions have, on occasion, been considerably worse in certain regions than they were in the early 1980s, yet fertility did not decline; actually, some regions, such as the Northeast, have maintained extremely high levels of fertility during periods of acute crises. Finally, the attribution of fertility decline to the deterioration of economic conditions is difficult to reconcile with data that show a consistent relation between higher income and lower fertility.

UNINTENDED AND UNANTICIPATED CONSEQUENCES OF POLICY

A major line of interpretation of the Brazilian fertility transition stems from the influential work by Faria (1989) (see also Faria and Barros e Silva 1983; Faria and Potter 1990 and 1994). It focuses on the unintended consequences for fertility behaviour of policies enacted in other domains. Faria argues that, although

Brazil has never enacted a family planning or population control policy, many government decisions in the economic and social domain have functioned as implicit population policies. His work relates Brazil's fertility decline to processes of institutional change affected by public policy. Most of these changes can be directly attributed to decisions made by the military government, which aimed at accelerating the modernization of the Brazilian economy after it assumed power in 1964.

Specifically, Faria analyses the role of the state in the evolution of what he calls 'proximate structural determinants of fertility'. He examines the relative effects, exerted singly and jointly, of four broad categories of institutional changes on fertility behaviour: the expansion of consumer society, the extension of social security coverage, the increase in mass communication, and the growing medicalization of society. His basic arguments are summarized in the following paragraphs.

Credit Policies and Increasing Consumption

From the mid-1950s until the early 1980s, the Brazilian state, particularly during the military regime (1964–85), was a primary instrument of administrative, financial, and economic modernization. It generally served as an agency for the promotion of institutional arrangements compatible with modern patterns of capital accumulation. To this end, it opened up market and investment opportunities for local and multinational capital, and it sought to alleviate social pressures and to control discontent. The state also played a significant role in the promotion of a consumer society and a national market. Its policies generally favoured the advancement of economically-based decisions and patterns of social orientation dictated by the rules of the market.

Within the range of economic measures aimed at promoting modernization, those that had the most significant (though unanticipated) impact on reproduction were credit policies aimed at urban lower-income social strata. In a context of widespread poverty and marked income inequalities, the ability to buy on the instalment plan had a large impact by integrating segments of the population into the consumer society. It allowed families to aspire to consumer goods and services they would not otherwise have been able to acquire. In short, it had the desired effect of raising expectations and increasing consumption among the urban masses.

Increased participation in the market economy, Faria argues, can be seen as conducive to fertility limitation. It imposes, on an everyday basis, the need for rational economic calculation as a means of social survival and family well-being. In the Brazilian case, the fact that credit facilities were oriented towards the purchase of certain consumer goods (clothes, appliances, automobiles) rather than to others that are more critical to the reproduction of the family (food, rent, transportation, education, medical services) further increased the cost of bearing and rearing children. Hence, various state policies in the economic domain played a strategic, though indirect and unintended, role in institutionalizing smaller family preferences.

The Spread of Mass Communications

The influence of the media on reproductive behaviour in Brazil stems mainly from the rapid spread of access to television, and from the nature of that vehicle's message (Faria and Potter 1994: *passim*). Heavy investments by the military regime in telecommunications equipped the country with an efficient and modern communications structure within a remarkably short time span. In the early 1960s, only 30 per cent of all households had a radio, while television reached only a small number of households in the main cities. By 1991, 76 per cent of households in the country had a radio and 78 per cent of urban households had a television set.

Television is now the most popular vehicle for entertainment and information throughout Brazil. It is particularly influential in opinion-formation because the great majority of the population do not read a daily newspaper. Television has contributed to the homogenization of culture and language; it is a prime source of information and is aggressively manipulated in the formation of public opinion.

Although there is no evidence that the mass media in Brazil ever contained explicit messages aimed at promoting changes in reproductive behaviour,[5] it is likely that it had a significant effect

[5] The director of the population control NGO called Population Communication International has often claimed to have a long-standing agreement with Roberto Marinho, the owner of the most influential television network in Brazil (TV Globo), to disseminate messages favouring the small-family norm in the Brazilian media. However, novela directors who convened to discuss this issue at the University of Campinas had never been given such a message; indeed, they had not the slightest idea that their product could be having any influence on fertility (Faria and Potter 1994:12)

on fertility regulation. First, as amply demonstrated in the communications literature, exposure to the media tends to change
people's perceptions of a wide range of social roles. In a traditionally sexist society such as Brazil, this is bound to have contributed to the erosion of male authority, as well as to a redef-
inition of sexual roles.

Second, viewers have favoured a particular genre of high technical and dramatic quality — the *novelas* — whose contents have
tended to favour nontraditional social norms. For instance, the
family image presented is typically that of the small, egalitarian,
and consumer-oriented unit. Moreover, new themes — such as
extramarital sex, family instability, female empowerment, and
non-traditional family arrangements — are frequently portrayed
on the screen and, as a result, have become part of daily discourse.
Similarly, various indirect messages, such as the advantages of
separating sexuality from reproduction, the cult of corporeal
beauty, and the advantages of remaining single and of working
outside the home, are also bound to influence values and aspirations. In recent years, questions of sexuality, health, and gender
relations have also been broached in regularly scheduled variety,
interview, or educational programmes. For instance, for several
years a female sexologist conducted a vastly popular sex education
programme, during which the entire spectrum of adolescent and
adult sexual and reproductive health issues was addressed. A
number of talk shows and live audience programmes have similarly dealt with issues related to sex, gender, and reproductive health.

Third, the mass media undoubtedly have been prime movers
in promoting consumption as a way of life. They do this directly
through publicity and propaganda, merchandizing, and marketing. In addition, the media serve as the main instrument of
integration of the population at large, though mostly in symbolic
terms, into the consumer society. In the Northeast, access to
information through newspapers, magazines, television, and radio
was found to be the most important predictor of fertility levels
among women aged 20–30 (Wong 1994:15).

The Medicalization of Health

The health policies implemented by the military regime promoted
the widespread medicalization of health in Brazilian society. Three
main approaches were employed: the expansion of curative/hospital

care at the expense of preventive medicine, promotion of private (though subsidized) medicine as the backbone of the health system, and significant expansion in the coverage of health services by coupling the social security system to the health system. This development of the public health system brought an increase in medical and paramedical personnel and a large increase in the number of persons covered by such services.

The expansion of the health system was crucial for institutionalizing the demand for fertility regulation. It greatly widened the sphere of social behaviour influenced by medical authority and resulted in the secularization of norms that regulated social behaviour in (*inter alia*) the reproductive sphere. The medicalization of reproductive behaviour inculcated values held by the medical establishment, such as the possibility and legitimacy of interfering in biological processes, the importance of taking care of one's body, and the belief in the efficacy of medical, surgical, and pharmaceutical interventions.

Although no efforts were made to intervene in the domain of fertility regulation, maternal and child health care eventually became an important issue. Medicalization weakened traditional authority in the realm of sexuality and reproduction, reduced the psychological costs of fertility regulation by legitimizing the use of modern birth control techniques, and increased the costs of bringing up children by defining new parameters of childcare.

Wider contact with the medical profession increased levels of information about and access to effective birth control. Moreover, the great majority of women who have been surgically sterilized in Brazil during the last two decades underwent the procedure in state-subsidized hospitals and clinics. Medical treatment for the complications of widely practiced self-induced abortion is generally available in such facilities. Finally, pharmacies are the main source of information about and acquisition of birth control pills. In short, changes in the health care domain were clearly instrumental in providing legitimacy, knowledge, motivation, and means, for fertility regulation.

The Social Security System

The policies implemented by the military regime greatly increased the coverage of the social security system, first in cities and later in rural areas. Some two-thirds of the economically active population are now covered by social security. As mentioned earlier, the social security system was linked to the health system: in order to have access to public medical assistance, one had to be a contributor to the social security system, a fact that effectively expanded the coverage of both. Under this arrangement, institutionalized social security gained greater visibility, establishing a socially guaranteed income during old age (despite its meagre levels and inequalities) as a basic right. The burden of responsibility for old-age security was thus shifted from the sphere of the family and community to that of the State.

Hence, expansion of the social security system helped redefine expectations and alter behaviour patterns in the area of reproduction. At the same time, it expanded the possibility of access to institutionalized medicine. None of these policies had population control as an objective. Indeed, until recently, the social security system in Brazil was explicitly pronatalist: levels of children's allowances, maternity assistance, and family wage benefits, were increased with the number of children in the household. Accordingly, the impact of the expansion of the social security system on reproductive change was not only unintended but contrary to the spirit of the law.

THE URBAN TRANSITION

Although urbanization is an integral part of the modernization theory's explanation of fertility decline, it has been largely ignored in the literature on the Brazilian decline. Recent information suggests that the pattern of urbanization in Brazil is as spectacular as its fertility reduction. The question that arises is: to what extent are the two processes interdependent?

Skeldon (1990) suggests that the demographic transition has to be separated into two components: the 'vital transition' and the 'mobility transition'. The two are intertwined and go through similar intermediary stages in the transition from late to advanced, though not necessarily with the same chronological timing.

This formulation seems particularly relevant to the Brazilian case. Indeed, its process of urban growth started earlier and has been much more rapid than in most developing countries. In 1940, 85 per cent of the population lived in rural areas and in towns or villages having less than 20,000 inhabitants. By 1991, this proportion had decreased to 41 per cent while 30 per cent lived in cities of one million or more inhabitants. In the meantime, the number of cities (20,000 or more inhabitants) also increased from 50 to 560 (Martine 1993: *passim*).

Moreover, the country has reached a stage of maturity that is unparalleled in the developing world outside Latin America. That is, Brazil is now in a 'Late Transitional Society' stage, in terms of the Skeldon model. According to the official definition of 'urban' (i.e. residents of the municipality or district seats), some 75 per cent of all Brazilians now reside in urban areas; this proportion is comparable to that of most North American or European countries. More importantly, urban growth has declined noticeably from its previous frenetic pace. During the 1980–91 period, the rate of urban growth was cut in half from previous levels. The reduction was significant in all city size classes, with the largest cities showing the biggest cutback in growth rates.

Both the trajectory of urbanization and its impacts on fertility in Brazil can be seen as one more instance of the unintended impacts of goverment policy. Rapid urbanization during the 1960s and 1970s was due to the combination of rapid population growth (caused by mortality decline) and to government-induced changes in the structure of agricultural production. In the mid-1960s, Brazil implemented a capital-intensive Green Revolution which further concentrated land tenure and expelled small farmers and rural workers. At the same time, the improvements in transport and communications (discussed above), stimulated and facilitated mobility. As a result, almost 30 million people (equivalent to more than one-third of the country's total population in 1970) migrated to the cities between 1960 and 1980 (Martine and Garcia 1987).

How is this urban transition related to rapid fertility decline? Cities are the places where changes in reproductive behaviour occur first and quickest. That is, urbanization is a central component in the motivation to adopt fertility because children present increased costs and reduced benefits in an urban ambience. Given rural/urban fertility differentials, a more urbanized country, or one which is experiencing a more rapid urban transition, can be expected to have a greater intensity and a wider range of rural-urban information flows and experience more rapid fertility decline. Thus, for instance, fertility in Korea and Taiwan fell more quickly, by comparison to China, in part because they had more rapid rates of urbanization (Johnson 1994:516). By the same token, more urbanized countries within Latin America had a relatively early fertility transition (Chackiel and Villa 1993).

The patterns of urban growth in Brazil go a long way towards explaining the rapidity of its fertility decline. The relationship can be seen as a two-way interaction. First, given the close-knit relation between modernization, urbanization and fertility, the decline began in urban areas of the more developed South and Southeast regions and then spread outward. It unquestionably spread out to rural areas as well so that, today, even remote rural areas now show considerably decreased fertility. Secondly, fertility decline in both rural and urban areas helped to drastically reduce the rate of urban growth and thus led to Brazil's early urban transition. The latter, in turn, itself had an additional self-acting and significant impact on the speed of the fertility decline.

In short, the significance of Brazil's urban transition has been insufficiently considered within the range of explanations which have been proffered for its fertility decline. In particular, the specificities of its urban growth go a long way towards explaining the rapidity of its fertility decline. It is interesting that, again, the root causes of Brazil's rapid urban growth and subsequent urban transition can be perceived as unintended consequences of government policy in other areas.

Evidently, like education, urbanization does not occur in a social, political, and economic vacuum; it must be understood within the particular historical conditions that gave it life and form. Urbanization contributed to the acceleration of the fertility decline in Brazil because it is associated with, inserted into, and a significant parcel of, a broad gamut of social, economic, and political changes that transformed the country during the last half-century.

SUMMARY AND CONCLUSIONS

Brazil's rapid fertility decline occurred during a period of far-reaching social change, which encompassed times of both rapid economic growth and economic crisis. Government-induced modernization, begun in the 1950s and intensified during the 1960s, changed the character and locus of economic activity, accelerated rural-urban migration, and promoted the development of a consumer society. As a result, the costs of rearing children increased, and family-size preferences rapidly declined.

Meanwhile, the institutional changes introduced by the military regime in the mid-1960s as part of its efforts to induce rapid modernization had several unintended consequences, both on people's motivation to control fertility and on their ability to do so. In turn, particular traits of the socio-economic and political framework of Brazilian society during this period reinforced the motivation for, and the effective practice of, birth control.

In this connection, the following characteristics of Brazil's fertility decline warrant highlighting. First, high rates of abortion and sterilization were the primary means by which the rapid fertility decline was achieved. This outcome is partly attributable to the interplay of attitudes, policies, and changing agendas of key social actors, which tended to limit the practical availability of other effective contraceptive methods. The increased motivation to control fertility is traceable to the indirect effects of institutional changes in the areas of health and social security that were implemented during the military regime. The influence of the mass media on social behaviour, including reproductive behaviour, is also noteworthy. Lastly, all of the other factors were catalyzed by a rapid urban transition — itself the product of the unintended impacts of social change.

Overall, the influence of explicit policies on fertility reduction has been negligible by comparison to the unplanned and unintended effects of a variety of public and private initiatives. The Brazilian government has never adopted a policy to control population growth, yet the impact of various macrolevel policies aimed at the modernization of social, political, and economic organization was probably greater than would have been the case had the state directly attempted to reduce fertility. The population establishment has never made much headway in convincing authorities of the need for encouraging the practice of birth control, let alone for establishing publicly financed contraceptive distribution programmes, yet it has probably had an important indirect influence on spreading awareness of the advantages of fertility limitation and on creating a favourable milieu for the practice of birth control. Other key actors in this process have similarly not fulfilled their own agendas, yet have contributed in unanticipated ways to the eventual fertility decline.

This story of indirect impacts and unintended consequences within a context of rapid social change is undoubtedly of great significance for a critical review of research and policy in this domain. It clearly demonstrates that fertility decline does not require large-scale family planning programmes. On the other hand, the Brazilian experience suggests that a 'market-based' or unassisted fertility reduction, whereby women use whatever methods are available, can have serious negative implications for women's health.

Finally, a critical nexus of research issues — involving changes in gender relationships, marital patterns, intergenerational transfer of resources, labour force participation, household composition, and urbanization — merits further study. Evidently, all of these factors have had a direct impact on the meaning of children in women's lives, on their families' ability to support children, and thus on the motivation for birth control.

ACKNOWLEDGMENT

The author thanks Carmen Barroso, Monica Das Gupta, Georgia Kaufmann, and Jonathan Simon for helpful comments on an earlier version of this article, as well as Kerry Malloy for assistance in the preparation of the figure and tables.

REFERENCES

Alencar, J.A. de and E.C. de Andrade (1989), 'A Esterilizacão Femenina no Brasil' (Female Sterilization in Brazil), *Anais do XVII Encontro Nacional de Economia*. ANPEC, vol. 2:1051–70. Rio de Janeiro.
—— (1991), 'A Esterilização Femenina no Brasil: Diferenças Sócio-econômicas, Individuais e Regionais' (Female Sterilization in Brazil: Socio-economic, Individual, and Regional Differences), *Relatrios de Pesquisa e Desenvolvimento*, No 9. UERJ/UFF.
Barbosa, Regina Maria and Margareth Arilha (1993), 'The Brazilian Experience with Cytotec', *Studies in Family Planning*, 24(4): 236–40.
Barros, F.C., J.P. Vaughan, C.G. Victoria and S.R.A. Hurtly (1991), 'Epidemics of Caesarean Sections in Brazil', *Lancet*, 338:167–9.
Barroso, Carmen (1984), 'Esterilizacão Feminina: Liberdade e Opressão' (Female Sterilization: Freedom and Oppression), *Revista de Saúde Pública*, 18:170–80.
—— (1987), 'Direitos Reprodutivos: A Realidade Social e o Debate Politico' (Reproductive Rights: Social Reality and Public Debate), *Cadernos de Pesquisa*, 62:52–9 (São Paulo: Fundacão Carlos Chagas).
—— (1988), 'Fertility Decline and Public Policies in Brazil', paper

presented at the American Assembly on US Policy Towards World Population Growth (Minneapolis: University of Minnesota).

Barroso, Carmen (1989), 'Fecundidade e Políticas Públicas' (Fertility and Public Policy), *São Paulo em Perspectiva*, 3(3):15–19 (São Paulo).

—— (1991), 'The Women's Movement, the State and Health Policies in Brazil', in G. Lycklama à Nijehdt (ed.), *Towards Women's Strategies in the 1990s: Challenging the Government and the State* (Worcester: Macmillan).

BEMFAM/DHS (1992), *Pesquisa Sobre Saúde Familiar no Nordeste Brasil 1991* (Investigation of Family Health in the Northeast, 1991) (Rio de Janeiro).

—— (1994), *Fecundidade, Anticoncepção e Mortalidade Infantil: Pesquisa Sobre Saúde Familiar no Nordeste 1991* (Fertility, Contraception, and Infant Mortality: An Investigation of Family Health in the Northeast, 1991) (Rio de Janeiro).

Bercovich, Alicia, Juarez de Castro Oliveira, and Marcia Martins S. Mendes (1993), 'Estimativas Preliminares de Fecundidade Considerando os Censos Demográficos, Pesquisas Por Amostragem e o Registro Civil' (Preliminary Estimates of Fertility, Considering the Demographic Census, Sample Surveys, and Vital Statistics) (Rio de Janeiro: IBGE/DPE).

Berquó, Elza (1980), 'Algumas Indicacães Sobre a Recente Queda da Fecundidade no Brasil' (Notes on the Recent Decline of Fertility in Brazil), paper presented to the CLACSO Working Group on the Process of Reproduction, Terespolis.

—— (1982), 'Os Corpos Silenciados' (The Silenced Bodies), *Novos Estudos CEBRAP*, 3:46–9.

—— (1985), 'Sobre o Declínio da Fecundidade e a Anticoncepção em São Paulo' (On Fertility Decline and Contraception in São Paulo), paper presented at the Harvard Seminar on Explanations of Fertility Decline in Latin America (Cambridge: Center for Population Studies, Harvard University).

—— (1993), 'Brasil, um Caso Exemplar: Anticoncepção e Partos Cirúrgicos—a Espera de uma Acão Exemplar' (Brazil, an Exemplary Case: Contraception and Caesarean Sections Awaiting an Exemplary Action), paper presented to the Seminar on the Situation of Women and Development (Campinas: Ministry of Foreign Affairs and NEPO/University of Campinas).

Berquó, Elza, Maria Coleta Oliveira, and Suzana M. Cavenaghi (1994), 'Family and Household Structure in Brazil, 1970–89' (Campinas: NEPO/UNICAMP), mimeograph.

Bongaarts, John (1978), 'A Framework for Analyzing the Proximate

Determinants of Fertility', *Population and Development Review*, 4(1):105–32.

Bravo, J.H. (1990), 'The Demographic Consequences of Structural Adjustment: The Case of Chile', paper presented to the IUSSP Seminar on the Fertility Transition in Latin America, Buenos Aires.

Camarano, Ana Amélia (1994), 'Os Determinantes Próximos da Fecundidade Nordestina: Uma Análise Agregada' (The Proximate Determinants of Fertility in the Northeast: An Aggregated Analysis), in *BEMFAM/DHS*.

——— (1996), 'Como Vai? Populacão Brasileira' (How is the Brazilian Population Doing?), *Tendências da Fecundidade Brasileira em N'vel Regional*, No. 1.

Carvalho, José Alberto, Paulo de Tarso Almeida Paiva, and Donald Rolfe Sawyer (1981), 'The Recent Sharp Decline in Fertility in Brazil: Economic Boom, Social Inequality and Baby Bust', Working Paper, Latin America and Caribbean Regional Office, the Population Council.

Carvalho, José Alberto and Laura Wong (1990), 'Transición de la Fecundidad en el Brasil' (Fertility Transition in Brazil), paper presented to the IUSSP Seminar on the Fertility Transition in Latin America, Buenos Aires.

Chackiel, Juan and Suzana Schkolnik (1990), 'América Latina: Transición de la Fecundidad en el Periodo 1950–1990' (Latin America: Fertility Transition in the 1950–1990 Period), paper presented to the IUSSP Seminar on the Fertility Transition in Latin America, Buenos Aires.

Chackiel, Juan and Miguel Villa (1993), 'América Latina y el Caribe: Dinámica de población y Desarrollo' (Latin America and the Caribbean: Population Dynamics and Development), paper presented to the Regional Conference on Population and Development: Latin America and the Caribbean (Mexico City).

Costa, Manuel (1991), 'A Esterilização Feminina no Brasil' (Female Sterilization in Brazil), *Texto Para Discussão*, No. 236 (Brasilia: IPEA).

De Souza e Silva, Rebeca (1992), *Aborto Provocado: Sua Incidência e Características São Paulo*, (The incidence and characteristics of abortion in São Paulo), Ph.D. dissertation, Faculty of Public Health, University of São Paulo.

Easterlin, R.A. and E.M. Crimmins (1985), *The Fertility Revolution: A Supply-Demand Analysis* (Chicago: University of Chicago Press).

Faria, Vilmar (1989), 'Politicas de Governo e Regulacão da Fecundidade: Consequências não Antecipadas e Efeitos Perversos' (Government Policies and Fertility Regulation: Unanticipated Consequences and Perverse Effects), *Ciências Sociais Hoje* (São Paulo: ANPOCS), Editora Revista dos Tribunais.

Faria, Vilmar and Pedro Luis Barros e Silva (1983), 'Transformaciones Estructurales, Politicas Sociales y Dinámica Demográfica: Discusión de un Caso, Brasil, 1950/1980' (Structural Transformation, Social Policy, and Population Dynamics: A Case Study of Brazil, 1950–1980), *Memorias del Congreso Latinoamericano de Poblacin y Desarollo* (Mexico City: El Colegio de México/UNAM/PISPAL), pp. 1009–60.

Faria, Vilmar and Joseph E. Potter (1990), 'Development, Government Policy, and Fertility Regulation in Brazil', Texas Population Research Center Papers, No 12.02 (Austin: University of Texas).

—— (1994), 'Television, Telenovelas and Fertility Change in Northeast Brazil', paper presented to the IUSSP Seminar on Values and Fertility Change, (Sion, Switzerland).

Faúndes, Anibal and J.G. Cecatti (1991), 'A Operacão Cesária no Brasil: Incidância, Tendâncias, causas, consequâncias e propostas de acão' (Caesarean Sections in Brazil: Incidence, Tendencies, Causes, Consequences and Proposals for Action), *Cadernos de Saúde Pública*, 7(2): 150–73 (Rio de Janeiro).

Ferraz, Elisabeth Anhel (1994), 'Dinâmica do uso da Anticoncepcão na Regiao Nordeste do Brasil — Uma Análise de Descontinuacão, Falha e Mudanca de Métodos com Tábuas de Mortalidade' (The Dynamics of Contraceptive Practice in the Northeast Region of Brazil: An Analysis of Discontinuation, Failures, and Change of Methods Using Life Tables), in *BEMFAM/DHS*.

Ferreira, Inez Quental (1994), 'Necessidade Insatisfeita e Demanda Total de Anticoncepcão no Nordeste do Brasil' (Unsatisfied Needs and Total Demand for Contraception in the Northeast of Brazil), in *BEMFAM/DHS*.

Fonseca Sobrinho, Delcio da (1993), *Estado e População: Uma Histria do Planejamento Familiar no Brasil* (State and Population: A History of Family Planning in Brazil) (Rio de Janeiro: FNUAP/Editora Rosa dos Tempos).

Frejka, T. and L. Atkin (1990), 'The Role of Induced Abortion in the Fertility Transition of Latin America', paper presented to the IUSSP Seminar on the Fertility Transition in Latin America, Buenos Aires.

Goldani, Ana Maria (1988), *Women's Transitions: The Intersection of Female Life Course, Family and Demographic Transitions in Twentieth Century Brazil.* Ph.D. dissertation (Austin: University of Texas).

Giffin, Karen and Sarah Costa (n.d.), 'As Práticas Contraceptivas e o Aborto no Brasil' (Contraceptive Practices and Abortion in Brazil), mimeograph.

Greene, Margaret E. and Vijayendra Rao (1992), 'The Marriage Squeeze and the Rise in Informal Marriage in Brazil', Population Research

Center Discussion Paper Series (Ogburn-Stouffer Center, NORC/ University of Chicago).

Henriques, M.H., N. do Valle Silva, and D. Wulf (1989), *Adolescentes de Hoje, Pais de Amanhã: Brasil* (Today's Adolescents, Tomorrow's Parents) (New York: The Alan Guttmacher Institute).

Johnson, D. Gale (1994), 'Effects of Institutions and Policies on Rural Population Growth with Application to China', *Population and Development Review*, 20(3):503–31.

Kaufmann, Georgia (1994), 'Family Planning in Urban Brazil: Gaps between Policy and Practice', Discussion Paper No. 39 (Sussex: Institute of Development Studies).

Lam, David, Guilherme Sedlacek, and Suzanne Duryea (1993), 'Increases in Education and Fertility Decline in Brazil', paper presented at the Annual Meeting of the Population Association of America.

Leite, Valéria da Motta (1981), 'Niveis e Tendencias da Mortalidade e da Fecundidade no Brasil a Partir de 1940' (Levels and Tendencies in Mortality and Fertility in Brazil since 1940), in *Annals of the II Meeting of the Brazilian Population Association* (ABEP), São Paulo, pp. 581–609.

Martine, George (1975), *Formacin de la Familia y Marginalidad Urbana en Rio de Janeiro* (Family Formation and Urban Marginality in Rio de Janeiro) (Santiago de Chile: CELADE).

—— (1993), 'The Recent Trend Towards Deconcentration and Demetropolization in Brazil', in *International Population Conference*, Montreal, vol. 2 (Liège: IUSSP), pp. 121–30.

—— and Ronaldo Garcia (1987), *Os Impactos Sociais da Modernizacão Agrícola* (The Social Impacts of Agricultural Modernization) (São Paulo: Caetes/Hucitec).

—— and Vilmar Faria (1988), 'Impacts of Social Research on Policy Formulation: Lessons from the Brazilian Experience in Population', *Journal of Developing Areas*, 23(1):43–62.

McDonough, L. and Amaury de Souza (1981), *The Politics of Population in Brazil: Elite Ambivalence and Public Demand* (Austin and London: University of Texas Press).

Merrick, Thomas and Elza Berquó (1983), *The Determinants of Brazil's Recent Rapid Decline in Fertility* (Washington, D.C.: National Academy of Science Press).

Paiva, Paulo (1984), 'The Process of Proletarianization and Fertility Decline in Brazil', *Textos Para Discussão*, No. 15 (Belo Horizonte: CEDEPLAR).

Paxman, J.M., A. Rizo, L. Brown, and J. Benson (1993), 'The Clandestine Epidemic: The Practice of Unsafe Abortion in Latin America', *Studies in Family Planning*, 24(4):205–26.

Perpétuo, Ignez Helena Oliva and Simone Wajnman (1992), 'A Mulher Que se Esteriliza no Brasil' (Women Who Undergo Sterilization in Brazil), in *Annals of the VII Meeting of the Brazilian Population Association* (ABEP), vol 2, pp. 23–35.

Pitanguy, Jacqueline (1994), 'Feminist Politics and Reproductive Rights: The Case of Brazil', in Gita Sen and Rachel C. Snow (eds.), *Power and Decision: The Social Control of Reproduction* (Boston: Harvard University Press).

Potter, Joseph E. (1990), 'Social and Economic Consequences of Rapid Fertility Decline in a Period of Economic Crisis', paper presented to the IUSSP Seminar on the Fertility Transition in Latin America (Buenos Aires).

Reher, D.S. and J.A. Ortega Osona (1990), 'Short-run Economic Fluctuations and Demographic Behaviour: Some Examples from Twentieth Century Latin America', paper presented to the IUSSP Seminar on the Fertility Transition in Latin America (Buenos Aires).

Rios Neto, Eduardo L.G., Stephen Dale McCracken, and Roberto Nascimento Rodrigues (1991), 'Contraceptive Use and Fertility in Brazil', in *Demographic and Health Surveys, World Conference, Proceedings*, vol. 1 (Columbia: IRD/Macro International), pp. 113–34.

Rocha, M.I.B. (1993), 'Politica Demográfica e Parlamento: Debates e Decisões Sobre o Controle da Natalidade' (Demographic Policy and Parliament: Debates and Decisions on Birth Control), *Textos NEPO*, 25, Campinas.

Rutenberg, N. and Elizabeth A. Ferraz (1988), 'Female Sterilization and its Demographic Impact in Brazil', *International Family Planning Perspectives*, 14(2):61–8.

Sawyer, Diana Oya (1988), 'As Mortes no Brasil: Mais ou Menos?' (Deaths in Brazil: More or Less?), paper presented at the Conference on the Demography of Inequality in Contemporary Latin America, Gainesville.

Silva, Nelson do Valle, Maria Helena Henriques, and Amaury de Souza (1990), 'An Analysis of Reproductive Behaviour in Brazil', *Demographic and Health Survey: Further Analysis Series*, No. 6.

Simões, Celso Cardoso da Silva and Luiz Antonio Pinto de Oliveira (1986), 'A Situacão da Fecundidade: Determinantes Gerais e Caracteristicas da Transicão Recente' (The Fertility Situation: General Determinants and Characteristics of the Recent Transition) (Rio de Janeiro: IBGE, Departamento de Estatisticas e Indicadores Sociais), mimeograph.

Singh, Susheela and Deirdre Wulf (1994), 'Estimated Levels of Induced Abortion in Six Latin American Countries', *International Family Planning Perspectives*, 20:4–13.

Skeldon, Ronald (1990), *Population Mobility in Developing Countries* (London and New York: Belhaven Press).

Townsend, Marcia et al. (1994), 'The Role of Not-for-Profit, Private Sector Organizations in Fertility Change in Latin America', in *The Peopling of the Americas, Proceedings*, vol. 3, pp. 117–34 (Vera Cruz: IUSSP).

United Nations (1995), *World Population Prospects: The 1994 Revision* (New York).

Verdugo Lazo, Aida (1994), 'Marital Fertility in Brazil: Differentials by Type of Union and its Importance in the Fertility Transition, 1976–1991', DHS Working Papers, No. 15 (Calverton, Maryland).

WHO/MHO/CEMICAMP (1994), 'An Assessment of the Need for Contraceptive Introduction in Brazil', mimeograph.

Wong, Laura Rodrigues (1994), 'A Queda da Fecundidade no Nordeste: Uma Aproximacão aos Determinantes' (Fertility Decline in the Northeast: Approximating the Determinants), in *BEMFAM/DHS*.

Wood, Charles and José Alberto M. de Carvalho (1988), *The Demography of Inequality in Brazil* (Cambridge: Cambridge University Press).

World Bank (1991), *Brazil: Women's Reproductive Health*. Report No. 8215–BR (Washington, D.C.).

—— (1992), *Population and the World Bank: Implications from Eight Case Studies* (Washington, D.C.: Operations Evaluation Department).

6

Demographic and Socio-economic Implications of Rapid Fertility Decline in Brazil: A Window of Opportunity

*José Alberto Magno de Carvalho and
Laura Rodríguez Wong*

INTRODUCTION

Rapid change in Brazil's demographic pattern over the last thirty years, produced by fertility decline, undoubtedly corresponds to one of the century's most important structural changes in that society. It is an irreversible and nonconjunctural process and its consequences have to be considered over the short, medium, and long range. Given their linkages to human life cycles and duration, demographic changes proceed at a slow pace; hence, decades will elapse before the consequences of current changes reach their fruition.

Between the 1940s and the 1960s, Brazil experienced a significant decline in mortality, while fertility remained relatively stable. This resulted in a rapid increase in the population growth rate without marked changes in the population age structure. Fertility decline since the late 1970s has already produced a reduction in the pace of population growth and a change in age distribution.

During the period of rapid mortality decline, it was widely believed that the country was condemned to endure a rapidly increasing and extremely young population over a long time. Few researchers entertained the possibility of a sustained decline in fertility without economic growth and redistribution. In the absence of a significant improvement in income distribution, there would be no reason for the poor, who comprise the majority of the population, to prefer a smaller family size.

Despite economic growth, income distribution in the country has not improved, and yet, fertility control has become widespread. The results of this phenomenon remain largely unknown to the general public and have not been taken into account in the formulation of social policies. The enormous changes in demographic growth rates and in the age structure of population are not being considered in the definition of social priorities.

The objective of this paper is to present the new Brazilian demographic reality and to assess the potential significance of changes in age structure for the solution of particular social problems. It also discusses the need to face the new context of social demands that the inevitable aging of the Brazilian population will create. The first part of the paper discusses the evolution of Brazilian demographic dynamics in the last five decades, as well as its prospective evolution until the year 2020. The main section of the paper deals with the consequences of the new demographic pattern on social demands by the young and elderly population. For a clearer understanding of changes in the age structure, the period considered here is 1920–2000.

THE DEMOGRAPHIC TRANSITION — RECENT TRENDS AND PERSPECTIVES

Over the first half of the twentieth century, high fertility gave Brazil's population a quasi-stable characteristic. Rapid fertility decline has altered this significantly, however. This section considers the more relevant changes by contrasting two periods: 1940–70 and 1970–90.

Quasi-stable Population and High Growth Rates: 1940–70

Brazil experienced a rapid demographic growth between 1940 and 1970, due to a high rate of natural growth. Population grew from 41 million to 93 million people, at an average annual growth rate of 2.8 per cent, with fluctuations from 2.4 per cent in the 1940s to 3.0 per cent in the 1950s. The increase in growth rate is almost entirely explained by mortality decline; life expectancy at birth increased from 44 to 54 years between 1940 and 1960. Three decades of constant downward trends indicated that mortality decline was a lasting phenomenon.

In the meantime, fertility remained at high levels, with a slight decrease in the total fertility rate from 6.3 to 5.8 children per woman. The differential evolution of both mortality and fertility caused a more rapid decline in the crude mortality rate than in the crude birth rate which resulted in a significant increase in the rate of growth (Carvalho 1988).

During these three decades, despite the rapid decline in mortality and the increase in the rate of growth, the relative age structure remained approximately the same. Around 52 per cent of the total population was under 20 years of age and 3 per cent above 65.

In the 1960s, high demographic growth rates in developing countries generated considerable concern in the First World. Fear of a population explosion, which would hinder development and cause serious internal social and economic problems, and put the international order at risk, were expressed. As a result, the need for population control policies received considerable support.

Fertility Decrease and Lower Growth Rates: 1970–90

The 1970 census results showed growth rates of 2.9 per cent for the 1960s; this is approximately the same level observed for the 1950s. The continuation of rapid growth rates came as no surprise since, in the light of existing theories, there was no reason to expect a decline in fertility in the country nor a consequent slower pace in demographic growth. However, the 1970 census did indicate divergent trends, with increased fertility in poorer regions and a slight decrease in others.[1]

Data collected during the 1970s, however, indicated that fertility was rapidly declining in the more developed regions and higher socio-economic strata, and that this decline was gradually spreading to the other regions and social strata. This phenomenon was irrefutably confirmed by the 1980 and 1991 censuses which showed that the growth rate had fallen to 2.4 per cent in the 1970s and to 1.9 per cent in the 1980s. The changes in the age distribution confirmed that declining fertility was responsible for the slow-down in population growth.

[1] See, for example, Carvalho 1974; Fernández and Carvalho 1986; Frias and Carvalho 1994.

Table 1 presents the total ferility rates of the several Brazilian regions in 1970 and 1980. Except for the North-northeast, with a lower but not negligible decline of 7 per cent, all other regions experienced a sharp drop in fertility in ten years only, with some of them showing a decline of over 30 per cent. Rural fertility decline was also generalized with an average decline of 22.4 per cent at the national level (Carvalho 1988).

TABLE 1: BRAZIL AND REGIONS: TOTAL FERTILITY RATE, 1970 AND 1980

Region	1970	1980	Variation
Amazonia	8.1	6.4	−21.0
North-northeast	7.3	6.8	−7.0
Central-northeast	7.8	5.8	−6.6
South-northeast	7.6	6.2	−18.4
East	6.5	4.3	−33.8
Rio de Janeiro	4.2	2.9	−27.5
São Paulo	4.2	3.2	−23.8
Paraná	6.5	4.1	−36.9
South	5.1	3.3	−35.3
Central-west	6.6	4.5	−31.8
BRAZIL	5.8	4.3	−25.9

Source: Carvalho 1988.
Estimates based on preliminary 1991 census returns indicate a total fertility rate of around 2.7 for Brazil in 1990 (Bercovich, Oliveira and Mendes 1994).

The magnitude of general fertility decline in Brazil which occurred during such a short period of time is surprising when compared with the historical experience of developed countries. Figure 1 compares the evolution of the TFR for two European countries and Brazil. It shows that Sweden and England took half a century (from 1870 to 1920) to reduce their total fertility rate by 53 per cent and 44 per cent, respectively. Brazil had a similar relative decline (45 per cent) in only 20 years (from 1970 to 1990). This decline is particularly noteworthy in view of the

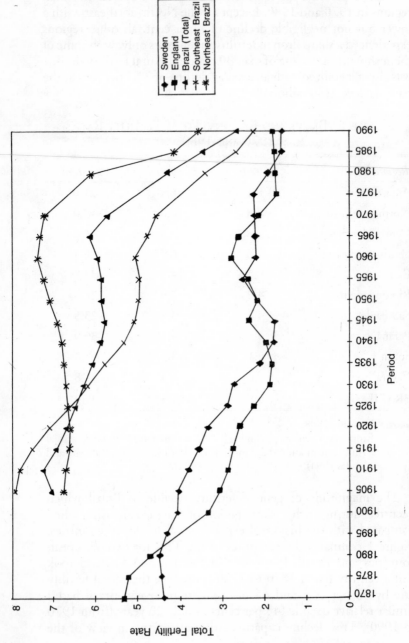

FIG. 1: *Sweden, England and Brazil (including Southeast and Northeast regions): Total fertility rate for selected periods*

fact that it occurred in a continental-sized country having a large heterogeneous population, and that it occurred in the absence of an official population policy.

Given that the majority of the Brazilian population is found in the lower income strata, such a decline in the average level of fertility could only occur if these strata were involved. Merrick and Berquó (1983) did indeed show that the greatest relative decline had occurred in the poorer income group of the population, i.e., in those families having a monthly income lower than one minimum wage. Figure 1 shows the patterns of decline in two Brazilian regions which have greatly differentiated levels of development, the Northeast and the Southeast.

Although the most obvious effect of fertility decline is the reduction in population growth rate, it can be observed that while the total fertility rate dropped 25 per cent, as shown in Table 1, the growth rate fell by only 14 per cent at the same time. This is due to the fact that in the 1970s, mortality decline partially outweighed the effects of fertility decline and that the fertility decline resulted in a narrower base of the age pyramid (population below 10), as well as a higher relative weight of the other age groups, including those of women in reproductive age groups. Thus, the annual number of births, as a proportion of total population, had a smaller decrease than that of the fertility decline.

Contrary to changes in mortality, fertility decline is conducive to significant changes in the age composition. Thus, the relative weight of children under 5 years of age decreased from 15 per cent in 1970 to 14 per cent and 11 per cent, respectively, in 1980 and 1991, and that of the age group of 5–9 dropped from 14 per cent to 13 per cent and 12 per cent, respectively. The population pyramids in Figure 2 clearly show the beginning of population aging as a consequence of fertility decline.

The Probable Trajectory of the Brazilian Population in the Next Decades: 1990–2020

In the following exercise, the Brazilian population was projected by adopting fertility and mortality functions for 1990–5 compatible with the 1991 census results. Functions were fixed for the period of 2015–20, producing a net reproduction rate equal to 1.0 (see Machado 1993). In other words, the Brazilian population was considered to be approaching an intrinsic growth rate equal to zero

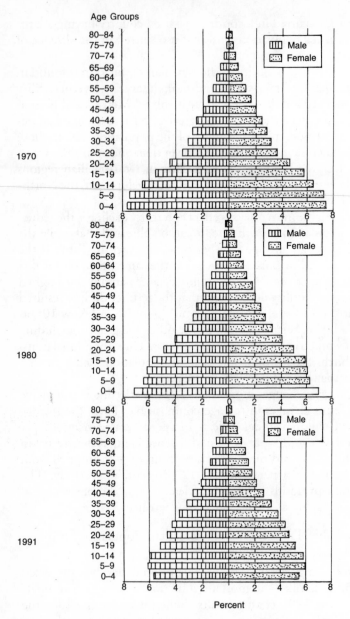

FIG. 2: *Brazil (1970/80/91): Relative age distribution*
Source: FIBGE — Demographic Census, Brazil 1970/1980/1991.

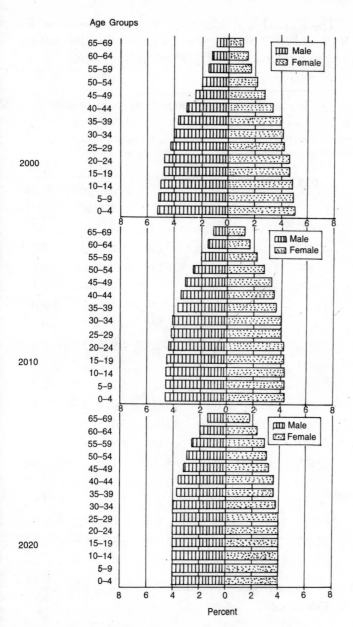

FIG. 3: *Brazil (2000/2010/2020): Relative age distribution*
Source: Machado (1993).

by 2015. The adjusted population for 1990, and that projected for 2000, 2010, and 2020, as well as average growth rates for each age group, are presented in Table 2. Figure 3 shows the projected population pyramids.

TABLE 2: BRAZIL: ESTIMATED POPULATION (IN THOUSANDS) IN 1990 AND PROJECTED POPULATION (IN THOUSANDS) AND GROWTH RATE FOR 2000, 2010, AND 2020

Age Groups	1990	2000	2010	2020	Annual Growth Rate 1990/ 2000	2000/ 2010	2010/ 2020
00–04	16043	17512	16466	16982	0.8	–0.6	0.3
05–09	17217	17041	17135	16479	–0.1	0.1	–0.4
10–14	16886	15732	17227	16245	–0.7	0.9	–0.6
15–19	14874	17096	16939	17046	1.4	–0.1	0.1
20–24	13384	16730	15609	17114	2.3	–0.7	0.9
25–29	12471	14679	16909	16786	0.7	1.4	–0.1
30–34	10914	13150	16489	15427	1.9	2.3	–0.1
35–39	9327	12182	14398	16645	2.7	1.7	1.5
40–44	7742	10569	12800	16123	3.2	1.9	2.3
45–49	6055	8918	11722	13934	4.0	2.8	1.7
50–54	5093	7264	9994	12193	3.6	3.2	2.0
55–59	4193	5515	8204	10889	2.8	4.1	2.9
60–64	3588	4425	6391	8916	2.1	3.7	3.4
65–69	2746	3395	4536	6871	2.1	2.9	4.2
70 or +	4261	5263	6656	9353	2.1	2.4	3.5
Total	144794	169471	191475	211003	1.6	1.2	1.0
05–14	34103	32773	34362	32724	0.3	0.5	–0.5
15–64	87641	110528	129455	145073	2.4	1.6	1.2
65 or +	7007	8658	11192	16224	2.1	2.6	3.8

Source: Machado (1993).

According to this set of assumptions, the Brazilian population would grow from 145 million in 1990 to 169 million in 2000, reaching 211 million in 2020. In contrast, official projections made in the beginning of the 1970s had predicted a total population of 201 million for the year 2000 (FIBGE 1974). The 32 million difference in the two projections is obviously due to the fertility decline occurring between 1970 and 2000. Actually the number of 'avoided' births is even larger, since the 32 million refer to 'survivors' in 2000.

According to Table 2, the population of individuals under age 15 will probably not increase between 1990 and 2020. Its component age groups will actually present negative growth rates in some quinquennia. The population between ages 15 and 65 will grow at above average rates during this period, though at a decreasing pace: this is because the generations born after the fertility decline will become an increasing part of this population. Younger age groups in the 15 to 65 population will actually show very low and even negative growth rates in the last two decades. The elderly population (65 and over) will grow at above average rates too, but at an increasing pace. By 2020, this group will still be made up only of the generations born before the decline in fertility.

Table 3 presents the Brazilian population projections to the end of the twenty-first century; therein the predetermined functions of fertility and mortality for 2015–20 being held constant.

TABLE 3: BRAZIL, 2020/2100: PROJECTED POPULATION, ANNUAL GROWTH RATE, AND RELATIVE AGE DISTRIBUTION

Period	Population (Thousands)	Annual Growth Rate	Relative Age Distribution		
			0–14	15–64	65 or more
2020	211002	1.10*	23.5	68.7	7.7
2040	236884	0.58	21.3	66.7	12.0
2050	242700	0.24	20.8	65.0	14.2
2060	244926	0.09	20.6	64.7	14.7
2080	245880	0.02	20.5	64.4	15.1
2100	246109	0.00**	20.5	64.2	15.3

Source: Machado (1993).
   * Growth rate for the period 2000/2020.
  ** Less than 0.01 per cent.

As can be observed, under these assumptions, the growth rate would decline rapidly from the second decade in the next century, reaching 0.2 per cent a year in mid-century, when Brazil would be reaching stationary population. Thus, from the year 2050, the Brazilian population would grow at rates close to zero and would be stabilized at under 250 million people. During the entire twenty-first century, the Brazilian population would grow from 169 million to 246 million, approximately the same absolute increase observed between 1940 and 1980.

CONSEQUENCES OF CHANGE IN THE BRAZILIAN DEMOGRAPHIC PATTERN ON THE DEMAND FOR SOCIAL SERVICES BY THE YOUNG AND ELDERLY POPULATION

At the outset, it should be pointed out that the expected trajectory of the Brazilian population for the next 25 years is not mere speculation: more than twenty-five years have elapsed since the beginning of the rapid decline in fertility. This is enough to support sound hypotheses. The decline represents an irreversible process that has already defined what will happen in terms of population and age distribution in the next few decades. It is surprising that such a significant change is being ignored by most Brazilian development planners and formulators of social policy projects.

However, some old and new preconceived notions persist. On the one hand, the idea that Brazil has a very young population and that it is in the throes of a population explosion remains in the mind of a good many planners. On the other hand, there exists an alarmist view which sees the growth of the elderly population as being so rapid that the state apparatus will not be able to support its social costs. Such ignorance of the new demographic reality leads people to overlook the opportunity to assist the country's poor, and to take advantage of favourable conditions which have been created. It also results in a lack of preparation with respect to other problems which will arise in the medium and long terms.

It is, of course, simplistic to believe that the reduction of fertility and the resulting relative decrease in the population growth will automatically solve Brazilian social problems: despite the significant decline in fertility in recent decades, problems such as that of homeless children and of juvenile delinquency in large cities have not been solved. On the contrary, the situation has worsened. Indeed, the favourable conditions created by the relative and even absolute reduction of the target populations to be reached by some social policies will only be fully explored if priorities are defined, decisions made, and programmes actually implemented. In a country with such great social needs, and which has undergone, during the last decade, a deep economic crisis, the definition of public policy must be selective, giving priority to those sectors which are able to guarantee better social yields in the medium and long terms.

Ongoing changes in the population age distribution, involving low growth rates at younger ages and high rates at older ages, evidently alter the profile of social demands. In the following analysis, the proportional distribution and annual average growth rates within the age groups 0–14 years, 15–64 years, and 65 years and older will be separately considered during the period 1920–2000. For a better understanding of the changes in the age structure, these same age groups are analysed within a longer term perspective (1920–2100). The consequences of the fertility decline in Brazil are analysed here in terms of aggregate dimensions, such as population size and age distribution.

Fertility decline has many consequences at the individual and family level as well. The current trend facilitates improvements in welfare: parents will be able to afford schooling for their children more easily due to later marriage (making for a better conjunction of schooling expenditures with the life cycle of income), better spacing between and a smaller number of children. Lower fertility will make for less health risk, particularly for mothers and infants, since parental resources for childcare will have a tendency to increase per child (United Nations 1984). There are also potential negative effects; among them, less support for the elderly if they have fewer children to look after them in the absence of a sound social security system.

Evolution of Demand: The Younger Population

As can be seen in Table 2, the infant population (individuals under five years of age) will increase at the very low average rate of 0.2 per cent between 1990 and 2020. There will be decades, however, in which the rate of growth will be significantly positive and others in which it will be negative. This will be due to oscillations caused by the combined effect of changes in fertility level and structure, as well as to changes in the age profile of women in reproductive age groups.

Until the 1970s, the 0–5 age group grew at a basically constant growth rate of over 2.5 per cent. From 1970 onwards, low, and oscillating rates have prevailed. The decrease in the rate of growth has been large and, as mentioned before, rates will be negative in the beginning of the twenty-first century. The decrease will be so dramatic that, in the year 2020, the absolute number of children under five will probably be only 6 per cent higher than in 1990. If the same average pace of growth observed between 1940 and 1970 was maintained, the increase would be 114 per cent. In absolute terms, the number of children under five in 2020 will be approximately 17 million. That is, there will be an increase of only one million in the 1990–2020 period, compared to the 18.4 million addition which would have occurred if the 1940–70 rates of growth had persisted.[2]

Public policies, directed to health, food, and other support for the youngest age groups, would greatly contribute to a qualitative difference in the new generations. Given its lower weight *vis- à-vis* the adult population that supports it, the younger population should, *ceteris paribus*, be in a position to receive better assistance at the societal and family levels. A national survey on health and nutrition, showed a significantly lower level of malnutrition among children under five years of age in 1989 than that observed in 1974. Given the severe economic crisis of the 1980s, this was an unexpected result. Part of the improvement can probably be explained by the decline in fertility that had as its consequence not only a smaller number of children per couple, but also a greater age difference among them (Peliano 1990). Another example can be found in the health services, where the possibilities of eradicating some diseases have improved. Thus, with little extra effort, if the trend towards declining fertility persists, total coverage of preventive care in many areas could soon be reached (Albuquerque and Duarte 1988). This would be the case for polio and measles, for instance, given that vaccination coverage is already reasonably high.

As for the population aged 5–14 years, the value of the growth

[2] The number of children in 2020, if there had been no fertility decline from the end of the 1960s, would have been even greater than 34.4 million, since the total number of children enumerated in 1990 (16 million) already incorporates the effect of the sharp decline in fertility between the end of the 1960s and 1990.

rate between 1980 and 1991 (1.6 per cent) was lower than that observed between 1940 and 1970 (2.8). Figures from Table 2 indicate that between 1990 and 2020, growth rate will experience a sharp drop, reaching negative values. However, there will be value oscillations between –0.5 per cent and 0.5 per cent. Had the same growth rate which prevailed between 1940 and 1970 continued between 1990 and 2000, the population of individuals aged 5–14 years would reach 77.8 million people in 2020, instead of the expected 32.7 million.[3]

The population aged 5–14 is covered by the elementary school system. The unusually favourable context for policy formulation in this age group which is presented by the change in age strucuture is self-evident. There is an excellent possibility that the country can now overcome the chronic shortcomings of its elementary school system, such as unsatisfactory coverage, high rates of grade repetition and drop out, and low wage for and poor qualification of educational staff.[4]

Given the absolute decrease in the size of the population entering elementary school in the present decade (see Table 2), the 1990s are of crucial importance for the definition and implementation of a new educational model for Brazil. The 1991 census showed that the number of children under five years of age is smaller than that of children between five and ten. As the pressure from increased numbers of children entering school lessens, more attention can be given to those children already enrolled, raising, for instance, the quality of teaching and the attainment levels of students. This would help reduce the currently high annual failure rates in primary schools and the concomitantly high dropout rates.[5] In this way, more financial

---

[3] The same observation made in the previous note is valid here.

[4] National statistics for primary school indicate about 27 students per classroom. This may not suggest an uncomfortable situation, at first glance. However, it is necessary to bear in mind that a Brazilian school very often runs two, three and even four shifts a day, and that a teacher often works in more than one or two classes during the same academic term. In addition, minimum supplies, such as chairs, tables or blackboards, are privileges of only 72 per cent of the students (estimates derived from figures published in FIBGE, 1993). Elementary school teachers are very poorly paid; and often earn less than the legal minimum wage per month (about US $100.00 in 1995).

[5] According to the Governor of São Paulo, the richest Brazilian state, '... out of every 100 children entering the first year of elementary school, only 33 successfully finish the eighth academic years required to complete primary school;

resources would be spared and re-routed to further improvements at the high school level, which now has a lower coverage than that of the elementary school.

The new educational model must be flexible enough so as to anticipate oscillations that will necessarily occur on the demand side, presenting both positive and negative growth rates in the country as a whole. At the local level, a continuous follow-up of demand will be even more important, since migration will play a more important role in the overall evolution of the school-age population there.

In short, changes in the demographic profile facilitate improvements in educational policies, as problems generated by quantitative pressure on the demand side will be reduced. Given the importance of education for Brazil's insertion into the international economic setting and the gravity of current problems in the educational system, a case can be made for the expansion of investment in the area, instead of reducing it because of decreasing demand and of the State fiscal crisis.

Qualitative Change in the Demands of Children

The actual reduction in absolute numbers does not mean that fewer children will demand public services since coverage does not presently reach 100 per cent of the population. Moreover, this reduction is a consequence of the fertility decline, which in turn is associated with increases in female participation in the labour force and with modernization. On the whole, the new process may generate an increase in the demand for some public services in spite of the decrease in population size. This is the case, for example, of preschools, nurseries, or daycare centres. Demand for these services can, theoretically, be better attended to due to the reduction in population size. However, the significant increase of female participation in the labour force, and the dissemination of modern ideas stimulating children to interact among themselves, in places other than their own residence, may increase such demands. Rosenberg (1995) forecasts a substantially

---

among these 33, only 5 spend 8 years time for obtaining the degree. In general, students that manage to finish primary school spend, on average, 12 years.' *Estado de Minas*, Sunday, 3rd of September, 1995, p. 2). Figures for the whole country are comparable: Among those enrolled in the first year of primary school, only 39 per cent reach the 5th academic year. (UNICEF 1995).

greater demand for preschool education; she points out the need for huge investments in developing skilled staff in order to meet this demand. Otherwise, the younger generations will risk perpetual confinement, thus developing or perpetuating adverse psychological and professional conditions.

As for health care issues, disease prevention oriented to children under five (a domain which is currently improving) is expected to undergo a further expansion following modernization diffusion. In that sense, media-propagated education will expand the demand for preventive rather than remedial medicine. For instance, more parents will look for nutritional information rather than oral rehydration treatment.

With respect to the school-age population, although lower rates of growth may ease education problems, it is worth recalling what Potter calls the 'perverse consequences' of the rapid fertility decline on educational levels in developed countries (Potter 1990). Preston (1984) argues that the rapid fertility change experienced in the United States contributed to the deterioration of child welfare. The reduced demand for teachers, due to the declining school-age population, also led to a decline in educational quality. 'This shift led to a lower wage for teachers, which induced a disproportionate number of the better teachers to leave the field or to avoid it altogether' (Preston 1984:449). This, however, may not be the case in Brazil where, as mentioned before, the deficit in school staff is chronic in both quantitative and qualitative terms.

Brazil should mirror the transition of East Asian countries, where the young population, still growing at relatively high rates, attained high skill levels through technical education and contributed to progress in those countries (Bowman 1987). The Brazilian economy will perform better if policies for technical training are reinforced, while the rate of growth of the youngest labour force is still high. According to Bowman, where there is already some diversity in economic activity and organization, and high rates of growth, of the youngest labour force (as in the Brazilian case) more doors are open for progress in formal schooling, for learning at work, and for the transmission of new ways of doing things.

Evolution of Demand by the Older Population

In the analysis of the evolution of social demand by the elderly, two important issues must be taken into account: 1) the absolute size of the group in question and its growth rate; 2) its relative size, particularly in relation to the labour force, since its constituents are not usually in productive activities, and they are supported directly or indirectly by the labour force.

While the total Brazilian population will grow at an average growth rate of 1.3 per cent between 1990 and 2020, that of 65 and over will continue to increase at about 2.8 per cent per annum. Such a rapid pace is due to the fact that, until the year 2030, it will continue to be made up of cohorts who were born before the decline in fertility and who benefited from the prior significant decline in mortality. From 2030 onwards, this group will present decreasing growth rates, because it will increasingly incorporate cohorts born after the decline in fertility. However, even in the long term, after it reaches a lower growth rate (close to zero), the relative weight of the elderly population will not be reduced. In fact, if we assume that Brazil will have an intrinsic growth rate of 0.0 from the year 2015 onwards, the population aged 65 or more will represent 14.2 per cent in the total population by 2050. This proportion would stabilize at about 15 per cent during the second half of the next century (Table 3). As population aging is a consequence of fertility decline, it will occur much more rapidly in Brazil than was the case in developed countries, since the former's fertility decline has occurred at a more rapid rate (Figure 1).

From 1990 onwards, the population above 65 will be increasingly comprised of generations of parents who were responsible for the fertility decline in Brazil. These are the people who initiated the fertility transition and who, thus, have a smaller number of children. Hence, the traditional role of family as supplier of the elderly's material and psychological necessities will be increasingly weakened. That is, even if there were no changes in the society concerning its attitudes towards parental solidarity, a smaller number of children would significantly increase the average burden per child in the case of assistance to parents.

A second major point in this discussion refers to the sex ratio among the elderly; already low, this ratio will tend to decrease even more in the future. In view of the higher male mortality at these ages, there will be relatively more surviving elder females than surviving elder males. That is, in a society which customarily discriminates women, there will be a growing female contingent exactly in those age groups which are more likely to be exposed to the social system's inequities.

Health Assistance to the Elderly

The morbidity profile of the elderly is completely different from that of the rest of the population, with a greater incidence of terminal diseases and a higher prevalence of chronic-degenerative diseases, the treatment of which, by its very nature, requires greater inputs of equipment, medicine, and specialized personnel (Jones 1975). Even if the Brazilian health system functioned well, increases in expenditure in the sector during the next thirty years would have to be above the value of growth rate of the total population. This is because the growth rate of the elderly (as shown in Table 2) will be significantly higher than the average, and the cost involved in supporting people aged 65 years or older is higher than that for the population at different ages. Given the current shortcomings of the public health system, the rapid pace of population aging emphasizes the need to redefine this sector's policies in order to prevent, or at least attenuate, the destitution of older generations.

The Retirement Question

Given the urgency of the current debate on the social security system in Brazil,[6] it is absolutely necessary to consider the new Brazilian demographic pattern and its consequences in the medium and long terms for the definition of an alternative system (Martine, Carvalho and Arias 1994). It is interesting that the need for a change in retirement age legislation has been justified with a demographic argument. That is, it is being argued that, in view of the increase in life expectancy of the Brazilian people, it is necessary to legally define a minimum retirement age (Moreira and Carvalho 1992).

In discussing this issue, it is worth recalling that there are two 'pure' social security systems: the so-called 'fully funded', and the

[6] The complex Brazilian social security system is one of the few in the world that does not impose a minimum age requirement for retirement. After 30 years (women) or 35 years (men) of social security contribution, anybody is entitled to retire. On the other hand, after at least 78 of monthly continuous contribution, one can apply for retirement at the age of 60 (women) or 65 (men). Furthermore, there are several professional groups that are allowed retirement after a shorter period of contribution, such as teachers of any level: 25 years (women) and 30 years (men).

'pay-as-you-go' system. In the fully funded system, the payments made by each contributor to the system constitute a fund which aims to insure her/his future benefits as a retired person. In this case, the average value of benefits will depend on the accumulated volume of contributions made in the past, the fund management, and the beneficiaries' expected number of surviving years. In this system the fundamental element of equilibrium, demographically speaking, is the life trajectory of each cohort, represented by it's life table.

The pay-as-you-go system must balance current revenues and expenditures. If the average value of benefit is the element that must adjust itself for the system's equilibrium, it will be defined by the number of contributors, beneficiaries, and average value of contributions. If the adjustment element is the average value of contributions, it will depend on the number of contributors and beneficiaries, as well as the average value of benefits.

The Brazilian social security system, as are all state-run social security systems, is a pay-as-you-go system, where the fundamental element of equilibrium, demographically speaking, is the age distribution of the population which defines at any given moment the ratio between beneficiaries (elderly population) and contributors (labour force).[7]

The age distribution of a population is only marginally dependent on its mortality levels; as was seen in first secton, it depends almost completely on past and recent fertility history. The present crisis of the Brazilian social security system is not related to the aging of the population, since the effect of fertility decline on the *inactive* (elderly people)-*active* (labour force) ratio was only marginal during the last decade, as can be seen in Table 4. However, given the present situation of financial disequilibrium in the Brazilian social security system, the country's demographic dynamics will inevitably aggravate the problems if nothing changes. If we consider a minimum age of 55 for retirement, the *inactive-active* ratio will rise by 56 per cent between 1990 and 2020; it will rise by 42 per cent if we consider the

---

[7] Only in the case of the stationary population would it be indifferent to consider, in both security systems, either the population age structure or the trajectory of a cohort defined by the life table. The reason being that, in this case, the actual age structure (from the given population) coincides with the L_x distribution (from the life table).

minimum age to be 65. The ratio for a minimum age of 55 in 1970 (0.15) will probably be equalled in 2020 with a minimum age between 60 and 65 (0.18 and 0.11, respectively).

TABLE 4: 'INACTIVE/ACTIVE' RATIOS
ACCORDING TO DIFFERENT AGE LIMITS

Period	55 or more/15–54	60 or more/15–59	65 or more/15–64
1970	0.15	0.10	0.06
1980	0.16	0.11	0.07
1990	0.19	0.13	0.08
2000	0.19	0.12	0.08
2010	0.23	0.14	0.09
2020	0.29	0.18	0.11
2020/1990	1.56	1.46	1.42

Source: 1970, 1980: FIBGE — Demographic Census. 1990 to 2020: Carvalho 1993.

In short, in discussing the definition of an alternative system for social security in Brazil, one cannot ignore the country's new demographic pattern since it will inevitably cause a relative aging of the Brazilian population in the next decades. In this context, it is indispensable to define a minimum age for retirement, a decision which, of course, does not depend exclusively on demographic variables.

THE GOLDEN AGE OF THE BRAZILIAN DEMOGRAPHIC TRANSITION

The coming years will present the most favourable scenario from the standpoint of the age composition of the Brazilian population. Prior sections pointed out the potential advantages of a reduction in the proportion of younger age groups in the total population and also warned of the extra burdens which higher proportions of elderly people impose. The comparison of the relationship between these 'dependent' groups and the 'productive' population over a longer period of time, may provide important insights for a better understanding of these changes.[8]

---

[8] The 'productive' population is defined here as the population aged 15–64.

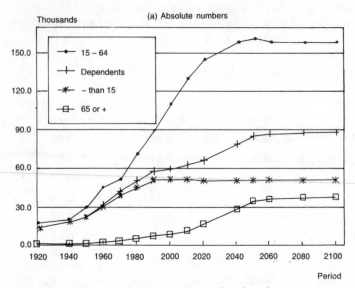

FIG. 4a: *Brazil, 1920/2100: Population by selected age groups,*
          absolute numbers

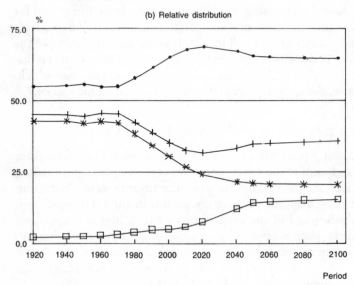

FIG. 4b: *Brazil, 1920/2100: Population by selected age groups,*
         relative distribution
Source: FIBGE (1987) and Machado (1993).

Changes in age structure due to mortality reduction and due to the dramatic fertility decline during the 1920–2100 period may be seen in Figure 4 (a & b), which portrays both the absolute and relative distribution of the population. The dependent population (children under 15, and people 65 or older) in Brazil made up nearly half of the total population at the beginning of the twentieth century; more than 90 per cent of the dependents were children below age 15. The decrease in the proportion of dependents began during the 1960s. By the end of the twentieth century, dependents would represent around only a third of the total population, the major portion constituted by individuals under 15 years of age. That proportion will probably start to increase again after 2020, which marks the lowest level of dependent population (31.3 per cent); by that time, three quarters of all dependents would be children. From that point onwards, the proportion of dependents would expand, reaching a level of 38 per cent by 2100. The increase would be totally explained by the growth of the weight of the elderly population which would constitute a proportion close to that of the children. Nevertheless, the proportion of dependents in the total population would probably never again reach the high values observed prior to the fertility transition.

The expected evolution of the Brazilian age structure, and the probable interaction between different age groups in the short, medium, and long terms, present several advantages. The proportion of children below age 15, as seen before, has been diminishing since the 1960s, and their absolute size has not increased since the 1980s. This means that the pressure for supporting young people has decreased in the recent past. Furthermore, according to the projected numbers plotted in Figure 4, this group is not expected to increase either in absolute or relative terms. Therefore, we should not expect demographic pressure in either the short, medium, or long terms for expanding resource expenditures. Instead, social pressure should stimulate the improvement of child welfare.

The population in economically active age groups, due to similar demographic dynamics — high fertility levels in the past and continuous improvements in survivorship — is still increasing. Although the proportion of the total population in this category will begin to decrease by 2020, it will continue to grow in absolute terms until Brazil reaches a nearly stationary growth, i.e., probably by 2050. In other words, despite the increase of the elderly, we can expect a long period in which population in the productive age group will increase both numerically and proportionally, as will its role in the economy. Figure 4 indicates that Brazil is currently entering this favourable phase: the weight of the population of working age is increasing fast, albeit at declining rates, and will probably continue to do so until 2020. From a demographic point of view, this large proportion of 'productive' population can better sustain dependents. The difference between population in the productive age groups and the dependent population started to grow during the 1970s, in relative terms. It is still expanding and it will remain substantial after reaching stability.

The dependency ratios,[9] shown in Figure 5, clarify the relationship between the different age groups mentioned. The burden on the

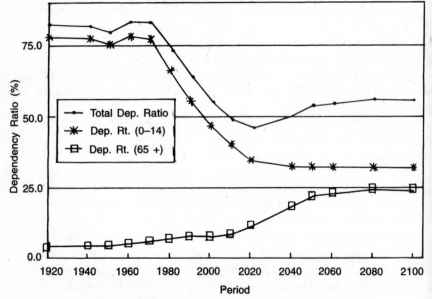

FIG. 5: *Brazil, 1920/2100: Dependency ratios*
Source: FIBGE (1987) and Table 5.

[9] We are considering:
   1. Children dependency ratio (CDR), as the number of people under 15, divided by the population aged 15–64.
   2. Elderly dependency ratio (EDR), as the number of people over 65, divided by the population aged 15–64.
   3. Total dependency ratio (TDR), as the sum of CDR and EDR.

the 'productive' population was heavy and approximately constant until 1970. The TDR has been decreasing since then, and can be expected to continue to decrease until 2020. It can be seen that the constraints expressed in these dependency ratios are at lower levels now than before, and will be even lower in the coming decades. The downward trend is defined by both the significant increase of adults and the stabilization of the population below age 15. It is worth noting that the TDR will probably never go back to the high levels it presented at the beginning of the twentieth century. In addition to the fact that the end of this century will be marked by an exceptional growth in the share of the working-age population (a consequence of the changing age structure), the labour force is expected to be further strengthened as a consequence of the increase in female labour force participation, partly due to the persistent decline in fertility.

CONCLUSIONS

It can be seen that Brazil is presently going through a rather favourable demographic process viewed in terms of ongoing changes in the structure and combination of various age groups. The country is about to achieve the lowest TDR in its history, due to the expansion of the labour force, the fast decrease in the proportion of young people, and the still relatively low growth rate of the elderly. This situation is encouraging from two standpoints.

Firstly, because in the short and medium terms, the smaller size of the current generation of children, which pushes down the TDR, makes it possible to reorient social expenditure towards greater efficacy of policies directed at children. At the same time, the increasing proportion of working-age population causes low demographic dependency ratios and should, in principle, relieve the burden of the current social welfare system for several decades. This situation creates favourable conditions for the reformulation of the present social security system, taking into consideration the irreversible process of population aging.

Secondly, given that the elderly dependency ratio will be rather high from 2020 onwards, and that the children of today (who belong to smaller generations than before) will be the labour force of tomorrow, a logical conclusion emerges: society vitally needs to invest in children today, particularly in the areas of health and education. This is not only a matter of human rights, but also because they (as part of smaller generations) will have to sustain a greatly expanded contingent of elderly people. Therefore, they will need to be better qualified than the previous generations.

Ignoring these new realities means wasting an opportunity to benefit the poor in the country. It would be naïve to believe that the relative decrease in the number of births and the subsequent reduction in the rate of population growth can automatically result in the solution of social problems. The opportunities presented by the new population dynamics should be effectively weighed while formulating social policies. It is urgent that priorities be redefined in the light of new demographic patterns and that resources be allocated to those sectors capable of guaranteeing higher social yields in the medium and long terms.

ANNEXURE

Data for Figure 1

Sweden, England, and Brazil (Including Southeast and Northeast Regions): Total Fertility Rate for Selected Periods

Period	Sweden	England	Brazil		
			Total	Southeast	Northeast
1870	4.37	5.31	–	–	–
1875	4.43	5.21	–	–	–
1890	4.49	4.70	–	–	–
1895	4.32	–	–	–	–
1900	4.08	3.34	–	–	–
1905	4.06	3.06	7.50	7.90	6.75
1910	3.80	2.86	7.25	7.80	6.70
1915	3.55	2.75	6.95	7.50	6.60
1920	3.36	2.60	6.70	7.10	6.60
1925	2.89	2.26	6.50	6.60	6.65
1930	2.76	1.88	6.30	6.20	6.70
1935	2.13	1.84	6.10	5.80	6.75

Period	Sweden	England	Brazil		
			Total	Southeast	Northeast
1940	1.82	1.99	5.90	5.35	6.80
1945	1.79	2.41	5.80	5.10	6.90
1950	2.20	2.18	5.90	5.00	7.10
1955	2.52	2.44	5.90	5.00	7.25
1960	2.24	2.81	6.00	5.10	7.40
1965	2.25	2.65	6.20	4.80	7.35
1970	2.27	2.17	5.76	4.60	7.25
1975	2.31	1.74	–	–	–
1980	1.94	1.79	4.35	3.45	6.13
1985	1.65	1.80	3.50*	2.70*	4.20*
1990	1.65	1.85	2.70**	2.30**	3.60

– N.A.   *   Estimated for 1984.   **   Preliminary estimations

Sources for Sweden:

1870–1905: Breckenridge, M.B., 1983. *Age, Time and Fertility: Applications of Exploratory Analysis.* Studies in Population, Academic Press, University of Wisconsin, Madison, Wisconsin.

1890–1910: Sveriges Offciella Statistik *Befolknings Statistik,* Statistiska Centralbyrans, Underdanigs Beratelse, Centralbyran; Stockholm.

1911–65: Sveriges Offciella Statistik *Befolkningsrorelsen au Statistiska.* (Folkmangden och dess Forandringar), Centralbyran; Stockholm.

1965 onwards: United Nations: *Demographic Yearbook,* Department of International, Economic and Social Affairs. Statistical Office, New York

Sources for England:

1870–1905: Keyfitz, N. and W. Flieger, 1968. *World Population: An Analysis of Vital Data.* University of Chicago, Chicago.

1905–20: The Registrar General: *Annual Report of the Registrar General of Births, Deaths and Marriages in England and Wales.* HMSO, London.

1921–69: The Registrar General: *Statistics Review of England and Wales.* Series: New Annual Series, Tables — Part I: Medical and II: Civil. London.

1970 onwards: Office of Population, Censuses and Surveys *Birth Status.* Series FM1 no. 13. Government Statistical Service, London.

234   Reproductive Change in India and Brazil

Sources for Brazil:

1905–65:   Frias, L.A. de M. and J.A.M. Carvalho, 1994. 'Fecundidade nas Regões Brasileiras a Partir de 1903 — Uma Tentativa de Reconstrução do Passado Através das Gerações'. *Anais do IX Encontro Associaçã o de Estudos Populacionais,* ABEP. Caxambú.

1970–80:   Leite, V. da M., 1981. 'Niveis e Tendências da Mortalidade e da Fecundidade no Brasil a Partir de 1940'. pp. 581–609. *Anais Segundo Encontro Nacional,* ABEP. Águas de São Pedrò.

1986:   Oliveira, L.A.P. and N.L.P. Silva, 1986. Tendências da Fecundidade nos Primeiros Anos da Década de 80. pp 213–31, *Anais V. Encontro Nacional,* ABEP. Águas de São Pedro.

1991:   Demographic and Health Surveys, Macro International Inc. & Sociedade Civil Bem-Estar Familiar no Brasil — BEMFAM 1992. *Nordeste, Brasil, Pesquisa Sobre Saúde Familiar no Nordeste Brasil — 1991* – Rio de Janeiro; and A. Bercovich, J.C. Oliveira, and M.M. Mendes, 1994. *Estimativas Preliminares de Fecundidade Considerando os Censos Demográficos, Pesquisas por Amostragem e o Registro Civil.* Rio de Janeiro: DEPOP/DPE/IBGE (unpublished).

Data for Figure 2

Brazil — 1970/1980/1991 — (First Pyramids set)

Age Group	1970		1980		1991	
	Male	Female	Male	Female	Male	Female
0–4	7.5	7.4	7.0	6.8	5.7	5.5
5–9	7.3	7.2	6.3	6.1	6.1	5.9
10–14	6.4	6.4	6.0	6.0	5.9	5.8
15–19	5.4	5.7	5.6	5.8	5.1	5.2
20–24	4.4	4.6	4.8	4.9	4.6	4.7
25–29	3.4	3.6	3.9	4.0	4.2	4.4
30–34	3.0	3.1	3.2	3.3	3.7	3.9
35–39	2.7	2.8	2.6	2.7	3.2	3.3
40–44	2.5	2.4	2.4	2.4	2.7	2.7
45–49	1.9	1.9	1.9	2.0	2.1	2.2
50–54	1.6	1.6	1.7	1.7	1.7	1.8

Age Group	1970		1980		1991	
	Male	Female	Male	Female	Male	Female
55–59	1.3	1.2	1.3	1.3	1.4	1.5
60–64	1.0	1.0	1.0	1.1	1.2	1.3
65–69	0.7	0.7	0.8	0.9	0.9	1.0
70–74	0.4	0.5	0.5	0.6	0.6	0.7
75–79	0.2	0.2	0.3	0.4	0.4	0.5
80–84	0.1	0.2	0.1	0.2	0.0	0.0
85–89	0.0	0.0	0.0	0.1	0.0	0.0

Data for Figure 3

Brazil — 2000/2010/2020 (Second Pyramids Set)

Age Group	2000		2010		2020	
	Male	Female	Male	Female	Male	Female
0–4	5.26	5.08	4.58	4.42	4.14	3.99
5–9	5.16	5.00	4.54	4.39	4.09	3.95
10–14	4.74	4.62	4.54	4.40	4.08	3.95
15–19	4.81	4.70	4.50	4.37	4.08	3.95
20–24	4.75	4.70	4.13	4.04	4.07	3.96
25–29	4.31	4.28	4.17	4.10	4.02	3.93
30–34	4.09	4.14	4.10	4.09	3.67	3.62
35–39	3.78	3.98	3.71	3.72	3.70	3.67
40–44	3.14	3.35	3.48	3.58	3.60	3.64
45–49	2.50	2.72	3.17	3.41	3.21	3.27
50–54	1.97	2.14	2.57	2.82	2.94	3.12
55–59	1.52	1.72	1.97	2.25	2.59	2.91
60–64	1.27	1.46	1.46	1.72	2.00	2.36
65–69	0.89	1.11	1.02	1.32	1.41	1.79

Data for Figure 4

A) Absolute Numbers

Period	15 to 64	Dependents	Less than 15	65 or More
1920	16771.1	13798.8	13078.3	720.5
1940	19623.5	18503.6	17523.6	980
1950	28854	22933.2	21669.8	1263.4
1960	44610	31769	29854	1915
1970	50900	42055.1	39130	2925
1980	71089	50230.4	45460	4770.4
1990	88677	57842	51042	6800
2000	109827	59261	51150	8111.2
2010	129633	62394	51350	11044.1
2020	144958	65832	49585	16247
2040	158467	78890	50460	28430
2050	160932	84940	50480	34460
2060	158467	86450	50450	36000
2080	158346	87530	50400	37130
2100	158000	88100	50450	37650

B) Relative Numbers

Period	15 to 64	Dependents	Less than 15	65 or More
1920	54.86	45.14	42.78	2.35
1940	55.01	44.98	42.60	2.38
1950	55.71	44.29	41.80	2.44
1960	54.59	45.41	42.67	2.74
1970	54.76	45.25	42.09	3.15
1980	57.75	42.25	38.24	4.01
1990	61.36	38.64	33.92	4.72
2000	64.95	35.05	30.25	4.80
2010	67.51	32.49	26.74	5.75
2020	68.44	31.56	24.09	7.47
2040	66.70	33.30	21.31	12.00
2050	65.00	34.80	20.80	14.20
2060	64.70	35.30	20.60	14.70
2080	64.40	35.60	20.50	15.10
2100	64.20	35.80	20.50	15.30

Data for Figure 5

Period	Total dependency ratio	0–14	65+
1920	82.27	77.98	4.29
1940	81.77	77.44	4.33
1950	79.49	75.11	4.38
1960	83.19	78.18	5.01
1970	82.63	76.88	5.75
1980	73.18	66.23	6.95
1990	62.97	55.28	7.68
2000	54.00	46.57	7.38
2010	48.13	39.61	8.52
2020	45.41	34.20	11.21
2040	49.89	31.90	17.99
2050	53.80	32.00	21.80
2060	54.50	31.80	22.70
2080	55.90	31.80	24.10
2100	55.70	31.90	23.80

REFERENCES

Alburquerque, S.P., and F.J. Duarte (1988), 'A Queda da Fecundidade e as Demandas Sociais Básicas: 1980–2000', (Fertility Decline and Social Demands: 1980–2000), *Anais do VI Encontro de Estudos Populacionais*, ABEP — Recife.

BEMFAM/IRD (1986), *Pesquisa Nacional Sobre Saúde Materno-Infantil e Planejamento Familiar (National Survey on Maternal-Child Health and Family Planning)*, PNSMIPF — Brazil, Rio de Janeiro.

Bercovich, A., J.C. Oliveira, and M.M. Mendes (1994), 'Estimativas Preliminares de Fecundidade Considerando os Censos Demograficos, Pesquisas por Amostragem e o Registro Civil' (Preliminary Fertility Estimates from Demographic Censuses, Surveys and Vital Registration Data) (Rio de Janeiro: IBGE/DPE/DEPOP), unpublished.

Bowman, M.J. (1987), 'Education, Population Trends, and Technological Change', in Espenshade and Stolnnitz (eds.), *Technological Prospects and Population Trends*. AAAS Selected Symposium — 103, Washington, D.C.

Carvalho, J.A.M. (1974), *Tendências Regionais de Fecundidade e Mortalidade no Brasil* (Regional Trends in Fertility and Mortality in Brazil) (Belo Horizonte: CEDEPLAR/UFMG), Monografia No. 8.

—— (1988), 'O Tamanho da População Brasileira e sua Distribuição Etária: Uma Visão Prospectiva' (Brazil's Population Size and Age Composition: A Prospective View), *Anais V Encontro Nacional de Estudos Populacionais* (São Paulo: ABEP).

—— (1993), 'Crescimento Populacional e Estrutura Demográfica no Brasil' (Population Growth and Demographic Structure in Brazil), Paper presented at the Seminar: Crescimento Populacional e Estrutura Demográfica, Ministério das Relações Exteriores/IBGE, Rio de Janeiro, May, Belo Horizonte: CEDEPLAR/UFMG.

Demographic and Health Surveys — Macro International Inc. & Sociedade Civil Bem-Estar Familiar no Brasil — BEMFAM (1992), *Nordeste, Brasil, Pesquisa Sobre Saúde Familiar no Nordeste Brasil — 1991.* (Survey of Family Health in Northeast Brazil, 1991) (Rio de Janeiro).

Estado de Minas — Ano LXVIII — Número 19.701 — Belo Horizonte, MG.

Fernández, R.E. and J.A.M. Carvalho (1986), 'A Evolução da Fecundidade no Brasil: Período de 1957–1979' (The Evolution of Fertility in Brazil between 1957–1979), *Revista Brasileira de Estudos de População*, Campinas, 3(3): 67–86, Jul./Dec.

FIBGE (1974), 'Projeção da População Brasileira por Idade e Sexo, 1975–2000' (Projection of the Brazilian Population by Age and Sex, 1975–2000), in *Revista Brasileira de Estatística*, 35(139):357–70 (Rio de Janeiro).

—— (1987), *Estatísticas Históricas* (Historical Statistics) (Part I) (Rio de Janeiro).

—— (1988), *Anuário Estatístico do Brasil* (Statistical Yearbook), 1987/1988 (Rio de Janeiro).

—— (1993), *Anuário Estatístico do Brasil* (Statistical Yearbook), 1993 (Rio de Janeiro).

Frias, L.A. de M. and J.A.M. Carvalho (1994), 'Fecundidade nas Regiões Brasileiras a Partir de 1903: Uma Tentativa de Reconstrução do Passado Através das Gerações' (Fertility in Brazilian Regions since 1903: An Attempt to Reconstruct the Past), *Anais do IX Encontro Associação de Estudos Populacionais* — ABEP. Caxambú.

Jones, G.W. (1975), 'Crecimiento de la Población y la Planificación de la Salud y de la Familia' (Population Growth and Planning for the Health and Family), in W.C. Robinson (ed.), *Planificación Para la Población y el Desarrollo* (New York: Population Council).

Machado, C.C. (1993) 'Projeçães Multirregionais de População: O Caso Brasileiro 1980/2020', (Multi-regional Projections: The Brazilian Case: 1980–2020), Belo Horizonte. Ph.D Thesis — Universidade Federal de Minas Gerais/CEDEPLAR.

Martine G., J.A.M. Carvalho, and A.R. Arias (1994), *Mudanças Recentes no Padrão Demográfico e Implicaçães Para a Agenda Social* (Recent Changes in Demographic Patterns and their Social Implications), Texto para Discussão N. 345. IPEA — Rio de Janeiro.

Merrick, T.W. and E.S. Berquó (1983), *The Determinants of Brazil's Recent Rapid Decline in Fertility* (Washington: National Academy Press) (Report, 23).

Moreira, M. M. and J.A.M. Carvalho (1992), 'Envelhecimento da População e Aposentadoria por Idade' (Population Aging and Age at Retirement), *Previdência em Dados*, Rio de Janeiro: 7(4):27–40, Oct./Dec.

Peliano, A.M., et al. (1990), *Pesquisa Nacional de Saúde e Nutrição* (National Survey on Health and Nutrition) (Brasilia: INAN/IBGE/IPEA).

Potter, J.E. (1990), 'Social and Economic Consequences of Rapid Fertility Decline in a Period of Economic Crisis', paper presented at Seminar on the Fertility Transition in Latin America, 2–5 April, Buenos Aires: IUSSP/CELADE/CENEP.

Preston, S.H. (1984), 'Children and the Elderly: Divergent Paths for America's Dependents', *Demography* — 21(4):435–57.

Rosenberg, F. (1995), 'Fecundidade, Educação Infantil e Gênero' (Fertility, Children's Education and Gender), paper presented at Seminar on Rapid Fertiltiy Decline in Brazil and India: Social Determinants and Consequences, 3–4 April, at Harvard Center for Population and Developments Studies, Cambridge, MA.

UNICEF (1995), *The State of the World's Children* (New York: Oxford University Press).

United Nations (1984), 'Population, Resources, Environment and Development', Proceedings of the Expert Group on Population, Resources, Environment and Development, 25–9 April, 1983 (Geneva: International Conference on Population).

Women's Position and Reproductive
Change

7

Gender and Reproductive Decision Making: The Contraceptive Choice of Women in a Brazilian *Favela*

Georgia Kaufmann

> Reproduction is governed by the interplay between biology and the social relations of gender, class, caste and race. While it has elements that are universal, it is, in fact, shaped by forces that are highly contextual and strongly politicized. Neither the role of economic factors nor the importance of gender ideology, and in particular, notions of what is or ought to be in the realms of sexuality and family, can be overstated. They drive the politics that push deeply into the public arena.
>
> Sen 1994:1–2

INTRODUCTION

The social construction of sexuality, gender, and family relations, influences both reproductive behaviour (including demographic outcomes) and the wider political context of reproductive rights. The purpose of this paper is to explore the relationship between gender, family formation, and contraceptive practice in a poor urban community in Brazil. It focuses on the role of women as the primary reproductive decision makers and the social construction and context of this role.

The chapter begins with a brief account of Brazilian population policy in order to describe the framework within which women's reproductive choices are made. Then, using data from fieldwork conducted in a *favela* (shanty town or slum) in Brazil in 1988, a

Thanks to George Martine and Lincoln Chen for their insights and encouragement.

brief analysis of gender relations as they pertain to sexuality and marriage is presented. This is followed by a discussion of the interplay between sexual behaviour and family formation in the *favela*. I argue that, as a result of the gender relations and the structure of families, reproductive decision making and subsequent action falls upon women. In the final section of the paper, the actual contraceptive choices of women in the *favela* study, and the rationale behind their actual contraceptive use, is presented.

The recent and rapid decline of Brazilian fertility is remarkable for its occurrence in the absence of a population policy and during a time of socio-economic crisis and instability (Merrick and Berquo 1983; Faria and Potter 1990; Martine 1995). Unlike many countries in the southern hemisphere, Brazil did not adopt a population policy in the 1960s or 1970s. The reasons for this are partly historical, partly political, and partly because rapid population growth was not considered a hindrance to development by the military government then in power (Silva 1986; Sobrinho 1993). Nevertheless, some NGOs were permitted to run localized family planning projects (Arruda et al 1987). In 1983, the government finally began to set about providing family planning nationwide with PAISM, a health programme for women which included information about and access to contraception. PAISM was established, however, after Brazil had already undergone its fertility transition (Sobrinho 1993). Women were already willing users or would-be-users of contraception and PAISM would have found a ready clientele had it progressed somewhat beyond the drawing board (Pitanguy 1994). For a variety of reasons, some of which will be explored below, the pill has become the most commonly used method with sterilization gaining increasing significance (Barroso 1989; Berquo 1993; Faria 1989). In fact, by 1990, 29.7 per cent of married women of reproductive age in Brazil were sterilized. This is a high level by international standards and by comparison, India and China, after many years under the influence of unambiguous family planning programmes, had 30.9 per cent and 36.9 per cent sterilization rates, respectively (Ross 1992:188).

Although sterilization is a technique sought by individual women, there has been a lot of political unease, particularly in the increasingly influential feminist lobby, regarding its high incidence in Brazil. In the late 1980s, there was popular outrage in Brazil against what was considered to be foreign intervention forcing poor black women to undergo sterilizations (Barroso 1987; Corrêa mimeo; Fernandes

1991; Guerra 1991). Eventually, a national commission of inquiry was set up to investigate 'the incidence of mass sterilization of women in Brazil'. The commission's findings were vague and unable to prove the more polemical points, but did point to the absence of a reproductive policy in the country (Comissão 1992).

Remarkably, fertility decline was the result not of interventions by the Brazilian government, but of the choices and actions of individuals themselves. More specifically, it was because women chose to limit their fertility and then acted upon that choice. The findings in this chapter do not draw a picture of women either being subjected to forced sterilizations or lacking the desire to contracept. They do suggest that, in this particular community, women as reproductive decision makers wanted to limit their fertility but did not have the options to do so. In the 1970s and 1980s, abortion, despite being illegal, probably accounted for much of the fertility decline (Merrick and Berquo 1983; Pitanguy 1994). More recently, women have faced a stark choice between abortion or sterilization and in the absence of alternatives, sterilization has increasingly become the preferred option.

There are several macro-level studies of the Brazilian fertility decline and discussions of its likely causes (see Martine 1995 for a full overview, and also Merrick and Berquo 1983; Wood and Carvalho 1988). However, there is less in the way of micro-level analyses of the influences directly affecting the actors in this social transition. It must be stated at the outset that an anthropological-demographic study of a single community such as this one cannot be used to represent Brazil as a whole. Even assuming the study to be internally consistent and the data good, it remains a snapshot of a small slice of a widely heterogeneous Brazilian society. Nevertheless, while no claim for representativeness is made, the *favela* is not atypical of the communities in which many Brazilians live. Brazil is one of the most urbanized countries in the developing world and many of the urban population are poor.

ALTO VERA CRUZ: SNAPSHOT OF A BRAZILIAN *FAVELA*

Throughout 1988, I lived in Alto Vera Cruz, a *favela*, conducting participant observation and a micro-demographic survey. The data presented here is the result of this fieldwork. In all, 76 women who had given birth in the year prior to the survey, were interviewed using a survey questionnaire. The sample was drawn from the records of a local residents' association and represents a fair cross-section of the *favela* population. It was not, however, a randomly drawn sample. Despite the small sample size, the use of non-parametric tests in the analysis ensured that statistical significance was measured. The demographic data was complemented by ethnographic information collected throughout the entire year.

Alto Vera Cruz was a *favela* nesting on the scarp slope that holds in the western edge of the city of Belo Horizonte, in central Brazil. Some three million people lived in Belo Horizonte with approximately 80,000 of them living in Alto Vera Cruz at the time of the survey. The *favela* encompassed a wide range of poor dwellings: from tents of black plastic sheeting strung over wooden poles and proverbial shanty huts constructed from discarded oil drums, tins, and doors, to robust two-storey houses, walled-in with car parking spaces, built up gradually over many years. Although the vast majority of people lived in densely inhabited, fragile structures of small one to three room dwellings, most had access to water, sewers, and electricity.

Favela life could best be described as marginal. The township sat on the edge of the city, and literally on the perimeter of municipal responsibility. The utility companies, although State monopolies, often declined to provide services for 'unurbanized' areas. While the majority of Alto Vera Cruz's inhabitants had access to water, sewers, and electricity, a significant minority had to improvise. One ploy, for instance, was for a legitimate user with official connections to the grid to establish himself as a nodal point. This user ran water pipes or electricity lines out of his home to his neighbours and then charged them for this service. This entrepreneurial spirit provided a service to its users at a costly rate. Health care was also hard to access. There were only three primary health care clinics in the *favela*, and all of them were understaffed and chaotically organized. None of them provided a dedicated family planning service, although they occasionally hosted educational sessions. For an individual intent on family planning, there was little by way of information or services within close proximity.

The poverty in infrastructure was reflected in the education and skills that women and men acquired. Less than 40 per cent of the women went beyond the third grade in school. As will be argued below, the differences between married, cohabiting, and single women were significant. Less than 30 per cent of the single and cohabiting women, but more than 50 per cent of the married wo-men, completed the fourth grade. A small minority of the married women completed their secondary education. The difference in education is reflected in employment patterns for women, which also varied according to marital status. Almost none of the cohabit-ing women worked outside of unpaid domestic labour at home. Nearly 80 per cent of the single mothers worked as cleaners in someone else's home. Only 40 per cent of the married women stayed at home; the rest were either self-employed, or had jobs as domestic maids or as skilled workers.

For men, job insecurity was a constant threat, although un-employment was relatively rare. Less than 5 per cent of the men were reported as unemployed. The lack of a job usually resulted in self-employment as a street vendor rather than unemployment. Over a third of the men worked as construction labourers; nearly another third worked as 'office boys' or waiters; while the remainder worked in various services. The majority of the men earned less than the legal minimum wage and married men tended to have a higher income than men in consensual unions.

With this representation of Alto Vera Cruz in mind, an account of the social construction of gender relations found in the township is provided. This is followed by an analysis of the relationship be-tween marital status and fertility, which, in turn, provides the set-ting for a discussion of contraceptive practice in Alto Vera Cruz.

GENDER AND SEX

Gender is the social construction of relations between the sexes. Nearly all human cultures divide themselves into male and female, but the exact constitution of these roles varies across and even within societies. In this section, the dominant characteristics of the gender roles I observed in Alto Vera Cruz are described. They are a local manifestation of Brazilian social history (colonization, slavery, Cath-olicism), African and Iberian cultural influence (Parker 1991), and the condition of social change and urbanization. Although social life was in a period of flux and change, the men and women interviewed during the course of the fieldwork held strong and clear ideas, based on traditional cultural norms, about how men and women should behave. They were aware, however, that these traditional 'ideal types' frequently diverged from practice and that changing social mores strained conformance to traditional behaviour. In the following passages I present a brief overview of the life history of gender roles in terms of an 'ideal type'.

A woman's ideal life, in the traditional view, is a straightforward and predictable progress from childhood to motherhood. As a child, a girl either stays at home in a protected environment playing with her siblings and cousins, or is accompanied to and from school. In her teens, she may begin to *namorar em casa* (be courted at home). If a suitable man comes along, they will become *noivos* (engaged), and then marry. Only then will she lose her virginity, since being a *virgem* is thought to be a necessary state for marriage. In her turn, she will bring up her own children. In all this time, the woman will live her life in one locus, *em casa* (at home). Although the actual house might change from her parents' home to her conjugal home, she will be restricted throughout her life to the domestic sphere. Her life will revolve around the transition from *virgem* to mother with the moment of becoming a woman defined as loss of virginity. For women, sex is ideally bound up with procreation. As women are confined as much as possible to the domestic world, their sexuality is domesticated and limited to reproductivity.

In polar opposition to the need for virginity and domesticated and controlled sexuality that is central to femaleness, virulent sexuality and energetic paternity characterize the ideal male: the *macho* or the he-man. A boy is initiated into manhood, often at the encouragement of older male relatives, by having sex (often with a prostitute). Sex usually precedes marriage, and it is not confined to marriage. The relationship between sex and paternity is, however, mediated by marriage. While a man will automatically assume the role of father to his legitimate offspring, children resulting from pre- and extramarital unions are not necessarily acknowledged.

In addition to not necessarily assuming responsibility for children born out of wedlock, men rarely take a precautionary approach to sex. Outside of marriage sex is practiced for pleasure, within marriage for procreation as well as recreation. Men scatter their seed quite liberally to the wind and this in turn confirms their masculinity with each child that is born. Although the man has no responsibilities outside of the family, within the family as father, he is the embodiment of the masculine virtues: control, authority, strength, and responsibility. Men are expected to be active and sexual at home and away. At home as the father and patriarch, away as a lover, a charmer. Responsibility versus amusement are the choices a man faces.

Several contrasts and contradictions which are salient to the theme of this paper can be drawn out through the juxtaposition of these male and female ideal types. Firstly, men are meant to have many partners, while women are to have just one. Men should have sex before marriage and play the field while women should wait. It would evidently be impossible for all men and all women to fulfil these roles. Some of the women surely lose their virginity before marriage, and some men probably do not. A structural motif underlying these ideals is that men are meant to be sexually active and women sexually passive (Parker 1991). Yet in the widest sense, women are responsible for reproduction (Sen 1994), which is in contradiction to their over-all position of passivity and domesticity.

Sex and Marriage

The interest of demographers in nuptiality is based on the assumption that, in most instances, exposure to sex is dependent on nuptial union. Hence, the treatment of fertile women is effectively the same, regardless of marital status. If, however, the advent of sexual activity is seen as something which is culturally determined, but most usually — though not necessarily — falling within a nuptial union, i.e., marriage, we can then explore the relationship between sexual activity and nuptiality and its implications for fertility. We need to question the impact of the loss of virginity before marriage if it is ideally to occur after marriage. Regardless of what men and women may do in an ideal world, what they actually do is quite different. In Table 1, the mean age at which women lost their virginity is presented according to their current age and marital status at the time of the survey.

Married women were consistently older than either the cohabiting or single women when they first had sexual intercourse. As I argued above, a woman ideally loses her virginity to her *noivo* (fiancé). The higher age of commencing sexual relations exhibited by the married women demonstrates the fact that the married women are at least delaying or waiting for the onset of sexual activities, and also that those who wait have a higher chance of

TABLE 1: MEAN AGE OF WOMEN AT LOSS OF VIRGINITY BY
MARITAL STATUS AND CURRENT AGE

Age in years	Married	Cohabiting	Single
15–19	15.0	16.0	14.3
20–24	18.1	15.1	15.6
25–29	19.4	12.2	19.3
30–34	21.3	17.0	17.4
35–39	29.0	23.5	–
Mean	19.9	15.8	16.8

marrying. The timing of this watershed event is determinant on
the subsequent marital status of the women.

By taking a processual approach, we can examine the relationship and sequence between these key events: the loss of virginity
(sx), moving in with a partner or getting married (chbt), and the
first birth (bth). In Table 2 below, the amount of time that elapses

TABLE 2: THE MEAN NUMBER OF YEARS BETWEEN SELECTED
PAIRS OF EVENTS BY MARITAL STATUS, ALTO VERA CRUZ[*]

Women	Sx-chbt	Sx-bth	Chbt-bth	N	Chbt-bth single	N
Total	2.09	2.91	0.95	58	0.89	49
Married	0.69	2.23	1.51	29	1.51	29
Cohabiting	3.25	3.13	–0.02	20	–0.02	20
Single	4.00	3.56	1.32	9		
Sign.	0.011		0.023		0.011	
F.	7.784		4.053		7.083	

Key: Sx-chbt   gap 1; first sex to first cohabitation/marriage
     Sx-bth   gap 2; first sex to first birth
     Chbt-bth   gap 3; first cohabitation/marriage to first birth
     Chbt-bth-single gap 3a; first cohabitation/marriage to first birth minus
                      single mothers
[*] The figures represent the mean number of years between a pair of events.
For example, '1.5' represents one and a half years. A negative figure, e.g.,
'–0.02', means that in fact the 'first' event occurred after the 'second', e.g.,
cohabitation followed a birth.

between these events is shown for the women according to different marital status. It is clear that there are definite and discrete patterns in the timing of these events according to women's marital status.

Looking at the first column in Table 2, we see that on average, the women have sex just over two years before their first cohabitation or marriage. Some 93 per cent of the married women said that their first sexual partner was their (future) husband, while only 40 per cent of the cohabiting women ended up living with the same man they lost their virginity to. The prenuptial sex for the married women happened, on average, eight months before marriage, while the cohabiting women first had sex on average three years before they first cohabited. A third of the single women had previously lived with a man (only one of them with the first sexual partner) and had started having sex, on average, four years prior to their period of cohabitation. For the rest, their first sexual encounter had been with either a boyfriend (40 per cent and 67 per cent of the cohabiting and single women, respectively), someone they knew, or they had been raped. A fifth of the single women had begun their sex lives with rape as did 15 per cent of the cohabiting women, while none of the married women had lost their virginity in this way. The average age of the women when they were raped was 13.5 years. There is thus a stark contrast between the women who held on to their virginity longer, giving it to the man they married, and the young girls who were raped, or seduced into early sex and ended up not marrying.

The significance of this result is confirmed by the Mann-Whitney U-Test (MWUT), which shows that the single and cohabiting women do not behave significantly differently from each other. Nevertheless, the long period of sexual activity before cohabitation is significantly different from the relatively short span of prenuptial sex engaged in by the married women. Nearly a third of the cohabiting women, and 37 per cent of the single women, had previously lived with a man (other than their current companion). Only 25 per cent of the single women were living with the father of their child at the time of the birth, and 45 per cent had subsequently split up (compared to 7 per cent of the cohabiting women). It is possible to conjecture that the single and cohabiting women represented one larger group of women oscillating between singleness and cohabitation. However, the consensual unions tended to be more stable than not.

GENDER AND MARRIAGE

From the above information, it is evident that initiation into sexual behaviour, combined with a normative moral order, has a determining influence on women's life chances. Only 24 per cent of the women who had prenuptial sex ended up in a marriage. It is also apparent that women who lost their virginity too soon lost their greatest asset in the marriage market. The normative order requires that men marry virgins; this has been stretched so that men often marry a woman whom they deflower themselves. But a woman's prospects of marriage greatly decrease if this first lover does not wed her.

The difference between marriage and cohabitation may not seem great from a demographic point of view, as both are instances of nuptial domestic union. But as shown above, married women are significantly better off (within the scope of poverty) than the cohabiting women. If we consider marriage as a desirable outcome, and the women who married as successful, we might expect them to be more successful in other spheres of their reproductive life, especially fertility control.

In the second column of Table 2, the gap between first sex and first birth is shown. The married women have the smallest gap between the two events. The MWUT revealed that there is a significant difference between the two years that married women waited to have the first child and the three and a half years on average that elapsed before single women became pregnant. As the next column shows, the relationships between conception and marriage, and conception and cohabitation, are quite distinct. Married women bore their first child, on average, a year and a half into matrimony, thereby not conceiving until well after the wedding. Cohabiting women began to co-reside about a week after the birth of their first child.

The majority of the single women had never co-resided. Just over one-third of the women who were single during the survey had previously lived with a man. But unlike the still co-residing women, the union was not tied to the birth of a child as co-residence usually preceded the birth. The MWUT not only supports this but also highlights the difference between the single and cohabiting women in this respect. Both groups of women had sex before marriage so neither of them were likely to marry. The cohabiting women were brought into the union by the birth of a child. Given the emphasis placed on paternity, once a man had assumed the responsibility for a child, the relationship had a chance of stability. The data do not suggest that fertility was the cause of cohabitation for the single women; without this cement, their relationships are more fragile.

Cohabiting and married women have distinct life courses. In the case of married women, marriage leads to procreation. Cohabitation, however, is more commonly the outcome of sexual relations that resulted in procreation. In one case, sex is an outcome of the process, while in the other it is the driving force. In practice, many married women wait until shortly before their wedding to start having sex. Engagement is taken seriously as it means that marriage is intended. Being a *noiva* (fiancée) is an accepted social status and *noivas* are given more freedom to be with their *noivo* (fiancé), because parents feel less protective and more sure of their daughter's future. It was not infrequent to hear a woman explaining that she had premarital sex with her *noivo*. In other words, once the couple have earnest intentions, which have been made public, and the wedding date has been fixed, then an engaged woman might cede to her *noivo's* (and her own) desires. They will then marry and, after an interval, she will have her first child.

If marriage is the desirable life course for the women, the cohabiting and single women make a strategic mistake. They have sex before they are engaged, or take engagement to mean legitimization of sex, but too early on, so that the man does not feel beholden to nor forced to marry them. In general, women are greatly pressurized by their boyfriends to have intercourse. Exceptionally, a man may decide that he wants to marry the woman, and then may choose to 'respect' her by not initiating premarital sex. More often, sexual behaviour involves negotiation, coercion, and/or frustration. The women's dilemma is not helped by the prevalence of naïvety combined with changing social mores.

Women (and men) are exposed to influences in stark contradiction to each other. It is, for example, a commonly held belief that only virgins can have a Christian wedding, as sex is seen as a matrimonial seal. As indicated, some women wait until their engagement is firmed up before they sleep with their *noivo*. Turning this practice on its head, it has now become commonplace for other young women to refer to their boyfriend as *noivo*, not because they plan to marry, but because they are already sexual partners. In the *favela*, these couples are unlikely to marry.

Some unmarried men, after the birth of their child, set up a home with the woman and child. Others desert the woman the moment she becomes pregnant (this was the most common complaint of the single women). The situations of the married and cohabiting women are, therefore, dissimilar. The married woman has planned her marriage, has sex with a man she trusts, and plans to have the baby after the wedding. The cohabiting woman has sex with a man before there are any such concrete plans and, through a probably unplanned pregnancy, ends up cohabiting. The woman who ends up single is more likely to become sexually active through rape or abuse, or even casually, but when pregnancy results the man leaves. Whatever the reason behind the man's departure, a woman has little chance of any permanent relationship and often slides into a series of temporary liaisons, sometimes briefly co-residing. In other words, these are discrete life courses that result from early actions or decisions. Although most women aspire to marriage, few actually succeed in their goal. In brief, a woman's chances of marriage are affected by whether or not she has premarital sex and, if so, with whom and when.

An initial observation of these differences suggests that single and cohabiting women may have more in common than do married and cohabiting women, apparently contradicting the findings of other studies. It is my contention, however, that each set of women has characteristics which distinguish them from the other two. The married women were clearly more careful than the other two groups about what they did and with whom. The cohabiting women tended to end up in fairly stable unions, but did not marry. There was some fluctuation between cohabitation and being alone for the single women, since a quarter had previously been living with the fathers of their children, but as I have previously suggested, the timing of the cohabitation is crucial. The partners of the cohabiting women on average moved in with them after the birth of their first child. In other words, the partners were assuming their responsibilities as fathers and 'husbands' by moving in. In such circumstances, it is presumably a thought-out decision. Paternity, when acknowledged, is generally taken seriously. The rest of the babies are then born into an established cohabiting union.

The single women, however, had often already been living with the man before the birth of the child. It seems plausible to suggest that if a woman offers a man uxorial services, including sexual ones, without the man having many responsibilities, then the risk of him running off at the onset of more onerous duties is high. Living together for sex is quite another matter from living together for child-rearing. Women bitterly related how men vanished as soon as they discovered that the women were pregnant.

If a woman's objective is marriage, she must choose to withhold herself and keep her virginity, until such time as her future with her husband-to-be is secure. Those women who yield early find it much harder to achieve the stability of the married women who waited. Sadly, none of the women whose first sexual encounter was rape ever successfully married. Those women who lose their virginity young have a much higher chance of having more than one mate. This is reflected in the fact that those who are very young when they first enter union have a much higher chance of going on to have a child with another man. These observations serve to strengthen my view that marriage is the outcome of planning and fortitude and not chance.

Despite the high proportion of women who had not married (over half), most of the women still considered it an ideal state. Amongst the benefits that came with marriage is greater social standing. Married women win more respect from others *and* their partners. While 41 per cent of married women worked for money, with the exception of one, none of the cohabiting women worked outside the home. The more ambiguous status of cohabitiation seemed to undermine the partner's sense of authority so that cohabiting women perversely lived more constrained and traditional lives than the married women.

From this presentation of the relationship between marital status, family formation, and fertility, the negotiation between the sexes is crucial. The culture of gender within the *favela* ascribes the ideal of virginity to young women and motherhood to married women. Men are offered the choice between responsible paternity within marriage and the pursuit of pleasure without. Presented with a pregnant girlfriend, men can choose to stay with the woman, *as if* they were married, and assume the burden of responsibility to the children and, therefore, the woman. Such couples rarely marry as it is not considered suitable. However, these unions are fairly stable since they are based on the assumption of paternity. But if a man chooses to leave a pregnant girlfriend, then the woman faces a life alone, interspersed with brief encounters. If men are reluctant to marry a woman they themselves deflowered or impregnated, how much more reluctant will they be if she is not the first?

MARITAL STATUS AND FERTILITY

The demographic approach to nuptiality likens marriage and cohabitation, which are comparable processes in so far as each describes a sexual and residential union. From an anthropological point of view, however, marriage and cohabitation differ sharply. Marriage is a transformation. Through it, a woman's social standing, status, and value, are radically changed. Cohabitation lacks this transformational power. In Alto Vera Cruz, and in many societies, moving in with someone is not the same as getting married to them. In the context of the analysis, the appearance of similarity between marriage and cohabitation depends upon the relative importance assigned to status, as opposed to process. The women in Alto Vera Cruz never confused their marital status. In a formal context, cohabiting women reported themselves as single rather than married (the legal alternatives). The meaning and status associated with getting married is not to be underestimated.

Any understanding of family planning should begin with an understanding of families. The shape and constitution of families is particularly relevant to the study of fertility and contraceptive practice because it is the presence and characteristic of conjugal relations that in many respects defines a family and, consequently, reproductive behaviour.

It is generally axiomatic in studies of fertility to assume that the factors affecting cohabiting and married women are the same in terms of fertility. Furthermore, in some instances, fertility data has been 'improved' by assuming that single women reported as fertile are in fact cohabiting and are, therefore, for all intents and purposes, like married women: 'In order to reduce the impact of underreporting of consensual unions, single women reporting a birth were considered married' (Merrick and Berquó 1983). From an anthropological perspective, as seen above, marital status is at least affected by differences in sexual comportment; demographers have overlooked the importance of marital status and have therefore missed key insights. I argued above that sexual behaviour is related to cultural norms. I will now extend this argument to fertility, namely,

reproductive behaviour. In Table 3, the ages of women at key events
in their lives are presented for each type of marital status.

TABLE 3: AVERAGE CURRENT AGE AND
AGE AT FIRST SEX, COHABITATION AND BIRTH, AND
AVERAGE NUMBER OF BIRTHS BY MARITAL STATUS

Women	Age	Sex	Cohab	Birth	N birth
Total	26.09	18.21	20.07	21.07	2.48
Married	27.50	20.18	20.87	22.38	2.76
Cohabit	25.06	16.29	19.36	19.34	2.45
Single	25.25	17.43	19.07	20.94	2.17
Sign.		0.004		0.05	
F.		6.09		3.13	

Note: The significance levels in this and the following tables are only shown if
the value is significant, i.e., less than 0.05; the means and significance
are the result of analysis of variance tests.

At first glance, it is apparent that married women pass through
all these events on average later than both the single and cohabiting women. But what is remarkable about these data is that, on
average, the single women also first experienced sex, and bore
their first child, later than the cohabiting women. This implies
that, although single women were different from married women,
cohabiting women were even more different. Cohabiting and
single women have more in common as groups than either have
with the married women. Further analysis of these data by way
of the Mann-Whitney U-Test (MWUT) confirms this difference
between the married and cohabiting women.

In overall terms, there was not a great variation in the level of
actual fertility between the groups. Single women had the lowest
number of offspring, but this is easily explained by a lower exposure
to the risk of conception. Only 17 per cent of the single women
had had sex in the previous four weeks, compared to 80 per cent
of the cohabiting women and 93 per cent of the married women.
The married women had, however, higher fertility than the cohabiting women. At first sight, this could be accounted for by the
fact that they were, on average, two years older than the other
women. But the cohabiting women started to reproduce when they

were on average 19 years old, three years earlier than the married women. Given that they were on average two years younger than the married women at the time of the survey, this means that they have had, on average, a whole year more during which to have another baby. I propose that the higher level of fertility exhibited by the married women is due to the fact that, although they begin their sexual lives later, they started with the intent of having a family and planned when to have children (in a batch). The cohabiting women started haphazardly, earlier, and then contracepted (less efficiently). Single women were therefore more open to chance.

Women who negotiate well sexually do better in life; they get married, which is a desirable state. For almost every social or economic indicator, married women are better off than unwed women. Given that the married women are better placed or able to negotiate the mating game, as well as being more materially successful, we must ask how this affects their contraceptive practice.

CONTRACEPTION IN A *FAVELA*

It was mentioned previously that the Brazilian government's approach to family planning had been reluctant. Yet in 1988, within a year after their last birth, the majority (78 per cent) of the reproductively active women in this poor township, without easy access to a family planning clinic, were seeking to control their fertility in some way. Overall, 42 per cent of women were taking the pill, 20 per cent were sterilized, 7 per cent were using IUDs, 5 per cent were using condoms, 3 per cent natural methods (i.e., the rhythm method), and only 2 per cent practiced coitus interruptus.

This differs somewhat from the pattern found in the 1986 national DHS/BEMFAM survey. In the national survey, 27 per cent of women aged 15–44 in unions were sterilized, greater than the 25 per cent using the pill, but less than the 34 per cent using no method. The rate of sterilization was even higher (30 per cent) for the urban populations in the survey (Arruda et al. 1987:10–78). The differences between the two surveys are not, however, startling, and are largely due to age differences: the Alto Vera Cruz survey population was somewhat younger than would be a truly representative cross-section of the 15–44 age group.

The focus of this paper is on the manifestation of gender relations, through marriage, on fertility and therefore contraception.

In Table 4 below, the pattern of contraceptive use by marital status is shown.

TABLE 4: PERCENTAGE OF WOMEN USING A CONTRACEPTIVE METHOD BY MARITAL STATUS

Women	%	ANOVA significance	ANOVA F	Mann-Whitney U-Test variables	MWUT sign.
All Women	78				
Marital Status					
Married	88	.0014	7.4317	married/single	.0068
Cohabiting	94			cohabiting/single	.0044
Single	50				

The MWUT shows that single women contracepted significantly less than married or cohabiting women. By definition, the single women were not in a permanent sexual union and therefore arguably less in need of protection (although it was the lack of protection in the past that resulted in them becoming single mothers). The difference between married and cohabiting women is striking. Despite the fact that they all lived in conjugal unions, the cohabiting women contracepted significantly less than did the married women. I argued above that the married women exhibited greater control in their sexual deportment, and that following marriage they controlled their fertility more effectively than the other women. But these data suggest that the cohabiting women have a different approach to contraception.

Married women appear to be in a position of the greatest relative security. They and their husbands sustained the highest levels of income, education, and security, in the survey. The women were also more independent than their cohabiting counterparts. The cohabiting women were more constrained in their domestic relations and were in a weaker position relative to their partners, lacking the advantage of a marriage certificate. This is reflected in contraceptive practices. The data from Alto Vera Cruz do show a pattern of variation in the choice of methods according to marital status.

In total, 78 per cent were contracepting: 42 per cent were taking the pill, 20 per cent were sterilized, and the remainder were using the various other methods. Pill use and sterilization, therefore, accounted for over 60 per cent of the women in the survey and nearly 80 per cent of the contracepting women. This pattern is not uniform if we consider marital status and gender relations. In Table 5 the data for contraceptive use by women's marital status is presented.

TABLE 5: PERCENTAGE OF WOMEN USING A
CONTRACEPTIVE METHOD BY MARITAL STATUS

Method	Marital status			
	Married	Cohabiting	Single	Total
Pill	64	31	67	53
IUD	0	19	11	9
Sterilized	27	31	11	26
Condom	5	6	11	6
Natural method	5	6	0	4
Withdrawel	0	6	0	2

Married women were twice as likely to use the pill than the cohabiting women, but pill use was highest amongst the single women. The most interesting pattern was the fact that a higher proportion of cohabiting as opposed to married women got sterilized and that none of the married women were using IUDs. In the following section, the pros and cons of the different methods will be discussed in the light of the different patterns of use within a *favela* setting.

CONTRACEPTIVE CHOICE

The Pill

The Pill was the most popular contraceptive choice in Alto Vera Cruz. The chief advantage of the pill over other methods was that it was readily available in practice and not too expensive. Of the women who had been using the pill in the year prior to the survey, only 32 per cent had been advised to do so by their doctor. The rest had followed the advice of friends and family, or their own initiative. The high rate of self-referral means that 60 per cent of the pill users (46 per cent of all women) had to buy their own pills; only those who saw a doctor first had prescriptions.

Because of the need to obtain the pill by medical prescriptions, many women were taking pills that might not have been suitable for them. Expectedly, many women had stopped using the pill previously, complaining of side effects. One woman alleged that the pills from the Red Cross were 'very strong, they made me feel ill, and in addition to that they don't have a name. You can't take medicines without knowing what you're taking, so I stopped taking them' (Rosa Maria).

The pill was the most reliable of the methods used by the women (68–76 per cent). Since the pill is theoretically 98 per cent reliable, this indicates that women were taking it inefficiently and incorrectly. When current pill users were asked how they were taking it, a wide disparity in the level of comprehension of the pill and how it worked became apparent. Only 68 per cent of the women were taking it according to the instructions on the packet, 4 per cent took it without interruption, 4 per cent only after sex, and 24 per cent according to their own ideas.

Despite the side effects, the pill is relatively cheap, and this was sometimes explicitly given as the reason for using this method (one informant, Maurisa, said that she used the pill because she could not afford condoms). Given the apparent availability, the greater reliability, and lower cost of the pill, it is not surprising to find it was the most popular contraceptive method.

Over 60 per cent of the married women and single women were using the pill, but not even a third of the cohabiting women opted for this method, despite its accessibility. Pill users were more likely to be self-starters, women seeking actively to control their fertility. It is thus fitting that the married women were more likely to be using it than the cohabiting women. The low efficiency rates of the method owe more to the lack of public health information than to the women's lack of willingness. The high use by single women is less easy to explain in terms other than availability.

The IUD

Of the other devices used to avoid conception, the IUD was marginally more popular than the condom. Some 8.5 per cent of the currently contracepting women interviewed were using the IUD, as compared to 6.4 per cent using condoms. The IUD, was well-known, but very few women knew where to get it (at government hospitals, health centres, and the Red Cross). Having the IUD fitted also required time and patience for all the various appointments necessary, in addition to regular check-ups thereafter.

In any event, while half the women thought there were no problems with it, 13 per cent thought that it created health problems and 37 per cent thought that it was not reliable. Although the IUD in theory has a 1.5 per cent failure rate, in practice the failure rate in the USA was marginally higher at 4 per cent (Boston Women's Health Book Collective 1984). It seems that the success rate of the IUD was actually low in Alto Vera Cruz, and the women were justified in their low expectations of it. The IUD must be fitted in properly sterile conditions by a skilled person. The Brazilian public health sector, which is the primary source of IUDs for poor people, is understaffed, underpaid, and ill-equipped. An IUD also needs to be properly monitored at least once a year. In such conditions, the procedures necessary for maintaining a well-fitted, reliable, and safe IUD are hard to ensure, so that despite the theoretical reliability of the IUD, it is not particularly popular.

None of the married women opted for this method, although nearly 20 per cent of the cohabiting women and 11 per cent of the single women were using the IUD. The IUD can only be used following medical intervention. Building on the hypothesis that married women are more in control of their lives than the other women, it is noteworthy that they did not use this 'risky' and unpopular method. I have characterized single and cohabiting women as less in control, more passive than active in running their lives, and the data show them to be more likely recipients of the IUD, a medical intervention.

The Condom

Only 6.4 per cent of the contracepting women and their partners were using condoms. Condoms come in three varieties in Brazil: imported, Jontex (made under licence from Johnson and Johnson), and local brands. The imported ones are very expensive and are found only in specialist 'sex' shops. Costing more than the price of a cheap prostitute, they are beyond the means of the *favela* inhabitants (*favelados*). The Jontex are widely available in supermarkets and upmarket pharmacies, but even they cost more than a dollar

apiece, still prohibitively expensive for the *favelados*. In the neighbourhood pharmacies, however, the local brands are available and
within the price range of the *favelados*. The drawback is that the
quality control is apparently not consistent and they are prone to
break. Given that they are bought locally, there is a further disin-
centive: shame. Several of the women who used condoms added that
they felt too ashamed to purchase them, so their partners' help was
necessary.

Condoms thus required the willing cooperation of men, not
just in use but also in acquisition. Male attitudes about sex and
contraception tended not to conform with women's, making such
cooperation unusual. This is the only method which the single
women were more likely to use than the other women. For men,
reproduction is the normative outcome of sex within marriage,
it is the causal force behind cohabitation, but it is not the necessary
aim of extramarital recreational sex. It is not without significance
that men more willingly used condoms with their girlfriends than
with wives and partners.

The least popular methods were coitus interruptus (6 per cent)
and the rhythm method (4 per cent), neither of which are particularly reliable. The alternatives to all of the above are sterilization,
abstention, pregnancy or, as a last resort, abortion.

Sterilization: Fertility Limitation

As of 1986, 27 per cent of all currently married Brazilian women
in reproductive age groups were sterilized by tubal ligation according to the Demographie and Health Survey of 1986. As
mentioned in the introduction to this chapter, such relatively
high rates have been the object of much controversy. In some
circles, the implication is that a large number of women have
somehow been coerced into sterilization against their will or
without their knowledge. The evidence from Alto Vera Cruz,
however, does not seem to indicate that any group was forced
into sterilization. On the contrary, many women were actively
seeking sterilization, or had already secured it.

In Alto Vera Cruz, only one-fifth of the women had been sterilized, but it is likely that this smaller proportion than the national
average is explained by a younger age distribution. The national
rates were highest amongst the 35–39 year old, an age group that

was underrepresented in the sample. Perhaps more important was the fact that, of the remaining women, nearly a third who were neither pregnant nor sterilized, wanted to be sterilized.

Nearly half of the women in Alto Vera Cruz who were sterilized underwent the procedure when they were less than 25 years old and had fewer than four children. Their young age belies the fact that the average duration of unions before sterilization was just over seven years. Figure 1 shows the proportion of women in different age groups at sterilization, and Figure 2 their parity at sterilization.

One of the contributing factors to the high rates of sterilization was the common practice of (repeated) delivery by caesarean section and subsequent sterilization. Medical training and the higher pay for caesarean over natural deliveries encouraged these high rates. Between 1971 and 1980, the percentage of caesarean births rose from 15 to 30 per cent in Brazil (Merrick and Berquó 1983). In Alto Vera Cruz, some 25 per cent of last births were by caesarean section. This implies that many of these mothers would likely be sterilized in the future; having had a caesarean procedure once, all subsequent births are similarly delivered. After two or three cae-sareans, sterilization is both the recommendation and the practice. This association between caesarean section and sterilization was

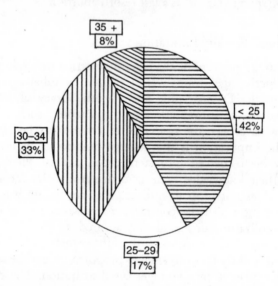

FIG. 1: *Age of women at sterilization*

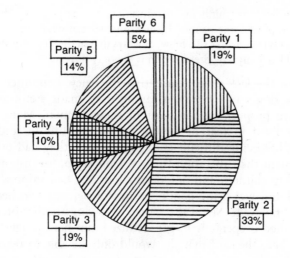

Fɪɢ. 2: *Parity of women at sterilization*

borne out in Alto Vera Cruz: 25 per cent of the women having had caesareans at their last birth were sterilized at the same time. An additional 16 per cent of the women had been sterilized since giving birth in the calendar year prior to the interview. Over 80 per cent of the women thought that they had had caesareans for medical reasons, while 17 per cent had them specifically for the purpose of getting access to sterilization.

More importantly, high levels of sterilization were attributable to the difficulties in getting access to effective contraception. Steriliza-tion was the common goal for many women because of its reliability. Many of the women were very dubious about the reliability of other methods:

> Sterilization is the only one that's any good. Because the IUD is abor-tive, it makes you abort once a month. The pill ruins a woman's health, but, unfortunately, it's the only one that is reliable, and the rhythm is far too risky. (Graça)

The need to contracept is great, otherwise: 'the little creatures will die of hunger' (Luceni). Fatima, one of the most educated respondents, was emphatic about the importance of sterilization:

> If you want contraception then you can get it, there are plenty of uneducated women who make sure that they don't get pregnant. But

the problem is mainly one of education. You can't get anything into the heads of some people. I know one woman who, every time her period is late, drinks this brew. She says that in the first month it's not a real baby anyway. Sterilization is the only way.

Thus, the lack of contraceptive efficiency, combined with a genuine desire to limit their family sizes, made sterilization an attractive proposition for most of these women. Many of the women lived in fear of having another mouth to feed; their current life being difficult enough as it was, they had no desire to augment their privation further. Conceição, for instance, had five living children and one dead child. She had stopped taking the pill and was using condoms but for her, sex had become a frightening event. She was terrified of having another pregnancy and wanted desperately to get sterilized, but her husband would not let her. She said that she would only be able to relax if she knew that she could not get pregnant again. A common predicament was that, depending on local regulations, a woman was required to be a certain age and parity before becoming eligible for sterilization. Unless a woman was lucky, the only way she could be sterilized was arranging with her doctor (having met all the official requirements) to have a caesarean delivery and have a tubal ligation at the same time. Several women explained to me that the only way they could guarantee limiting their family size was to get pregnant again in order to arrange to be sterilized. There were instances when women, who previously arranged for sterilization during birth, delivered in the hospital when their doctor was not on call. Much to their chagrin, they underwent the caesarean delivery without having their tubes tied.

On the other hand, many of the women who reported that they wanted to and knew how to get sterilized, had not done so, as of the survey date. Figure 3 shows the reasons for this apparent failure. Nearly 40 per cent of these women had their intentions thwarted by medical and institutional objections, and 31 per cent were trying to have the operation done outside of the state system, i.e., privately, but didn't have enough money for it.

In summary, far from finding a situation in which large numbers of women were being led out of ignorance or reluctance to have their tubes tied, many women were actively seeking or had already secured sterilization, seeing it as a solution to the problems of increasing numbers of mouths to feed.

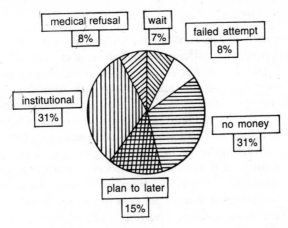

FIG. 3: *Percentage of women by reason for not getting sterilized*

It is interesting that more cohabiting women had caesareans and underwent sterilization than married women. The incidence of caesareans at last birth ranged from 21 per cent amongst married women to 30 per cent amongst cohabiting women. Rates of sterilization were 21 per cent among married women and 26 per cent among cohabiting women.

Given the fact that cohabiting women rarely worked outside the home, and in many respects were governed more authoritatively by their partners than a married woman by her husband, it is curious that cohabiting women were more successful in gaining access to an effective and seemingly universally-desired method. This may be explained by the fact that, although tubal ligation is the most reliable method, it's emotional finality is less pleasing. Married women, who tended to have more stable relationships and better economic situations, had more contraceptive options and ended up choosing other methods in preference to sterilization. The cohabiting women were less consistent in their family planning efforts and, thus, tended to the use of IUDs and sterilization. In other words, the desirability of sterilization was inversely related to the ability of women to contracept efficiently.

In brief, if there was any coercion regarding sterilization, it came not from outside pressure groups, but rather from the practical lack of effective alternatives to fertility regulation, given the circumstances in which women lived.

ABORTION: THE LAST RESORT

For all women, when contraception failed or was not used, an unwanted pregnancy offered two choices: abortion, or another mouth to feed. It was not easy to get accurate measurements of the incidence of abortion (Kaufmann 1991). Abortion is illegal in Brazil, except if the woman's life is endangered by the pregnancy, or if the pregnancy is the result of a rape. Only 4 per cent of the women in the survey admitted to having had abortions, although several more mentioned experiencing 'miscarriages'. Outside of the formal question and answer sessions of the survey, I found that abortion was far from infrequent. Moreover, an earlier survey revealed that 35 per cent of women in other *favelas* in Belo Horizonte had had abortions. The women interviewed always knew of 'someone else' who had had one:

> Life is so hard that we have to take precautions. If you're single you try everything to avoid getting pregnant. But if you're married . . . I know lots of women who've had 5 abortions. I never have, I'm frightened of dying. (Maurisa)

The likely explanation for low abortion rates in Alto Vera Cruz is a reluctance to disclose the perpetration of a legally and seemingly morally-censured act. There is much debate in Brazil about the morality of abortion and in Alto Vera Cruz, abortion can be loudly condemned:

> Abortion is unjust. A while ago they found a 3 kg baby in the toilet; its back was broken in an attempt to push it down. Dead. It's wrong. (Elisabeth; the toilet referred to was a communal toilet for several families)

One of the questions asked during the survey was about knowledge of other contraceptive techniques. Respondents often mentioned abortion brews or douches; teas made with cloves, cinnamon, or fennel seeds, are thought to be abortifacients. Alternatively, it was common to drink alcohol in excess in order to 'bring on' the menstrual period. Drugs sold over the pharmaceutical counter (ostensibly for other purposes) were also taken as abortifacients. Finally, if all else failed, a woman may have resorted to a back street abortionist who inserts a probe into her uterus. Doing so, a woman risks infection, injury, as well as potentially being discovered. For example, one of my informants began by taking pills which did not work. She already had two children that she could barely support and out of desperation, she borrowed money to visit an abortionist. The price was more than one-third of the legal minimum monthly salary. The abortionist inserted a probe into her uterus but it fell out the following day so she had to go back. Two days later she went into labour and aborted a live foetus/infant that soon died. It was thrown away on the extended area of wasteland above Alto Vera Cruz:

> I threw it into a hole above the waste. I couldn't bury it because I was afraid to get caught. There, no one would suspect it was me . . . everyone is already commenting that my stomach has got flatter.

In short, where contraception is hard to get or difficult to use easily or effectively, if the women do not want children they turn to abortion as a last resort regardless of its legality or risks. Abortion appears to be something that most women knew how to obtain either through self-help or by knowing where to go. The woman in the above example went to an abortionist that a friend of hers had gone to three times before.

Whatever the rights and wrongs of abortion, the failure of alternative means of family planning is creating a continuous stream of women who risk their lives and break the law in order to obtain a clandestine abortion. The fact that abortion is illegal simply increases the risk and the sense of degradation that these women experience on a daily basis. The costs of clandestine abortions also impose high costs on the health service. The lack of hygiene and medication associated with backstreet abortions results in high rates of infection and greater demand for hospital care.

Abortion and infanticide are ancient human practices that are often, although not always, the result of choice. The reasons a woman chooses abortion as a method of controlling the number of her progeny will vary between cultures. Amongst the factors that a woman considers are the other possibilities of family planning available to her. In Alto Vera Cruz, contraception was available but often inaccessible. As we have seen, failure to employ other legitimate methods of contraception, and resorting to backstreet abortions, are a testament to women's desire to limit their fertility.

GENDER AND CONTRACEPTIVE CHOICE

Gender relations were an important aspect of the limited choices facing women in Alto Vera Cruz. The attitude of men was an additional cultural constraint and one of the reasons that women ended up having to choose between the grim alternatives of sterilization, abortion, or unwanted pregnancy (Kaufmann 1991). Both men and women agreed that contraception was a female responsibility, but for different reasons. In general, the women felt that men did not like to assume any of the responsibility of conception, particularly if the woman was unmarried. As one woman put it, 'it's the women who should take precautions; because men .have children without being responsible' (Ana Maria). The men's lack of responsibility continued beyond contraception, to child-rearing: 'men don't like saying the kids are theirs. They avoid responsibilities. They'll go as far as to threaten the mothers' (Margaret).

This was one of the few points that men and women agreed upon, despite their different reasoning. As one man put it, 'It's really the woman's responsibility. It's her who is the progenitrix (*progenitora*). She's the one who's going to give it life, you know? She's got to be more responsible . . . '. He explained at some length, that being open-minded, he always explained the risks to a woman, but 'if she insisted' he was willing to get his fun.

We have established that most women want to, and many try to, limit their fertility. The differences in contraceptive use seem to relate to a sense of control, with the women in the most secure positions (those who are married) more likely to use the pill, and the less secure opting for sterilization and other one-time methods.

The influence of gender relations cannot be ignored. The lack of trust that cohabiting men display for their partners is mirrored in the lack of control these women experience. Additionally, in a culture where men accrue status by having offspring, poorer unmarried men gain status through the control of their women and the display of their sexual force. Therefore, they do not consider it in their interest to contracept.

Married women and men exhibited greater degrees of cooperation and control in their lives, and most often chose to use the most efficacious reversible method, the pill. Their status was secured in other respects, and it is clear that the relative sharing of power, status, and control, i.e., gender relations, arguably has a direct bearing on contraceptive practice within families.

CONCLUSION

The 1994 International Conference on Population and Development (ICPD) held in Cairo was a significant step forward in terms of population advocacy. The influence of women's movements was critical in shifting the dominant agenda from demographic targets to reproductive rights and free choice. However, free choice has a different meaning in countries that have had long-standing state-supported family planning programmes. This is especially true in a country such as Brazil, where fertility decline originated in 'market' factors. Brazil is different from countries like India or Bangladesh, where reproductive rights are about the provision of free choice, because in Brazil there is a major need that has been somewhat satisfied but at a great cost to women's health and welfare.

Contraceptive use in Alto Vera Cruz is a perfect example of this. Contraception was theoretically available; in order to get it, however, would-be users actively had to seek it at a considerable cost to their time and/or their purse. Women with many children and a low income are in a weak position in such a situation. High rates of sterilization and abortion are a reflection of the fact that this demand is not being adequately met.

The women who were most secure, in the most controlled environment, were also the most effective contraceptors. The more precarious her sexual relationship, the harder for a woman to obtain the necessary contraceptive means, and the less likely she would feel able to have any effective role in her life. The more educated and better-off women blamed others for being ignorant and not caring. The degree to which women had control over their lives, or were more empowered, affects their level and type of contraceptive practice.

Following Cairo, the emphasis on the reproductive rights of women has become more realistic. In Brazil, as in many other cultures, reproductive responsibility is considered the domain of women. Here, I have argued that the underlying system of gender relations influences the sexual and reproductive choices and behaviour of women. In other words, women's reproductive behaviour cannot be viewed in isolation from men's. In Brazil, concepts of masculinity (*machismo*) are forceful, and are deeply entwined with notions of fecundity and paternity. In this cultural milieu, men do not consider it in their interest to engage in family planning. This arena is entirely female, and because of men's disinterest, women are left to act alone. In the past they sought the help of backstreet abortionists and now, increasingly, they are seeking the permanent solution of sterilization. Women's needs must be met, and men's cooperation must be sought.

The current challenge to meet the need for reproductive rights and family planning in Brazil is simple: listen to the women and provide them with what they want. It must be one of the few instances of a developing country where the population needs to persuade the government rather than the other way round.

REFERENCES

Arruda, M., N. Rutenberg, L. Morris, and E.A. Ferraz (1987), *Pesquisa Nacional Sobre Saúde Materno-Infantil e Planejamento Familiar: PNSMIPF — Brasil, 1986* (Rio de Janeiro: BEMFAM)

Barroso, C. (1987), 'Direitos Reprodutivos: A Realidade Social e o Debate Político', *Cadernos de Pesquisa,* (62):52–9 (São Paulo)

—— (1989), 'Fertility Decline and Public Policies in Brazil', Presented at the American Assembly on US Policy towards World Population Growth, 26th–28th October at Hubert M. Humphrey Institute of Public Affairs (Minneapolis: University of Minnesota).

Berquóo, Elza (1993), 'Brasil, um Caso Exemplar — Anticepção e Parto Cirúrgicos — À Espera de uma Ação Exemplar', paper presented at the Seminário A Situação da Mulher e o Desenvolvimento, 1–2 July, NEPO, Unicamp, Brazil.

Boston Womens' Health Book Collective (1984), *The New Our Bodies Ourselves* (New York: Simon and Schuster).

Comissão Parlamentar Mista de Inquérito (1992), 'Relatorio Final do Comissão Parlamentar Mista de Inquérito', Destinada a examinar a Incidência da Esterilização em Massa de Mulheres no Brasil (Brasilia).

Corrêa, S. 'Not Exactly a Choice: Sterilization in Brazil', mimeo.

Daly, H.E. (1985), 'Marx and Malthus in Northeast Brazil: A Note on the World's Largest Class Difference in Fertility and its Recent Trends', *Population Studies,* 39(2):329–38.

Faria, V.E. (1989), 'Políticas de Governo e Regulação da Fecundidade: Consequencias não Antecipadas e Efeitos Perversos'. Ciências Sociais Hoje.

Faria, V.E., and J.E. Potter (1990), 'Development, Government Policy and Fertilty Regulation in Brazil', Texas Population Research Center Papers, No. 12.02 (Austin: The University of Texas).

Faria, V.E., and J.E. Potter (1994), 'Television, Telenovelas, and Fertility Change in Northeast Brazil', paper presented to IUSSP Seminar on Values and Fertility Change (Sion, Switzerland).

Fernandes, B. (1991), 'Alceni Cura Tudo', *Istoé/Senhor.* 6 February, 1115:47.

Guerra, K. (1991), 'Polêmica Fértil: Governo e Entidade Discutem o Aumento das Taxas de Esterilização Feminina', *Istoé/Senhor.* 2 February, 1115:24–5.

Kaufmann, G. (1991), 'Family Formation and Fertility in a *favela* in Belo Horizonte', Brazil: An Analysis of Cultural and Demographic Influences', D.Phil., Oxford University.

Martine, G. (1995), 'Brazil's Remarkable Fertility Decline: A Fresh Look at Key Factors'. Harvard Center for Population and Development Studies, Working Paper Series No. 95.04 (Cambridge, MA.: Harvard Center for Population and Development Studies).

Merrick, T.W., and E. Berquó (1983), *The Determinants of Brazil's Recent Rapid Decline in Fertility.* Committee on Population and Demography Report CM 22 (Washington, D.C.: National Academy Press).

Pacheco, Mário Victor de Assis (1984), *Racismo, Machismo e 'Planejamento Familiar',* 3rd edn. (Petropolis: Vozes).

Parker, R.G. (1991), *Bodies, Pleasures and Passions: Sexual Attitude in Contemporary Brazil* (Boston: Beacon Press).

Pitanguy, J. (1994), 'Feminist Policies and Reproductive Rights: The Case of Brazil', in G. Sen, and R. Snow (eds.), *Power and Decision: The Social Control of Reproduction* (Boston: Harvard School of Public Health), pp. 101–22.

Prado, D. (1986), *O Que é Aborto,* 2nd edn. (São Paulo: Brasiliense).

Ross, J. A. (1992), 'Sterilization: Past, Present, Future', *Studies in Family Planning,* 23(3):187–98.

Sen, G. (1994), 'Reproduction: Policies and Politics', in G. Sen, and Rachel Snow (eds.), *Power and Decision: The Social Control of Reproduction* (Boston: Harvard School of Public Health), pp. 1–4.

Silva, Léa Melo da (1986), 'A Mulher e o Planejamento Familiar', Cadernos do Nucleo de Estudos e Pesquisas Sobre a Mulher: 2 (Belo Horizonte: UFMG).

Sobrinho, Délcio da Fonseca (1993), *Estado e População: Uma História do Planejamento Familiar no Brasil* (Rio de Janeiro: Rosa dos Tempos).

Wood, C.H. and José Alberto Magno de Carvalho (1988), *The Demography of Inequality in Brazil* (Cambridge: Cambridge University Press).

8

Female Participation in Health and Education: A Leading Factor in Fertility Reduction in India

D. Narayana

1. INTRODUCTION

Early writers on fertility decline (Thompson 1929; Davis 1945, 1955, 1963; Notestein 1945, 1953; Freedman 1961–2) emphasized broad forces of modernization, such as urbanization, industrialization, shifts to nonagricultural labour, and increased literacy, as bringing about changes in traditional structures. The neoclassical theoreticians shifted the focus to the microlevel and translated the changes in macro conditions into individual and household level calculations. Both these strands of theoretical work have come under attack in recent years. Among the macrolevel changes, one force of change which has shown robust association with fertility decline is female literacy (Levine et al 1993; Visaria 1995). However, a question raised in this context is: how is it that 'the level attained in a few years of attendance at low-quality schools during her childhood could be retained by the average woman in her childbearing years and have an impact on her child health care and reproduction sufficient to affect birth and death rates' (Levine et al 1994:186)? Answering this question would require measuring literacy skills, such as reading and decontextualized language ability, directly, 'which has not been done in demographic research to date' (Levine et al, ibid. 186).

The Princeton University-based European Fertility Project, while instrumental in undermining the faith in classic demographic

This paper was written when the author was Visiting Fullbright Fellow at the Harvard Center for Population and Development Studies.

transition theory, suggested that fertility was significantly related to 'culture', defined operationally as language, ethnicity, or geographical region. This has been interpreted as diffusion of ideas — thinkability of fertility control — and contraceptive technology. This diffusion is thought to occur through social networks (Watkins 1987). But what are these networks, and how do they facilitate diffusion? Do all social networks facilitate diffusion, or do some inhibit it? These are important questions which arise in this context and to which answers have not yet been provided.

It has been suggested that *gender equity* in the formal sector is one important macrolevel factor common to developing countries demonstrating rapid fertility decline (Narayana 1995). This is an aspect ignored by the two schools of demographic thought mentioned above. This paper tests the hypothesis that female participation in the formal sector is a leading factor in fertility reduction. Female participation in the formal occupations is closely associated with female literacy and may be viewed as a measure of the proportion of females in the labour force who are actually using literacy skills, such as reading and decontextualized language ability, in their daily work. Firstly, women working in the education and health sectors can be seen as being actively involved in generating the decontextualized language dominant in the discourse of health in the clinics and in the classrooms. Secondly, inasmuch as participation in the formal sector means entry into respected occupational groups in a modernizing society, these women become peers in the social networks that are formed, thus facilitating the diffusion of ideas and technologies. This paper further hypothesizes an inverse relationship between female participation in the formal sector and fertility. This hypothesis is tested in the context of recent Indian fertility decline.

Section 2 of this paper defines the hypothesis and proposes a method to test the impact of female participation in the formal sector as distinct from female literacy. Section 3 tests the hypothesis at the state level, which provide clearly marked geographical and language units. This level of analysis allows for the cultural explanations of fertility, assuming that higher female participation in the formal occupations in a particular state is a cultural phenomenon. In section 4, analysis is carried out at the level of districts for Kerala, Tamil Nadu, and Punjab, which have shown varying levels of fertility decline. If the levels of female participation differ across states and are associated with the fertility levels, yet within states show fairly similar levels across districts, then cultural explanations of fertility decline may be valid. If intrastate or interdistrict variation in fertility is high and correlated with female participation, then the cultural explanations become less certain. In Section 5, the districts of Maharashtra are analysed to show the striking differences in female participation and fertility across the districts within a fairly homogeneous cultural unit. Section 6 concludes by drawing together the main findings.

Gender Equity and Social Networks

The rapidity and pervasiveness of fertility decline in countries that differ in economic conditions, social structures, political regimes, national history, and culture, suggests that it is an outcome of profound changes in 'ideas, aspirations, and attitudes rather than techniques', and that some mechanism of diffusion was involved. What was being diffused, in Coale's terminology, was the thinkability of fertility control (Watkins 1987). Beckman (1983) described friends and neighbours as the most frequent sources of information and influence regarding contraception. Later, referring to Lee's (1979) work on Korea, she says 'a woman is more likely to adopt family planning if women in her social network have already done so. Peer contacts provide women not only with information but also with emotional support' (p. 429). Who are these friends and neighbours who think of fertility control in the first place? It may be hypothesized that they are the educated women who have entered those occupations such as physicians, teachers, and modern production workers, that have a modernizing influence on society. Entry of women into these occupations is a significant part of the modernization that is taking place in society. New networks form around them and they become the peers who are instrumental in providing information and emotional support to the women in their social network. Thus, the emphasis is on opinion leadership, social networks, and social process in shaping ideas, attitudes, and behaviour (Retherford and Palmore 1983).

The role of social networks in shaping ideas is not new to the societies and communities undergoing fertility change. Every society has its social networks, but there is something specific to the social networks in societies undergoing fertility change; these networks are receptive to changes in ideas, aspirations, and attitudes, and do not inhibit certain kinds of changes. In this connection, the empirical regularity of gender equity in employment in the formal occupations, observed in the developing countries undergoing rapid fertility decline, becomes relevant. The entry of women into these occupations is itself an innovation. What they do and profess often has great influence on others as they are often looked upon as role models by the other young women and girls.

Shamiran's story from Bangladesh, quoted in Pollak and Watkins (1993), illustrates this idea. Two key societal changes underlying the story are: girls going to school in large numbers; and a woman appointed as a community-based family planning worker. Although, initially there was strong disapproval to the presence of women family-ly planning workers — a result of existing social networks diffusing ideas opposed to the entry of women into new occupations — their trustworthiness and credibility was soon established. With it, a new network of information and exchange of ideas was established with the family planning worker at one end, receiving new knowledge from outside, and the young women and girls at the other end. Similar networks also form around women physicians and teachers who command even more respect and influence in this regard.

Note some of the reactions of the young girls in Shamiran's story to the presence of Mukti Ma, the family planning worker: 'this lady is wearing her sari the way I have seen my relatives, who live in the city, wear their saris'; 'she earns a good amount of money'; and 'I would like to work as she does'. These reactions would be equally true with regard to the female teachers and physicians working in the villages, who supplant the traditional influence of elders. The younger women who become teachers, physicians, and family planning workers form the peer group for the younger women and the schoolgirls. Quite often, discussions take place in the school, as in the case of Shamiran's story, and the school becomes an effective base for forming further networks.

Assuming entry into formal occupations as conditional upon a certain level of education, does the often-used female literacy variable capture this particular aspect of new social networks? Theoretically, it may not, as there are several problems in using female education as a gross measure of modernization in society. Firstly, 'loss of literacy is fairly common among people who have no reason to use the skill, even in societies where reading material is widely available' (Jeffrey 1987:11). Obviously, participating in the education process for a few years at a young age and returning to the traditional modes of life does not give the education much opportunity in reality. This is the same question posed by Levine et al. (1993) as to how much of school learning is retained by the woman in her child-bearing years. Secondly, there is the related aspect of utility of content and how marketable the skills are in education. This has been considered a reason for the decline in school attendance in Punjab over a century ago by Leitner (quoted in Jeffery op. cit.). One of the important reasons parents send their daughters to school is to improve their chances of obtaining a job (Caldwell et al. 1988:174–5; Knodel et al 1987:129). The social process by which women enter the formal occupations, as teachers, physicians, and production workers, not only empowers women and brings about gender equity but may also build lasting social networks.

The simple education process wherein girls enter the school system and become literate, must be contrasted with the process in which women are also employed in the formal occupations, in particular, in the school system as teachers and in the health system as physicians. In the latter process, a group of women become active participants in passing on new knowledge. They also realize that their literacy is a useful and marketable skill that is valued and respected in society. Female literacy, thus becomes an active force in social change. Further, female teachers become role models for girls.

In general, female employment as school teachers and as physicians and health workers is distinctly superior to female employment in the formal sector, for two important reasons. First, female employment in the schools and hospitals involves a wider geographical spread. Second, it inherently involves a greater process of socialization, as teachers and physicians must continuously interact with students and patients, which is not true of other formal sector employment. For this process to be effective, it is necessary to enlist the teachers and physicians to work in their local areas so they can communicate more effectively (El-Sanabary 1993:164). In schools, female teachers can play an effective role in pupil motivation, achievement, and attainment:

> Teachers often perpetuate sex-role stereotypes directly and indirectly through what they teach and through their behaviour, their interactions with pupils, and their assumptions about the skills and abilities of girls and boys. Female teachers may inspire girls to high achievement

and accomplishment or direct them toward conformity with prevailing domestic ideals (El-Sanabary 1993:165).

Undoubtedly, the prevailing socio-ideological situation itself shapes the education process. In the context of fertility decline, the presence of female health workers and female physicians also has wide geographical coverage. That is why this paper emphasizes three occupations: teachers, physicians, and health workers.

The entry of women into the teaching and health professions within rural societies represents a structural break in traditional society. Inasmuch as they form the nucleus of new networks and become effective channels for the diffusion of information and technologies, these women can potentially be considered as determinants of fertility and related changes.

How is the entry of women into these three occupations to be captured in an empirical analysis? One obvious measure is the proportion of female workers to the total population of workers. However, the proportion of female workers to the total is related to the level of female literacy itself. At very low levels of female literacy, the proportions of workers would be low and with an increase in literacy the proportion would tend to increase. The relationship between female literacy and the proportion of female workers may be formalized in the case of schoolteachers, as follows. At low levels of female literacy, the proportion of female teachers in the school system would be low; at very high levels of female literacy, the proportion is unlikely to be higher than one-half. This assumption is based on the fact that the proportion of female teachers in the total for the developed countries, in 1985, was well below one-half. In 1965, the proportion of female teachers in the teaching force were 0.63, 0.37, 0.18 at the primary, secondary, and higher levels, respectively, for the upper-middle-income countries. By 1985, these proportions increased to 0.65, 0.47, 0.28, respectively. The proportions are much lower for the lower-income and lower-middle-income countries (King and Hill 1993:11). The relationship between female literacy level and the proportion of female teachers in the schools may, thus, be expressed as follows:

$Y = F(L)$ Y: Proportion of female teachers
               L: Level of female literacy

Following from the above, terminal values may be set as follows:

$$Y = 0 \text{ at } L = 0 \text{ and } Y = 0.5 \text{ at } L = 1.$$

A simple functional form satisfying the above condition is $Y = A + \beta^L$. At $L = 0$, $A + 1 = 0$ or $A = -1$; at $L = 1$, $-1 + \beta = 1/2$ or $\beta = 1.5$. The above functional form with the coefficients generated by the terminal conditions taken as the norm allows us to see how states have performed on this count. One way to do it is by running a regression of percentage of female teachers on female literacy and then testing the estimated value of β for its difference from 1.5. If it is higher, then the state is doing better in terms of female participation in relation to its female literacy; if it is lower, then the state is doing poorly. If the value of β does not differ from 1.5, then using female literacy is equivalent to using the proportion of female teachers. No similar formalization of the relationship between female literacy and the proportion of female physicians or female health workers can be attempted, because both are highly specialized and no data are available to set the terminal values.

There is a problem with the levels of aggregation at which data must be handled. The level of literacy should be at the overall level (rural + urban) and the proportion of female teachers should be of rural areas only. Historically, rural literacy has followed urban literacy and rural teachers, in the first instance, receive their education in the urban areas. Further, the argument developed above is primarily about rural societies and one of the aspects emphasized is the geographical spread. The reason for not using aggregate proportion of female teachers is that the higher proportion of female teachers in the urban areas clouds the picture.

At a second level, the relationship between fertility levels and the proportion of female teachers may be tested. The proportion of female teachers, by itself, does not tell us much about the coverage of the school system. To take that into account, a measure of spread, such as the proportion of villages having a school or educational institute, must be incorporated. In order to carry out testing, a sufficiently large number of observations are needed: this is possible only in a disaggregated analysis, which is carried out for the Indian states in the next section. In the following sections, further disaggregation at the level of districts, within the states of Kerala, Tamil Nadu, Punjab, and Maharashtra, is attempted.

3. The Indian Experience — Analysis at the State Level

Given that India is a large country with diverse regions and diverse fertility experiences, it is essential to carry out our analysis at the level of the states. The states differ in terms of urbanization, industrialization, female literacy, and female participation in the formal occupations. However, all the states have a common long history of family planning programmes, beginning in the 1950s with the adoption of the First Five-Year Plan. After some experimentation, an extension approach, wherein health workers visit women in the reproductive ages, has been implemented since 1966–7 (P. Visaria and L. Visaria 1994). What impact the programme has had on fertility can only be assessed by the observed decline in fertility.

Table 1: Fertility, Urbanization, and Female Literacy in the Indian States

States	CBR 74–80	CBR 84–90	% change	% urban	Female Literacy 1961	Female Literacy 1981	Female Literacy 1991	Gender gap 1991
Andhra Pradesh	33.5	28.2	15.9	23.3	12.0	24.2	32.7	22.5
Bihar	38.2	37.0	3.1	12.5	0.7	16.5	22.9	29.5
Gujarat	34.2	28.8	15.8	31.1	19.1	38.5	48.6	24.0
Haryana	35.9	33.0	7.9	21.9	–	6.9	40.5	27.0
Himachal Pradesh	32.7	27.8	15.2	7.6	0.6	37.7	52.1	22.1
Karnataka	32.2	28.0	13.1	28.9	14.2	33.2	44.3	23.0
Kerala	25.0	20.3	18.7	18.7	38.9	75.7	86.9	7.6
Madhya Pradesh	39.2	37.2	5.1	19.9	0.7	19.0	28.9	29.0
Maharashtra	30.5	28.8	5.5	35.0	16.8	41.0	52.3	24.0
Orissa	33.3	30.4	8.8	11.8	0.9	25.1	34.7	28.0
Punjab	30.4	27.2	10.6	27.7	14.1	39.6	50.4	14.0
Rajasthan	40.5	37.0	8.6	21.0	0.6	14.0	20.4	34.3
Tamil Nadu	28.2	21.9	22.3	33.0	18.2	40.4	52.3	22.6
Uttar Pradesh	42.0	38.1	9.4	17.9	0.7	17.2	25.3	29.4
West Bengal	31.1	28.9	7.1	26.5	17.0	36.1	46.6	20.0
Pondicherry	28.5	23.0	19.3	52.3	–	53.0	65.6	18.1
Goa	25.5	18.3	28.0	32.0	–	52.2	67.1	16.5

Sources: Bhat, P.N. Mari 1994, 'Levels and Trends in Indian Fertility: A Reassessment', *Economic and Political Weekly*, 29(51&25):3273–80. Centre for Monitoring Indian Economy, *Basic Statistics: States* 1994.

TABLE 2: FEMALE PARTICIPATION IN THE
TEACHING AND HEALTH OCCUPATIONS, 1981

States	% Female physicians	% Female health workers	% Female teachers	% FT Expected	Difference	Change in % female teachers
	(1)	(2)	(3)	(4)	(5)	(6)
Andhra Pradesh	4.09	40.07	16.9	10.3	6.6	4.4
Bihar	1.88	35.08	8.9	6.9	2.0	4.0
Gujarat	4.59	37.67	25.0	16.9	8.1	11.6
Haryana	2.87	32.97	16.1	11.5	4.6	−0.6
Himachal Pradesh	2.98	37.17	19.2	16.5	2.7	11.1
Karnataka	4.15	50.10	14.9	14.4	0.5	7.9
Kerala	13.69	69.44	47.1	35.9	11.2	4.8
Madhya Pradesh	3.28	34.06	7.3	8.0	−0.7	3.3
Maharashtra	5.01	36.67	15.8	18.1	−2.3	6.7
Orissa	1.58	26.95	7.9	10.7	−2.8	5.7
Punjab	4.8	48.72	29.8	17.4	12.4	16.3
Rajasthan	3.04	31.69	7.7	5.8	1.8	3.5
Tamil Nadu	8.98	46.43	28.9	17.8	11.1	9.4
Uttar Pradesh	1.79	33.25	7.0	7.2	−0.2	1.8
West Bengal	1.7	34.46	9.8	15.8	−6.0	5.6
Pondicherry	5.92	35.01	28.7	24.0	4.7	17.6
Goa	11.17	63.13	48.8	25.1	23.7	17.9

Source: *Population Census 1981, General Economic Tables.*
Notes: Column 4 is computed taking the female literacy for 1981. Column 6 is based on the age distribution of teachers as of 1981.

An interstate comparison of fertility trends in relation to urbanization, female literacy, and female participation in the three occupations, is attempted at the outset. The data are provided in Tables 1 and 2. As regards urbanization in relation to fertility decline, no clear relationship seems to exist. There are three groups of states in terms of the range of crude birth rates 1984–90 (CBR84–90)[1], and within each group, states show varied levels

[1] The reason for using CBRs is the availability of comparable figures computed by Mari Bhat. He uses the reverse survival technique taking the population Census data.

of urbanization. The states within the group having low CBRs had levels of urbanization ranging from below 20 per cent to above 50 per cent; in the moderate CBR group, urbanization varied from below 10 per cent to above 40 per cent; in the high CBR group, urbanization varied from around 10 per cent to around 30 per cent. In fact, 13 of the 17 states had proportions of urban population within a narrow range of 18 and 36 per cent, with CBRs ranging from 18.3 to 38.1.

The inverse relationship between female literacy and CBR is better defined. However, closer examination shows patterns inconsistent with the overall relationship. Goa and Pondicherry both have comparable levels of female literacy, yet their CBRs differ by five. The case of Andhra Pradesh, Orissa, and Haryana is similar. Much worse was the case of the middle seven states, all of which had comparable levels of female literacy in 1981, but only Tamil Nadu had a CBR of below 22 in 1987 (CBR 1984–90), having experienced one of the most rapid declines between 1974–80 and 1984–90. Punjab, Himachal Pradesh, and Gujarat had fairly high rates of decline; Maharashtra and West Bengal, despite fairly high levels of urbanization, had the lowest declines in fertility. Further, in each of the six states, female literacy had increased by about 30 percentage points between 1961 and 1991, with the exception of Himachal Pradesh, where the increase was a phenomenal 51.5 percentage points. Secondary school enrolment of girls in 1987–8 ranged between 61 and 71 per cent in the six states, with the exception of Himachal Pradesh where it was 81 per cent, next only to the highest percentage of 98 in Kerala. In Karnataka, it was 56 per cent. The gender gap in literacy in 1991 in these states varied between 20 to 24 percentage points, except in Punjab where it was only 14 percentage points. Thus, whichever aspect of female literacy is analysed, there is little difference among these states yet fertility decline has varied very widely.

In 1981, numbers of women teaching in the rural areas among the states showed wide variation. At the top were Goa and Kerala with proportions of female teachers around 48 per cent; at the bottom were Uttar Pradesh, Rajasthan, Orissa, and Madhya Pradesh, with proportions around 8 per cent. Among the seven states with comparable levels of female literacy, secondary school enrolment of girls, gender gaps in literacy, and participation of women in teaching, showed wide variation: it was highest at 29 per cent for Tamil

Nadu and Punjab, and lowest at 9.8 and 15.8 per cent for West Bengal and Maharashtra repectively. To assess whether participation is high or low, a norm in relation to female literacy is needed. Using the relation posited in section 2 above, when the expected proportions were computed for the states, it was seen that the actual proportion was significantly higher than the expected proportion in the case of the three high literacy states: Goa, Kerala, and Pondicherry. For the four low literacy states, the actual proportions were approximately the expected levels. Among the seven states with comparable levels of female literacy, in Punjab, Tamil Nadu, and Gujarat actual proportions were significantly higher than the expected proportions; Himachal Pradesh had female participation slightly higher than the expected level, even when it had one of the most rapid increases in female literacy; Karnataka had an actual proportion just equal to the expected level; and Maharashtra and West Bengal had actual proportions significantly lower than expected.

With regard to the relationship between female participation in teaching and fertility reduction, the four categories of states in terms of female participation in teaching mentioned earlier become ordered in terms of their fertility performance, with Haryana still standing in a different class of its own. In comparison with the relationship between fertility and female literacy, the relationship between fertility and female participation in teaching is clearer. The problem with a cluster of seven states having the same level of female literacy but behaving differently in terms of fertility levels or fertility reduction is obviated. The states with higher female participation have reported larger fertility declines. Some of them have reached fairly low levels of fertility (Tamil Nadu), while others are on their way to lower levels (Punjab, Gujarat, and Himachal Pradesh). The states with lower levels of female participation in teaching have all reported fairly low reductions in fertility (Maharashtra and West Bengal, in addition to the large North Indian states). How much of the variation in fertility across the states is explained by the proportion of female teachers? As is evident from the regression results shown in Table 3, the coefficient of the proportion of female teachers (Y) in Model I is significantly different from unity and 83 per cent of the variation is explained. The addition of the variable, proportion of villages having an educational institution, improved the R^2; but the coefficient itself was not significantly different from unity (Model II). Thus, it may be concluded that the proportion of female teachers is a leading factor in explaining the decline in fertility.

TABLE 3: DETERMINANTS OF CRUDE BIRTH RATES
IN THE INDIAN STATES

	Model I		Model II	
	B	t	B	t
F.T.	0.225	4.333	0.247	3.247
P.V.	—	—	0.907	0.604
Constant	38.3		40.1	
R²	0.822		0.827	
F	69.46		33.55	
N	17		17	

Sources: Tables 1 and 2.
Registrar General of India, *Study on Distribution of Infrastructural Facilities in Different Regions and Levels and Trends of Urbanisation,* Occasional Paper 1 of 1986.

Note: Model I : CBR = $A B^Y$; Y: Proportion of Female Teachers.
Model II: CBR = $A B^Y C^V$; V: Proportion of villages having an educational institution.

However, a closer look at the data raises a few questions. Punjab and Gujarat report proportions of female teachers comparable to that of Tamil Nadu, and yet Tamil Nadu alone reported a rapid decline. The answer may lie in the process by which the proportion of female teachers in 1981 was achieved. It is possible that the proportion was low at an earlier date, say in 1961, but rapidly increased between 1961 and 1981; or, it could be that the proportion was high in 1961 and has remained high since then. These two different situations will not produce similar fertility reductions. It may be expected that a state which had a higher proportion at an earlier date will have a lower fertility rate compared to a state which had a lower proportion earlier and a rapid increase more recently. In other words, those states which had a longer history of higher female participation will show a higher fertility decline as compared to those with a shorter history.

From the data on age distribution of teachers in 1981, the proportion of female teachers in 1961 and the change in the percentage over 1961–81 were computed (Table 2). It may be seen that the change in the percentage was fairly high for Gujarat, Himachal Pradesh, Punjab, Tamil Nadu, Pondicherry, and Goa; it was low for Uttar Pradesh, Rajasthan, Madhya Pradesh, and Haryana; and was of a moderate magnitude for the remaining states. Thus, there are basically four categories of states: those where female participation in teaching has been high (over 20 per cent) for a long time (Kerala, Tamil Nadu, and Goa); those which have shown significant improvement over 1961–81 (Gujarat, Himachal Pradesh, Punjab, and Pondicherry); those which have shown moderate improvement (Andhra Pradesh, Bihar, Karnataka, Maharashtra, Orissa, and West Bengal); and those which have shown low levels of change (Madhya Pradesh, Rajasthan, and Uttar Pradesh). Haryana does not fall into any of these categories. This would probably explain the rapid fertility decline in Tamil Nadu compared with Punjab, Gujarat, or Himachal Pradesh.

Although our hypothesis centres on three occupational categories — health workers, physicians, and teachers, this section focuses primarily on teachers. A functional relationship can be posited between female literacy and the proportion of female teachers. Similar relationships cannot be posited for the proportion of female physicians and the proportion of female health workers. A further reason is the strong correlation of the proportion of female health workers and physicians with the proportion of female teachers. The correlation coefficient between the proportion of female teachers and the proportion of female physicians is 0.921, and that between the proportion of female teachers and the proportion of female health workers is 0.865. Consequently, the independent effects of gender equity in the employment of health workers and physicians cannot be estimated. To put it another way, when we claim that the proportion of female teachers plays an important role in fertility decline, we are, in fact, referring to a composite which includes the proportion of female physicians and female health workers.

Examining the proportion of female physicians and female health workers across the states of India shows that Kerala and Goa report not only high proportions of female teachers but also high proportions of female health workers and female physicians (Table 2). Tamil Nadu, Punjab, and Karnataka have moderately high proportions of female health workers; the rest of the states report proportions of female health workers between 30 and 40 per cent. Orissa is at the bottom, with a figure below 30 per cent. As regards the proportion of female physicians, it is important to note that Tamil Nadu reported a figure slightly lower than that of Goa. The rest of the states fall into two categories with the proportion slightly higher than four per cent for Andhra Pradesh, Gujarat, Karnataka, Maharashtra, Punjab, and Pondicherry. The contrast between Punjab and Tamil Nadu is striking: both the states report comparable proportions of female health workers and teachers, but Tamil Nadu reports a significantly higher proportion of female physicians. This would suggest a significant role for the proportion of female physicians in the rapid decline of fertility in Tamil Nadu.

It may be concluded that female participation in the health and education sectors plays an important role in the fertility reduction of Indian states. In a country committed to an antinatalist policy for over three decades, where states with comparable levels of female literacy and urbanization show significant reduction in fertility only in the presence of relatively high female participation in the occupations of teaching and physicians, it can be concluded that gender equity in these occupations is a very potent factor. The entry of women in large numbers into these occupations facilitates the formation of social networks for the diffusion of information and technologies. Nevertheless, the analysis carried out in this section cannot rule out a cultural explanation of fertility change. It could also be argued that the higher female participation is just an aspect of the 'culture' of the concerned states. To address this issue we now carry out our analysis at the level of districts within the states.

4. KERALA, TAMIL NADU, AND PUNJAB: COMPLEMENTARITIES AND FERTILITY DECLINE

In the previous section, it was shown that Tamil Nadu and Punjab were comparable in terms of many indicators, but that their fertility behaviour differed greatly. Female literacy and female participation in teaching in the two states are comparable. Female participation in teaching in relation to female literacy is well above the expected norm. Although the proportion of female health workers in the two states are comparable, the proportion of female physicians is higher in Tamil Nadu when compared to Punjab. Kerala reported higher levels of female literacy, female participation in teaching, proportion of female health workers, and proportion of female physicians. Turning to fertility behaviour, Kerala reported a crude birth rate (CBR) of 25.4 in 1974–80, which declined to 20.3 in 1984–90. Tamil Nadu reported 28.2 in 1974–80 and 21.9 in 1984–90. The decline in Kerala was 18.7 per cent, and in Tamil Nadu much higher at 22.3 per cent. Punjab reported a CBR of 30.4 in 1974–80, declining to 27.2 in 1984–90; the decline was only 10.6 per cent.

As is evident, the levels and declines vary greatly across the states. How much of these interstate differences are explained by the intrastate differences in female participation in the three occupations mentioned? As the Indian states are large, and composed of a large number of diverse districts, an analysis of the patterns across the districts within a state will elucidate the observed fertility behaviour. If the interdistrict differences in CBRs within a state are low, especially in the presence of wide interdistrict variation in female participation in health and education, then cultural explanations assume significance. However, existence of wide differences in fertility across the districts within a state cannot have a satisfactory cultural explanation; other explanatory variables such as female literacy, or female participation in formal occupations, must be considered.

The need for an interdistrict analysis is evidenced by the coefficient of variation of the CBRs of districts which are relatively high in Kerala (around 17 per cent), slightly lower in Tamil Nadu (around 12 per cent), and very low in Punjab (around 5 per cent). The coefficient of variation was basically the same in 1974–80 and 1984–90 in these states. This means that the fertility trends observed within the state across the districts varied within a narrow range of the state average in all the three states, with Kerala showing the widest variation.

The relationship between female literacy and the proportion of female teachers must be discussed at the outset. As is evident from the regression results shown in Table 4, the coefficient B was significantly greater than 1.5, indicating that the proportion of female teachers in the schools in these states is well above that expected for the levels of female literacy prevailing in the states. Analysing the three states together, or Kerala and Tamil Nadu combined, or Tamil

Nadu and Punjab combined, provided similar results. Note that the coefficients reported here are much above those reported for the all-India regression, as is to be expected by the very high differences between observed and expected values of the proportion of female teachers reported in Table 2 for these states.

TABLE 4: REGRESSION OF PROPORTION OF FEMALE TEACHERS ON FEMALE LITERACY, 1981

Districts of	Coefficient B	t value	R^2	F	No. of observations
Kerala, Tamil Nadu, and Punjab	1.830	10.154	0.525	42.02	39
Kerala and Tamil Nadu	1.822	8.434	0.593	37.87	27
Tamil Nadu and Punjab	1.849	7.227	0.300	5.94	27

Source: Same as Tables 1 and 2.

Having shown that the relationship between female literacy and the proportion of female teachers is well above the norm, a detailed discussion of the participation of women in the selected occupations is in order. The average proportion of female teachers in Kerala is 20 percentage points higher than that in Punjab and Tamil Nadu (Table 5). The coefficient of variation (percentage) of the proportions is highest in Tamil Nadu, followed by Kerala, and is the lowest in Punjab. The proportion of female health workers is also higher in Kerala by over 20 percentage points, compared to Tamil Nadu and Punjab. The coefficient of variation is low in all three states. The proportion of female physicians is significantly higher in Kerala, moderate in Tamil Nadu, and lower in Punjab. The coefficient of variation of the proportion of female physicians is higher than the coefficient of variation of the other two categories in all three states, and among the states is significantly higher in Punjab. As regards female participation in the selected occupations, the interdistrict variation is insignificant in the case of health workers in all three states, and for teachers in Punjab. The interdistrict variations are considerable in all three states in the case of physicians, and for teachers in Kerala and Tamil Nadu.

TABLE 5: INTER-DISTRICT VARIATION IN
FEMALE PARTICIPATION, 1981

	FPh	FHW	FT
Kerala			
Mean	14.15	69.45	47.59
CV (%)	33.21	11.50	22.92
Corr. Coeff. with FT	0.581	0.582	1.00
Tamil Nadu			
Mean	8.81	46.29	28.48
CV (%)	34.05	18.47	30.06
Corr. Coeff. with FT	−0.252	0.371	1.00
Punjab			
Mean	5.15	50.10	29.16
CV (%)	46.80	16.75	13.17
Corr. Coeff. with FT	0.128	0.273	1.00
Maharashtra			
Mean	4.46	36.20	15.22
CV (%)	75.19	15.06	35.48
Corr. Coeff. with FT	0.327	0.558	1.00

Source: Same as Table 2.
Notes: FPh: Percentage of female physicians in total.
FHW: Percentage of female health workers in total.
FT : Percentage of female teachers in total.

Do the interdistrict variations in female participation in the three occupations have any relationship between themselves? An indication of this is given by the correlation coefficients shown in Table 5. The relationship between the proportion of female teachers and the proportion of female health workers is positive in all three states, and is stronger in Kerala than in the other two states. It may be inferred that the districts with higher proportions of female teachers have higher proportions of female health workers.

However, this is not the relationship between the proportion of female teachers and the proportion of female physicians in all three states. In Kerala, the districts with a higher proportion of female teachers have a higher proportion of female physicians and the relationship is strong; in Punjab, the relationship is similar to that of Kerala but not as strong; but in Tamil Nadu, the correlation coefficient has a negative sign indicating that the districts with a higher proportion of female teachers have a lower proportion of female physicians. To clarify this relationship, the distribution of districts by the proportion of female teachers and the proportion of female physicians is presented in a two-way table (Table 6). It is evident from Table 6 that, in both Kerala and Punjab, there is a clustering of the districts and a positive bias in the relationship between the two proportions, whereas Tamil Nadu showed a dispersion wherein the districts reporting a lower proportion of female teachers show a higher proportion of female physicians. Thus, the pattern observed in Tamil Nadu is distinct from that observed at the all-India level, or in Kerala or Punjab.

The relationship between the proportion of female teachers and physicians with fertility decline may be inferred from Table 6. In both Kerala and Punjab, districts with higher proportions of female teachers and physicians have reported lower CBRs compared to the

TABLE 6: DISTRIBUTION OF DISTRICTS BY PERCENTAGE OF FEMALE TEACHERS AND FEMALE PHYSICIANS, KERALA, TAMIL NADU, AND PUNJAB, 1981

Percentage of female physicians	Percentage of female teachers			
	>45	30 to 45	25 to 30	<25
>10	17k 17k 17k 19k 20k 20k	23k	24t 26t	25t 27p
7.5 to 10	20t 23k	20t 21k 22t 27p 30k	17t 22k	19t 21t 22t
5 to 7.5		23t 25t 25p 26p	27p	21t 26t
<5		23t 28p 28p	27p 28p 28p 31p	28p

Note: Figures in the Table are crude birth rates from Mari Bhat (1994).
k: Kerala, t: Tamil Nadu, and p: Punjab.

districts with lower proportions of female teachers and physicians. Such a clear pattern is not seen in Tamil Nadu, where the districts are spread out in terms of the combination of proportion of female teachers and proportion of female physicians as well as the CBRs. This distinct pattern observable in Tamil Nadu has led to a rapid fertility decline at lower levels of female participation in teaching and among physicians as compared to Kerala.

Based on the district-level analysis of Kerala and Punjab, the conclusion can be made that female participation in the formal occupations is a leading factor in fertility decline. This section concludes that there are no general state-level factors — linguistic and cultural — which bring down fertility evenly. Fertility decline operates through such factors as the proportion of female teachers or female physicians. A low proportion of female teachers and/or female physicians in a district, such as Malappuram with a CBR of thirty in Kerala, which is showing a rapid decline does not necessarily alter its position. One conclusion of section 3 is modified by the findings of this section. On the basis of a high correlation between the proportion of female teachers and female physicians, and between the proportion of female teachers and female health workers, it was argued that the proportion of female teachers can be used as a composite index of gender equity in formal occupations. The reality of Tamil Nadu shows that this need not be the case; a lower proportion in one occupation may be complemented by a higher proportion in another leading to a rapid decline in fertility. However, the fact that fertility decline was rapid across the districts and that interdistrict variation was narrow despite the wide variations in female participation in the formal occupations in all the three states, does not allow us to rule out cultural explanations. Only the Kerala experience would be an exception to the cultural explanation with its wide interdistrict variation in fertility, female participation in the formal occupations, and a much longer history of fertility decline.

5. Why has Maharashtra Fallen Behind?

The low interdistrict variation in CBR and the proportion of females in the formal occupations in the three states analysed in section 4 leaves the discussion open to both cultural and gender equity explanations of fertility change, except for the evidence from

Kerala. The evidence from Kerala, especially the higher CBRs in a few districts and the near-replacement levels in many others, is not consistent with a cultural explanation of fertility change. However, the evidence from both Tamil Nadu and Punjab is consistent with both cultural and gender equity explanations.

It is in this context that an analysis of Maharashtra becomes relevant. Maharashtra is comparable to Tamil Nadu in two important respects. Urbanization is similar in both the states (it was 35 per cent in Maharashtra and 33 per cent in Tamil Nadu, in 1981) and female literacy is comparable (41.0 per cent in Maharashtra and 40.4 per cent in Tamil Nadu, in 1981) (Table 1). Increases in female literacy experienced between 1981 and 1991 and enrolment of girls in the 10–14 age group in 1987–8 is also comparable in the two states. The 1970s saw Maharashtra bring down its TFR from about 4.5 in the early 1970s to around 3.5 by the late 1970s. During the same period, Tamil Nadu showed only a slight decline in fertility. But the 1980s witnessed a reversal of the trends: Maharashtra virtually stagnated and Tamil Nadu showed a rapid decline. The question is, therefore , why has Maharashtra fallen behind.

Let us first look at how Maharashtra performed on the employment of women in schools. In order to test this, a regression of the form $Y = -1 + \beta L$ was run using the data for the districts of the state. The estimated coefficient was tested for its value = 1.5. The t value was 2.2337 and the coefficient was significantly higher than 1.5, which may be interpreted as good performance based on the criterion set above. However, when the same equation was re-run dropping the four districts with the highest values of the proportion of female teachers in schools, the t value of the coefficient dropped to 0.620 showing that the coefficient is not significantly different from 1.5.

	Coefficient β	t Value	R²	DF
All Districts	1.5751	2.2337	0.465	24
Four Districts Less	1.5186	0.6200	0.395	20

Female literacy (rural + urban) was low in many districts in 1981: above 30 per cent in 13 districts, between 20 per cent and 30 per cent in eight districts, and below 20 per cent in four districts, excluding Greater Bombay which is entirely urban. Moreover, as seen above, the proportion of female teachers has been in accordance with female literacy and are generally at low levels.

The diverse nature of the districts in terms of female participation in the teaching and health sectors is evident from the coefficient of variations (percentage) shown in Table 5. The coefficient of variation of the proportion of female teachers is 35 per cent, one of the highest among the four states. The coefficient of variation of the proportion of female physicians is extremely high at 75 per cent (Table 5), and the proportion itself is above 5 per cent in only nine districts. Female participation among the health workers alone did not show much variation across the districts of the state. The districts reporting higher proportion of female teachers generally reported higher proportion of female physicians, as evidenced by the correlation coefficient of 0.327. Such a close relationship between female participation in teaching and among the physicians has its impact on fertility. The CBR is generally lower in districts where female participation is higher and vice versa (Table 7). While the northwest corner in Table 7 reports CBRs below 30, it is much higher in the southeast corner.

TABLE 7: DISTRIBUTION OF DISTRICTS BY PERCENTAGE OF FEMALE TEACHERS AND FEMALE PHYSICIANS, MAHARASHTRA, 1981

Percentage of female physicians	Percentage of female teachers		
	>20	10 to 20	<10
>10		26 25	
7.5 to 10	24 27	30	
5 to 7.5	30	30 25	36
<5	28	32 26 27 31 29 37 31 27 31 27 29	36 37 33 33

Source: Same as Table 6.

The slow decline of fertility in Maharashtra is thus related to the generally low female participation in teaching and among physicians. The participation in teaching is in accordance with female literacy, except in a few districts where it is higher. Female participation among physicians follows female participation among teachers and, in this regard, Maharashtra is no different from Kerala or Punjab, and distinctly differs from Tamil Nadu. Female participation in Maharashtra is generally in accordance with the low level of female literacy. As shown above, the number of districts reporting female literacy between 20 and 30 per cent is eight, and that below 20 per cent is four. Thus, almost 50 per cent of the districts in Maharashtra report extremely low levels of female literacy and female participation. The lack of decline in almost half the number of districts of the state is a drag on the overall CBR in the state.

The Maharashtra case clearly cannot be explained in cultural terms. The state has districts which are well advanced in fertility decline at one end, and districts which have not yet begun the fertility decline at the other end, with a whole spectrum in between. The districts showing fairly rapid decline in fertility are not geographically contiguous. The lowest CBR (21.8) has been reported by the metropolitan area of Greater Bombay; but none of the districts around Bombay has reported a rate below 27. Then there are two groups of four districts each at the South-western and the Northeastern corners of the state reporting CBRs ranging between 24 to 27, and 25 to 28, respectively. The levels of female participation among teachers and physicians is comparatively higher in these districts, lending credence to the gender equity explanation of fertility decline.

6. CONCLUSION

Female literacy is an entry condition for female participation in the formal occupations. The possibility that female participation can vary greatly at given levels of female literacy led to the setting up of a model to evaluate female participation in relation to female literacy. Analysing state-level data on female participation showed that states reporting higher levels of female participation, which are significantly above the norm corresponding to their literacy levels, had shown significant fertility decline. Analysis at the district-level in three states (Kerala, Tamil Nadu, and Punjab), showed that female participation was generally high. Fertility decline was evident in all the districts but at varying rates. The district-level analysis of Maharashtra showed that female participation was significantly above the norm in only a few districts, while the rest of the districts had low female participation and in accordance with their low levels of female literacy. Fertility decline in Maharashtra was confined to the few districts with higher levels of female participation in the selected occupational category.

Do the above findings lend support to the gender equity hypothesis of fertility decline? Analysis at the level of Indian states, though strikingly different in terms of female participation in formal occupations, lends credence to the cultural explanations. District-level analysis within states showed low variation in fertility across the districts, despite the existence of wide variation in female participation in Tamil Nadu and Punjab, also supporting the cultural explanation. But Kerala, with its long history of female participation and fertility decline, showed wider variation in fertility decline at the district-level which were strongly related to female participation. This situation cannot be consistent with the cultural explanation.

Maharashtra provides conclusive evidence against a cultural explanation. This state, with its strong language identity, has experienced wide variation in CBRs across the districts. The districts reporting lower birth rates are not marked by geographic contiguity, but female participation in the formal occupations was distinctly higher in these districts. This seems to support the gender equity explanation of fertility decline.

Overall, the two theories of fertility decline, the female literacy strand and the diffusion strand, cannot be viewed as contending positions, as there is a very close and intricate relation between the two through female participation in the formal occupations. Female participation among teachers, physicians, and health workers are important social forces of gender equity, empowerment of women, and modernization in largely agricultural and rural societies. Women in these occupations become peers and opinion leaders to other women in their community. The process of modernization occurs through the networks formed around these women. The thinkability of fertility control, like many other ideas, obviously, diffuses through these networks. The large interdistrict variation in fertility within the states, which represent language and cultural units, raises serious questions about purely cultural explanations of fertility decline. The fact of female participation in occupations explaining fertility decline, while strengthening the diffusion perspective, clearly points to the need to have substantial bases at the societal level to build networks for this diffusion to take place.

NOTE ON THE DATA

The statistical analysis carried out in this paper uses the CBRs computed by Mari Bhat for the period 1974–80 and 1984–90 based on the 1981 and 1991 Population censuses. The data on female literacy (rural and urban) and proportion of female teachers, physicians, and health workers in the rural areas are from the Population censuses; the latter are drawn from the General Economic Tables reporting occupational data computed to the two-digit level. Although the occupational data does give the age distribution as of 1981, they cannot be used with certainty to project backwards for the reason that we do not have information on the turnover by age.

REFERENCES

Beckman, L.J. (1983), 'Communication, Power and the Influence of Social Networks in Couple Decisions on Fertility', in R.A. Bulatao and R.D. Lee (eds.), *Determinants of Fertility in Developing Countries* (New York: Academic Press).

Bhat, P.N. Mari (1994), 'Levels and Trends in Indian Fertility: A Reassessment', *Economic and Political Weekly*, 29(51 & 52).

Caldwell, J.C. (1982), *Theory of Fertility Decline* (New York: Academic Press).

Caldwell, J.C., P.H. Reddy, and P. Caldwell (1988), *The Causes of Demographic Change: Environmental Research in South India* (Madison, WI: University of Wisconsin Press).

Centre for Monitoring Indian Economy, *Basic Statistics: States* 1994.

Coale, A. J. (1973), 'The Demographic Transition Reconsidered', in *International Population Conference, Liege, 1973*, vol. I (Liege: International Union for the Scientific Study of Population).

Davis, K. (1945), 'The World Demographic Transition', *Annals of the American Academy of Political and Social Science*, 273.

—— (1955), 'Institutional Patterns Favouring High Fertility in Underdeveloped Areas', *Eugenics Quarterly*, 2(1).

—— (1963), 'The Theory of Change and Response in Modern Demographic History', *Population Index*, 29(4).

El-Sanabary, N. (1993), 'Middle East and North Africa', in E. King and

M.A. Hill (eds.), *Women's Education in Developing Countries* (Baltimore: The John Hopkins University Press).

Freedman, R. (1961–2), 'The Sociology of Human Fertility', *Current Sociology*, 10 & 11 (2).

Jeffery, R. (1987), 'Governments and Culture: How Women Made Kerala Literate', *Pacific Affairs*, 60(3).

King, E., and M.A. Hill (eds.) (1993), *Women's Education in Developing Countries* (Baltimore: The John Hopkins University Press).

Knodel, J., A. Chamratrithirong, and N. Debavalay (1987), *Thailand's Reproductive Revolution: Rapid Fertility Decline in a Third-world Setting* (Wisconsin: University of Wisconsin Press).

Lee, S.B. (1979) 'Communication Networks and Family Planning in Korean Villages', Seoul: Korean Institute for Family Planning.

Levine, R.A., et al. (1993), 'Schooling and Survival: The Impact of Maternal Education on Health and Reproduction in the Third World', in L.C. Chen, A. Kleinman, and N.C. Ware, *Health and Social Change in International Perspective* (Boston: Harvard School of Public Health).

—— (1994), 'Maternal Literacy and Health Care in Three Countries: A Preliminary Report', *Health Transition Review*, 4(2).

Narayana, D. (1995), 'Asian Fertility Transition: Is Gender Equity in Formal Occupations an Explanatory Factor?', mimeo.

Notestein, F.W. (1945), 'Population — The Long View', in T.W. Schultz (ed.), *Food for the World* (Chicago: University of Chicago Press).

—— (1953), 'Economic Problems of Population Change', in *Proceedings of the Eighth International Conference of Agricultural Economists* (London: Oxford University Press).

Pollak, R.A., and S.C. Watkins (1993), 'Cultural and Economic Approaches to Fertility: Proper Marriage or Misalliance?', *Population and Development Review*, 19(2).

Retherford, R. and J.A. Palmore (1983), 'Diffusion Processes Affecting Fertility Regulations', in R.A. Bulatao and R.D. Lee. (eds.), *Determinants of Fertility in Developing Countries*.

Thompson, W.S. (1929), 'Population', *American Journal of Sociology*, 34.

Visaria, P. (1995), 'Demographic Transition and Policy Responses in India', Presidential Address, Eighteenth Annual Conference of the Indian Association for the Study of Population.

Visaria, P., and L. Visaria (1994), 'Demographic Transition: Accelerating Fertility Decline in 1980s', *Economic and Political Weekly*, 29(51 & 52):3280.

Watkins, S.C. (1987), 'The Fertility Transition: Europe and the Third World Compared', *Sociological Forum*, 2.

9

Fertility Transition in India: Implications for Social Policies

Anrudh Jain

INTRODUCTION

R apid population growth is, at one time or another, blamed for most of the social ills facing the human race, including global warming, environmental degradation, tribal and racial conflicts, widespread hunger, and poverty. Furthermore,it is assumed that rapid population growth in a country impedes its economic development and, therefore, its ability to provide basic services and to improve the conditions of its people. One of the main rationales[1] behind the investment of public resources in family planning programme is the belief that a decline in the population growth rate would lead to a faster rate of economic development and, thus, would also enhance a country's ability to improve the condition of its people. This belief is based on the reasoning that a growing base of the population pyramid (size of the cohort aged 0 to 4 years) requires increasing resources to provide essential basic services such as education and health. Governments are unable to allocate these resources because of slow economic growth. Poor health and education of the labour force, in turn, slows the pace of economic development even further. Thus, per capita availability of resources for health and education would increase even in the absence of any increase in the total allocation of government resources for these services.

Now that the fertility transition in India has been ongoing for the past twenty years, can it contribute to just social policies, for

[1] Other rationale for investing public resources in family planning programmes include the improvements in maternal and child health and the basic human right to have access to the means of regulating one's own fertility.

example, those oriented to the reduction of gender and regional disparities in health or education? The analysis presented in this paper suggests that while the recent changes in the age distribution of the Indian population can enhance the government's potential ability to improve the well-being of Indian people, it cannot solely depend upon these changes to achieve the overall objective of improving the health and education conditions of its people throughout India.

My conclusion is based on various observations. Social justice and fertility decline are closely interlinked, but the degree varies from state to state. Reduction in infant mortality, an improvement in female education, and a decrease in gender disparity are among the conditions that contribute to fertility decline. Changes in age structure are much more pronounced in states which have already achieved higher education, lower infant and child mortality, and gender equality. In other states, however, we find that both social justice and fertility decline are relatively less advanced. The state of Kerala made tremendous progress in education while experiencing the fastest growth in population, whereas the state of Uttar Pradesh made little progress in education, even during its period of slow population growth. Thus, improvements in female education, for example, would require more than a decline in population growth rate. It would require a commitment to this objective and education policies that give priority to the achievement of this objective.

The policy and budgeting framework of India today means, however, that potential savings due to changes in the age distribution in the resources required for education and health in one state cannot be transferred to another state. Policies and mechanisms must be developed that allow those transfers and determine priorities within each state for more investment.

Within the Indian context, education and health — the levels and distribution of which are key indicators of social justice — are under the domain of the state government. I conclude that the progress made in closing the gap of regional disparities in infant mortality is to some extent the result of centrally-sponsored and financed activities such as the universal immunization programme. Given the variable degree of background gender equality, levels of resources allocated to education and commitment to girls' access to schooling, improvements in female education across the states would likely require a similar centrally-sponsored and financed programme. Such a programme could mitigate the effects of state-level variation in social and cultural factors that impede female education and undercut universalizing primary education, especially among girls living in rural areas.

These observations are based on the analysis presented in the subsequent three sections. The first section analyses the state-level data from the National Family and Health Surveys (NFHSs) to identify some of the key determinants of fertility. The second analyses the data from censuses, Sample Registration System (SRS), and NFHS to show the extent of the progress made in terms of improving equality in education and health in selected states. The last section brings together these data to identify the implications of India's fertility decline for future social policy.

DETERMINANTS OF FERTILITY

Conditions that promote high fertility include disparities within and among households. Parents are believed to have large families in order to enhance their own welfare, i.e., for reasons such as old age security, to provide extra help in domestic and field work, and to care for other siblings. Thus, a shift in parents' thinking toward an improvement in the welfare of children, and a more equitable sharing of the costs and benefits of children between men and women, would create conditions conducive to fertility decline.

There is no unique set of prerequisites necessary for fertility decline to occur and fertility has declined under a variety of conditions. While socio-economic development ultimately would lead to fertility decline, and family planning programmes have been shown to decrease fertility even under poor conditions, the ideal situation is one in which a good programme operates in a favourable social environment. Conditions conducive to fertility decline include:

a. A family planning programme that offers services and information of good quality;
b. A health system that results in low infant and child mortality; and
c. An educational system that results in high female literacy and education, at least up to the primary level.

The role of social development (female education and health) in Kerala's fertility transition is well established (see, for example,

Krishnan in this volume). How social development has influenced the course of fertility decline in other states is less well documented. This section briefly outlines the roles of infant mortality and female education in fertility transition in India.

The National Family and Health Survey (NFHS) conducted in 1992–3 confirmed that fertility in India has declined. Not only has it declined in Southern states like Kerala and Tamil Nadu, but it has also declined in Northern states like Uttar Pradesh. In fact, fertility declined throughout the country during the 1980s. The total fertility rate (TFR) in India, according to the Sample Registration System (SRS), declined from 5.7 births per woman in 1970–2 to 4.5 in 1980–2 and to 3.7 in 1990–2. The TFR estimated by NFHS for the 1990–2 period, however, was 3.4 births per woman. Notwithstanding the difference in the TFR estimates of SRS and NFHS, it is certain that fertility in India has declined during the last 20 years by about two births per woman.[2]

Table 1 shows the classification of 16 major states by the level of infant mortality and female education (percentage of married women aged 15–49 years who have at least primary level education). The TFR for each state is shown within parentheses. The TFR is less than 3.1 births per woman in states where *both* the infant mortality rate (IMR) is low to medium (i.e., less than 75), and female education is medium to high (i.e., more than 27 per cent). There are two exceptions to this rule — Orissa and Haryana. The TFR in Orissa is lower than what would be expected on the basis of levels of infant mortality and female education, while the situation is reversed in Haryana. The level of IMR in Rajasthan is medium but the level of female education is low, whereas the level of female education is medium in Assam and the level of IMR is high. The TFR in these two states is lower than the level in the remaining three states — Bihar, Madhya Pradesh, and Uttar Pradesh — where

---

[2] The National Family Health Survey (NFHS), carried out between April 1992 and September 1993, included a nationally representative sample of 89,777 ever-married women in the age group 13–49 years from 24 states and Delhi. It collected information on fertility, family planning, mortality, and maternal and child health. The Sample Registration System (SRS) was initiated in 1964–5 on a pilot basis and on a full-scale in 1969–70 to provide dependable estimates of vital rates at the national and state levels. Initially, the SRS underestimated the 'true' level of birth and death rates. The accuracy of SRS estimates is believed to have improved over time (see Mari Bhat in this volume and Jain, 1996 for further details).

both female education is low and infant mortality is high. A reduction in infant mortality and an increase in the level of female education in these three states will help them move rapidly toward the replacement level fertility.

TABLE 1: CLASSIFICATION OF 16 MAJOR STATES BY LEVEL OF FEMALE EDUCATION AND INFANT MORTALITY RATE, 1992–93

Female education (% of married women in reproductive age with at least primary level education)	*Infant mortality rate per 1,000 live births*		
	High (85–112)	*Medium (65–75)*	*Low (24–55)*
Low (19–23%)		Bihar (4.0)	Rajasthan (3.6)
	M.P. (4.0)		
	Orissa* (2.9)		
	U.P. (4.8)		
Medium (27–36%)	Assam (3.5)	A.P. (2.6)	
		Gujarat (3.0)	
		Haryana* (4.0)	
		Karnataka (2.9)	
		W.B. (2.9)	
High (39–45%)	Tamil Nadu (2.5)	Jammu (3.1)	
			Maharashtra (2.9)
			Punjab (2.9)
			Kerala (2.0)

Total fertility rate for each state is shown in parentheses.
* The levels of TFR in Orissa and Haryana are different than what would be expected on the basis of the levels of infant mortality and female education in these states.

Source: NFHS 1992–93.

The Role of Infant and Child Mortality

Fertility decline observed during the last twenty years has been accompanied by a substantial decline in infant and child mortality. The overall IMR in India, according to SRS estimates, has declined from 132 to 80 deaths per 1,000 births between 1970–2 and 1990–2, while TFR declined from 5.7 to 3.7 births per woman. The overall relationship between state-level IMR and TFR is reflected by the correlation coefficient of 0.619 between the two, which suggests that states with high infant mortality also have high fertility. There is a two-way connection between infant mortality and fertility.

The implication of high infant and child mortality for fertility behaviour is reflected by a gap between the average number of surviving children and the average number of live births per woman. For example, the average number of children born and surviving among women aged 40 to 44 years, according to NFHS, were 4.8 births and 4.0 children, respectively. The difference between the two in Uttar Pradesh, with high infant mortality, however, was much higher than in Kerala which had low infant mortality (1.2 vs. 0.2 births). The number of births a woman has is included in the numerator for estimating indices of fertility such as TFR and CBR. However, when a woman says that she wants a certain number of children, she refers to *surviving* children and not to live births. This means that a reduction in infant and child mortality would reduce the number of births she must have to reach her desired number of surviving children, which in turn would reduce TFR without reducing the desired family size.

This connection between IMR and TFR reflects both the biological and behavioural effects of high infant mortality on fertility. For example, the duration of breast-feeding for a child who dies in infancy is considerably shorter than for the child who survives for a longer period. Thus, the birth interval in the absence of contraceptive use following an infant death is usually shorter than that following the child who survives for more than one year. Moreover, a desire to replace a lost child in the subsequent birth interval may be implemented by adjusting the timing and frequency of coitus.

The relationship between IMR and TFR also reflects the fact that high fertility in a community means a higher proportion of high-parity births and that IMR is also high among high-parity births. Hence, a reduction in TFR achieved through a reduction of high-parity births would also reduce infant mortality. However, direct interventions to reduce infant mortality at all parities, and especially at the first parity, are most likely to reduce TFR. Such policies need special attention in Assam, Bihar, Madhya Pradesh,

Orissa, and Uttar Pradesh, where the level of IMR is estimated to be as high as 85 deaths or more per 1,000 births.

The Role of Female Education

Female education has been found to be associated with a decrease in fertility and mortality indicators in many societies, and, India is no exception. The assumption about the fertility reduction effect of education is based on the observation that the advancement in female education leads to: (i) a decrease in the demand (ideal or desired) for children; (ii) an increase in age at marriage; (iii) an increase in the use of contraception; and (iv) a decrease in the incidence and duration of breast-feeding and post-partum abstinence (see Table 2). The total fertility rates by female education for 16 major states in India, according to NFHS, are shown in Figure 1. In all states, TFR decreases with an increase in female education. There is no state in which TFR among females with little education is higher than that among women with no education. Even if there was such a state, state resources are wasted and social justice goals failed if girls' dropout rates from grades one to four are not minimized. Thus, even without the amply demonstrated fertility decline rationale, policies must work to increase the proportion of girls completing primary level of schooling (Jain 1981).

TABLE 2: TOTAL FERTILITY RATE AND ITS
PROXIMATE DETERMINANTS BY LEVEL OF
FEMALE EDUCATION IN INDIA, 1992–93

Female education	Fertility rate			Contra-ceptive Prevalence Rate	Median age at marriage among women 25–29 years of age	Median number of months of post-partum non-suscep-tible period
	Total	Wanted	Un-wanted			
Illiterate	4.03	3.15	0.88	33.9	15.3	11.4
Literate	3.01	2.31	0.70	50.4	17.1	9.2
Middle school	2.49	1.95	0.54	50.8	18.7	7.9
High school & above	2.15	1.78	0.37	54.7	21.7	6.2
Total	3.39	2.64	0.75	40.6	16.6	10.2

Source: NFHS 1992–93.

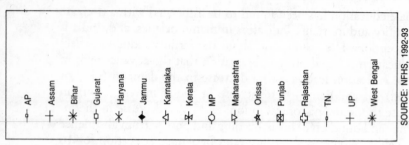

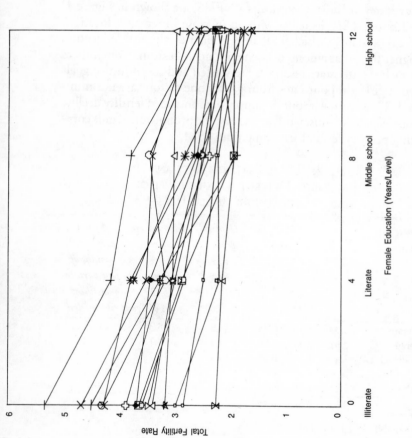

FIG. 1:   *Total fertility rate by female education for major states in India: 1990–92*

The effect of education on fertility is measured by the slope in a regression equation, which has been found to vary from state to state in India (see Figure 1). For example, TFR in Uttar Pradesh decreases from 5.4 births among women with no education to 2.6 births among women with at least high school education, which implies a regression coefficient of –0.220. In comparison, Kerala's TFR decreases from 2.3 to 2.0 births per woman with a regression coefficient of –0.029. The effect of female education measured by the slope of the regression equation in Kerala is lower than in Uttar Pradesh (–0.029 vs. –0.220). This is what would be expected at different stages of demographic transition. At the beginning of demographic transition, TFR is likely to be uniformly high in all education groups. As women with better education start to regulate their fertility, the relationship between TFR and education becomes pronounced, as depicted by the pattern in Uttar Pradesh. Toward the end of the demographic transition, the fertility becomes uniformly low in all education groups as shown by the pattern in Kerala.

If the relationship between female education and fertility simply reflects the stage of demographic transition, will improvement in female education in, for example, Uttar Pradesh reduce fertility? The answer depends upon a better understanding of why the effect of education on fertility varies from state to state. Two distinct situations under which the individual-level effect of education on fertility could vary among countries or communities within a country are schematically shown in Figures 2(a) and 2(b).

In the pattern shown in Figure 2(a), the average fertility of women with little or no education is similar across countries, whereas, fertility of educated women differs markedly across countries. In this pattern, the variation in the effect of education on fertility is due to the variation in the fertility of educated women. The variation in the fertility of educated women across communities could reflect differences among communities in factors, such as levels of economic development, opportunities for and actual participation by educated women in the paid labour force and, therefore, to differences in the economic value of education. If so, an increase in female education is unlikely to reduce fertility, without simultaneous improvements in economic opportunities. This is the most prevalent interpretation about the differential effect of female education on fertility.

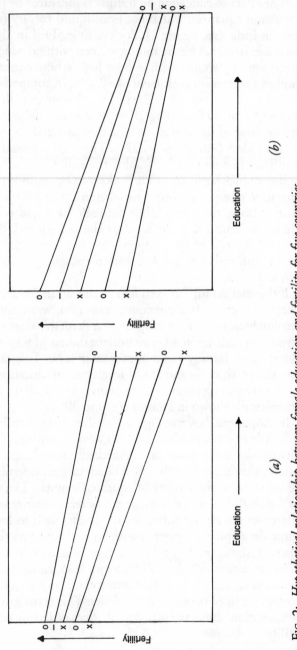

Fig. 2: *Hypothetical relationship between female education and fertility for five countries*

In the pattern shown in Figure 2(b), the average fertility of educated women is similar across communities, whereas fertility of women with little or no education differs markedly across communities. In this pattern, the variation in the effect of education on fertility is due to the variation in the fertility of women with no education. The fact that the fertility of educated women is similar across communities with different opportunities would imply that fertility behaviour of women, in part, depends upon their education. In this case, attention must be given to the causes of differences among communities in the fertility behaviour of women with no education. Such differences could reflect the impact of variations in postpartum amenorrhoea and abstinence, differences in infant mortality, and the differential impacts of family planning programmes, i.e., differential use of contraception among women with no education.

The pattern in India (Figure 1) is similar to the one shown in Figure 2(b). While TFR among women with no education varies from a low of 2.3 in Kerala to a high of 5.4 in Uttar Pradesh, TFR among women with at least high school level education is quite close to 2 except in Bihar, Haryana, Karnataka, Madhya Pradesh, and Uttar Pradesh. In these states, TFR varies between 2.6 in Bihar and Uttar Pradesh, and 3.0 in Karnataka. Thus, the difference between regression coefficients for Kerala and Uttar Pradesh (−0.029 vs. −0.220) is primarily due to the difference in fertility among women with no education (5.4 vs. 2.3) rather than to the difference in fertility among educated women (2.6 vs. 2.0).

Women with a high school education appear to be more similar across state boundaries than women with no education (the standard deviation of TFRs among women with no education is 0.79 in comparison to 0.42 among those with high school education). This means that there might be something more to female education (that holds across state boundaries) than an increase in their potential to participate in economic activities (which varies among states). Improvements in female education, therefore, can be expected to influence fertility behaviour, even without simultaneous changes in other factors such as increased opportunities for participation in the paid labour force.[3] A similar conclusion was drawn by an analysis conducted with data from eleven countries (Jain 1981).

[3] Improvements in girls' education will reduce fertility as they move through their reproductive period. Will children's education reduce parental fertility in the short run? This is unlikely to be the case in high fertility societies, especially

Potential Effect of Improvement in Female Education

What can be achieved by focusing upon female education? To address this question I compare two states, Kerala and Uttar Pradesh, in regards to the effect of female education on total and wanted fertility rates and infant mortality rates. The results, from NFHS, are shown in Table 3; panel A for total fertility rate, panel B for wanted fertility rate, and panel C for infant mortality rate.

Seventy-six per cent of women of reproductive age in Uttar Pradesh have no education, compared to 16 per cent in Kerala. If the education of women in Uttar Pradesh was the same as that of women in Kerala, the overall TFR in Uttar Pradesh would have been 3.9 instead of 4.8 births per woman. This means that, out of a difference of 2.8 births in TFR between Uttar Pradesh and Kerala, 0.9 births are explained by the fact that women in Uttar Pradesh have less education than those in Kerala. The remaining difference of 1.9 births reflects the effect of differences between Kerala and Uttar Pradesh in education specific fertility rates. Women in Uttar Pradesh exhibit higher fertility than women with similar education in Kerala. The differences between the two states, however, decreases from 3.1 births for women with no education to 0.6 births for women with a high school education. The narrowing of fertility differences with improvement in education suggests that the differential effect of

the short run? This is unlikely to be the case in high fertility societies, especially if laws about compulsory education and prohibition against child labour cannot be enforced. There are two reasons for not expecting a feedback loop of children's education to parental fertility. The first reason is based on demographic realities, and the second on the belief that parents in high fertility societies tend to maximize their own welfare rather than their children's.

In high fertility societies, by the time the eldest child is likely to complete primary education, the mother would be about 30 years of age and, on average, would have completed about 70 per cent of her marital fertility. If the effect of a child's education on parent's fertility is postponed until s/he completes secondary school, the mother will be close to completing her childbearing process.

If benefits to parents from their children's education are higher than the corresponding costs, they are unlikely to reduce their fertility because more children would mean higher benefits. On the other hand, if benefits from their children's education are lower than the corresponding costs, the outcome is likely to be no education for children rather than high education for children and low fertility for parents. In brief, children's education is unlikely to have a negative feedback effect on parent's fertility unless parents are assumed to maximize the welfare of their children at an early stage of childbearing. But if that were the case, parents would already be having small families (Jain 1982: 186–7).

TABLE 3: TOTAL AND WANTED FERTILITY RATES AND
INFANT MORTALITY RATES BY FEMALE EDUCATION IN
KERALA AND UTTAR PRADESH, 1992–93

Education	Kerala	Uttar Pradesh	Ratio
(1)	(2)	(3)	(4) = (2)/(3)
A. Total Fertility Rate			
Illiterate	2.27	5.36	0.424
Literate	2.16	4.16	0.519
Middle school	1.95	3.81	0.512
High school	1.95	2.55	0.0765
Total observed	2.00	4.82	0.415
*Total estimated**	2.00	3.92	0.510
Constant	2.26	5.29	
Regression coefficient	−0.029	−0.220	
B. Wanted Fertility Rate			
Illiterate	1.98	4.30	0.0460
Literate	1.92	3.30	0.582
Middle school	1.81	3.00	0.603
High school	1.86	2.10	0.886
Total observed	1.82	3.80	0.479
*Total estimated**	1.82	3.13	
Constant	1.96	4.21	
Regression coefficient	−0.012	−0.173	
C. Infant Mortality Rate			
Illiterate	60.4	127.4	0.474
Literate	33.6	72.7	0.462
Middle school	22.7	83.0	0.273
High school	14.5	54.6	0.266
Total	23.8	99.9	0.238
Constant	55.1	115.6	
Regression coefficient	−3.72	−5.20	

Source: NFHS 1992–93.

* Assumes that the education composition of women in Uttar Pradesh was
the same as that of women in Kerala.

macro-level factors on TFR between the two states is more pronounced among women with no education than among the educated women. The lower fertility of women with no education in
Kerala might reflect the fact that health and family planning services
in Kerala are better than in Uttar Pradesh. Simultaneous improvements made in Uttar Pradesh in the quality and availability of
education, health, and family planning services would, therefore,
contribute to the reduction of overall TFR in the state. These improvements are not interchangeable. Simultaneous improvements
in female education and a reduction in infant mortality would
decrease wanted fertility or desired family size (see discussion
below), and improvements in family planning services would enhance women's ability to carry out their desires to regulate fertility.

The wanted fertility in Uttar Pradesh decreases from 4.3 among
women with no education to 2.1 among those with at least high
school level of education.[4] It is of interest to note that the desired
fertility level among women with a high school education in Uttar
Pradesh is quite close to the corresponding level among women
with no education in Kerala. In both groups the infant mortality
level is also similar. Thus, wanted fertility decline would require a
substantial decrease in infant mortality or a substantial increase in
female education. However, improvements in both female education and health would perhaps decrease wanted fertility faster than
the improvements in either one of these.

As far as the reduction in infant and child mortality is concerned,
the effect of female education is complementary to that of health
services. In fact, under certain circumstances, the effect of the two
factors may even be synergistic, as both facilitate changes in
health seeking behaviour. This point can be illustrated by comparing

---

[4] Unwanted births are excluded from the numerator in calculating wanted
fertility rate. According to NFHS: 'a birth is considered unwanted if the number
of living children at the time of conception was greater than or equal to the current
ideal number of children, as reported by the respondent. Women who gave a
non-numeric response to the question on the ideal number of children were
assumed to want all their births.' This procedure estimated that 24 per cent of
TFR was unwanted. Distribution of births during the four years preceding the
survey and current pregnancies by fertility planning status indicated that only 9
per cent of births were unwanted and an additional 14 per cent were ill-timed.
The difference in unwanted fertility between the two procedures may reflect the
effect of post-facto rationalization, i.e., women are unwilling to call a child already
born as 'unwanted'.

education-specific infant mortality rates between Kerala and Uttar Pradesh. The infant mortality rate in Kerala declines from a level of 60, among women with no education, to 14, among those with at least a high school education. In comparison, IMR in Uttar Pradesh decreases from 127 among women with no education, to 55, among those with at least high school education. The effect of education on infant mortality measured by the slope of the regression equation is −3.72 in Kerala and −5.20 in Uttar Pradesh. This means that improving female education in Uttar Pradesh will reduce the overall IMR. However, even if all women in Uttar Pradesh receive a high school education and health services remain the same, the overall IMR is likely to be reduced to 55, the current level among high school graduates. In order for the IMR to decline further, there must be improvements in other factors including health services.

The gross effect of health services can be measured by differences in the education-specific ratios of IMR (shown in column 4, panel C of Table 3). The effect of health services on IMR decreases with an increase in education. This means that the effect of health services on IMR among women with no education is much more pronounced than that among educated women. In other words, an increase in the coverage of health services would reduce the effect of female education on infant mortality because women with no education would also be able to access these services. The education-specific ratios of IMR may overestimate the effect of health services because other factors, such as poverty, are not included in these comparisons. Nevertheless, these comparisons make it clear that simultaneous improvements in both education and health services would reduce infant mortality faster than concentrating on just one of the two.

As far as the reduction in total fertility is concerned, the effect of female education is complementary to that of contraceptive and health services: improvements in female education reduces the desired family size (see panel B in Table 3) and improves women's ability to regulate their fertility. Furthermore, improvements in contraceptive services provide women with the means to transform their desires into practice. Similarly, reductions in infant and child mortality and in fertility are mutually supportive. In sum, a faster decline in IMR, a faster increase in female education, in conjunction with a good quality family planning programme is likely to accelerate the ongoing fertility transition in India.

MAXIMIZING THE SOCIAL BENEFITS OF FERTILITY DECLINE

When considering the consequences and benefits of fertility decline, it is necessary to think of consequences at different levels: the macro (all-India) level, the regional (or state) level, the family level, and the individual level. It is also necessary to consider whether the cost of fertility reduction and potential benefits are proportionately distributed among different segments of the population. For example, the cost of fertility reduction and the benefits derived from low fertility may not be shared equally between rich and poor households, or even between the man and the woman in the same household. This might happen when poor households (or women) are asked to reduce their fertility while the other government policies tend to favour the middle class and the rich (or men).

While some of the assumptions about adverse economic consequences of rapid population growth have recently been questioned, they were recognized by Indian economic planners as early as the 1950s. Even the eighth Five-Year Plan document considered the implications of the rapid population growth of the past:

> The [population] growth started increasing rather fast after 1951 and reached a peak of 2.22 per cent during the decade 1971–81. It is tempting to think that if only India had succeeded in containing her population growth rate after 1951 to around one per cent per annum i.e. the rate China has achieved, how much difference this factor alone would have meant in terms of per capita income, consumption, and levels of living. (GOI: Planning Commission 1992: 22–3)

A recent study (Drèze and Sen 1995), however, suggests that if India could cut its population growth to China's level, its annual per capita GDP growth would rise slightly from 3.1 per cent to 3.8 per cent. In other words, a reduction in the population growth rate would have little effect on the pace of economic development. The authors, however, support policies to reduce the rate of population growth on other grounds.

The effect of fertility decline on a government's ability to invest in human development, as mentioned above, is mitigated through changes in the age distribution of the population. While India still has a young population, its age composition has begun to change. The age composition had been quite stable until 1971, due to high fertility: with about 41 per cent between 0 to 14 years of age; about 5 to 6 per cent over the age of 60 years; and the remaining 53 to

54 per cent in the working ages (15 to 59 years). The effect of the recent fertility decline on age composition has begun to show in terms of a slight decrease in the per cent of population aged 0–14 years (from 41 per cent in 1971 to 36 percentage in 1991) and a corresponding increase in the working age population from 54 per cent in 1971 to 58 per cent in 1991 (see Table 4). Consequently, the dependency ratio has decreased from 0.85 in 1971 to 0.72 in 1991. The overall dependency ratio is made up of two components: dependency burden of the young (0 to 14 years) population and

TABLE 4: AGE DISTRIBUTION OF POPULATION IN INDIA AND SELECTED STATES, 1961–91

Age (Years) (1)	1961 Census (2)	1971 Census (3)	1981 Census (4)	1991 SRS (5)	1992/93 NFHS (6)
India					
0–14	41	41	38	36	38
15–59	53	54	56	58	54
60+	6	5	6	6	8
Total	100	100	100	100	100
Kerala					
0–14	42	40	35	30	30
15–59	52	54	57	62	62
60+	6	6	8	8	8
Total	100	100	100	100	100
Uttar Pradesh					
0–14	41	42	42	39	42
15–59	53	51	51	55	50
60+	6	7	7	6	8
Total	100	100	100	100	100
Tamil Nadu					
0–14	37	38	35	31	32
15–59	57	54	59	62	60
60+	6	6	6	7	8
Total	100	100	100	100	100

the dependency burden of the old (60 years or more) population. The first component has decreased from 0.76 to 0.62 during the last 20 years, whereas the second component has slightly increased from 0.09 to 0.10.

There are two important implications of the young population in India. First is the phenomenon of momentum, meaning that even if fertility is instantaneously reduced to replacement level, the population will continue to grow until children who are already born pass through their reproductive period. This effect is minimized by increasing the length of the generation, which can be done by delaying the age at first birth, and by increasing the interval between subsequent births. The second issue has to do with the provision of health and education services. While the size of the cohort becoming eligible for education has started to decline in terms of the proportion of the total population, the absolute number of children becoming eligible for primary education is likely to continue to grow. On the other hand, while the proportion of elderly (60 or more years of age) has remained constant, the absolute number of elderly has increased substantially because of the growth in the total population size. Health and other needs of this elderly population will become an increasingly important area of public expenditure. How to meet the growing demands of the increasing elderly population on public expenditures without reducing the resources required to meet the needs of children is a critical policy issue to be addressed by Indian policy-makers.

These effects would be different in each state, because of differences in the changes in age distribution. It is important to consider state-level differences because both education and health are state domains, with the state government investing the majority of resources required to improve the education and health conditions of its people. Under the current scheme, the savings realized from education of young children as a consequence of the fertility reduction in one state are not transferable to another state.

The age distributions of three states are compared in Table 4 to illustrate this point: Kerala and Tamil Nadu with low fertility, and Uttar Pradesh with high fertility. The age distributions in all three states were quite similar till 1971. The age distribution in Uttar Pradesh shows a very slight change since then, whereas the proportion of the population in the young age group, 0 to 14 years, in both Kerala and Tamil Nadu has declined substantially. The dependency burden of the young population in Kerala has declined markedly from 0.74 to 0.48, and in Tamil Nadu, it has declined from 0.70 in 1971 to 0.50 in 1991. The dependency burden of the young population in Uttar Pradesh has declined slightly from 0.82 to 0.71. On the other hand, the dependency burden of the young population in Uttar Pradesh in 1991 was similar to what it was in Kerala and Tamil Nadu in 1971. The education and health conditions of the people at present in Kerala and Tamil Nadu are quite different from those in Uttar Pradesh and, therefore, the implications of the changing age distributions for the future would be quite different.

DIFFERENTIAL PROGRESS MADE IN EDUCATION AND HEALTH

Since the key determinants of fertility decline include infant mortality and female education, we have selected these indicators to show the progress made in the health and education sectors. In terms of education, we have focused on the percentage of population aged 15 to 19 years which has completed primary level schooling. I have selected this age group because children would have ample time to complete primary level schooling by the age of 15 years even if they started their schooling much later than age five. Moreover, these ages mark the beginning of the reproductive period for women.

The infant mortality rate in all three states has declined during the last twenty years (see Table 5). However, IMR in Tamil Nadu in 1991 was about the same as it was in Kerala in 1971. IMR in Uttar Pradesh in 1991 was even higher than what it was in Kerala, but lower than what it was in Tamil Nadu in 1971. All three states have also made considerable progress in terms of education (see Table 6). Almost all persons (93 per cent) in the 15–19 year age group in Kerala had completed primary level schooling in 1991, in comparison to 72 per cent in Tamil Nadu, and 56 per cent in Uttar Pradesh. In 1991, this level in Uttar Pradesh was about the same as it was in Tamil Nadu in 1971, but lower than what it was in Kerala then.

Disparities in these education and health indicators are computed at three levels: regional (among states), residential (between rural and urban areas within a state), and gender (between male and female). Instead of or in addition to gender disparities at the individual level, class, religion, or caste disparities could also have been considered in the achievement of good health and education.

TABLE 5: INFANT MORTALITY RATE PER 1,000 BIRTHS FOR
INDIA AND SELECTED STATES BY PLACE OF RESIDENCE AND
GENDER, 1970–72 TO 1990–92

Period	Place of Residence				Gender		
	Total	Rural	Urban	Residential disparity (rural-urban)	Male	Female	Gender disparity (female-male)
(1)	(2)	(3)	(4)	(5)	(6)	(7)	(8)
India							
1970–72	132	141	86	55	131	134	3
1980–82	110	119	64	55	110	110	0
1990–92	80	86	52	34	81	80	−1
Kerala							
1970–72	58	61	44	17			
1980–82	36	38	27	11			
1990–92	17	17	15	2	17	16	−1
Uttar Pradesh							
1970–72	174	184	116	68			
1980–82	152	160	98	62			
1990–92	98	103	73	30	95	100	5
Tamil Nadu							
1970–72	120	131	84	47			
1980–82	89	101	57	44			
1990–92	58	67	40	27	60	54	−6

Source: SRS.

I have selected gender to show the extent of disparity at the individual level because women have disproportionately borne the
cost of fertility reduction in India. This is shown by the fact that
out of 36.2 per cent of couples who were using a modern method
of contraception according to NFHS, only 5.8 per cent were using
a male method. The remaining 30.4 per cent were using a female
method — mainly female sterilization (27.3 per cent).

TABLE 6: PERCENTAGE OF PERSONS AGED 15–19 YEARS
WHO HAVE COMPLETED AT LEAST PRIMARY LEVEL SCHOOLING
FOR INDIA AND SELECTED STATES BY GENDER AND
PLACE OF RESIDENCE, 1971–92/93

	Rural			Urban			Total		
Period	Male	Female	Total	Male	Female	Total	Male	Female	Total
(1)	(2)	(3)	(4)	(5)	(6)	(7)	(8)	(9)	(10)
India									
1971	49	23	36	76	62	70	55	31	44
1981	51	27	40	76	65	71	58	37	48
1992/93	68	40	54	84	75	80	73	50	61
Kerala									
1971	80	71	75	86	80	83	81	71	77
1981	88	84	87	91	89	90	89	85	87
1992/93	92	93	93	94	94	94	92	94	93
Uttar Pradesh									
1971	45	13	31	66	50	59	51	19	37
1981	53	17	37	65	52	59	56	24	42
1992/93	70	32	51	76	66	71	71	40	56
Tamil Nadu									
1971	55	33	43	79	65	72	63	42	52
1981	71	49	60	81	70	75	75	56	65
1992/93	76	56	65	87	84	85	80	66	72

Source: Census for 1971 and 1981; NFHS for 1992/93.

Regional Disparity

The regional disparity is measured by the difference in the state level IMRs or primary school completion rates (see Table 7). While the regional disparities in IMR have declined over twenty years, disparities in education have remained about the same. For example, the regional disparity in IMR between Uttar Pradesh and Kerala has declined from about 116 points in 1971 to 81 points in 1991, and between Uttar Pradesh and Tamil Nadu it has declined from 54 to 40 points. The regional disparity in education, on the other hand, has remained around 40 points between Uttar Pradesh and Kerala, and around 15 points between

Uttar Pradesh and Tamil Nadu. It is possible that a reduction in regional disparities in IMR reflects the fact that interventions to reduce IMR, such as the Universal Immunization Programme (UIP) got impetus under the centrally-sponsored schemes like Maternal and Child Health (MCH) and Child Survival and Safe Motherhood (CSSM) Programme. It is possible that these programmes disproportionately focused on states with high infant and child mortality and, thus, minimized the effect of biases in the allocation of state resources to primary health care. No such central scheme is active to universalize primary education.

TABLE 7: REGIONAL DISPARITIES IN INFANT MORTALITY RATE
AND EDUCATION BY PLACE OF RESIDENCE, 1970/72 TO 1990/92

	Disparity in infant mortality rate by place of residence			Disparity in education by place of residence		
Period	Total	Rural	Urban	Total	Rural	Urban
(1)	(2)	(3)	(4)	(5)	(6)	(7)
	Uttar Pradesh–Kerala			*Kerala–Uttar Pradesh*		
1970–72	116	146	72	40	44	24
1980–82	116	122	71	45	40	31
1990–92	81	86	58	37	42	23
	Tamil Nadu–Kerala			*Kerala–Tamil Nadu*		
1970–72	62	70	40	25	32	11
1980–82	53	63	30	22	27	15
1990–92	41	50	25	21	28	9
	Uttar Pradesh–Tamil Nadu			*Tamil Nadu–Uttar Pradesh*		
1970–72	54	76	32	15	12	13
1980–82	63	59	41	23	13	16
1990–92	40	36	33	16	14	14

Source: Tables 5 and 6.

Residential (Rural-Urban) Disparity

The rural-urban disparity in IMR in Kerala has virtually disappeared during the period 1971–91 (see column 5 in Table 5). It

has declined quite considerably in both Tamil Nadu (from 47 points in 1971 to 27 points in 1991) and Uttar Pradesh (from 68 points in 1971 to 30 points in 1991). The rural-urban disparity in education also follows the same pattern (see column 5 in Table 8): it has completely disappeared in Kerala and has declined in both Tamil Nadu (from 29 points to 20 points) and Uttar Pradesh (from 28 points to 20 points) between 1971 and 1991. Thus, it appears that the potential benefits of fertility decline in terms of improved health and education are being shared with people living in rural areas. This, however, is not the case with gender differences.

TABLE 8: GENDER AND RESIDENTIAL DISPARITY IN PRIMARY EDUCATION ATTAINMENT FOR INDIA AND SELECTED STATES, 1971–92/93

Period	Gender disparity (male–female)			Residential disparity (urban–rural)	Combined disparity (urban male–rural female)
	Rural	Urban	Total		
(1)	(2)	(3)	(4)	(5)	(6)
India					
1971	26	14	24	34	53
1981	24	11	21	31	49
1992/93	28	9	23	26	44
Kerala					
1971	9	6	10	8	15
1981	4	2	4	3	7
1992/93	1	0	–2	1	1
Uttar Pradesh					
1971	32	16	32	28	53
1981	36	13	32	21	48
1992/93	38	10	31	20	44
Tamil Nadu					
1971	22	14	21	29	46
1981	22	11	19	15	32
1992/93	20	3	14	20	31

Source: Table 6.

Gender Disparity

Rapid population growth can affect gender disparity due to a gender bias in the allocation of government resources and gender bias within the family. Large family size is assumed to adversely effect the allocation of parental resources for health and education of children within the family. It is, therefore, logical to expect that a decline in family size would improve parental allocation of financial and other resources per child. However, it raises the important question of whether these benefits are shared equally between male and female children.

There is very little information on this subject. Das Gupta and Mari Bhat (1995) showed intensification of gender bias in terms of sex selected abortions as a result of fertility decline during the 1980s. Jejeebhoy (1993) showed that female children in rural Maharashtra did not benefit as a consequence of a decreased family size, whereas male children did. According to the author, her study raises 'the alarming possibility that with the increasing prevalence of small families, gender disparities in outcomes for children will widen'. To counteract these adverse consequences of fertility decline on gender disparities would require formulation and implementation of gender sensitive public policies in education, health, and other spheres.

Women's Health

As mentioned earlier, women have disproportionately borne the cost of fertility regulation. Have they benefited in terms of better health?

The life expectancy at birth in India — one indicator of better health — has increased for both males and females from about 23 years at the beginning of this century to about 60 years at present. The life expectancy at birth for females is estimated to be about 61 years in comparison to 60 years for males. This is in contrast to countries in East Asia where the life expectancy for females was estimated to be about 74 years in comparison to 70 years for males. Evidently, women in India are relatively disadvantaged as far as overall mortality is concerned.

High maternal morbidity and mortality are other indicators of low female health status and their lack of access to health resources in India. Information on these two indicators of maternal health is lacking. Recently, Mari Bhat et al. (1995) estimated maternal mortality ratios by using indirect methods of estimation and data from SRS. According to these estimates, the maternal mortality ratio for India is estimated to be 580 deaths per 100,000 live births for the 1982–6 period. The maternal mortality ratio is estimated to be higher in rural than in urban areas (638 vs. 389 deaths per 100,000 live births). There are some regional variations as well. For example, the state of Assam has an estimated 1,068 maternal deaths per 100,000 live births for the same time period and 207 maternal deaths were recorded for Punjab. Other states which show high maternal mortality are Uttar Pradesh, Bihar, Orissa, and Rajasthan. Lower maternal mortality levels are reported for southern and western Indian states.

According to the NFHS conducted in 1992–3, the average maternal mortality ratio at the national level for the two-year period prior to the survey date is estimated to be 437 deaths per 100,000 live births. The rate for rural areas is estimated to be higher than for urban areas (448 vs. 397). The extent to which the difference between the indirect estimate derived by Mari Bhat et al. for 1982–6 and the NFHS estimate for 1990–1 reflects a real decline in the risk of maternal deaths between the two time periods cannot be ascertained.

In addition to the risk of maternal deaths, women also suffer a high risk of morbidity related to reproduction. However, the knowledge about reproductive morbidity and its determinants in India is virtually nonexistent (see Jejeebhoy and Rama Rao 1995 for an excellent review of the available material). There are two studies which indicate a high level of reproductive morbidity among Indian women. Bang et al. (1989) found that 55 per cent of women belonging to the Gond tribe in a Maharashtra village reported gynaecological complaints. Another recent study in Karnataka (Bhatia and Cleland 1995) found that approximately one-third of all women reported at least one current symptom indicating morbidity such as conditions of anaemia, menstrual disorders, lower reproductive tract infection, and acute pelvic inflammatory disease.

While reproductive health in regions with low fertility may be better than those with high fertility, the levels of maternal morbidity and mortality may still be unacceptably high. For example, according to Mari Bhat et al. (1995), the maternal mortality ratio, even in the state of Kerala, which has a slightly below replacement level fertility and very low infant mortality, was as high as 235 deaths per 100,000 births for the 1982–6 period. It should be noted that other indicators of health care in Kerala in terms of antenatal care received at the time of birth are quite high (see Table 9): among births during 1988–9, i.e., four years prior to the interview in NFHS, about 90 per cent of mothers received antenatal care and about 90 per cent of babies were born in medical institutions and/or attended by a health professional. The reasons for high maternal mortality in Kerala despite this good health care system remain unknown. As expected, these indicators of health care in Uttar Pradesh are extremely low, while Tamil Nadu seems to have made good progress in this regard.

TABLE 9: SELECTED INDICATORS OF HEALTH CARE
FOR INDIA AND SELECTED STATES

Indicators	India	Kerala	Uttar Pradesh	Tamil Nadu
(1)	(2)	(3)	(4)	(5)
Percentage of births during four years prior to NFHS whose mothers received:				
Antenatal Care	62.3	97.3	44.7	94.2
Two dosages of tetanus toxoid vaccine	53.8	89.8	37.4	90.1
Iron/Folic tablets	50.5	91.2	29.5	84.2
Percentage of births during four years prior to NFHS delivered in medical institutions	25.5	87.8	11.2	63.4
Percentage of deliveries assisted by health professionals	34.2	89.7	17.2	71.2
Maternal mortality ratio per 100,000 births	580	247	920	372
Maternal death rate per 100,000 women	82	21	160	38

Source: NFHS for health care indicators; Mari Bhat et al. (1995) for maternal mortality.

While fertility decline contributes to improvements in women's health by eliminating high-parity births and increasing intervals between subsequent births, additional interventions will also be required to improve women's health. These interventions should be oriented to reduce the risk of maternal mortality and morbidity during the gestation period and at the time of pregnancy termination, and to reduce maternal morbidity associated with the use of contraception. The median age at sterilization for Indian women is slightly less than 27 years. This means that these women remain exposed to the risk of disease for at least another 18 years of their reproductive life, with no contact with the health system which is oriented to provide contraceptive services and health services for mothers and children.

Infant and Child Mortality

Male infant mortality, in the absence of gender bias, should be slightly higher than female infant mortality. While IMR has declined over the last twenty years, the decline at the all-India level has been of the same order of magnitude for males and females. Time trend data for gender-specific IMR for each state are not available. However, at present, the gender disparity in the risk of infant death has more or less disappeared in Andhra Pradesh, Karnataka, and Orissa. The gender disparity in IMR remains quite pronounced in Bihar, Haryana, Punjab, and Uttar Pradesh. In the remaining states, IMRs for males and females are about the same.

While the effect of gender bias on the risk of infant death can be minimized through such public interventions as universal immunization, this may not happen for the risk of death beyond the first year of life. During this period of life, the effect of behavioural factors, such as neglect of female children (allocation of food and utilization of health services), on their chances of survival may become more pronounced. However, while the age-specific death rate in the 0–4 year age group has declined, the extent of gender bias in child survival at the all-India level has not changed much, that is, the child mortality rates have remained about the same for both male and female children. In some states like Uttar Pradesh, the gender bias in child mortality has declined both in absolute and relative terms. The child mortality rate (0–4 age group) in Uttar Pradesh in the mid-1970s was about 65 for males and 97 for females. In the early 1990s, these rates declined to about 30 and 37, respectively. The effect of gender bias on child survival remains particularly serious in Bihar, Haryana, Madhya Pradesh, Punjab, and Uttar Pradesh (SRS 1993; Das Gupta and Mari Bhat 1995).

Girls' Education

The gender differences in education tell quite an interesting story. The gender disparity in education is measured by the difference between the percentage of males and females aged 15–19 who have completed primary-level schooling. Table 8 shows the gender disparities in education separately for rural and urban areas. Gender disparity in education in Kerala was low to begin with, and has now disappeared from both rural and urban areas. The overall gender disparity in education in Tamil Nadu has decreased from 21 points to 14 points over a period of twenty years. This decline appears to have accelerated during the 1980s, which may have contributed to a faster fertility decline in Tamil Nadu during this period. However, almost all of this decline is accounted for by a decrease in gender disparity in urban areas of the state. In rural Tamil Nadu, the gender disparity in education has remained virtually constant around 20 points. The overall gender difference in Uttar Pradesh, on the other hand, has remained virtually constant at about 30 points, having decreased in urban areas from 16 to 10 points, but increased in rural areas from 32 to 38 points, during the period 1971–91. Thus, rural females in Uttar Pradesh have not done as well in education as rural males or urban females.

The joint effect of disadvantage due to the place of residence (urban or rural) and gender on the completion of primary school education can be measured by the difference between urban males (the most privileged) and rural females (the least privileged). The value of this index has declined from 15 points to 1 point for Kerala, from 46 to 31 points for Tamil Nadu, and from 53 to 44 points for Uttar Pradesh and the country as a whole. The regional disparities (differences among states) for male education is much lower than that for female education, especially in rural areas. Moreover, the regional disparities in education among rural females has either remained constant or increased somewhat during a period of twenty years. In contrast, the regional disparity among rural males has declined over this period (these results are not shown in a table, but could be calculated from Table 6). Tamil Nadu, Uttar Pradesh, and perhaps all other major states, have a long way to go to address these disparities in female education. Removal of these disparities may be facilitated by changes in age distribution in Tamil Nadu, but not so much in Uttar Pradesh. In addition, the removal of gender disparities in these and other states would require adoption and implementation of educational policies that would disproportionately favour rural females and allocate adequate resources for this purpose.

CONCLUDING REMARKS

A rationale for reducing population growth through fertility reduction is to improve the social and economic conditions of people — referring both to level and distribution of socially valued outcomes. Thus, it is important to ascertain the extent to which the ongoing fertility transition has contributed to the reduction of disparities among people. To address this question one must first demonstrate that there has been a reduction in disparities and then ascertain whether that reduction is a cause or consequence of fertility reduction.

I have found that some significant disparities persist or even increase as fertility declines. In terms of disparities, regional (between states), residential (between rural and urban), and gender disparities in infant and child mortality and education were examined. The regional and residential disparities in the risk of infant and child death have declined over the past twenty years, to some extent a function of fertility decline. The gender disparity in child mortality has declined in some states, but not in others. While rural-urban differences in education have declined, the regional disparity and educational attainment has remained the same and, with regard to gender, we find that girls in rural areas do less well than girls in urban areas or boys in rural areas.

It is very difficult to ascertain whether reduction in these disparities is a cause or consequence of fertility reduction. Conditions conducive to low fertility include low infant and child mortality and high female education at least up to the primary school level. The gender disparities in health and education are also low in states with low infant and child mortality and with high female education. A reduction in gender disparities in education and health, thus, could be included among the conditions conducive to fertility decline.

It should be noted that a tremendous progress in education was made in Kerala during its period of highest population growth. The annual exponential population growth rate in Kerala was over two per cent during 1941–71 before it declined to 1.74 per cent during 1971–81 (see Table 10). The female literacy rate increased from 32 per cent in 1951 to 54 per cent in 1971. In comparison, while the annual population growth rate in Uttar Pradesh was low, it experienced very little progress in education. The annual exponential population growth rate in Uttar Pradesh was 1.12 per cent during 1941–51, and it increased to 1.79 per cent during 1961–71. The female literacy rate, however, increased from 4 per cent in 1951 to 11 per cent in 1971. The age distributions of population in both states were similar until 1971, but they made differential progress in improving female education.

TABLE 10: POPULATION GROWTH RATE AND FEMALE LITERACY RATE IN KERALA AND UTTAR PRADESH DURING 1941–91

Period	Annual exponential population growth rate		Female literacy	
	Kerala	Uttar Pradesh	Kerala	Uttar Pradesh
1941–51	2.08	1.12	32	4
1951–61	2.24	1.54	39	7
1961–71	2.26	1.79	54	11
1971–81	1.74	2.29	65	14
1981–91	1.34	2.27		

Note: Female literacy rates are shown for the ending year of each decade.

The progress in education in Kerala, therefore, cannot be attributed to fertility decline and to changes in its age distribution. Kerala allocated 35 per cent of its resources to education, and a bulk of it to primary school education, which was not the case in Uttar Pradesh. A decline in the population growth rate in Uttar Pradesh, without concomitant changes in its education policies, therefore, is unlikely to improve conditions for females, especially for those living in rural areas.[5]

[5] The reasons why Uttar Pradesh does not allocate as much funds to education as does Kerala are quite complex and may be rooted in cultural differences

The recent changes in the age distribution of the Indian population as a result of fertility decline should facilitate the efforts of the Government of India (GOI) to improve the well-being of the Indian people, releasing resources that might have been needed for a larger younger population. However, this demographic dividend will not translate into social justice without specific policies. Girls' education will especially suffer in backward states in the North without rethinking how to transfer potential savings from fertility decline from one state to another.

With special measures, India has made good progress in reducing regional and urban-rural disparities in infant mortality. The changing age distribution is likely to further facilitate the reduction of these disparities, especially if centrally-sponsored programmes like the MCH and CSSM direct a disproportionate share of resources to states with high infant mortality.

I am less optimistic that this reduction in disparities will occur rapidly in the case of female education. Changes in age structure are much more pronounced in states which have already achieved higher education and gender equality. For example, the potential saving in resources required for primary education is likely to be realized in states like Kerala which have already achieved almost universal primary education. In contrast, the need for resources for primary education will continue to be high in states like Uttar Pradesh which have low levels of education and have shown very little change in the age distribution. There is also an 'age disparity issue' as well as a 'gender disparity issue' to consider. The welfare of children in the age group 0–4 is receiving some attention in all states through the centrally-sponsored health and nutrition programmes. However, in the absence of any centrally-sponsored scheme to universalize primary education, children aged 5 to 9 years do not receive the same attention in all states in terms of their schooling needs. Investment in the education of this age group, especially focused on girls living in rural areas, would accelerate the ongoing fertility transition, and would contribute to the reduction of gender disparities. The achievement of both the goals of fertility transition as well as improvements in gender

---

between states. Low level of female education in Uttar Pradesh may not simply be a function of inadequate resources allocated to female education. Both may reflect the fact that females in Uttar Pradesh have a lower status and value than females in Kerala.

equality will, therefore, require the implementation of gender sensitive social policies in the areas of education and health.

In sum, so great and persistent are the disparities between states with respect to gender equity and education that we must create policy mechanisms to transfer potential savings in state-controlled resources from one state to another: it is imperative that a centrally-sponsored and financed scheme to improve female education at the primary level, especially in rural areas, is created.

REFERENCES

Bang, R.A., M. Baitule, S. Sarmukaddam, A.T. Bang, Y. Choudhary, and T. Tale (1989), 'High Prevalence of Gynaecological Diseases in Rural Indian Women', *Lancet*, 1(8629):84–8.

Bhat, P.N. Mari (1996), 'Contours of Fertility Decline in India: As Revealed by the 1991 Census'.

Bhat, P.N. Mari, K. Nowaneetham, and S.I. Rajan (1995), 'Maternal Mortality in India: Estimates from a Regression Model', *Studies in Family Planning*, 26(4):217, 232.

Bhatia, J.C. and J. Cleland (1995), 'Self-reported Symptoms of Gynecological Morbidity and their Treatment in South India', *Studies in Family Planning*, 26(4):203:216.

Das Gupta, M. and P.N. Mari Bhat (1995), 'Intensified Gender Bias in India: A Consequence of Fertility Decline', Working Paper No. 95–03. Center for Population and Development Studies (Cambridge, MA.: Harvard University).

Drèze, J. and A. Sen (1995), *Indian Economic Development and Social Opportunity* (New Delhi: Oxford University Press), pp. 78–9.

GOI: Planning Commission (1992), *Eight-Five-Year-Plan 1992–97 WCI* (New Delhi: Planning Commission).

GOI: Registrar General, India (1962), *Census of India 1961: Final Population Totals*, Paper No. 1 of 1962, (New Delhi: Registrar General, India).

——— (1976), *Census of India 1971: Social and Cultural Tables*, Series 1, Part II-C (ii) (New Delhi: Registrar General, India).

——— (1983), *Census of India 1981: Key Population Statistics Based on 5 Per cent Sample Data*, Paper No. 2 of 1983 (New Delhi: Registrar General, India).

——— (1987), *Census of India 1981: Social and Cultural Tables*, Series 1, Part IV A, (Tables C1 to C6) (New Delhi: Registrar General, India).

——— (1993), *Sample Registration System: Fertility and Mortality Indicators* (New Delhi: Registrar General, India).

GOI (1995), *Sample Registration Bulletin*, 29(2) (New Delhi: Registrar General, India).

Jain, A.K. (1981), 'The Effect of Female Education on Fertility: A Simple Explanation', *Demography*, 18(4):577–96.

—— (1982), 'Education Sector Policies, Educational Attainment and Fertility: A Case Study for India', in R. Barlow (ed.), *Case Studies in the Demographic Impact of Asian Development Project* (Ann Arbor, Michigan: University of Michigan's Center for Research on Economic Development).

—— (1996), 'Consistency between Contraceptive Use and Fertility in India', Presented at the 1996 Annual Meeting of the Population Association of America (New Orleans).

Jejeebhoy, S.J. (1993), 'Family Size, Outcome for Children, and Gender Disparities: The Case of Rural Maharashtra', in C.B. Lloyd (ed.), *Fertility, Family Size, and Structure: Consequences for Families and Children* (New York: The Population Council).

Jejeebhoy, S.J., and S.R. Rao (1995), 'Unsafe Motherhood: A Review of Reproductive Health', in M. Das Gupta, L.C. Chen, and T.N. Krishnan (eds.), *Women's Health in India: Risk and Vulnerability*, (Bombay: Oxford University Press).

Krishnan, T.N. (1996), *The Route to Social Development in Kerala*.

National Family Health Survey (1995), *National Family Health Survey 1992–3: India, and State Reports* (Bombay: International Institute of Population Studies).

10

Mortality, Fertility, and Gender Bias in India: A District-Level Analysis

Mamta Murthi, Anne-Catherine Guio, and Jean Drèze

INTRODUCTION

India is a country of striking demographic diversity. Even broad comparisons between its states bring out enormous variations in basic demographic indicators. At one end of the scale, Kerala has demographic features that are more typical of a middle-income country than of a poor developing economy, including a life expectancy at birth of 72 years, an infant mortality rate of 17 per thousand live births, a total fertility rate (1.8 births per woman) below the replacement level, and a ratio of females to males in the population well above unity (1.04). At the other end, the large North.Indian states find themselves in the same league as the world's least-developed countries in terms of the same indicators. In Uttar Pradesh, for instance, the infant mortality rate is six times as high as in Kerala, the total fertility rate is 5.1, and the female-male ratio (0.88) is lower than that of any country in the world.[1]

India is also, increasingly, a country of rapid demographic change. As in many other developing countries, mortality rates in India have declined significantly in recent decades; the infant mortality rate, for example, has decreased by about 50 per cent

This essay first appeard in the December 1995 issue of *Population and Development Review*.

[1] The figures cited in this paragraph (with 1991 as the reference year in each case) are taken from Drèze and Sen (1995): Statistical Appendix, and are based on data from the census and the Sample Registration System. A few countries of West Asia (e.g. Kuwait and the United Arab Emirates) actually have a lower female-male ratio than Uttar Pradesh, but this is due to exceptionally high levels of male immigration.

between 1961 and 1991. The same period has seen a sustained decline in fertility, particularly in the South Indian states (in Tamil Nadu, the total fertility rate declined from 3.5 to 2.2 during the 1980s). There have also been significant changes in the relative survival chances of men and women.[2]

Apart from being of intrinsic interest, these inter-regional and inter-temporal variations provide useful opportunities to study the determinants of demographic outcomes in India. This article examines some of the relevant relationships based on a cross-section analysis of district-level data from the 1981 Census of India.[3]

Our sample consists of 296 districts for which detailed information is available. The demographic outcomes under study are the child mortality rate, the total fertility rate, and the relative survival chances of male and female children. The choice of explanatory variables is partly guided by recent analyses of the determinants of demographic behavior, but also reflects the limitations of available statistical sources. Particular attention is paid to the influence of per capita income, male and female literacy, female labour force participation rates, levels of urbanization, availability of health care facilities, and related socio-economic variables. We begin with a brief discussion of the relevance of different explanatory variables, before turning to the presentation and interpretation of our results.

ISSUES AND HYPOTHESES

In this section we discuss some plausible relationships between demographic outcomes and basic personal and social characteristics. We start with mortality and fertility and then take up the issue of gender bias.

Demographic change (in particular, the 'demographic transition' from high to low levels of mortality and fertility) is sometimes thought of as a byproduct of economic growth and rising incomes.

[2] On this point, see, e.g., I. Sen (1986), Karkal (1987), Dyson (1988), Miller (1989), Kundu and Sahu (1991), Srinivas (1991), Nanda (1992), Rajan et al (1991, 1992), and Raju and Premi (1992).

[3] Earlier investigations of this type, for India, have often been based on state-level data, involving a much smaller number of observations; see, e.g., Jain (1985), Bourne and Walker (1991), Reddy and Selvaraju (1993), and Tulasidhar and Sarma (1993). Analyses based on district-level data include Rosenzweig and Schultz (1982), Gulati (1992), Kishor (1993), Guio (1994), and Khemani (1994).

Certainly a broad inverse association can be observed, at the international level, between per capita gross national product on the one hand, and mortality and fertility levels on the other. Evidence of a causal relationship abounds, with rising incomes typically leading to some reduction of mortality and fertility. But recent research suggests that the 'income effect' can be quite slow and weak, and that other personal characteristics such as female literacy often have a more powerful influence on demographic outcomes.

The limited explanatory power of per capita income and related variables can be illustrated by considering the relationship between child mortality and the incidence of poverty (as measured by the 'head-count ratio') in different states of India. The relevant

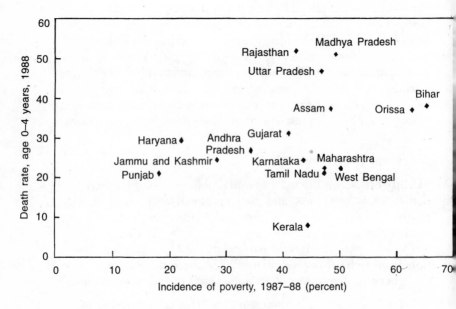

FIG. 1: *Relationship between poverty and child mortality in 16 Indian states*

Note: The measure of poverty is the head-count ratio, which indicates the proportion of the population living in households with per capita expenditure below a specified poverty line.

Source: Minhas, Jain, and Tendulkar 1991; Government of India 1990: Statement 39, p. 48.

information is presented in Figure 1.[4] The association between the two variables is clearly weak. Some aspects of this weakness of association are striking; for instance, rates of child mortality are more than six times higher in Uttar Pradesh than in Kerala, even though the head-count ratios are similar and close to the all-India average in the two states. This need not mean that income and expenditure have no effect on child mortality and related demographic outcomes. There is plenty of evidence, for India as for many other countries, that mortality declines with higher income (this elementary relationship also emerges in the empirical analysis presented below). The point is that many other factors, not all of which are themselves strongly correlated with income, also have a strong influence on demographic outcomes.

THE ROLE OF LITERACY

Among the factors other than private income that have a strong influence on fertility and mortality, basic education, especially female education is now widely considered one of the most powerful. The close relationship between education and demographic change has clearly emerged in recent empirical studies.[5] A wide range of theoretical analyses from different disciplines points in the same direction.[6]

Considering fertility first, economic, demographic, and anthropological studies suggest specific ways in which female education contributes to fertility reduction. At a general level, it is useful to distinguish between the influences of female education on (1) desired family size, (2) the relationship between desired family size and planned number of births, and (3) ability to achieve the planned number of births.

[4] 1987–8 is the latest year for which state-specific estimates of the head-count ratio are available.

[5] On the international evidence, see Caldwell (1979, 1986), Behrman and Wolfe (1984, 1987), Ware (1984), Cleland and van Ginneken (1987, 1988), United Nations (1987), Cleland (1990), Bhuiya and Streatfield (1991), Thomas et al (1991), Barro and Lee (1993a, 1993b), and Subbarao and Raney (1994). For studies related to India, see Vlassoff (1980), Jain (1985), Jain and Nag (1985, 1986), Nag (1989), Beenstock and Sturdy (1990), Bourne and Walker (1991), Satia and Jejeebhoy (1991), United Nations (1993), International Institute for Population Sciences (1994), and Basu and Jeffery (forthcoming).

[6] See, e.g., Dasgupta (1993) and the literature cited therein.

Female education can be expected to reduce desired family size for several reasons. First, educated women are more likely to voice resentment at the burden of repeated pregnancies and to take action to lighten that burden. This may occur because educated women have other sources of prestige and fulfilment besides reproductive performance, more control over household resources and personal behaviour, and greater involvement in reproductive decisions (Dyson and Moore 1983; Cain 1984). Second, educated women are likely to be less dependent on their sons as a source of social status and old-age security, and this too may lead to a reduction in desired family size. Third, educated women often have higher aspirations for their children, combined with lower expectations from them in terms of labour services provided (United Nations 1993). This may reduce desired family size if there is a perceived tradeoff between the number of children and their personal achievements. Fourth, the opportunity cost of time tends to be comparatively high for educated women, and this creates an incentive to minimize such time-intensive activities as child-bearing and child-rearing.[7] Further links of this kind have been found to have empirical relevance, usually implying a negative association between female education and desired family size.

Female education also affects the relationship between desired family size and the planned number of births. Specifically, since better maternal education reduces infant and child mortality (as discussed below), educated mothers are able to plan fewer births in order to achieve a particular family size. Maternal education also helps in achieving the planned number of births, by facilitating knowledge and command of modern contraceptive methods. This reduction of unplanned pregnancies is another basis of the negative relationship between female education and fertility.[8]

[7] Some formal economic models in the neoclassical tradition have analysed the relationship between education and fertility in terms of standard income and substitution effects (see, e.g., Becker 1960 and Olsen 1994 for a review). If children are 'normal goods' intensive in the use of the mother's time, then the income effect of a rise in female education (implying a rise in the mother's 'shadow wage') raises the demand for children while the substitution effect lowers it. If the analysis is extended so that parents derive utility from both the number of children and child 'quality' (also likely to be intensive in the use of time), the income effect on the demand for children is attenuated and the substitution effect strengthened.

[8] There are some effects in the other direction, too. For instance, the duration

Some of the effects described in the preceding paragraphs, for example the reduction of fertility through lower child mortality, also suggest a negative link between paternal education and fertility. But it is clear that many of the links between education and fertility are likely to be much weaker for male than for female education.[9] In the statistical analysis below, we attempt to identify the separate contributions of male and female education to fertility reduction.

The relationship between maternal education and child mortality requires comparatively little elaboration. At the most obvious level, educated women are likely to be more knowledgeable about nutrition, hygiene, and health care. This aspect of maternal education may be particularly significant given the remarkably uninformed and deficient nature of child care practices in large parts of rural India. In villages of Uttar Pradesh, for instance, it is still common for cooked food to be left uncovered for long hours, for umbilical cords to be cut with unsterilized sickles, for children to be left unimmunized, and for extraordinary beliefs to be entertained about the causes of simple childhood diseases such as tetanus and diarrhoea.[10] In addition, basic education can be important in helping mothers to demand adequate attention to children's needs by other members of the household, to take advantage of public health care services, and generally to pursue their aspirations (including the well-being of children) in the family and society in a more informed and effective way.

In assessing the relationship between education, mortality, and fertility, it is important to remember that mortality and fertility tend to be positively related, in the sense that, other things being equal, mortality is likely to have a positive effect on fertility and vice versa. High fertility rates, for instance, are typically associated with short birth spacing, which is often detrimental to child health.

---

of breast-feeding often declines with maternal education, lowering the duration of post-partum amenorrhoea, and post-partum abstinence taboos tend to be less influential among educated women. But these effects are unlikely to be strong enough to dominate the negative links between maternal education and fertility.

[9] In the neoclassical framework mentioned in note 7, male education has an income effect only (assuming that fathers have little involvement in child care). The direction of the income effect is ambiguous, as it depends on the relative strengths of the demands for child 'quantity' and 'quality'.

[10] Personal observations. For a telling study of maternal perceptions of marasmus in Pakistan, see Mull (1991).

338 Reproductive Change in India and Brazil

Similarly, high child mortality rates raise the number of births required to achieve a given desired family size (in terms of surviving children), and this has the effect of elevating fertility. These interaction effects are also relevant in assessing the influence of other explanatory variables on mortality and fertility. We return below to their implications for estimation procedures and interpretation.

OTHER INFLUENCES

Aside from the demographic impact of income and education, the influences of several other variables on mortality and fertility can be usefully investigated on the basis of district-level data for India.

One relationship of interest is that between female labour force participation and child mortality. It is difficult to determine *a priori* whether the effect of higher female labour force participation on child survival is likely to be positive or negative.[11] In the case of boys, two important effects work in opposite directions. First, involvement in gainful employment often enhances the effectiveness of women's agency roles in society and family, including those connected with child care. Second, the 'double burden' of household work and outside employment can impair women's ability to ensure the good health of their children, if only by reducing the time available for child care activities (since men are typically reluctant to share the domestic chores).[12] In the case of girls, a third consideration is that higher levels of female labour force participation may enhance the importance attached to the survival of a female child. The net result of these different effects remains a matter of empirical investigation.

[11] The variable we use to measure female labour force participation is the ratio of female 'main workers' (women engaged in 'economically productive work' for at least 183 days in the year) to the total female population. The instructions to census investigators state that unpaid 'household duties' are not to be counted as economically productive work. The census definition of 'economically productive work', while questionable, serves our purpose since we are interested in the relationship between child survival and women's independent income-earning opportunities (rather than their economic contribution generally, whether or not rewarded).

[12] For useful empirical analyses of this 'maternal dilemma' in the Indian context, see Basu (1992) and Gillespie and McNeill (1992). On the international evidence, see Leslie (1988), Leslie and Paolisso (1989), and the literature cited therein.

The effect of female labour force participation on fertility is more predictable. Generally, we expect greater female labour force participation to have a negative impact on fertility, since the double burden of household work and gainful employment makes repeated child-bearing particularly stressful. It is, of course, also possible that fertility affects female labour force participation, since having many children makes it more difficult for women to take up gainful employment. This effect may not be important in India, where other social and economic factors are likely to be far more crucial determinants of female labour force participation. If the effect is important, however, some bias will be involved in using female labour force participation as an exogenous explanatory variable in analysing the determinants of fertility (and also of mortality, given the interaction effects mentioned earlier). We, therefore, also present results based on treating female labour force participation as an endogenous variable (this essentially involves dropping female labour force participation from the set of explanatory variables in the 'reduced form' equations).

The availability of health care services can reasonably be expected to have a negative impact (if any) on child mortality. However, the functioning of health services can be as important as their availability. Many studies have demonstrated the poor functioning of health services in large parts of India, especially the big North Indian states.[13] Many empirical studies have noted the widespread diversion of rural health care services to family planning campaigns.[14] In the absence of statistical information on these and other qualitative aspects of health care provision, quantitative indicators of available health facilities are likely to provide imprecise measures of the services actually supplied, and the relationship between health care provision and child mortality may be hard to identify. Similar caveats apply in the case of fertility. The fact that rural health services have given overwhelming priority to family planning in many Indian states may suggest

[13] See particularly the evaluations carried out by the Operations Research Group (including Khan and Prasad 1983; and Khan et al 1980, 1983, 1986, 1988, 1989) and by the Public Systems Group (Indian Institute of Management 1985; Shah 1989). For some fairly damning case studies see Budakoti (1988), Prakasamma (1989), and Indian Council of Medical Research (1989).

[14] See, e.g., Iyengar and Bhargava (1987), Jeffery et al (1989), Prakasamma (1989), Priya (1990), Jesani (1990), Gupta et al (1992), and the studies cited in note 13.

a strong negative relationship between the availability of health services and fertility levels. But the validity of this inference is far from obvious, given the ineffective and even counterproductive nature of the top-heavy tactics that have often been used in rural India to promote family planning.

Another issue of interest is whether the identified relationships between demographic and socio-economic variables are roughly the same in urban and rural areas. It is quite possible for urbanization to influence fertility and mortality independently of the other variables included in the analysis, through, for example, better access to various types of relevant information in urban areas.[15] Similarly, it is worth investigating whether the identified relationships vary significantly between social groups. In India, the contrast between 'scheduled castes', 'scheduled tribes', and other sections of the population is of particular interest.

Finally, the relationship between poverty, on the one hand, and mortality and fertility, on the other, deserves careful examination. We have already noted that the bivariate association between poverty and child mortality appears to be weak in India, judging from broad interstate comparisons (Figure 1). The question remains whether poverty has a strong effect on mortality or fertility after controlling for other explanatory variables. Also, quantitative estimates of that effect are of interest, especially in comparison with the effects of other variables. These estimates give us an idea of the relative effectiveness of different means of intervention aimed at more rapid reductions of mortality and fertility.

GENDER BIAS

Relatively little is known about the antecedents of gender bias in child survival in India. The existence of a female disadvantage (FD) in large parts of the country has been clearly identified, and the regional patterns (see Figure 2) are well-known.[16] But the

[15] Analyses of fertility in the neoclassical tradition also point to the lower costs of children in rural compared with urban areas, given the opportunities for rural children to contribute to household production and to acquire training and skills cheaply within the household. See Schultz (1981, 1994).

[16] In 1991, the death rate in the 0–4 year, age group (per thousand population) was 25.6 for males and 27.5 for females at the all-India level. The female mortality rate in this age group was lower than the male rate in the southern states of Andhra

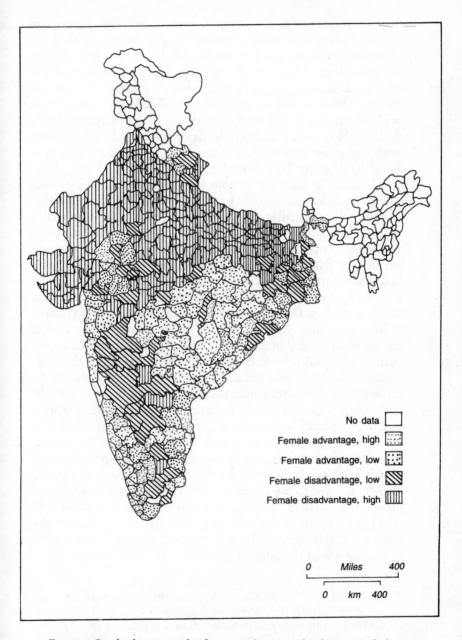

FIG. 2: *Gender bias in under-five mortality rates, by district: India 1981*

Notes: Female disadvantage, high FD > 5; female disadvantage, low, 0 < FD < 5; female advantage, low –5 < FD < 0; female advantage, high FD < –5. For the definition of FD, see Table 1.

social, economic, and cultural factors underlying these sharp regional contrasts remain a matter of speculation. In fact, the literature contains a number of contradictory claims and findings on this subject.[17] It has been suggested, for instance, that gender bias tends to diminish with higher female literacy (Bourne and Walker 1991) as well as with lower female literacy (Basu 1992); with higher levels of poverty (Krishnaji 1987; Dasgupta 1993; Miller 1993) as well as lower levels of poverty (Agarwal 1986); with higher levels of fertility (Das Gupta 1993, 1994) as well as lower levels of fertility (Basu 1992).

There are at least two reasons for this confusion. First, with respect to theoretical analysis, it is often difficult to predict whether the effect of a particular variable on gender bias in child survival is likely to be positive or negative, and plausible arguments can often be presented in both directions. Consider, for instance, what happens to the relative survival chances of boys and girls as a household's access to medical facilities improves. It has often been argued that, in a situation of widespread son preference, this improved access to medical facilities is likely to enhance the survival chances of boys more than those of girls (because of an anti-female bias in the use of additional health care facilities), and therefore to accentuate gender inequality in child survival. However, it has also been argued sometimes by the same authors that greater scarcity of medical facilities exacerbates gender bias, because boys are given priority in the use of limited resources. Both lines of reasoning are plausible, but, in any particular context, only one can be correct. Similarly, when other constraints on household opportunities are relaxed (e.g., through higher parental literacy or higher per capita income), it is difficult to predict whether the improved opportunities are likely to be used to the advantage of boys, and therefore to accentuate gender bias, or whether they will reduce the force of discriminatory practices that were initially caused by the limited nature of available opportunities. Different authors have tended to emphasize one or the other of these two plausible effects.

Pradesh, Kerala, and Tamil Nadu, but higher in all other major states except Assam and Himachal Pradesh. The female mortality disadvantage was most pronounced in the northcentral and northwestern states of Bihar, Madhya Pradesh, Punjab, Rajasthan, and Uttar Pradesh. See Government of India (1993): Table 7.

[17] For recent reviews of this literature, see Guio (1994) and Kishor (1995).

Second, when it comes to empirical investigation, the findings often depend on which variables are included in the analysis. It has been observed, for instance, that gender bias in child survival tends to be relatively low among poor households, among disadvantaged castes, and among households with high levels of female labour force participation.[18] But we also know that there is a good deal of colinearity between these three variables; only multivariate analysis can tell us whether, say, poverty has a positive or negative effect on gender bias independently of the influence of caste or female labour force participation. Similarly, an examination of the relationship between parental literacy and gender bias in child survival can be misleading if it fails to take into account other relevant variables. Indeed, if gender bias is lower among poorer households, it would be quite possible, in principle, to find a positive bivariate association between parental literacy and gender bias (given the positive correlation between poverty and illiteracy), even if literacy reduces gender bias at any given level of poverty.

Clearly, then, empirical investigation in a multivariate framework has much to contribute to the identification and quantification of relevant relationships. Two earlier studies illustrate the point. In a pioneering study, Rosenzweig and Schultz (1982) examined the relationship between differential adult employment opportunities and intrafamily resource allocation between girls and boys. Based on a multivariate statistical analysis of district-level census data for India in 1961 (supplemented with a similar analysis of household survey data collected by the National Council of Applied Economic Research), they found that improved employment opportunities for adult women tended to raise the relative survival chances of girls. This is in line with the predictions of the human capital approach adopted in that study. Most of the other variables included in the analysis did not have a statistically significant effect on relative survival chances.

More recent work by Kishor (1993, 1995) investigates the determinants of gender bias in child survival using district-level data from the 1981 Census of India. The author examines the relevance of two hypotheses, respectively stressing the influence of daughters' 'economic worth' and 'cultural worth' on their

[18] See, e.g., Miller (1981) on the caste factor, Krishnaji (1987) on the poverty factor, and Bardhan (1974) on the female labour force participation factor.

relative survival chances *vis-à-vis* male children. Economic worth is measured by female labour force participation. The incidence of patrilocal exogamy (measured, roughly speaking, as the proportion of women not born in their village of enumeration) is taken as an inverse indicator of cultural worth, which essentially refers to the influence of kinship systems on the valuation of female survival. Kishor finds that the relative survival chances of girls strongly depend on both economic and cultural worth (i.e., survival chances tend to be higher in districts where female labour force participation is higher, and where the incidence of patrilocal exogamy is lower).

The soundness of this dichotomy between economic worth and cultural worth (and of the identification of these notions with female labour force participation and patrilocal exogamy, respectively) is not entirely clear. It can be argued that both female labour force participation and patrilocal exogamy (or, more generally, kinship systems) have an economic as well as a cultural basis.[19] Similarly, both variables may influence the relative survival chances of girls through economic as well as cultural links.[20] Be that as it may, Kishor's study represents a major achievement in clarifying the respective influences of female labour force participation and kinship systems on relative female survival chances. It also yields insights into the relationship between gender bias in child survival and a range of other variables such as mortality and fertility levels, development indicators, and geographical location.

Many of these relationships also emerge in the analysis presented here. Although Kishor's analysis of gender bias and our own differ in approach, the results are broadly consistent, and the two studies can usefully be treated as complementary. Some of the important similarities and differences will be mentioned as we go along.

---

[19] It has been suggested, for instance, that patrilocal exogamy in rural India can be usefully interpreted as an insurance mechanism, which facilitates risk sharing between households living in diverse agro-climatic zones (Rosenzweig 1988, 1993; Rosenzweig and Stark 1989). On the other side, female labour force participation is closely linked with the practice of female seclusion, which may be as much a cultural phenomenon as an economic one.

[20] To illustrate: patrilocal exogamy can reduce the returns to parental investment in female child survival (an economic link), and female labour force participation can raise the general perception of women's role and value in society (which is part of the local culture).

CLAIMS AND COUNTERCLAIMS

Before presenting our own results, it may be worth commenting further on the issues that have emerged from earlier studies of the relationship between gender bias in child survival and particular economic and social variables. The following discussion concentrates on the possible influence of four variables: female labour force participation, female literacy, poverty, and fertility.

Perhaps the only uncontroversial finding of earlier studies is that female labour force participation tends to be associated with lower levels of female disadvantage in child survival. The empirical studies of Rosenzweig and Schultz (1982) and Kishor (1993) both confirm this hypothesis. What remains unclear, however, is the precise mechanism underlying that relationship. There are a number of possibilities, including that female labour force participation: (1) raises the returns to 'investment' in girls; (2) raises the status of women in society, and therefore the value attached to young girls; (3) lowers dowry levels, and therefore reduces the costs of rearing daughters; (4) makes women less dependent on adult sons for security in old age, and therefore reduces son preference; and (5) raises the bargaining power of adult women and their ability to resist male pressure to discriminate in favour of boys. As things stand, there is little evidence to distinguish between these alternative hypotheses.

The link between adult female literacy and gender bias in child survival is far from clear. In her analysis of data from the Khanna Study in Punjab, Das Gupta (1987) found a positive bivariate association between anti-female bias and maternal education, and she suggested that educated women are in a better position to 'keep the mortality of undesired children high by withholding the requisite care' (p. 84). It is hard to believe, however, that it takes good education to discriminate between boys and girls. A different line of explanation, pursued in greater depth by Das Gupta and Mari Bhat (1995), is that educated mothers have lower fertility, which tends to be accompanied by higher gender bias.

Other studies have yielded a wide range of results. Empirical investigations have suggested that the relationship between maternal education and gender bias in child survival may be: (1) positive, as originally argued by Das Gupta (Bhuiya and Streatfield 1991); (2) positive in North India, but negative in South India (Basu

1992); (3) generally negative, but possibly positive in South India (Bourne and Walker 1991); (4) negative in the case of first daughters but positive for higher-parity daughters (Amin 1990); (5) negative (Simmons et al. 1982).[21] Other studies find, or suggest, that no simple relationship between the two can be established (Chen et al. 1981; Sen and Sengupta 1983; Caldwell, Reddy, and P. Caldwell 1989). The debate continues.

As to the influence of *poverty*, there is a widespread hunch that discrimination against female children is less intense among poorer households. Arguments along those lines have been advanced by Miller (1981, 1993), Krishnaji (1987), and Dasgupta (1993) among others. Some authors have distanced themselves from this hypothesis (Agarwal 1986), or have suggested that poverty may not be a major determinant of gender bias in child survival (Chen, Huq, and D'Souza 1981; Harris 1990; Das Gupta 1987). Unfortunately, detailed empirical investigations of this issue are few.[22]

One noteworthy exception is Krishnaji's (1987) discussion of the relationship between the female-male ratio and per capita expenditure, based on National Sample Survey data. Krishnaji observed that the female-male ratio is higher at lower levels of per capita expenditure, suggesting that anti-female discrimination is less intense in poorer households. But the author qualified this conclusion, pointing out that households with a high female-male ratio may be concentrated at the lower end of the per capita expenditure scale simply because females have more-restricted earning opportunities than males.

In short, there is some evidence that gender bias in child survival is lower among poorer households, and no sound evidence of the opposite pattern. But the empirical basis for these observations remains limited. We concur with Kishor's (1995) judgment that

[21] Unfortunately, Kishor (1993) does not include female education in her analysis. Rosenzweig and Schultz (1982) find no statistically significant relationship between female education and the relative survival chances of female children.

[22] Poverty is not among the explanatory variables included in the multivariate statistical analyses of Rosenzweig and Schultz (1982) and Kishor (1993). Rosenzweig and Schultz (1982) found a positive association between landlessness and the relative survival chances of female children based on district data, but found the reverse relationship based on household data. In Kishor's (1993) study, the variable most closely related to poverty is the proportion of agricultural labourers in the population, but this variable is not statistically significant.

'we do not as yet have any conclusive evidence that poorer house-holds are necessarily less discriminatory'.

The relationship between *fertility* and gender bias in child survival is complex. One major insight comes from Das Gupta's (1987) finding that, in rural Punjab, the female disadvantage in child survival is particularly pronounced among children of higher birth parity.[23] From this 'parity effect', it is tempting to conclude that fertility decline would generally contribute to reducing gender bias in child survival.

This conclusion receives further support from the argument that high fertility and excess female mortality in childhood derive from a common root, namely the economic and other advantages of having male children (Basu 1991, 1992). A similar argument is advanced by Dyson and Moore (1983), who see the low status of women in society as a common cause of high fertility and gender bias in child survival. Here again, one might expect fertility and gender bias to move in the same direction.

In a recent study, however, Das Gupta and Mari Bhat (1995) argue that the intensification of gender bias in India (specifically, the decline in juvenile female-male ratios between 1981 and 1991) is 'a consequence of fertility decline'. They argue that the 'parity effect' is outweighed by an 'intensification effect', which renders parity-specific gender bias more pronounced at lower levels of fertility. That pattern, according to the authors, can be observed in the Khanna Study. Their explanation for the intensification effect is that, in many situations, the desired number of sons declines less rapidly than the desired number of children.

The general validity of this argument, however, calls for further empirical investigation. There is, for instance, some indication from cross-sectional data that one force in the direction of fertility decline in India may be the gradual displacement of 'two sons, one daughter' by 'one son, one daughter' as the most widely preferred family pattern.[24] In this case the desired number of sons declines more rapidly than the desired number of children, contrary to the suggested basis of the intensification effect.

[23] This finding is based on data from the Khanna Study. For similar findings in rural Uttar Pradesh, see Khan et al (1989).

[24] For some relevant evidence, see the studies cited in Basu (1991) and the more recent information from the National Family Health Survey (International Institute for Population Sciences 1994).

Das Gupta and Mari Bhat refer to the recent spread of sex-selective abortion in China, South Korea, and India, as further evidence of the strength of the intensification effect. Selective abortion of female foetuses, however, has a direct and obvious effect on the female-male ratio in the population, whether or not it also contributes to the reduction of fertility, and there is no great advantage in seeing that direct effect through the prism of fertility decline. One difficulty in this discussion is that fertility decline can have many causes, not all of which would have the same influence on gender bias. While it is easy to see that sex-selective abortion would often lead simultaneously to fertility decline and lower female-male ratios, the same pattern need not apply to a reduction of fertility due, say, to more widespread literacy or a more equal valuation of boys and girls (fertility decline, for instance, has not 'caused' an intensification of gender bias in Kerala — on the contrary). To put it another way, there is some danger in treating 'fertility' as an exogenous variable in any analysis of gender bias in child survival.

INTERPRETATION OF THE ESTIMATES

As we discussed earlier, mortality and fertility influence each other. This complicates the analysis if, for example, we are interested in estimating the effect of fertility on mortality, or the effect of female education on mortality, other than through reduced fertility. Thinking in terms of a simple linear framework, if we include fertility as an explanatory variable when estimating the equation for mortality, the estimated coefficient is not easily interpretable (does it measure the effect of fertility on mortality or that of mortality on fertility?). Moreover, the use of an endogenous variable as a regressor induces a correlation between the error term and the explanatory variables. Under these circumstances, the ordinary least squares estimates will be inconsistent, and the estimated coefficients will not approach their true values even in very large samples. In principle, if we can find suitable instruments (variables that are correlated with the endogenous variable but uncorrelated with the error term), we can estimate the relevant coefficients consistently. In practice, finding suitable instruments may not be an easy task for reasons of both theory and data availability.

We, therefore, concentrate on the reduced forms that relate the dependent variables of interest (child mortality, fertility, and gender bias in child survival) to exogenous variables alone.[25] The estimated coefficients thus measure the total effect of each explanatory variable on each endogenous variable, without determining the relative importance of the endogenous mechanisms through which this effect operates.[26] For instance, the estimated coefficient on female education in the equation for mortality measures the total effect of female education, including its effect on child mortality through fertility reduction.

DATA AND ESTIMATION

The analysis that follows is based on a sample of 296 districts for which adequately detailed information is available. These districts are located in 14 of India's 15 most populous states. These states contained 326 districts in 1981 and accounted for 94 per cent of India's total population. The missing state is Assam, where the 1981 census was not conducted.

Fertility is measured by the total fertility rate (TFR), which represents the number of children that would be born to a woman if she lived to the end of her childbearing years and bore children at each age in accordance with the prevailing age-specific fertility rates. The age-specific fertility rates are derived from responses to the census question on births during the last year.[27] For our purposes, the total fertility rate is a more useful measure of the fertility level than, say, the crude birth rate, since it is independent of the age structure of the population. The child mortality variable (Q5) is the probability that a child will die before attaining the age of five years. It is based on census questions on the number

[25] Given the possibility that female labour force participation is endogenous, we also treat it as a fourth endogenous variable in some of the regressions presented later.

[26] Formally, the model can be written as $Y = AY + BX$, where Y_{ij} is the value of the ith endogenous variable in the jth district and X_{kj} is the value of the kth exogenous variable in the jth district (A is a square matrix with as many rows and columns as there are endogenous variables). Provided that the matrix $[I A]$ is invertible, Y can be written as $Y = [I A]^1 BX$, which is the 'reduced form'.

[27] Estimates of birth rates obtained in this way are normally adjusted upward to compensate for potential underestimation (see Government of India 1989). In this analysis we use the adjusted series given in Sharma and Retherford (1990).

of children ever born and the number of children surviving.[28] Gender bias in child mortality is measured as FD = 100 (Q5F–Q5M)/Q5F, where Q5F is mortality among female children and Q5M is mortality among male children. For convenience, we refer to this measure of gender bias as 'female disadvantage' (or FD for short). Negative values of this measure indicate female advantage. TFR, Q5, and FD are the three endogenous variables of interest.

Turning to the exogenous variables, our indicator of female literacy is the crude female literacy rate, defined as the proportion of literate females in the total population, and similarly with male literacy.[29] Female labour force participation, where included, is the proportion of female 'main workers' in the total female population (on the definition of 'main workers' see note 11). Urbanization is measured by the proportion of the total population living in urban areas.[30] We use the distributionally sensitive Sen index as an indicator of poverty.[31] The availability of health care services is measured by the proportion of villages with medical facilities. In addition to these, we include two variables relating to the composition of the population: the proportion of 'scheduled castes' and the proportion of 'scheduled tribes' in the population. Finally, three dummy variables are used to identify regional patterns: South, for Andhra Pradesh, Karnataka, Kerala, and Tamil Nadu; East, for districts in Bihar, Orissa, and West Bengal; and West, for Gujarat and Maharashtra.[32] A list of the

[28] Estimates of Q5 are 'graduated' to remove inconsistencies between the estimated probabilities of death at different ages. We use graduated estimates from Government of India (1988).

[29] Literacy is defined in the Census of India as the ability to read and write with understanding in any language.

[30] Settlements counted as urban areas in the 1981 census were those with a population exceeding 5,000; those with a municipality, corporation, or cantonment board; those with a population density greater than 1,000 per square mile; and those with at least 75 per cent of the male labour force in the nonagricultural sector.

[31] On the definition and properties of the Sen index, see Sen (1976). Another measure of economic status is average per capita expenditure. The Sen index has the advantage of being more sensitive to what happens at the lower end of the per capita expenditure scale (where child mortality tends to be heavily concentrated). In any case, the results obtained by replacing the Sen index with average per capita expenditure are very similar to those we present here.

[32] The control region thus consists of Haryana, Punjab, Madhya Pradesh,

variables, their definitions, and sources is given in Table 1, which also presents summary statistics for our sample. Table 2 gives the mean values of these variables in the 14 Indian states and for all of India.

TABLE 1: VARIABLE DEFINITIONS AND
SAMPLE SUMMARY STATISTICS

Variable	Definition	Mean	Standard deviation
TFR	Total fertility rate, 1981	5.0	1.0
Q5	Under-five mortality rate, 1981: probability that a child will die before the fifth birthday (x 1,000)	156.9	42.8
FD	Female disadvantage in child survival, 1981, defined as FD = 100 (Q5F–Q5M)/ Q5F (per cent)	5.4	10.7
Female literacy	Crude female literacy rate, 1981 (per cent)	22.0	13.7
Male literacy	Crude male literacy rate, 1981 (per cent)	44.8	12.2
Female labour force participation	Proportion of 'main workers' in the female population, 1981 (per cent)	14.5	10.5
Urbanization	Proportion of the population living in urban areas, 1981 (per cent)	19.8	12.0
Poverty	Sen index of rural poverty, 1972–3 for the 'region' in which the district is situated (x 100)	17.6	8.5
Medical facilities	Proportion of villages with some medical facilities (per cent)	21.4	20.5

Table 1 (cont.)

Rajasthan, and Uttar Pradesh. The regional partition used here is essentially the same as that used in the Sample Registration System (see, e.g., Government of India 1993: 39), except that we have merged the SRS's 'Central' and 'North' regions and have taken this merged unit as the control region.

Variable	Definition	Mean	Standard deviation
Scheduled caste	Proportion of scheduled-caste persons in the population, 1981 (per cent)	16.0	6.9
Scheduled tribe	Proportion of scheduled-tribe persons in the population, 1981 (per cent)	8.0	13.5
South	Dummy variable, with value 1 for districts in Andhra Pradesh, Karnataka, Kerala, and Tamil Nadu	0.23	0.42
East	Dummy variable, with value 1 for districts in Bihar, Orissa, and West Bengal	0.16	0.37
West	Dummy variable, with value 1 for districts in Gujarat and Maharashtra	0.14	0.35

Sources: TFR: Sharma and Retherford (1990); Q5, Q5F, and Q5M (FD is calculated from the last two): Government of India (1988); Female literacy, Male literacy, Female labour force participation: Government of India (1981); Urbanization: Government of India (1982); Poverty: Jain, Sundaram, and Tendulkar (1988); Medical facilities: Government of India (1986); Scheduled caste and scheduled tribe: Government of India (1984).

Most of the information used in this analysis is derived from the 1981 census and is available in published census reports (see Table 1 for sources). The main exception concerns the Sen index, which requires further comment.

District-specific indicators of income or expenditure are not available in India. The standard source of information on per capita expenditure, the National Sample Survey (hereafter NSS), does not generate district-specific estimates, because the sample size is too small for many districts. Instead, the NSS divides the country into a number of 'regions', based on agro-climatic and socio-economic criteria, and permits reasonably reliable region-specific estimates of average per capita expenditure and related indicators. The NSS region is essentially an intermediate unit between the district and the state, with each region consisting of

TABLE 2: STATE-LEVEL AVERAGES OF THE REGRESSION VARIABLES

	TFR	Q5	FD	Female literacy	Male literacy	Female labour force participation	Urbanization	Poverty	Medical facilities	Scheduled caste	Scheduled tribe
Andhra Pradesh	4.35	138.6	-6.2	19.4	38.4	27.5	22.8	15.8	25.9	15.0	6.4
Bihar	5.24	141.1	14.4	13.4	37.6	8.6	11.6	24.8	18.1	14.9	1.8
Gujarat	4.80	126.1	6.2	30.9	53.1	10.7	28.2	15.5	28.2	7.4	11.0
Haryana	5.40	139.0	17.5	21.5	48.0	4.5	21.4	3.7	58.2	18.9	0.0
Karnataka	4.68	142.3	-3.4	27.1	48.0	19.9	24.5	14.5	13.4	14.2	5.1
Kerala	3.40	81.2	-10.5	66.0	75.4	13.1	17.9	20.9	95.8	10.4	0.9
Madhya Pradesh	5.57	202.9	4.4	14.5	38.5	20.3	19.6	19.3	5.8	14.9	21.1
Maharashtra	4.34	155.7	-2.0	31.8	56.4	26.2	26.2	25.1	18.3	7.3	10.1
Orissa	4.81	175.7	-4.2	18.9	44.9	11.8	11.6	37.8	10.8	14.2	24.9
Punjab	3.26	110.6	10.6	33.4	47.4	2.4	26.7	3.8	26.8	26.7	0.0
Rajasthan	6.05	174.6	9.8	10.5	34.4	9.6	19.2	13.2	16.7	16.7	14.2
Tamil Nadu	3.92	126.8	-2.8	35.7	58.5	22.7	32.3	17.6	32.6	17.6	1.1
Uttar Pradesh	5.89	185.6	15.3	14.7	50.2	8.0	17.3	13.0	11.8	20.8	0.5
West Bengal	4.57	123.0	1.0	28.2	46.6	7.1	23.3	28.4	15.2	22.9	7.2
All-India	5.02	156.5	5.3	22.1	44.7	14.3	20.7	17.9	21.4	15.9	8.0

Note: For definition of variables see Table 1.
Sources: See Table 1. The state-level averages presented here are calculated by aggregating the relevant district-level figures.

several districts within a particular state, and each of the major states being divided into several regions. The 14 states included in this study contain 51 regions. For these regions, estimates of average per capita expenditure, the head-count ratio, and the Sen index are available for 1972–3 (rural areas only) from Jain, Sundaram, and Tendulkar (1988), based on the 27th round of the NSS. The poverty indicator used here for each district is the Sen index of rural poverty for the region in which the district is situated. For want of information on the level of poverty in rural and urban areas combined, we have included a separate variable indicating the level of urbanization.

Two caveats are in order. First, the reference year for the poverty variable is 1972–3, rather than 1981 (as with the other variables). The justification for using 1972–3 for the poverty variable is that the 1981 mortality estimates are based on birth and death information pertaining to the late 1970s, and poverty levels during that period must have been quite close to those observed in 1972–3. Fortunately, the relative position of different regions in terms of poverty levels seems to be fairly stable over time. In fact, replacing the Sen index for 1972–3 with the Sen index for 1987–8 (also available for NSS regions) has little effect on the results presented here.[33]

Second, the use of the regional poverty estimate for each district within a region involves the implicit assumption that intra-regional variations in poverty are small. This is plausible, since the NSS regions are meant to be relatively homogeneous in terms of agro-climatic and socio-economic features. However, some loss of information is certainly involved here, and the results presented below have to be interpreted bearing in mind the imprecise nature of the district poverty indicators.

One way of dealing with this second limitation of the poverty variable is to carry out the entire analysis at the level of 'regions' rather than of districts. Although this approach has the advantage of generating a more accurate poverty indicator for each observation, reducing the number of observations from 296 to 51 also entails a

[33] To our knowledge, 1972–3 and 1987–8 are the only two years for which poverty indicators have been calculated for the NSS regions. The 1987–8 estimates are available from unpublished tabulations of the National Sample Survey performed by P.V. Srinivasan (Indira Gandhi Institute of Development Research, Bombay).

major loss of information. As it turns out, the broad conclusions of this alternative approach are similar to those obtained on the basis of district-level analysis. In the following, we focus primarily on the district-level results, but the region-level results are also presented.

Cross-section, analysis is standardly based on the assumption that the error terms are independently and identically distributed. In this case, there is a possibility of spatial correlation in the error terms. Spatial correlation refers to the positive or negative correlation of a variable between neighbouring regions of a surface, such as contiguous districts of a map.[34] Spatial correlation in the errors may arise because of unobserved (or unobservable) variables that may themselves be spatially correlated. In our context, for instance, spatial correlation may result from the influence of unobserved cultural factors on mortality or fertility.[35] If the regression errors are spatially correlated, then the standard assumption of a diagonal error covariance matrix fails to hold. We, therefore, adopt a standard technique of spatial econometrics, which consists of modeling the spatial structure of the errors by parametrizing the error covariance matrix as a function of a spatial dependence parameter, l, and estimating the model using maximum likelihood estimation. We test whether $l = 0$, that is, whether spatial correlation in the errors is negligible (in which case the properties of the ordinary least squares estimator are restored). The test fails in all cases, confirming the need to take spatial correlation into account. For further details of the estimation procedure, and diagnostics, see Murthi, Drèze, and Guio (1995).

BASIC RESULTS

Table 3 presents the main results. Apart from indicating the signs of the coefficients and whether they are statistically significant, Table 3 makes it possible to assess the quantitative effects of different variables on fertility, child mortality, and gender bias, by combining the given information with the mean values presented in Table 1.

[34] The analogy with time-series data is that of serial correlation. The main difference is that time provides an ordering to the data so that earlier disturbances can affect later disturbances, but not vice versa; space provides no such ordering, so that a disturbance at one point affects neighbours in all directions.

[35] On cultural influences on demographic behaviour in India, see Sopher (1980a, 1980b), Dyson and Moore (1983), and Basu (1992).

TABLE 3: DETERMINANTS OF FERTILITY,
CHILD MORTALITY, AND FEMALE DISADVANTAGE:
MAXIMUM LIKELIHOOD ESTIMATES OF REDUCED FORMS

Independent variable	Dependent variable		
	TFR	Q5	FD[a]
Constant	6.60	205.82	0.86
	(23.10)*	(14.37)*	(3.00)*
Female literacy	−0.03	−0.87	−0.04
	(−4.28)*	(−2.45)*	(−4.46)*
Male literacy	−0.005	−0.49	0.01
	(−0.70)	(−1.40)	(1.97)*
Female labour force	−0.02	0.44	0.02
participation	(−3.57)*	(1.82)**	(−3.85)*
Poverty	0.007	0.53	−0.02
	(1.14)	(1.76)**	(−3.13)*
Urbanization	−3.9E−04	−0.31	0.005
	(−0.15)	(−2.40)*	(1.73)**
Medical facilities	−0.002	−0.25	0.005
	(−1.04)	(−2.23)*	(1.84)**
Scheduled tribe	−0.01	−0.60	−0.01
	(−3.40)*	(−3.57)*	(−3.96)*
Scheduled caste	−0.007	0.55	−0.007
	(−1.23)	(1.89)**	(−1.13)
South	−0.55	−41.50	−0.82
	(2.60)*	(−3.85)*	(−4.91)*
East	−0.25	−38.08	0.15
	(−0.99)	(−2.91)*	(0.81)
West	−0.38	−12.24	−0.15
	(−2.06)*	(−1.32)	(−0.87)
λ	0.82	0.84	0.61
	(25.95)*	(28.07)*	(11.00)*
Mean squared error	0.31	15.15	0.39
Adjusted R^2	0.89	0.87	0.81
Log likelihood	−155.95	−1310.26	−190.80
Sample size	296	296	296

a The dependent variable is a logistic transform of FD.
Notes: Asymptotic *t*-ratios in parentheses. * significant at 5 per cent;
   ** significant at 10 per cent. For definition of variables see Table 1.

In arriving at the estimates in Table 3, we began with general specifications that included quadratic terms (for nonlinearities) and cross-products. We found no evidence of nonlinearities, except in the equation for female disadvantage. Visual inspection and non-parametric estimation suggested that the relationship between this variable and the individual explanatory variables follows a logistic pattern, so we used a logistic transform of this variable as our dependent variable in Table 3. We present no cross-product terms at this stage, in order to keep the discussion relatively straightforward, but we later discuss some results relating to cross-product terms.

The estimates in Table 3 treat female labour force participation as an exogenous variable, but, as discussed earlier, that variable may both influence and be influenced by the fertility rate and is therefore potentially endogenous. In Table 4, we exclude female labour force participation as an explanatory variable in recognition of its endogeneity. In general, the conclusions that follow from Table 3 are upheld by Table 4.

We first comment on the influence of different explanatory variables on child mortality and female disadvantage, before turning to fertility.

TABLE 4: DETERMINANTS OF FERTILITY,
CHILD MORTALITY, AND FEMALE DISADVANTAGE,
EXCLUDING FEMALE LABOUR FORCE PARTICIPATION:
MAXIMUM LIKELIHOOD ESTIMATES OF REDUCED FORMS

	Dependent variable		
Independent variable	*TFR*	*Q5*	*FD* [a]
Constant	6.38	210.72	0.66
	(21.90)*	(14.09)*	(2.21)*
Female literacy	−0.02	−1.01	−0.03
	(−3.52)*	(−2.88)*	(−3.46)*
Male literacy	−0.01	−0.35	0.01
	(−1.49)	(−1.03)	(1.01)
Female labour force participation	—	—	—
Urbanization	1.7E–04	−0.32	0.01
	(−0.06)	(−2.46)*	(1.88)**

Table 4 (contd.)

	Dependent variable		
Independent variable	TFR	Q5	FD [a]
Medical facilities	−0.002	−0.24	0.005
	(−1.07)	(−2.21)*	(1.92)**
Poverty	0.007	0.53	−0.02
	(1.14)	(1.73)**	(−3.05)*
Scheduled tribe	−0.01	−0.56	−0.01
	(−3.68)*	(−3.37)*	(−4.11)*
Scheduled caste	−0.005	0.50	−0.004
	(−0.82)	(1.72)**	(−0.54)
South	−0.66	−37.91	−1.02
	(−3.01)*	(−3.58)*	(−5.77)*
East	−0.11	−40.42	0.26
	(−0.42)	(−3.10)*	(1.21)
West	−0.41	−11.09	−0.23
	(−2.17)*	(−1.19)	(−1.26)
λ	0.84	0.83	0.68
	(28.43)*	(27.66)*	(14.05)*
Mean squared error	0.31	15.26	0.39
Adjusted R^2	0.89	0.87	0.81
Log likelihood	−162.05	−1311.91	−197.24
Sample size	296	296	296

a   The dependent variable is a logistic transform of FD.

Note: Asymptotic *t*-ratios in parentheses. * significant at 5 per cent; ** significant at 10 per cent. For definition of variables see Table 1.

Child Mortality and Female Disadvantage

With respect to child mortality and female disadvantage, the following observations are particularly noteworthy:

Female literacy has a negative and statistically significant effect on child mortality. It has a negative effect on both male and female child mortality, but the effect on female child mortality is larger. This is why female literacy also has a negative (and statistically significant) effect on FD, the extent of female disadvantage in child survival. The last result contrasts with the hypothesis, advanced by several other researchers, that higher female literacy is often a tool of intensified discrimination against female children.

Higher female literacy reduces child mortality and anti-female bias in child survival independently of male literacy. Male literacy also has a negative effect on child mortality (independently of female literacy), but its effect is much smaller than that of female literacy, and is not statistically significant. Male literacy has a significant effect on the extent of gender bias in child survival, in the direction of enhancing female disadvantage (because male literacy reduces male child mortality more than female child mortality). Interestingly, the last statement remains true even if female literacy is dropped from the regression.

We tested the hypothesis that the effect of female literacy on gender bias varies between regions by introducing additional interaction terms involving the female literacy variables and regional dummies. None of the coefficients of these interaction terms is statistically significant. In particular, we find no support for the notion that the effect of female literacy on gender bias is positive in the North but negative in the South, or vice versa.

Higher *female labour force participation* reduces the extent of gender bias in child survival, and this effect is statistically significant. This result is in keeping with the findings of earlier studies. Although higher levels of female labour force participation are clearly associated with reduced anti-female bias in child survival, the relationship between female labour force participation and absolute levels of male and female child mortality is more complex. The results presented in Table 3 suggest that higher female labour force participation is associated with higher levels of male and female child mortality. When examining the effects of female labour force participation on child mortality, however, it is important to control carefully for the economic and social disadvantages that motivate many women to seek gainful employment. In particular, it is important to control for the level of poverty; given the aforementioned limitations of our measure of poverty, the effect of female labour force participation on absolute levels of child mortality requires further scrutiny. We return to this issue below.

Urbanization has a negative and statistically significant effect on child mortality. The effect on male mortality is larger than that on female mortality; therefore, urbanization is associated with higher levels of female disadvantage in child survival. The last effect is statistically significant at the 10 per cent level, but not at the 5 per cent level.

Medical facilities have essentially the same effects as urbanization: they reduce child mortality, but amplify the female disadvantage in child survival. Here again, the last effect is statistically significant at the 10 per cent level.

As expected, higher levels of *poverty* are associated with higher levels of child mortality. This variable is not significant at the 5 per cent level, although it is significant at 10 per cent.[36] Less evidently, there is a negative and statistically significant relationship between poverty and FD: higher levels of poverty are associated with lower levels of female disadvantage in child survival. This is consistent with the hypothesis, discussed earlier, that anti-female discrimination is particularly strong among privileged classes.[37]

A higher proportion of *scheduled tribes* in the population reduces the extent of anti-female bias in child survival, and this effect is statistically significant. It is interesting that this variable has a significant effect even after controlling for female labour force participation, which is generally higher among scheduled tribes than in the population as a whole. This suggests that tribal groups have other features that enhance the relative survival chances of female children, for example kinship systems and property rights.[38]

It is also noteworthy that the absolute levels of child mortality are relatively low in districts with a high proportion of scheduled tribes, after controlling for poverty and literacy. This is consistent with the common notion that tribal lifestyles have some healthy aspects; for example, relatively low levels of crowding and pollution. But the precise basis of this statistical association requires further investigation.

There is no significant association between the proportion of *scheduled castes* in the population and the extent of female disadvantage in child survival. This is consistent with recent research on gender inequality among scheduled castes, particularly relating to trends in sex ratios. Until recently, the female-male ratio in the population was considerably higher than average among disadvantaged castes, including those now classified as 'scheduled'.

[36] The absence of statistical significance at the 5 per cent level may reflect the lack of precision of the poverty variable, as discussed above.

[37] On this, see our earlier discussion, as well as Drèze and Sen (1995): ch. 7.

[38] Kishor (1993) finds that the statistically significant association between gender bias in child survival and the proportion of tribal groups in the population disappears after her 'patrilocal exogamy' variable is included in the regression.

Many observers have attributed this contrast to the relatively egalitarian character of gender relations within these castes. In recent decades, however, there has been a striking decline of the female-male ratio within scheduled castes, so that by 1991 this ratio (0.922) was very close to the ratio in the population as a whole (0.927).[39] In other words, differences in gender relations between the scheduled castes and the rest of the population appear to have narrowed, and have disappeared altogether as measured by the female-male ratio, a basic indicator of gender inequality.[40]

Finally, with regard to *regional dummies*, even after controlling for the other variables, the southern region has considerably lower levels of child mortality. This is particularly the case for girls; indeed, female children have a survival advantage over boys in that region (see Table 2). With respect to both child mortality and gender bias, the contrast between the southern region and the rest of the country is statistically significant.

The demographic features of South India, including the relatively favourable survival chances of female children, have been much discussed in the literature.[41] The findings presented in Table 3 suggest that the demographic contrast between South India and the rest of the country cannot be explained entirely in terms of female literacy, female labour force participation, and other variables included in the regression.[42] This is consistent with the view that differences in kinship systems, property rights, and related features of the economy and society not captured in this analysis (for lack

[39] On this, see Agnihotri (1994) and Drèze and Sen (1995): ch. 7.

[40] The 'Sanskritization' process, involving the emulation of high-caste practices by members of the lower castes as a means of improving their social status, suggests an explanation for the recent convergence of female-male ratios in the two groups. Indeed, restrictions on the lifestyle and freedom of women have often played a prominent part in this process. However, there are other lines of explanation. For instance, the sharp decline of female-male ratios among scheduled castes may simply reflect the combination of (1) upward economic mobility among the scheduled castes, and (2) a positive link between economic affluence and gender inequality (due to economic or other factors that may have little to do with caste as such). This alternative line of explanation need not invoke 'Sanskritization' as an important influence.

[41] See, e.g., Karve (1965), Bardhan (1974, 1984, 1988), Sopher (1980a, 1980b), Miller (1981), Dyson and Moore (1983), Mandelbaum (1988), Basu (1992), Gupta et al (1993), and Kishor (1993).

[42] For a similar finding (even after including 'patrilocal exogamy' as an additional explanatory variable) and further discussion, see Kishor (1993).

of adequate statistical information), play an important role in the North-South contrast.[43]

FERTILITY

Tables 3 and 4 include further results related to the determinants of the total fertility rate. Female literacy and female labour force participation have a negative and statistically significant effect on TFR. Fertility is also significantly lower in the southern and western regions and in districts with a high proportion of scheduled tribes. None of the other variables is statistically significant.

FURTHER RESULTS AND EXTENSIONS

Poverty and Female Labour Force Participation

Earlier we commented on some limitations of our variable for measuring poverty. We noted, in particular, that the reference year for this variable is 1972–3, rather than 1981 (as with the other variables), and also that the available poverty indicators relate to NSS regions rather than to individual districts.

These limitations may lead to inaccurate estimates of the effect of poverty on demographic outcomes. They may also lead to bias in the estimated coefficients of variables that are strongly correlated with poverty. One important example concerns female labour force participation, in particular the relationship between that variable and child mortality. As we discussed earlier, in estimating the effect of female labour force participation on child mortality and other demographic outcomes, it is important to control for the incidence of poverty. Indeed, female labour force participation in India is often a reflection of economic hardship, and failure to control for this factor may lead, for instance, to a spurious positive relationship between it and child mortality (implicitly reflecting, in fact, the positive association between poverty and child mortality).[44]

In view of these considerations, we have explored alternative ways of dealing with the poverty variable. As for the reference year,

[43] On these and related influences, see Basu (1992), Kishor (1993), and Agarwal (1994), and the studies cited in Drèze and Sen (1989, 1995), Gupta et al. (1993), and Dasgupta (1993).

[44] This argument holds whether or not female labour force participation is exogenous.

we have examined the effects of replacing the 1972–3 poverty estimates with the corresponding 1987–8 estimates. The basic results presented above continue to hold; hence the choice of reference year for the poverty variable does not seem to be a major issue.

Regarding the use of region-level (as opposed to district-level) poverty estimates in the regressions, one way of investigating whether this procedure leads to serious bias is to re-estimate the regression equations using region-level estimates for all variables listed in Table 1. Region-level estimates can easily be obtained by aggregation, as weighted averages of the district-level values. While this method leads to a sharp reduction in the number of observations (from 296 to 51), it eliminates any bias arising from the fact that the poverty variable and other variables relate to different levels of territorial aggregation. The corresponding results are presented in Table 5.

TABLE 5: DETERMINANTS OF FERTILITY,
CHILD MORTALITY, AND FEMALE DISADVANTAGE, NSS REGIONS:
MAXIMUM LIKELIHOOD ESTIMATES OF REDUCED FORMS

Independent variable	Dependent variable		
	TFR	Q5	FD
Female literacy	−0.04	−1.84	−0.69
	(−2.47)*	(−2.41)*	(−4.57)*
Male literacy	0.020	1.17	0.38
	(1.09)	(1.41)	(2.24)*
Female labour force participation	−0.03	−0.34	−0.31
	(−2.82)*	(−0.65)	(−3.56)*
Urbanization	−0.005	−0.39	0.03
	(−0.080)	(−1.27)	(0.47)
Medical facilities	0.002	−0.29	0.08
	(0.46)	(−1.29)	(1.84)**
Poverty	5.6E–04	0.74	−0.16
	(0.06)	(1.73)**	(−1.61)
Scheduled tribe	−0.01	0.09	−0.29
	(−1.54)	(0.24)	(−3.95)*
Scheduled caste	−0.02	1.04	−0.01
	(−1.78)**	(1.63)	(−0.41)

Table 5 (cont.)

Independent variable	Dependent variable		
	TFR	Q5	FD
South	−0.25	−12.29	−8.34
	(−0.77)	(−0.72)	(−4.19)*
East	−0.29	−30.04	−2.96
	(−0.92)	(−1.82)**	(−1.44)
West	−0.44	2.94	0.50
	(−1.65)**	(0.22)	(0.24)
λ	0.59	0.66	−0.41
	(4.45)*	(5.42)*	(−1.98)*
Mean squared error	0.36	18.14	3.71
Adjusted R^2	0.74	0.68	0.79
Log likelihood	−23.45	−223.23	−140.17
Sample size	51	51	51

Notes: Asymptotic *t*-ratios in parentheses. * significant at 5 per cent; ** significant at 10 per cent. For definition of variables see Table 1.

The results of the region-level analysis (Table 5) are similar to those of the district-level analysis (Table 3). One difference is that the *t*-ratios tend to be lower in the region-level regressions than in the district-level regressions, and, accordingly, some variables that were statistically significant in the latter are not significant in the former (this applies, for instance, to the South 'dummy' in the mortality and fertility regressions). This is not surprising, since the region-level regressions are based on a smaller number of observations and reflect a considerable loss of information.

Aside from this, the main difference between the two sets of regressions is that, in the region-level regressions, higher female labour force participation is associated with lower child mortality (both sexes combined). Although this association is not statistically significant, it suggests that the positive association between these two variables obtained in the district-level regressions may reflect a failure to adequately control for poverty.[45]

[45] Kishor (1993) found that female labour force participation had a positive and statistically significant effect on both female and male child mortality. In that study, too, the positive association between female labour force participation and child mortality may reflect the lack of adequate control for poverty (the regressions

Fertility and Gender Bias in Child Mortality

As we discussed earlier, the links between fertility and gender bias in child survival are unclear. To shed light on this issue, we have included the total fertility rate as an additional regressor in the equation for female disadvantage.[46] We find that higher fertility is associated with *higher* female disadvantage in child survival, and the association is statistically significant.[47] Thus, it appears that, after controlling for other pertinent factors, the relative survival chances of girls are lower in areas of high fertility. These results contribute to dispelling any fear that rapid fertility decline in India might entail some intensification of gender bias in child survival.

Interaction between Female Literacy and Medical Facilities

One way in which female literacy may help reduce child mortality is by enabling women to take better advantage of available medical facilities. If that hypothesis is correct, then we might expect female literacy and medical facilities to have synergistic effects on child mortality, in the sense that the influence of one of these two variables is stronger when the other is also at work. We test this hypothesis by including an interaction term in the regression for child mortality, as an additional right-hand variable. This interaction term (the product of 'female literacy' and 'medical facilities') allows the effect of medical facilities to vary with the level of female literacy, and vice versa. We find the coefficient of this interaction term to be negative and statistically significant, suggesting that medical facilities and female literacy do have synergistic effects in reducing child mortality.[48]

---

presented there included only rough proxies for 'level of development'). An additional reason may be the omission of female literacy from the analysis (bearing in mind that there is likely to be a negative correlation between female literacy and female labour force participation).

[46] This procedure assumes, in line with the literature on the subject, that level of fertility affects the relative survival chances of girls but is not affected by it.

[47] The coefficient on the total fertility rate is 0.13, and it's t-ratio is 2.04. None of the other coefficients changes very much, nor are there important changes in levels of statistical significance.

[48] The coefficient on the interaction term is -0.011, with a t-ratio of -2.55. The statistical significance of the other variables remains unchanged.

Structural Change

Another issue of interest is the stability of the estimated relationships over time. When detailed results of the 1991 census are available, it will be possible to carry out regression exercises similar to those presented here and to compare them with the 1981 results. Meanwhile, we attempt a tentative assessment of structural change as follows.

We estimated an additional regression equation, with crude birth rate (CBR) as the dependent variable, using 1981 district-level data. We retained all explanatory variables in Table 3 except 'medical facilities'.[49] This equation was used to 'predict' the CBR in 1991, using the 1991 values of the independent variables. In the absence of district-level information for 1991, this could only be done at the state-level. These predicted CBRs were then compared with the actual figures derived from the 1991 census.[50]

This comparison indicates that our regressions under-predict the decline of the CBR between 1981 and 1991 in each of the 14 states considered. The difference between predicted and actual CBR (expressed as a proportion of actual CBR) is very small for Madhya Pradesh (1.1 per cent) and also relatively small (less than 10 per cent) for Haryana, Rajasthan, and Uttar Pradesh, but particularly large for West Bengal (21 per cent), Punjab (24 per cent), Andhra Pradesh (25 per cent), Kerala (41 per cent), and Tamil Nadu (46 per cent). The under-prediction of CBR decline in all states suggests that structural change during 1981–91 has reinforced cross-sectional effects identified in this study. Further, the state-specific patterns are consistent with recent evidence of an accelerated demographic transition in Southern India, contrasted with much greater inertia in the large Northern Indian states.[51]

Sex Ratio and Child Mortality

Finally, we examined the hypothesis that, even for given values of the explanatory variables included in this analysis, child mortality

[49] The reason for dropping this variable is that 1991 information on medical facilities was not available at the time of writing.

[50] The 1991 CBR estimates were calculated by P.N. Mari Bhat (Population Research Centre, Dharwad). We are grateful to him for making these unpublished estimates available to us.

[51] On this see particularly P. Visaria and L. Visaria (1994).

is higher in areas of higher gender inequality. The idea is that high levels of gender inequality tend to suppress the agency of women in society, one consequence of which may be higher levels of child mortality (insofar as the health of children in India depends greatly on women's initiative).

To test this hypothesis, we used the juvenile sex ratio (number of females per thousand males in the 0–10-year age group) as an additional right-hand variable in the equation for child mortality.[52] The juvenile sex ratio is interpreted here as a rough indicator of gender inequality.[53] Holding other factors constant, we find that child mortality is higher in districts with a lower juvenile sex ratio, and this effect is statistically significant.[54] This lends some support to the proposed hypothesis.

DISCUSSION

Women's Agency and Demographic Outcomes

The findings of this study clearly demonstrate the role of women's agency and empowerment in reducing mortality, fertility, and gender inequality.

Consider, for instance, the determinants of gender bias in child mortality. It is striking that, while the variables directly related to women's agency (specifically, the female literacy rate and female labour force participation) have a strong and statistically significant negative impact on female disadvantage, those relating to the society's general level of economic development and modernization (e.g., poverty, urbanization, male literacy, and medical facilities) do nothing to improve the relative survival chances of girls *vis-à-vis* boys. In fact, to the extent that these variables have a statistically significant influence on female disadvantage in child survival, this influence operates in the 'wrong' direction in each case: higher levels of male literacy and urbanization, lower levels of poverty, and

[52] As with similar exercises presented in this section, the validity of this procedure requires that the added variable (in this case, the juvenile sex ratio) is not affected by the left-hand variable (in this case, the child mortality rate).

[53] The reason for using the juvenile sex ratio, rather than the sex ratio in the population as a whole, is that the latter can be sensitive to migration patterns at the district-level (Miller 1981).

[54] The coefficient on the juvenile sex ratio, measured as the ratio of girls to boys in the 0–10 years age group, is –0.166, with a *t*-ratio of –3.23.

improved access to medical facilities, are all associated with a larger female disadvantage (see Tables 3, 4, and 5 for details). The reason is that these variables reduce male child mortality more than female child mortality. Insofar as a positive connection exists in India between the level of development and reduced gender bias in survival, it seems to work through variables that are directly related to women's agency, such as female literacy and female labour force participation.

Similarly, while indicators of development such as male literacy, reduced poverty, greater urbanization, and the spread of medical facilities, do have positive effects on absolute levels of child survival, these effects are relatively small compared with the powerful effect of female literacy. This point is illustrated in Table 6, which indicates how the predicted values of Q5 and FD respond to changes in female literacy when the other variables are kept at their mean value (responses to male literacy and poverty are also shown in the table).[55] The influence of female literacy on child mortality and gender bias is quite large, especially in comparison with the influence of male literacy or poverty.

The same point emerges in connection with the determinants of fertility. In this case, in fact, none of the variables related to the general level of development and modernization is statistically significant. By contrast, female literacy and labour force participation appear to be crucial determinants of the total fertility rate. As shown in Table 6, for instance, female literacy alone exerts considerable force in reducing fertility. Here again, the message seems to be that some variables related to women's agency (in this case, female literacy) play a much more important role in demographic outcomes than do variables related to the general level of development.

Cross-section and Time-series Analysis

As we discussed in the preceding section, our results lend little support to the notion that gender bias in India automatically declines

[55] The simulations in Table 6 concerning the effect of changes in the level of poverty are based on equations in which the head-count ratio of poverty is used as an explanatory variable in place of the Sen index. The substitution was made because percentage changes in the head-count ratio are more straightforward to interpret. The use of the head-count ratio in place of the Sen index makes little overall difference to the estimates.

TABLE 6: EFFECTS OF SELECTED INDEPENDENT VARIABLES (FEMALE LITERACY, MALE LITERACY, AND POVERTY) ON CHILD MORTALITY (Q5), FEMALE DISADVANTAGE (FD), AND FERTILITY (TFR)

Assumed level of independent variable (per cent)	Predicted values of Q5, FD, and TFR when the female literacy rate takes the value indicated in the first column			Predicted values of Q5, FD, and TFR when the male literacy rate takes the value indicated in the first column			Predicted values of Q5, FD, and TFR when the proportion of the population below the poverty line takes the value indicated in the first column[a]		
	Q5	FD	TFR	Q5	FD	TFR	Q5	FD	TFR
10	166.4	10.7	5.38	172.9	-2.0	5.18	151.5	9.8	4.79
20	157.7	5.9	5.07	168.0	-0.1	5.13	152.7	8.5	4.85
30	149.0	1.1	4.76	163.1	1.8	5.08	153.8	7.1	4.91
40	140.2	-3.3	4.45	158.2	3.9	5.03	154.9	5.8	4.97
50	131.5	-7.1	4.15	153.3	5.9	4.98	156.0	4.4	5.03
60	122.8	-10.3	3.84	148.4	8.0	4.93	157.2	3.1	5.09
70	114.0	-12.8	3.53	143.5	10.1	4.88	158.3	1.8	5.15
80	105.3	-14.8	3.22	138.7	12.2	4.83	159.5	0.5	5.21

a   For convenience of interpretation, the 'Sen index' has been replaced here by the 'head-count ratio' (i.e., the proportion of the population below the poverty line). The figures presented in these three columns are based on the same regressions as in Table 3, with the Sen index replaced by the head-count ratio.

Note: For definition of variables see Table 1.

with economic development (except insofar as the latter enhances female literacy and female labour force participation). This may seem surprising, but it is worth noting that our finding is consistent with the widely discussed phenomenon of sustained decline in India's ratio of females to males since the beginning of this century.[56]

In 1901, the ratio of females to males in the Indian population was 0.972. From then, the female-male ratio declined almost monotonically until 1991 (the last year for which census estimates are available), when it reached the lowest-ever recorded value of 0.927.[57] The causes of this decline are a matter of debate, and the results we presented here are of some relevance in this context. The regressions presented in Table 3 suggest that the only important force that may have worked to reduce gender bias over this period is the expansion of female literacy. Most other developments, including the expansion of per capita income, medical facilities, and male literacy, would have worked in the other direction, if our cross-section results are any guide to the corresponding effects over time.[58]

These observations should not be taken to imply that economic development in India is comprehensively detrimental to the position of women in society. Such a conclusion, if drawn, would require at least three qualifications. First, our results suggest that gender bias is reduced by an expansion of female literacy, and that expansion is part of economic development. Even female labour force participation can be expected to increase in the future, and that too is likely to reduce gender bias.

Second, the relationship between gender bias and level of economic development may well be nonlinear, with the relative position of women first declining and later improving as, say, per capita income increases. Some authors have indeed stressed

[56] On this issue, see Drèze and Sen (1995): ch. 7, and the literature cited therein.

[57] For the latest figures on female-male ratios in India and Indian states since 1901, see Nanda (1992): 102–3.

[58] One qualification concerns time trends in female labour force participation. Given the frequent changes in definition and treatment of women's work in Indian censuses, it is difficult to state with confidence whether female labour force participation rates in India have increased or decreased since the beginning of this century (see, e.g., Duvvury 1989 for further discussion). It is unlikely, however, that a major *increase* in female labour force participation has taken place over that period.

the plausibility of such a nonlinear relationship (see particularly Kishor 1995). In our own work, we have found no evidence of this type of nonlinearity, but this may reflect the fact that India is still at an early stage of development. The relationship between gender bias and economic variables may well change.

Third, our investigation has been confined to one aspect of gender bias — differences in mortality rates between boys and girls. Obviously, all aspects of gender inequality need not move in the same direction, and it would be difficult to deny that some aspects of the condition of Indian women have improved considerably in the recent years. [59]

Demographic Change

Since population growth in India is often of intense concern, it is worth reiterating that the only variables we found to have a significant effect on fertility are female literacy and female labour force participation. In addition, of course, there is likely to be a significant causal link between mortality and fertility, with the latter going down as mortality declines. The direct promotion of child health, female literacy, and female labour force participation is likely to be more conducive to lowering fertility than are indirect interventions based on promoting economic development.

It would, of course, be helpful to know more about the precise links between fertility and child mortality. The problem is that there are simultaneous causal links in both directions; links that are difficult to estimate. We made one attempt at such estimation, based on two-stage least squares estimation of the fertility equation (with child mortality as an additional right-hand variable in the fertility regression). Identifying the effect of child mortality requires the inclusion in the model of at least one exogenous variable that influences child mortality but not fertility. 'Availability of drinking water' seemed like a plausible candidate, but tentative estimates based on using it as an instrument for child mortality gave no useful results. This is an important area for further research.

[59] The gender gap in literacy, for instance, has narrowed somewhat between the 1981 and 1991 censuses. Similarly, the survival advantage of women in the older age groups has noticeably increased since 1971, and the age at which that advantage begins has also declined; as a result, female life expectancy has recently overtaken male life expectancy (see Karkal 1987; Dyson 1988; and Rajan et al 1992).

ACKNOWLEDGEMENT

The authors are grateful to Satish Agnihotri, Sudhir Anand, Jean-Marie Baland, Peter Boone, Monica Das Gupta, Angus Deaton, Tim Dyson, Michel Garenne, Haris Gazdar, Stuti Khemani, Sunita Kishor, P.N. Mari Bhat, Jean-Philippe Platteau, Rohini Somanathan, and P.V. Srinivasan, for helpful discussions and comments. They also thank the International Development Research Centre (IDRC, Canada) for supporting this collaborative work.

REFERENCES

Agarwal, Bina (1986), 'Women, Poverty and Agricultural Growth in India', *Journal of Peasant Studies*, 13(4):165–220.

—— (1994), *A Field of One's Own: Gender and Land Rights in South Asia* (Cambridge: Cambridge University Press).

Agnihotri, Satish (1994), 'Missing Females: A Disaggregated Analysis', mimeograph, University of East Anglia (forthcoming in *Economic and Political Weekly*).

Amin, S. (1990), 'The Effect of Women's Status on Sex Differentials in Infant and Child Mortality in South Asia', *Genus*, 46(34): 55–69.

Bardhan, Pranab (1974), 'On Life and Death Questions', *Economic and Political Weekly*, 9, Special Number.

—— (1984), *Land, Labour and Rural Poverty* (New York: Columbia University Press).

—— (1988), 'Sex Disparity in Child Survival in Rural India', in T.N. Srinivasan and P.K. Bardhan (eds.), *Rural Poverty in South Asia* (New York: Columbia University Press).

Barro, Robert J., and Jong-Wha Lee (1993a), 'Losers and Winners in Economic Growth', Working Paper 4341, National Bureau of Economic Research.

—— (1993b), 'International Comparisons of Educational Attainment', Paper presented at a conference on 'How do National Policies Affect Long-run Growth?' (Washington, D.C.: World Bank).

Basu, Alaka M. (1989), 'Is Discrimination in Food Really Necessary for Explaining Sex Differentials in Childhood Mortality?', *Population Studies*, 43(2):193–210.

—— (1991), 'Demand and its Sociocultural Context', in J.K. Satia and S.J. Jejeebhoy (eds.), *The Demographic Challenge: A Study of Four Large Indian States* (Bombay: Oxford University Press).

—— (1992), *Culture, the Status of Women and Demographic Behaviour* (Oxford: Clarendon Press).

Basu, Alaka M. (1993a), 'Women's Roles and the Gender Gap in Health and Survival', mimeograph (Delhi: Institute of Economic Growth).
—— (1993b), 'Fertility Decline and Increasing Gender Imbalances in India: Including the South Indian Turnaround', mimeograph, Institute of Economic Growth, Delhi University.
Basu, Alaka M. and Roger Jeffery (eds.) (forthcoming), *Girls' Schooling, Women's Autonomy and Fertility Change in South Asia* (New Delhi: Sage).
Becker, G. (1960), 'An Economic Analysis of Fertility', in *Demographic and Economic Change in Developed Countries* (Princeton: Princeton University Press).
Beenstock, M. and P. Sturdy (1990), 'The Determinants of Infant Mortality in Regional India', *World Development*, 18(3): 443–53.
Behrman, J.R. and B.L. Wolfe (1984), 'More Evidence on Nutrition Demand: Income Seems Overrated and Women's Schooling Underemphasized', *Journal of Development Economics*, 14:105–28.
—— (1987), 'How Does Mother's Schooling Affect the Family's Health, Nutrition, Medical Care Usage, and Household Sanitation', *Journal of Econometrics*, 36:185–204.
Bhuiya, A. and K. Streatfield (1991), 'Mothers' Education and Survival of Female Children in a Rural Area of Bangladesh', *Population Studies*, 45(2):253–64.
Bourne, K. and G.M. Walker (1991), 'The Differential Effect of Mothers' Education on Mortality of Boys and Girls in India', *Population Studies*, 45(2):203–19.
Budakoti, D.K. (1988), 'Study of the Community and Community Health Work in Two Primary Health Centres in Chamoli District of Uttar Pradesh', M. Phil dissertation, Centre for Social Medicine and Community Health, Jawaharlal Nehru University, New Delhi.
Cain, Mead (1984), 'Women's Status and Fertility in Developing Countries: Son Preference and Economic Security', World Bank Staff Working Papers, No. 682.
Caldwell, John C. (1979), 'Education as a Factor in Mortality Decline: An Examination of Nigerian Data', *Population Studies*, 33(3):395–413.
—— (1986), 'Routes to Low Mortality in Poor Countries', *Population and Development Review*, 12(2):171–220.
Caldwell, John C., P.H. Reddy, and Pat Caldwell (1982), 'The Causes of Demographic Change in Rural South India: A Micro Approach', *Population and Development Review*, 8(4):689–727.
—— (1989), *The Causes of Demographic Change* (Madison: University of Wisconsin Press).
Chen, Lincoln C., Emdadul Huq, and Stan D'Souza (1981), 'Sex Bias in

the Family Allocation of Food and Health Care in Rural Bangladesh',
Population and Development Review, 7(1):55–70.

Cleland, J. (1990), 'Maternal Education and Child Survival: Further
Evidence and Explanations', in John C. Caldwell et al. (eds.), *What
We Know About Health Transition: The Cultural, Social and Behavioural Determinants of Health* (Canberra: Health Transition Centre,
Australian National University).

Cleland, J. and J. van Ginneken (1987), 'The Effect of Maternal Schooling on Childhood Mortality: The Search for an Explanation', paper
presented at a conference on Health Intervention and Mortality
Change in Developing Countries, University of Sheffield.

——— (1988), 'Maternal Education and Child Survival in Developing
Countries: The Search for Pathways of Influence', *Social Science and
Medicine*, 27(12):1357–68.

Das Gupta, Monica (1987), 'Selective Discrimination Against Female
Children in Rural Punjab, India' *Population and Development
Review*, 13(1):77–100.

——— (1993), 'Fertility Decline in Punjab, India: Parallels with Historical
Europe', mimeograph (Center for Population and Development
Studies, Harvard University).

——— (1994), 'What Motivates Fertility Decline? Lessons from a Case
Study of Punjab, India', mimeograph (Center for Population and
Development Studies, Harvard University).

Das Gupta, Monica and P.N. Mari Bhat (1995), 'Intensified Gender Bias
in India: A Consequence of Fertility Decline', Working Paper No.
95.02 (Harvard Center for Population and Development Studies).

Dasgupta, Partha (1993), *An Inquiry into Well-being and Destitution* (Oxford: Clarendon Press).

Drèze, Jean and Amartya Sen (1989), *Hunger and Public Action* (Oxford:
Oxford University Press).

——— (1995), *India: Economic Development and Social Opportunity* (Oxford and New Delhi: Oxford University Press).

Duvvury, Nata (1989), 'Women in Agriculture: A Review of the Indian
Literature', *Economic and Political Weekly*, 28 October.

Dyson, Tim (1988), 'Excess Female Mortality in India: Uncertain Evidence on a Narrowing Differential', in K. Srinivasan and S. Mukerji
(eds.), *Dynamics of Population and Family Welfare 1987*, (Bombay:
Himalaya).

Dyson, Tim and Mick Moore (1983), 'On Kinship Structure, Female
Autonomy, and Demographic Behavior in India', *Population and
Development Review*, 9(1):35–60.

Gillespie, S. R. and G. McNeill (1992), *Food, Health and Survival in India
and Developing Countries* (Delhi: Oxford University Press).

Government of India (1981), *Census of India 1981*, Series 1, Part II-B(i), Primary Census Abstract, General Population (New Delhi: Office of the Registrar General).

—— (1982), 'Final Population Totals', *Census of India 1981*, Series 1, Paper 1 (New Delhi: Office of the Registrar General).

—— (1984), *Census of India 1981*, Series 1, Paper 2 (New Delhi: Office of the Registrar General).

—— (1986), 'Study on Distribution of Infrastructural Facilities in Different Regions and Levels of Urbanization', *Census of India 1981*, Occasional Paper 1 (New Delhi: Office of the Registrar General).

—— (1988), 'Child Mortality Estimates of India', *Census of India 1981*, Occasional Paper No. 5 (New Delhi: Office of the Registrar General).

—— (1989), 'Child Mortality, Age at Marriage and Fertility in India', *Census of India 1981*, Occasional Paper No. 2 (New Delhi: Office of the Registrar General).

—— (1990), *Sample Registration System: Fertility and Mortality Indicators 1988* (New Delhi: Office of the Registrar General).

—— (1993), *Sample Registration System: Fertility and Mortality Indicators 1991* (New Delhi: Office of the Registrar General).

Guio, Anne-Catherine (1994), 'Aspects du Sex Ratio en Inde', unpublished M.Sc. thesis, Université de Namur, Belgium.

Gulati, S.C. (1992), 'Developmental Determinants of Demographic Variables in India: A District Level Analysis', *Journal of Quantitative Economics*, 8(1):157–72.

Gupta, D.B., A. Basu, and R. Asthana (1993), 'Population Change, Women's Role and Status, and Development in India: A Review', mimeograph (Delhi: Institute of Economic Growth).

Gupta, N., P. Pal, M. Bhargava, and M. Daga (1992), 'Health of Women and Children in Rajasthan', *Economic and Political Weekly*, 17 October.

Harris, Barbara (1990), 'The Intrafamily Distribution of Hunger in South Asia', in J.P. Drèze and A.K. Sen (eds.), *The Political Economy of Hunger* (Oxford: Clarendon).

Indian Council of Medical Research (1989), *Evaluation of Quality of Maternal and Child Health and Family Planning Services* (New Delhi: ICMR).

Indian Institute of Management (1985), *Study of Facility Utilization and Programme Management in Family Welfare* (Ahmedabad: Public Systems Group, Indian Institute of Management).

International Institute for Population Sciences (1994), *National Family Health Survey: India 1992–93* (Bombay: IIPS).

Iyengar, Sudarshan and Ashok Bhargava (1987), 'Primary Health Care and Family Welfare Programme in Rural Gujarat', *Economic and Political Weekly*, 4 July.

Jain, Anrudh K. (1985), 'Determinants of Regional Variations in Infant Mortality in Rural India', *Population Studies*, 39(3):407–24.

Jain, Anrudh K. and Moni Nag (1985), 'Female Primary Education and Fertility Reduction in India', Working Paper No. 114, Center for Policy Studies (New York: The Population Council).

—— (1986), 'Importance of Female Primary Education for Fertility Reduction in India', *Economic and Political Weekly*, 6 September.

Jain, L.R., K. Sundaram, and S.D. Tendulkar (1988), 'Dimensions of Rural Poverty: An Inter-regional Profile', *Economic and Political Weekly*, Special Number, November.

Jeffery, P., R. Jeffery, and P. Lyon (1989), *Labour Pains and Labour Power: Women and Child-bearing in India* (London: Zed).

Jesani, Amar (1990), 'Limits of Empowerment: Women in Rural Health Care', *Economic and Political Weekly*, 19 May.

Karkal, M. (1987), 'Differentials in Mortality by Sex', *Economic and Political Weekly*, 8 August.

Karve, Irawati (1965), *Kinship Organisation in India* (Bombay: Asia Publishing House).

Khan, M.E., C.V.S. Prasad, and A. Majumdar (1980), *People's Perceptions about Family Planning in India* (New Delhi: Concept).

Khan, M.E. and C.V.S. Prasad (1983), *Under-utilization of Health Services in Rural India: A Comparative Study of Bihar, Gujarat and Karnataka* (Baroda: Operations Research Group).

Khan, M.E., C.V.S. Prasad, and N. Qaiser (1983), 'Reasons for Underutilization of Health Services: Case Study of a PHC in a Tribal Area of Bihar', paper presented at the ICMR/Ford Foundation Workshop on Child Health, Nutrition and Family Planning.

Khan, M.E., S.K. Ghosh Dastidar, and R. Singh (1986), 'Nutrition and Health Practices among the Rural Women: A Case Study of Uttar Pradesh', *Journal of Family Welfare*, 33(1):320.

Khan, M.E., R.B. Gupta, C.V.S. Prasad, and S.K. Ghosh Dastidar (1988), *Performance of Health and Family Welfare Programme in India* (Bombay: Himalaya Publishing House).

Khan, M.E., R. Anker, S.K. Ghosh Dastidar, and S. Bairathi (1989), 'Inequalities between Men and Women in Nutrition and Family Welfare Services: An In-depth Enquiry in an Indian Village', in J.C. Caldwell and G. Santow (eds.), *Selected Readings in the Cultural, Social and Behavioral Determinants of Health*, Health Transition Series No. 1 (Canberra: Health Transition Centre, Australian National University).

Khemani, Stuti (1994), 'Neoclassical vs. Nash-bargained Model of Household Fertility: Evidence from Rural India', undergraduate thesis, Department of Economics, Mount Holyoke College.

Kishor, Sunita (1993), '"May God Give Sons to All": Gender and Child Mortality in India', *American Sociological Review*, 58(2):247–65.

Kishor, Sunita (1995), 'Gender Differentials in Child Mortality in India: A Review of Evidence', in M. Das Gupta, T.N. Krishnan, and Lincoln Chen (eds.), *Women's Health in India: Risk and Vulnerability* (Bombay: Oxford University Press).

Krishnaji, N. (1987), 'Poverty and Sex Ratio: Some Data and Speculations', *Economic and Political Weekly*, 6 June.

Kundu, Amitabh and Mahesh Sahu (1991), 'Variation in Sex Ratio: Development Implications', *Economic and Political Weekly*, 12 October.

Leslie, Joanne (1988), 'Women's Work and Child Nutrition in the Third World', *World Development*, 16(11):1341–62.

Leslie, Joanne, and Michael Paolisso (eds.) (1989), *Women, Work and Child Welfare in the Third World* (Boulder: Westview).

Mandelbaum, David G. (1988), *Women's Seclusion and Men's Honor: Sex Roles in North India, Bangladesh and Pakistan* (Tucson: University of Arizona Press).

Miller, Barbara D. (1981), *The Endangered Sex: Neglect of Female Children in Rural North India* (Ithaca: Cornell University Press).

—— (1989), 'Changing Patterns of Juvenile Sex Ratios in Rural India, 1961 to 1971', *Economic and Political Weekly*, 3 June.

—— (1993), 'On Poverty, Child Survival and Gender: Models and Misperceptions', *Third World Planning Review*, 15(3): iii–viii.

Minhas, B.S., L.R. Jain, and S.D. Tendulkar (1991), 'Declining Incidence of Poverty in India in the 1980s', *Economic and Political Weekly*, 613, July.

Mull, Dorothy (1991), 'Traditional Perceptions of Marasmus in Pakistan', *Social Science and Medicine*, 32(2): 175–91.

Murthi, Mamta, Jean Drèze, and Anne-Catherine Guio (1995), 'Mortality, Fertility and Gender Bias in India: A District Level Analysis', Discussion Paper 61, Development Economics Research Programme, STICERD, London School of Economics.

Nag, Moni (1989), 'Political Awareness as a Factor in Accessibility of Health Services: A Case Study of Rural Kerala and West Bengal', *Economic and Political Weekly*, 25 February.

Nanda, Amulya Ratna (1992), 'Final Population Totals: Brief Analysis of Primary Census Abstract', Census of India 1991, Series 1, Paper 2 of 1992 (New Delhi: Office of the Registrar-General).

Olsen, R.J. (1994), 'Fertility and the Size of the U.S. Labour Force', *Journal of Economic Literature*, 32:60–100.

Prakasamma, M. (1989), 'Analysis of Factors Influencing Performance of Auxiliary Nurse Midwives in Nizamabad District', Ph.D. thesis (New Delhi: Centre for Social Medicine and Community Health, Jawaharlal Nehru University).

Priya, Ritu (1990), 'Dubious Package Deal: Health Care in Eighth Plan', *Economic and Political Weekly*, 18 August.

Rajan, S.I., U.S. Mishra, and K. Navaneetham (1991), 'Decline in Sex Ratio: An Alternative Explanation?', *Economic and Political Weekly*, 21 December.

—— (1992), 'Decline in Sex Ratio: Alternative Explanation Revisited', *Economic and Political Weekly*, 14 November.

Raju, S. and M.K. Premi (1992), 'Decline in Sex Ratio: Alternative Explanation Re-examined', *Economic and Political Weekly*, 25 April.

Reddy, K.N. and V. Selvaraju (1993), 'Determinants of Health Status in India: An Empirical Verification', mimeograph (New Delhi: National Institute of Public Finance and Policy).

Rosenzweig, Mark (1988), 'Risk, Implicit Contracts and the Family in Rural Areas of Low-income Countries', *Economic Journal*, 98:1148–70.

—— (1993), 'Women, Insurance Capital, and Economic Development in Rural India', *Journal of Human Resources*, 28(4): 735–58.

Rosenzweig, Mark and T. Paul Schultz (1982), 'Market Opportunities, Genetic Endowments, and Intrafamily Resource Distribution: Child Survival in Rural India', *American Economic Review*, 72:803–15.

Rosenzweig, Mark and Oded Stark (1989), 'Consumption Smoothing, Migration, and Marriage: Evidence from Rural India', *Journal of Political Economy*, 7:905–26.

Satia, J.K., and S.J. Jejeebhoy (eds.) (1991), *The Demographic Challenge: A Study of Four Large Indian States* (Delhi: Oxford University Press).

Schultz, T. Paul (1981), *Economics of Population* (Reading: Addison-Wesley).

—— (1994), 'Sources of Fertility Decline in Modern Economic Growth: Is Aggregate Evidence on Demographic Transition Credible?', mimeograph (Yale University).

Sen, A.K. (1976), 'Poverty: An Ordinal Approach to Measurement', *Econometrica*, 44:219–31.

Sen, A.K. and S. Sengupta (1983), 'Malnutrition of Children and the Rural Sex Bias', *Economic and Political Weekly*, Annual Number.

Sen, Ilina (1986), 'Geography of Secular Change in Sex Ratio in 1981: How Much Room for Optimism?', *Economic and Political Weekly*, 22 March.

Shah, M.H. (1989), 'Factors Responsible for Low Performance of Family

Welfare Programme', in B. Jena and R.N. Pati (eds.), *Health and Family Welfare Services in India* (New Delhi: Ashish).

Sharma, O.P. and Robert D. Retherford (1990), 'Effect of Female Literacy on Fertility in India', Occasional Paper No. 1 (New Delhi: Office of the Registrar-General).

Simmons, G.B., C. Smucker, S. Bernstein, and E. Jensen (1982), 'Postneonatal Mortality in Rural India: Implications of an Economic Model', *Demography*, 19(3): 371–89.

Sopher, David (ed.) (1980a), *An Exploration of India: Geographical Perspectives on Society and Culture* (Ithaca: Cornell University Press).

Sopher, David (1980b), 'The Geographical Patterning of Culture in India', in Sopher 1980a.

Srinivas, K. (1991), 'The Demographic Scenario Revealed by the 1991 Census Figures', *Journal of Family Welfare*, 37.

Subbarao, K. and L. Raney (1994), 'Social Gains from Female Education: A Cross National Study', World Bank Discussion Paper No. 194.

Thomas, D., J. Strauss, and M.H. Henriques (1991), 'How does Mother's Education Affect Child Height?', *Journal of Human Resources*, 26:183–211.

Tulasidhar, V.B. and J.V.M. Sarma (1993), 'Public Expenditure, Medical Care at Birth and Infant Mortality: A Comparative Study of States in India', in P. Berman and M.E. Khan (eds.), *Paying for India's Health Care* (New Delhi: Sage).

United Nations (1987), *Fertility Behaviour in the Context of Development: Evidence from the World Fertility Survey* (New York: United Nations).

—— (1993), *Women's Education and Fertility Behaviour: A Case-Study of Rural Maharashtra, India* (New York: United Nations).

Venkatachalam, R. and V. Srinivasan (1993), *Female Infanticide* (New Delhi: Har-Anand).

Visaria, Pravin and Leela Visaria (1994), 'Demographic Transition: Accelerating Fertility Decline in 1980s', *Economic and Political Weekly*, 1724, December.

Vlassoff, Carol (1980), 'Unmarried Adolescent Females in Rural India: A Study of the Social Impact of Education', *Journal of Marriage and the Family*, 42(2): 427–36.

Ware, Helen (1984), 'Effects of Maternal Education, Women's Roles, and Child Care on Child Mortality', in W. Henry Mosley and Lincoln C. Chen (eds.), *Child Survival: Strategies for Research*, supplement to *Population and Development Review*, 10:191–214.

11

The Reproductive Health of Brazilian Women During the 'Lost Decade'

Elza Berquó

INTRODUCTION

Given the rapid decline in the average number of children per woman and the high rate of contraceptive use which prevails in Brazil, one might easily surmise that Brazilian women enjoy full reproductive health and rights. Though its total fertility rate is still considerably higher than the 1.7 value found in countries from the Northern hemisphere, Brazil did show a decline of more than 50 per cent between 1970 and 1991 and its TFR has now passed the 2.5 barrier. Furthermore, some regions and certain population segments already exhibit rates below the minimum replacement level. In addition, 70 per cent of all women in child-bearing ages use contraceptive methods, which brings Brazil close to the 74 per cent contraceptive prevalence rate found in more developed countries.

Nevertheless, Brazil's accentuated fertility decline does not necessarily denote a marked improvement in reproductive health. Absolute levels of maternal mortality and morbidity have evidently declined as a result of reduced exposure to child-bearing, but relative levels have shown little improvement. This is because fertility decline occurred, at least in part, in a context marked by severe economic and social difficulties which had serious negative impacts on women's health. Much of the period in which fertility declined at a rapid pace was characterized by a great instability in economic growth processes, which led to the stagnation of average income, to an increase of poverty, and to a gradual reduction in public funds allocated for health care. Conflicts of interest within the private sector retarded the implementation and regulation of the Unified Health System (whose intent it was to decentralize health care, to extend treatment to all segments of the population, and to create an administrative hierarchy in health care). Moreover, the country never developed any sort of adequate public reproductive health programme, a fact which explains the preponderant use of just two fertility regulation methods (the pill and sterilization), as well as the high incidence of clandestine and unsafe abortions (Berquó 1993).

Considering that a large portion of the Brazilian population, especially women, depends exclusively upon the public sector for health care, there is no doubt that this scenario has had serious repercussions upon the health of the female population. The initial section of this paper documents the social debt to women's health through an analysis of existing health and social indicators and tendencies. The next section examines changes in the institutional structure which relate to reproductive health. The central section of the paper addresses contraception and women's health in the Brazilian context, and the main findings are brought together in a concluding summary.

IMPOVERISHMENT

The 1980s began with great expectations, based on the hope that the high rates of economic growth which had marked the preceding years would continue. Starting in 1968, the remarkable growth period of the so-called 'Brazilian miracle' decisively set the tone for the economy in the 1970s. Between 1970 and 1980, per capita income increased significantly, having positive consequences for all social strata. During this period, according to Barros and Mendonça (1995), all the deciles of the income distribution showed annual average rates of growth above 5.5 per cent (Figure 1), with the greatest increase occurring at the extremes of the distribution, that is, among the poorest and the richest.

Unfortunately, this exuberant pace of growth was not maintained in the 1980s; actually, the remarkably high growth rates of the 'miracle' period lasted only until 1976. According to Barros and Mendonça, the Brazilian economy went through an unequal process of decline during the 1980s, with the losses concentrated among the poorer segments of the population (Figure 2). As a

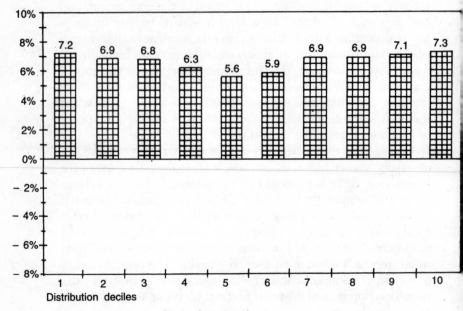

FIG. 1: *Income growth rate (1970–80)*
Source: Barros and Mendonça 1995.

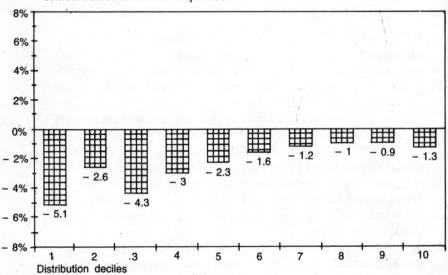

FIG. 2: *Income growth rate (1980–90)*
Source: Barros and Mendonça, op. cit.

result, the 1980s bore witness to great instability, increasing impoverishment, and deterioration of welfare.

Though several efforts at economic stabilization and inflation control were attempted, such as the 'Cruzado Plan' of 1986 (which momentarily raised per capita income to the 1980 level), Brazil entered a period of prolonged economic stagnation. As can be seen from Table 1, 1983 was the worst year of this recession period, showing a decline of 13.1 per cent in the real per capita income as compared to 1980.

TABLE 1: BRAZIL: EVOLUTION OF REAL PER CAPITA INCOME
AND OF THE PROPORTION OF THE POPULATION
BELOW THE POVERTY LINE, 1960-88

Years	PCI (1980=100)	Poverty (%)
1960	45.3	41.4
1970	55.3	39.3
1980	100.0	24.4
1983	86.9	41.9
1986	99.6	28.4
1987	101.0	35.9
1988	98.9	39.3

Source: Singer 1995.

Analysing this same time period from a poverty perspective, that is, the proportion of the population earning incomes below the minimum required to provide an individual's basic necessities (Romao 1991), there is strong evidence of impoverishment. While between 1970 and 1980, a rapid decline in the portion of the population residing below the poverty line had been observed (from 39.3 per cent to 24.4 per cent), this number rebounded to an alarming level during the worst year of the recession. Thus, in 1983, four out of every ten Brazilians found themselves below the poverty line. This level improved in response to signals of economic recovery, but while per capita income in 1986 reached the same level as in 1980, poverty levels did not recede in the same proportion. In the years that followed, when the economy assumed a stationary condition, poverty continued to increase, growing from 35.9 per cent to 39.3 per cent between 1987 and 1988. In other words, by 1988, the country's poverty levels had practically returned to the high levels experienced in 1983.

In terms of its regional distribution, poverty reaches its heaviest concentration in the Northeast, afflicting 60 per cent of the population in 1989. The Northern and Central-Western regions followed with 49 per cent. Even in the Southeast, with a heavy concentration of investment and a large industrial park, 31 per cent of the population failed to meet their minimum basic needs (Lopes 1993).

CHANGES IN THE HEALTH SYSTEM[1]

The end of the 'miracle' period, economic recession, as well as a growing inflation rate which exploded from 100 per cent to 1000 per cent a year between 1982 and 1988, not only caused a deterioration in living conditions but also had serious repercussions upon the health system. During the period of the 'economic miracle', a new government agency of great relevance to reproductive health was conceived, the National Institute for Medical Care and Social Security (INAMPS). This agency was created independently of the Health Ministry, and was intended to provide medical care to workers covered by Social Security, using funds from compulsory contributions by workers and employers. Established in 1974, INAMPS directed its operations towards contracting health services, through cooperative agreements with third-party health operators.

In response to the opportunities created by this new system, group medicine and a network of associated private hospitals and clinics grew rapidly. By 1981, 71 per cent of INAMPS' spending was channeled towards payment for services provided by the private sector. In addition, the government directed considerable investment toward the expansion and modernization of this sector's existing capacity.

These changes in the direction of public support for the health sector heightened a characteristic that had always dominated public health care in Brazil, namely the emphasis on curative rather than preventive medicine. Thus, spending in the curative areas grew from 36 per cent in 1965, to 85 per cent by the end of the 1980s, with the majority of these funds directed to the hospital sector.

[1] This section is based on Berquó, E., M.J. Araujo, and S.R. Sorrentino, 'Fecundidade, Saude Reprodutiva e Pobreza na America Latina', 1994.

Constant delays by INAMPS in honouring its financial commitments with associated sectors generated a growing apathy among health professionals in the hospital network and created financial difficulties in maintaining hospitals with up-to-date basic equipment and medical supplies. This led to a rapid deterioration of the health care network available to the country's working population. The structure of payments made by INAMPS to doctors within this system led to serious abuses such as 'phantom' surgeries, unnecessary operations, or, in many cases, operations carried out at rates incompatible with a competent and secure practice. One blatant example of this situation is the abuse of caesarean sections, which began to grow when INAMPS decided to pay out more money for surgical than for vaginal births. As described below, this decision has had an enormous impact on reproductive health.

The 1988 Federal Constitution transferred INAMPS from the Social Security to the Health Ministry and created the Unified Health System (*Sistema Único de Saúde*, hereafter SUS), with the intent of offering an alternative to the earlier privatizing and curative orientations of the public health system. Based on the principles of decentralization, universal care, and community participation, SUS re-established public health as a social right, wherein the public sector would play a fundamental role in strengthening a suitable approach to health. Theoretically, SUS should have been introduced to each Brazilian municipal district as of 1990, but this actually took place in only a few states.

The result has been a long, drawn-out transition, marked both by conflicts of interest within the private sector, and the lack of a clear orientation for the coordination and regulation of actions at the federal, state, and municipal levels. Another major reason why the implantation of SUS has proved so slow stems from the fact that when the Health Ministry absorbed INAMPS, its financial resources remained in the Ministry of Social Security. One can thus conclude that the operationalization of a municipal and universal health care, as proposed by the SUS system, is still far from becoming a reality. Moreover, given the strength of group medicine lobbies in Congress, it is not impossible that the process of constitutional revision now underway will bring new surprises in this area.

Only 25 per cent of the population possesses a private health care plan, of which 17 per cent corresponds to employer health insurance and 8 per cent to individual insurance plans. This, along with the fact that US $6.6 billion, a figure equivalent to 88 per cent of the Health Ministry's total budget for 1993, moved through the private sector in 1994, indicates the seriousness of the health situation among the remaining 75 per cent of the population. Worse yet, federal spending in health care dropped from US $11.3 billion in 1989 to 7.5 billion in 1993. As a result, per capita spending on health, already tiny when compared to the US $1,500 to which First World citizens have a right, fell from US $80 to US $48 between 1989 and 1993.

CONTRACEPTION IN THE BRAZILIAN CONTEXT

Unfortunately, national-level information on contraceptive use in Brazil is dated: the most recent available data are from 1986 (PNAD-86 FIBGE and PNSMIPF-BENFAM 1986). At that time, Brazil exhibited a high overall rate of usage: some 70 per cent of married or cohabiting women from 15 to 54 years of age were using some contraceptive method. For all women, regardless of marital status, this figure was 43 per cent. Among the methods used, female sterilization was at the top of the list and was followed by synthetic hormones; together, these two made up 85 per cent of the methods used. Among the methods considered to be highly effective in avoiding pregnancy, intra-uterine devices were used by only 1.5 per cent of women, while fewer than 1 per cent of the women had vasectomized partners. The so-called less efficient methods were used by 10.4 per cent of women, with periodic abstinence being the primary method. In spite of regional and state-level differences in rates of sterilization and of pill use, there is no doubt that when one refers to contraception in Brazil, one is talking about the pill or tubal ligation. The Northeast and the state of Goiás led the country in rates of tubal ligation.

In the 1990s, two studies — one in the Northeast in 1991 (DHS 1991) and the other in the city of São Paulo in 1992 (CEBRAP 1992) — provide comparable information on the situation of birth control in these two highly-differentiated regional contexts.[2] They also allow us to assess whether the contraceptive picture has changed over the past five years. Much of the arguments made throughout the remainder of this paper will

[2] In the case of São Paulo, the 1992 study refers to the municipality, and the 1986 study to the state.

draw upon data from these two studies. The Northeast study showed that 54.3 per cent of all women had used at least one contraceptive method and that 39.1 per cent were doing so at the time of the survey (Table 2). The figures were much higher in the São Paulo study, where 58.3 per cent of the women interviewed stated that they were currently using a contraceptive method, and 76.8 per cent had used one at some point during their child-bearing years. Table 2 shows that, despite increased use, the picture has not changed since 1986 in terms of method mix. In other words, birth control continued to be virtually limited to two methods: the pill and sterilization of women. Taken together, these two methods were used by 74.7 per cent of all female users of contraceptive methods in São Paulo, and 85.9 per cent of those in the Northeast.

TABLE 2: PERCENTAGE DISTRIBUTION OF ALL WOMEN OF CHILDBEARING AGE USING SOME KIND OF CONTRACEPTIVE METHOD, ACCORDING TO METHOD USED, IN THE NORTHEAST REGION AND THE MUNICIPALITY OF SÃO PAULO.

Methods	São Paulo[1] 1992	Northeast[2] 1991
Female Sterilization	36.1	62.9
Pill	38.6	23.0
Condoms	6.2	2.8
Vasectomy	4.5	0.2
Injections	2.8	1.8
IUD	2.2	0.8
Vaginal Methods	0.3	0.0
Coitus Interruptus	3.8	4.1
Periodic Abstinence	2.3	4.3
Other	3.2	0.1
Total	100.0	100.0
Number of women	1,026	6,222
% using a method	58.3	39.1
% having used at some time	76.8	54.3

[1] 'Pesquisa sobre Saúde Reprodutiva da População Negra', CEBRAP, 1992.
[2] 'Pesquisa sobre Saúde Familiar no Nordeste', Brasil 1991.
Source: E. Berquó (1993).

In São Paulo, as had been the case in 1986, the pill had a slight lead over tubal ligation, while in the Northeast, ligations were more common, accounting for 62.9 per cent of all contraceptive users, compared to 47.2 per cent of users in 1986. On the other hand, use of the pill in the Northeast decreased from 32.1 per cent in 1986 to 23 per cent in 1991.[3] In other words, in the poorest region of Brazil, the practical range of alternatives for contraception was narrowed even further. This is noteworthy, considering the growing list of options for controlling conception. It is estimated that of the 10,487,909 women aged 15 to 49 years in the Northeast in 1991, between 2.3 and 2.5 million had been sterilized.

These two studies from the 1990s also reveal some of the characteristics of sterilized women in the two regions and point to changes in these characteristics over time. In the Northeast, 19 per cent of all women had been sterilized before reaching the age of 25, as compared to 10 per cent in São Paulo. However, the median age at sterilization was quite similar in the two studies: 29.7 and 31 years, respectively. It is astonishing to observe how the age for definitive interruption of childbearing dropped so drastically over the course of just five years. Indeed, in 1986, only 5 per cent and 3 per cent of women had been sterilized by the age of 25 in the Northeast and São Paulo, respectively. Median age at sterilization was 36.6 and 38.2 years respectively; in other words, in both cases there was an abrupt drop of some seven years!

The median number of children born before sterilization is also quite similar in the two contexts: 2.7 for São Paulo and 3.0 for the Northeast. However, in the Northeast, the proportion of women sterilized after bearing a maximum of two children increased from 15 per cent in 1986 to 22 per cent in 1991; with a maximum of three children, the figure increased from 40 per cent to 49 per cent. The median number thus decreased from 3.6 to 3 children. Meanwhile, in São Paulo, the median number of children at sterilization remained virtually stable. In the Northeast there was a slight proportional increase in prevalence of sterilization with an increase in schooling, while the São Paulo study found no correlation between sterilization and education. In both studies, practically 50 per cent of the ligations had occurred in the last five years.

[3] Preliminary data from the 1991 National Census.

Concerning the relationship between race and contraception, the following results are worth highlighting. First, as concerns the propensity to undergo sterilization, no significant difference in sterilization was found between white and black women, either in the Northeast or in São Paulo. No statistical differences were associated with race with respect to contraceptive prevalence either; 63.2 per cent of white women and 53.4 per cent of black women in São Paulo were currently using any method. Among white users, 22.0 per cent were sterilized and 24.0 per cent were using the pill. Among black users, 20.9 per cent were using the pill and 20.1 per cent had been sterilized. Table 3 shows the proportion of sterilized women by race and level of education. As can be seen, no statistical difference was found between blacks and whites for three different levels of instruction. It is worth noting however that, for black women, the percentage of sterilization decreases as the level of education increases, while among white women it is highest in the intermediate educational category.

TABLE 3: PROPORTION OF STERILIZED WOMEN BY RACE, FOR DIFFERENT LEVELS OF EDUCATION, SÃO PAULO, 1992

Level of Education	Black	White	X^2	P-values (%)
Less than Primary School	24.6	20.0	1.08	0
Primary School to High School	20.5	28.1	2.69	10
College or more	15.2	18.1	0.53	40

Source: 'Pesquisa sobre Saúde Reprodutiva da População Negra', CEBRAP, 1992.

Similarly, no statistically significant difference was found between sterilized blacks and whites by level of monthly income per capita measured in fractions of minimum wage (Table 4).

These findings have important implications in view of the serious polemic surrounding the issue of sterilization by race in Brazil.[4]

The São Paulo study also identified the most frequent reason cited by women for having undergone sterilization. Some 61.6

[4] Blacks constitute 50 per cent of the Brazilian population and some black segments view sterilization as an attempt to reduce the black population.

per cent stated that they no longer wanted to have children, while 25 per cent referred to health problems. The change in women's discourse in the past few years is worthy of note. In 1986, the proportion of Brazilian women who stated they had submitted to tubal ligation, because they had already borne the ideal number of children, varied from 18 per cent to 48 per cent in different states. Evidently, none of these figures compares with the 61.6 per cent who declared this to be the case in the São Paulo study. Moreover, in 1986, the most frequently cited reason by women for undergoing sterilization was related to health problems; this proportion ranged from 32 per cent to 54 per cent between states. At that time we argued that this frequency of 'health problems' probably reflected the influence of physicians over women's decisions, since according to the Brazilian code of medical ethics, sterilization can only be performed in exceptional cases of serious health problems among women (Berquó 1989).[5] In the final analysis, it is likely, these women were repeating what they were expected and allowed to say. Be that as it may, the proportion citing health reasons as their reason for undergoing tubal ligation was only 25 per cent in the 1992 São Paulo study.

TABLE 4: PROPORTION OF STERILIZED WOMEN BY RACE, FOR DIFFERENT LEVELS OF MONTHLY INCOME PER CAPITA, SÃO PAULO, 1992

Income in minimum wage	Black	White	X^2	P-values (%)
0–¼	27.4	20.5	1.04	31
¼–½	28.2	21.6	1.32	25
½–1	19.2	21.9	0.36	55
1–2	14.6	22.7	2.10	15
2–3	12.5	28.6	2.77	10
3 or more	6.2	18.5	1.26*	26

* For Fisher exact test, P = 39 per cent.
Source: 'Pesquisa sobre Saúde Reprodutiva da População Negra', CEBRAP, 1992.

[5] Chapter VI of the 'Medical Code of Ethics: On the physician's responsibility'. Article 52: 'Sterilization is a crime, but it may be performed in exceptional cases when there is a precise prescription, approved by two physicians heard jointly'.

The fact that, in 1992, women were much more directly explicit about not wanting any more children reflects an important change of attitude among women. They feel that they have already had as many children as they want, and that they have the right to express this. This is due unquestionably to an atmosphere created in the country by women's movements in defense of reproductive rights. Of course, if women had knowledge about and access to other contraceptive methods, they could exercise their reproductive rights without necessarily having to rely on an irreversible method applied *en masse*. In this sense, it is of no small import that the Northeast study showed that, while nearly 100 per cent of women had heard of the pill and tubal ligation, and over 80 per cent knew where to obtain them, only 50 per cent had heard of the IUD and over 76 per cent did not know where to obtain it. Worse yet, only 37 per cent had heard of vaginal methods and 79 per cent did not know where to get them.

WOMEN'S HEALTH
On Pre-Natal Care

Among Brazilian child-bearing women, an average of 70 per cent receive pre-natal care on at least one occasion. Those who do not receive such treatment are usually members of poorer segments of the population. Among women whose monthly income falls below the minimum wage, 50 per cent did not receive any professional medical attention during their pregnancies. Regional differences on this score are also alarming: a comparison of the country's richest region, the Southeast, to the poorest regions, the North and Northeast, reveals a disparity of 75 per cent to 48 per cent of pregnant women who benefit from pre-natal services in their respective regions.

Some 39 per cent of all pre-natal services were provided by INAMPS, while state and municipal public health units accounted for another 24 per cent. Deficient pre-natal care also results from an insufficient number of visits with physicians, the absence of laboratory tests and vaccinations, and in the case of high-risk pregnancies, the lack of qualified background. It is worth stressing, for example, that only 62 per cent of pregnant women are vaccinated against tetanus.

On Deliveries

Three-quarters of all deliveries in Brazil take place in hospitals, but this proportion varies greatly among regions and between rural-urban areas. In the Southeast region, 99 per cent of all children are born in hospitals, against only 76 per cent in the Northeast. In cities, 93 per cent of all deliveries occur in hospitals, in contrast to 64 per cent in rural areas. Among North-eastern states, the presence of a physician at delivery varies from 26 per cent to 66 per cent, while the remaining children are delivered by midwives or nurses, who in effect account for most attendance of deliveries. This regional and urban-rural disparity helps explain why 18 per cent of all deaths linked to pregnancy are the result of complications at delivery, in spite of the high rate of hospital births on a national level.

Another related factor is the reduced number of hospital beds available for obstetrics and gynaecology, especially in high-risk cases, when both mother and newborn baby need special care or protracted hospital stays. A study conducted in the municipal district of São Paulo, by the Assesoria da Mulher da Secretaria Municipal de Saude de São Paulo 1989, showed that women in labour had to pass through an average of three hospitals before finding an available bed. This evidently increases health risks to the mother, which is exactly what many of these women had sought to avoid through pre-natal care. Part of this shortage of hospital beds is due to the commitment of available beds for longer periods for women recovering from caesarean sections. In this case, the date, place and time of birth is scheduled in advance by doctors and their patients; this relative advantage of convenience may be another factor which reinforces the preference for caesarean sections. As will be seen below, many hospital beds are also occupied by women who have undergone illegal and otherwise unsafe abortions.

Altogether, obstetrical practices in Brazil have evolved into a serious abuse of surgical deliveries. From 15 per cent of all deliveries in 1970, caesarean sections jumped to 31 per cent by 1980 (Granada-Neiva 1992), reaching 34 per cent in 1990. In some states, caesareans accounted for as many as 69 per cent of all deliveries in 1991 (Jorge et al. 1992). In the state of São Paulo, this rate amounted to almost half of all deliveries in 1993, while in some regions of the state it reached 70 per cent! Paid for by the public health system (SUS), caesarean sections approach 400,000 per year, considerably raising the cost of hospital services for childbirth, given the need for anaesthetics and longer stays in the hospital. High rates of caesarean section also reduce the availability of beds for natural childbirth. Even more importantly, the risk of maternal death is 2.9 times greater for caesareans, when compared to normal births (Costa 1991). The growth of this practice has much to do with the fact that having a caesarean section provides an appropriate surgical opportunity for tubal ligations.

Caesareans and Sterilization

The course of sterilization in Brazil has generated its own culture, inducing an increasing number of women every year to put an end to their ability to reproduce. In the Northeast, 54 per cent of all sterilized women underwent the operation in the last five years, and São Paulo exhibits similar figures. Such statistics speak of a veritable culture of sterilization. In São Paulo, 52 per cent of sterilized women are daughters or sisters of other sterilized women, and there are cases of families where the mother and two or three of her daughters have had tubal ligations. In addition, of those who have not yet undergone sterilization, 42 per cent are members of families where the mother or a sister has already had this procedure.

When asked if they would recommend tubal ligation to other women, 65 per cent of those who had already undergone the operation said yes, justifying their answer on the basis of financial difficulties in raising many children (40 per cent), safety in the method (37 per cent), and not harming one's health like the pill does (18 per cent). This last reason demonstrates yet again that women only have two options available: the pill or sterilization, of which the former is often considered unacceptable.

Some 89 per cent of the women interviewed in São Paulo said they were satisfied with sterilization, the main reasons being not having to worry about using other methods and the fact that they already had the ideal number of children. For those who regretted having submitted to sterilization, the reasons they cited are similar to those found in other studies: death of children, new marriages, wanting to have more children, and health problems (Grubb et al. 1985; Pinotti et al. 1986). Among those who had not undergone sterilization, 39 per cent of married (or cohabiting) women expressed the intent to be sterilized in the future, with the highest proportion found among women in the 15 to 24 years age bracket. In the Northeast, among the currently married women who were not using any contraceptive method, 31 per cent stated that they intended to submit to sterilization over the next twelve months and 36 per cent intended to do so later on.

Because sterilization is forbidden under the Brazilian Penal Code[6] and the Medical Code of Ethics, physicians perform tubal ligations during caesarean sections. In this case, the patient's hospital costs as well as the doctor's fees are covered by INAMPS (the Social Security system), and the additional cost of sterilization is paid for 'under the table' by the patient (Barros et al. 1991; Faúndes and Cecatti 1991). This practice explains why, in 1986, 75 per cent of tubal ligations were performed along with the woman's last delivery, that is, at the time of a caesarean section. The recent study in São Paulo revealed that 80 per cent of tubal ligations had been done during caesarean sections.

The economics associated with this procedure are revealing. Some 55 per cent of sterilized women stated that they had paid the physician for the operation in cash: furthermore, in 11 per cent of the cases, in addition to coverage paid through INAMPS or health insurance, women also paid a portion in cash. Health insurance or INAMPS covered the entire cost for 11 per cent of the women. However, it is worth noting that 23 per cent of the tubal ligations were performed free of cost — they were paid for by some source that the women were unaware of.

Arrangements for sterilization are often made with physicians during pre-natal visits. Osis[7] and collaborators interviewed 3,703 women of child-bearing age in 1988 in the state of São Paulo and found that 87 per cent of the women discussed tubal ligation with their physicians during pre-natal visits. The 1992 study estimated this number to be about 50 per cent of all cases. Another 10 per cent of such agreements are reached just prior to childbirth, and 11

[6] According to the Brazilian Penal Code (promulgated in 1940), Article 29, paragraph 2-III, sterilization is a crime, since it constitutes serious bodily injury, resulting in the loss of reproductive function. The corresponding sentence is two to eight years in prison.

[7] M.J.D. Osis, et al, 1990, 'Laqueadura Tubária Nos Serviços de Saúde do Estado de São Paulo', *Revista de Ginecologia e Obstetrícia*, 1 (3), pp. 195–204.

per cent of the sterilized women stated that the physician-patient decision had been reached during labour! It is also highly revealing that 32 per cent of the women stated that they had gotten pregnant in order to be sterilized during a caesarean section childbirth!

The fact that caesarean sections are used as a vehicle to perform sterilizations is highlighted by the fact that in São Paulo (1992), the proportions of caesareans in the last delivery was 80 per cent among sterilized women and 33 per cent among non-sterilized women. In the Northeast, too, the proportion of caesarean sections for the last live birth for those women who had at least one live delivery in the last five years was 52 per cent for sterilized women and 21 per cent for non-sterilized women. The incidence of Caesarean sections in the last childbirth actually increased with level of schooling for the patients, thus confirming previous studies (Faúndes and Cecatti 1991). This trend is true for both sterilized and non-sterilized women.

Just as the desire or need for sterilization leads women to submit to caesarean sections as described above, the abuse of such surgical deliveries by obstetricians also leads many women to submit to sterilization, since they have already undergone several caesareans and run the risk of a ruptured uterus during childbirth. This causal factor is present in Brazil, and contributes to the high prevalence of tubal ligations.

The above discussion clearly shows that there is an abuse of modern reproductive technology in Brazil where an extremely high rate of caesarean sections is coupled with surgical sterilization. The significant association between the two constitutes a serious public health problem and status quo directly affects both reproductive morbidity and mortality and the conditions of neonates. Furthermore, it feeds rising hospital costs in the Social Security system. Without a doubt, the main issue at stake is the position taken by physicians, particularly obstetricians/gynaecologists. This specialty knows quite well that the reasons for Brazil's caesarean epidemic go far beyond clinical indications pertaining to either the mother or the foetus; still, they continue to prefer surgical deliveries, either out of convenience or a lack of ability to perform vaginal deliveries. Faúndes and Cecatti (1991), in a thorough study on the subject, discuss the institutional, legal, and clinical obstetrical factors influencing the high incidence of caesareans. They enumerate and demonstrate the serious health consequences of unindicated caesareans for both the neonate and the mother.

On a more general level, the well-known lack of coverage in the public health system for reproductive health care, which deprives women of their reproductive rights, is of no less importance. In short, Brazilian women — especially those from lower income groups who constitute the vast majority — are facing a serious dilemma in the area of reproductive health. The pill is really their only reversible method of contraception; and can be purchased in drugstores without a doctor's prescription, which often leads to undesirable side-effects. Not having access to legal abortion to back up occasional contraceptive failures, women see sterilization as a 'lifesaver', given the lack of choices they experience in reproductive health. But in order to obtain this 'lifesaver', they must pay the physician 'under the table' and submit to a caesarean, even if there is no clinical recommendation for it. Sometimes they are forced to accept the procedure because of the abuse of previous caesareans performed by physicians for reasons which have little to do with their health.

On Post-Natal Care

Another alarming statistic has to do with the low frequency of post-natal check-ups of women attended by the public health care system. Of those who go through pre-natal care, only 2 per cent return for post-partum care, leaving the remaining 98 per cent exposed to post-delivery complications such as infections, lung disorders, and toxaemia, which are usually avoidable with appropriate treatment.

Maternal Mortality

Since maternal mortality is directly related to living conditions and to the quality of medical care received during pregnancy and childbirth, high mortality rates among child-bearing women are to be expected in the light of the foregoing picture, especially among the female population which is being simultaneously neglected from an economic, social, and health perspective. The most recent available official statistics on maternal mortality (from 1988), show a rate of 134.7 per 100,000 live births. This rate is fourteen times greater than that of the United States, and thirty-four times that of Canada.

Regional variations in maternal mortality are also very large; the difference between the north and the south was 298.3 per thousand against 110.2 in 1987. It is true that the high rate in the northern region might also reflect the impact of a 70 per cent increase in malaria in the area between 1983 and 1987 (Araújo and Sorrentino 1994).

Though maternal mortality rates declined somewhat in the early 1980s, it is critical to observe that these rates practically stabilized as of 1985. Figure 3 shows the contrast between recent trends in maternal mortality with the accentuated and systematic decline in fertility.[8] In other words, the decline in fertility failed to lead to a significant improvement in pregnancy and delivery-related risks. Even in the state of São Paulo, where maternal mortality rates are far below the national average, this index barely shifted between

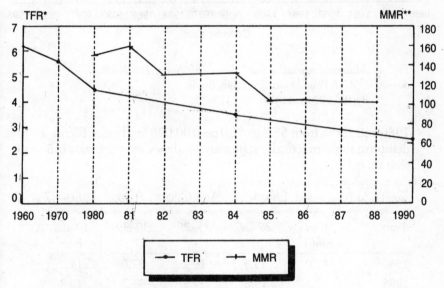

FIG. 3: *Total fertility rate and maternal mortality rate,*
          Brazil, 1960–90
Source: Ministry of Health.
    *   Total Fertility Rate.
    **   Maternal Mortality Rate by 100,000 live births.

[8] In this figure, maternal mortality rates are not corrected by an under-reporting factor, since the Health Ministry does not possess a corrected historical series. Hence the graph should be read for the tendencies and not the levels it describes.

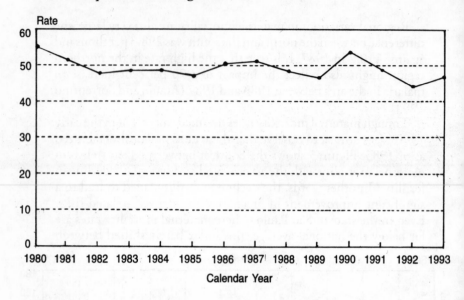

Fɪɢ. 4: *Maternal mortality rate*, São Paulo State, 1980–93*
Source: SEADE Foundation, São Paulo, Brazil.
      * By 100,000 live births.

1980 and 1990, from 55.2 to 54.0 per 100,000 live births. Figure 4 demonstrates a practically stationary tendency over the past thirteen years.[9]

TABLE 5: MATERNAL DEATHS, BY AGE GROUP, BRAZIL, 1980–87

Years	19 and under	20–24	25–29	30–39	40 and over
1980	12.0	19.5	19.2	37.0	11.2
1985	12.6	19.8	22.5	33.7	10.3
1987	13.1	22.2	20.0	34.2	9.4

Source: Mortality Statistics, Health Ministry.

Table 5 offers a glimpse of the age distribution of maternal mortality, which changed slightly over the period under consideration.

[9] This graph too should be read for the tendencies and not the levels it describes.

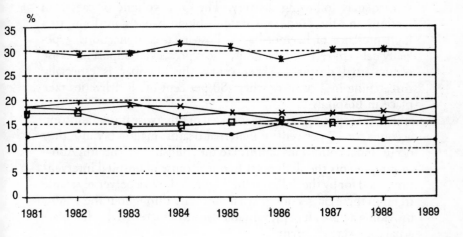

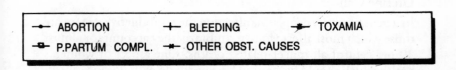

Fɪɢ. 5: *Deaths by causes associated to pregnancy delivery and post-partum, Brazil, 1981–89*
Source: Ministry of Health (1994).

Maternal deaths among younger women increased overall, while the relative weight of older women declined.

The most frequent cause of maternal mortality is pregnancy-related toxaemia which accounts for 30 per cent of all deaths. This disorder can be easily controlled during the pre-natal stage through simple and inexpensive procedures, such as the observation of weight and blood pressure. Hence, toxaemia's elevated incidence as cause of death among mothers proves symptomatic of the deterioration of health services and of the poor quality of pre-natal care.

Haemorrhages linked to pregnancy, childbirth, and post-delivery, constitute the second most frequent cause of maternal mortality, accounting for 18 per cent of all deaths. This cause is directly related to the quality of medical attention during and immediately following delivery. The great volume of caesarean sections and the precarious state of blood banks contribute to a high presence of haemorrhages. Post-natal complications, especially delivery-related infections, also represent an important cause of maternal deaths (15 per cent); this number is especially threatening in a country where 80 per cent of all deliveries take place in hospitals.

Deaths resulting from self-induced or otherwise unsafe abortion account for 12 per cent of maternal deaths, mainly because they occur under conditions harmful to the child-bearer's health. Abortion represents the sixth most frequent cause of hospital interventions paid for by the SUS system. Figure 5 shows a perversely stable trend in these causes of maternal mortality throughout the 1980s, providing a portrait of preventable causes of maternal death if maternal care were different.

Uterine Cancer Morbidity and Mortality

In a general sense, neoplasms affecting the reproductive system are those which most affect women. In Brazil, they account for almost 30 per cent of all cancer-related deaths. One aspect of women's health which should be stressed here has to do with uterine cancer, since this is an illness that can be detected early under favourable clinical and gynaecological conditions, thus preventing unnecessary deaths.

Table 6 shows another example of the perverse stability in health indicators over the 1980s. It indicates that trends in the relative weight of uterine cancer among neoplasm-related hospital entries, as well as in the specific mortality rates due to this type of cancer, have stabilized in recent years.

Though simple and inexpensive, gynaecological examinations are accessible to only a small part of the female population. In the Northeast, for example, 43 per cent of all women underwent this examination at least once in their lifetime, while only 22 per cent received gynaecological care in 1991, a percentage that dips to 10 for the rural area.[10] Furthermore, a gynaecological appointment does not mean that Pap smears are always done. Even in São Paulo,

---

[10] 'Pesquisa Sobre Saúde Familiar no Nordeste', BENFAM, 1991.

TABLE 6: UTERINE CANCER AMONG WOMEN AGED 10 AND
OVER. BRAZIL, 1984–90

Year	% Hospital entries for Neoplasms	Deaths per 10,000 women	% of Total deaths of women hospitalized for this cause
1984	6.5	4.7	12.4
1985	7.2	4.2	11.7
1986	7.4	4.4	12.7
1987	7.0	4.3	11.7
1988	6.3	4.6	11.3
1989	6.3	4.3	10.0
1990	6.4	4.6	10.0

Source: Health Ministry (1994).

this examination is carried out for only 4 per cent of all women undergoing gynaecological examinations.

Unfortunately, national statistics on sexually-transmitted diseases with direct consequences upon women's reproductive health, including chronic infections which elevate the chances of uterine cancer, are not available (except for AIDS). What we do know through a few isolated studies is that the incidence of the silent infection Chlamydia has been increasing.

Finally, another point worth adding to this already bleak picture is that the great number of women sterilized each year, due to lack of information, believe that they no longer need to seek health services regularly.

CONCLUSION

In this paper, we have sought to show that the decline in fertility that began during the period of the 'economic miracle' gained strength throughout the so-called 'lost decade' of the 1980s. The economic problems endured by the country during this latter period contributed to the deterioration of the public health system, with serious implications for health conditions, especially among the poorer population. This situation has direct and negative consequences for women's reproductive health.

The relative drop in the number of child-bearing women should have led to an improvement in pre-natal, delivery, and post-partum services. Unfortunately, this is not what happened, as demonstrated by the high levels of maternal mortality due to avoidable causes. At the same time, resources saved from reduced child-bearing loads could have been channeled to gynaecological treatment, thus alleviating morbidity and mortality rates related to avoidable causes; again, this did not take place.

In sum, the 1980s, which have been described in Latin America as 'a lost decade' from several standpoints, can also be considered as a loss from the health standpoint, in the sense that the potential for improving the reproductive health of women — a potential generated by the rapidly declining fertility rates experienced in all regions of the country — was not taken advantage of. Theoretically, more resources should have been available for investment in critical areas of the reproductive health sector. That this did not occur is partly a function of the protracted economic crisis which the country has suffered since the early 1980s. However, it is also a function of the vicissitudes of the Brazilian public health sector and of the manner in which it has interacted with the private sector.

REFERENCES

Araújo, M.J.O., and S.R. Sorrentino (1994), 'O Sistema de Saúde no Brasil' (The Health System in Brazil), in *A Transição da Fecundidade*, p. 77.

Barros, F.C., J.P. Vaughan, C.G. Victoria, and S.R.A. Huttly (1991), 'Epidemics of Caesarean Sections in Brazil', *The Lancet*, 338(20):167–9.

Barros, R.P. and R.S.P. Mendonça (1995), 'A Evolução do Bem-estar, Pobreza e Desigualdade no Brasil Desde 1960' (The Evolution of Welfare, Poverty and Inequality in Brazil since 1960), *Pesquisa e Planejamento Econômico*, 25(1):115–64.

BEMFAM/IRD (1986), 'Pesquisa Nacional Sobre Saúde Materno-Infantil e Planejamento Familiar' (National Survey of Maternal-Child Health and Family Planning), PNSMIPF Brasil (Rio de Janiero).

Berquó, E. (1989), 'A Esterilização Feminina no Brasil Hoje' (Female Sterilization in Brazil Today), paper presented at the International Meeting, Women's Health: A Right to be Won, promoted by the Conselho Nacional dos Direitos da Mulher (National Council for Women's Rights), Brasília, June 5–6.

—— (1993), 'Contraception and Caesareans in Brazil: An Example of

Bad Reproductive Health Practice in Need of Exemplary Action', *Revista de Estudos Feministas*, 1(2): 461–72 (Rio de Janeiro).

CEBRAP (1992), 'Pesquisa Sobre Saúde Reprodutiva da População Negra' (Research on Reproductive Health of the Black Population) (São Paulo).

Costa, C.F.F. (1991) 'Via de Parto e Mortalidade Materna' (Childbirth and Maternal Mortality), in A. Faúndes and J.G. Cecatti, *Morte Materna: Uma Tragédia Evitável* (Campinas: Editora da Unicamp).

Demographic and Health Surveys — Macro International Inc. & Sociedade Civil Bem-Estar Familiar No Brazil — BEMFAM (1992), 'Pesquisa Sobre Saúde Familiar no Nordeste Brasil, 1991' (Survey of Family Health in Northeast, Brazil, 1991), Rio de Janiero

Faúndes, A. and J.G. Cecatti (1991), 'A Operação Cesárea no Brasil. Incidência, Tendências, Causas, Consequências e Propostas de Ação' (Caesarean Sections in Brazil: Incidence, Trends, Causes, Consequences and Action Proposals), *Cadernos de Saúde Pública*, 7(2):150–73 (Rio de Janeiro).

FIBGE (1986), 'Pesquisa Nacional por Amostra a Domicilios' (National Household Survey).

Granada-Neiva, J.G. (1992), 'Operação Cesária no INAMPS' (Caesarean Sections in INAMPS), *Jornada Brasileira de Ginecologia e Obstetrícia*, XXVI (Rio de Janeiro).

Grubb, G.S., H.B. Peterson, P.M. Layde, and G.L. Rubin (1985), 'Regret After Decision to have a Tubal Sterilization', *Fertility and Sterility*, 44(2).

Jorge, Mello M.H. et al. (1992), *O Sistema de Informaçóo Sobre Nascidos Vivos*, (The information system on live births) (São Paulo: CBCD, n.7).

Lopes, J.R.B. (1993), 'Brasil, 1989: Um Estudo Sócio-econômico da Indigência e da Pobreza Urbanas' (Brazil, 1989: A Socio-economic Study and Indigency and Urban Poverty), *Caderno de Pesquisa Nepo-Unicamp*, no. 25, Campinas.

Municipio de São Paulo (1989), 'Diagnóstico de Saúde da Mulher no Município de São Paulo' (A Diagnosis of Women's Health in the Municipality of São Paulo), Assessoria da Mulher da Secretaria Municipal de Saúde de São Paulo.

Osis, M.J.D. et al. (1990), 'Laqueadura Tubária nos Serviços de Saúde do Estado de São Paulo' (Tubal Ligations in Public Health Services in the State of São Paulo), *Revista de Ginecologia e Obstetrícia*, 1(3):195–204.

Pinotti, J.A. et al. (1986), 'Identificação de Fatores Associados à Insatisfação Após Esterilização Cirúrgica' (Identification of the

Factors Associated with Insatisfaction after Surgical Sterilization), *MIGin. Obst. Bras.* 9(4):304.

Romão, M.C. (1991), 'Distribuição da Renda, Pobreza e Desigualdades Regionais no Brasil' (Income Distribution, Poverty and Regional Inequalities in Brazil), in J.M. Camargo and G. Giambiagi (eds.), *Distribuição de Renda no Brasil,* Rio de Janeiro, Paz e Terra,

Singer, P.I. (1995), 'Um Mapa da Exclusão Social no Brasil' (A Map of Social Exclusion in Brazil), unpublished paper presented at the 'Social Exclusion in Brazil: Diagnosis and Possibilities' Seminar, CEBRAP, 18 February.

Name Index

Subject Index